The New Cultures of Food

To 'cousin' Helge – AL
To my parents Jean and Graham – MKH

The New Cultures of Food

Marketing Opportunities from Ethnic, Religious and Cultural Diversity

Edited by
ADAM LINDGREEN and **MARTIN K. HINGLEY**

Routledge
Taylor & Francis Group

LONDON AND NEW YORK

First published in paperback 2024

First published 2009 by Gower Publishing

Published 2016 by Routledge
4 Park Square, Milton Park, Abingdon, Oxon OX14 4RN

and by Routledge
605 Third Avenue, New York, NY 10158

Routledge is an imprint of the Taylor & Francis Group, an informa business

Gower Applied Business Research
Our programme provides leaders, practitioners, scholars and researchers with thought provoking, cutting edge books that combine conceptual insights, interdisciplinary rigour and practical relevance in key areas of business and management.

British Library Cataloguing in Publication Data
The new cultures of food : marketing opportunities from
  ethnic, religious and cultural diversity
  1. Ethnic food industry 2. Food – Social aspects 3. Food
  preferences 4. Minority consumers
  I. Lindgreen, Adam II. Hingley, Martin
  381.4'1'089

Library of Congress Control Number: 2008942220

ISBN : 978-0-566-08813-1 (hbk)
ISBN : 978-1-03-283806-9 (pbk)
ISBN : 978-1-315-55521-8 (ebk)

DOI: 10.4324/9781315555218

Contents

List of Figures

List of Tables

About the Editors

Adam Lindgreen

After graduating with degrees in chemistry, engineering, and physics, Dr Adam Lindgreen completed an MSc in food science and technology at the Technical University of Denmark. He also finished an MBA at the University of Leicester, as well as a one-year Postgraduate Program at the Hebrew University of Jerusalem. Professor Lindgreen received his PhD in marketing from Cranfield University. Since May 2007, he has served as a Professor of Strategic Marketing at Hull University Business School.

Professor Lindgreen has been a Visiting Professor with various institutions, including Georgia State University, Groupe HEC in France, and Melbourne University; in 2006, he was made an honorary Visiting Professor at Harper Adams University College. His publications include more than 65 scientific journal articles, 6 books, more than 30 book chapters, and more than 75 conference papers. His recent publications have appeared in *Business Horizons, Industrial Marketing Management,* the *Journal of Advertising,* the *Journal of Business Ethics,* the *Journal of the Academy of Marketing Science,* the *Journal of Product Innovation Management, Psychology & Marketing,* and *Supply Chain Management*; his most recent books are *Managing Market Relationships* (2008) and *The Crisis of Food Brands* (2009), both with Gower Publishing. The recipient of the 'Outstanding Article 2005' award from *Industrial Marketing Management,* Professor Lindgreen also serves on the board of several scientific journals; he is the editor of the *Journal of Business Ethics* for the section on corporate responsibility and sustainability. His research interests include business and industrial marketing management, consumer behavior, experiential marketing, and corporate social responsibility.

Adam Lindgreen has discovered and excavated settlements from the Stone Age in Denmark, including the only major kitchen midden – Sparregård – in the south-east of Denmark; because of its importance, the kitchen midden was later excavated by the National Museum and then protected as a historical monument for future generations. He is also an avid genealogist, having traced his family back to 1390 and publishing widely in scientific journals related to methodological issues in genealogy, accounts of population development, and particular family lineages.

Martin K. Hingley

Dr Martin K. Hingley has degrees from three U.K. universities: He first graduated (Agricultural and Food Marketing, BSc Honours) from the University of Newcastle upon Tyne; he has an MPhil in marketing from Cranfield University; and he received his PhD in marketing from the Open University. Dr Hingley is a reader in marketing and supply chain management at Harper Adams University College, the leading university in the United Kingdom specializing in agri-food business. He is also a Visiting Fellow to the

University of Hull Business School and has previously held a Fellowship endowed by Tesco Plc. Dr Hingley has wide-ranging business experience in the international food industry and has spent some time in provision of market and business analysis with the Institute of Grocery Distribution, a leading UK research and training organization.

Dr Hingley's research interests are in applied food industry marketing and supply chain relationship management. He has presented and published widely in these areas, including in the *British Food Journal*, *Industrial Marketing Management*, and the *Journal of Marketing Management*. His most recent book is *The Crisis of Food Brands* (2009, Gower Publishing). He serves on the board of several scientific journals and also regularly guest edits such journals.

About the Contributors

Luís Kluwe Aguiar is a senior lecturer in marketing and international business at the Royal Agricultural College and an associate lecturer with the Open University Business School. Mr Aguiar received a MSc degree in Agricultural Economics from the University of London-Wye College. Prior to becoming a full-time academic, he worked for many years in both the private and public sectors and lectured on a part-time basis. His extensive international research and consultancy work has driven his main research interests, including marketing and consumer studies, especially relating to ethical consumerism.

Dr Marcia Dutra de Barcellos is an assistant professor in marketing and business strategy at the Pontifical Catholic University of Rio Grande do Sul (PUCRS). She is also a postdoctoral researcher at MAPP (Centre for Research on Costumer Relations in the Food Sector), Aarhus University. Dr de Barcellos received her PhD from the Federal University of Rio Grande do Sul (UFRGS). During her studies, she was a visiting researcher at Wageningen University and at the University of New England. She has published in international conference proceedings (*Agri-Food Chains and Networks, Asociación Latino-Iberoamericana de Gestión Tecnológica, Council of Learning Assistance and Developmental Associations, International Food and Agribusiness Management Association*, the *International PENSA Conference on Agri-Food Chain/Networks Economics and Management, Simpósio de Administração da Produção, Logística e Operações Internacionais*, among others) and in journals including *Agroanalysis, Brazilian Administration Review, Organizações Rurais & Agroindustriais* and *Revista Faces* (Fundação Mineira de Educação e Cultura), among others. Her research interests include food marketing and innovation, consumer behaviour, applied market research, branding, agri-food supply chain management and business strategy. Dr de Barcellos serves on the board of the *Brazilian Angus Association and Beef Information Service*.

Sean Beer is a senior lecturer in the School of Services Management at Bournemouth University. His primary research interests relate to the food supply chain, consumer behaviour and the nature of object and existential authenticity. He is extensively involved in promoting local and regional food and drink in the south-west of England. Mr Beer is a Winston Churchill Fellow and a Nuffield Scholar.

Dr Lorraine Brown works in the School of Services Management at Bournemouth University as programme leader for the Tourism Masters Framework, as well as study support lecturer for international postgraduate students. She has just completed her PhD thesis on the experiences of international students adapting to life in the United Kingdom. Her research interests include cross-cultural interaction, cultural dissonance, Islamophobia and role and identity conflict.

Dr Stephen Dann is a senior lecturer in the School of Management, Marketing and International Business at the Australian National University. His research has been published in the *Journal of Public Affairs, Monash Business Review, Quality Assurance in Education* and *Social Marketing Quarterly*. He has published several marketing textbooks, including *Strategic Internet Marketing* and *Competitive Marketing Strategy*, and he is a regular contributor to the *Australian and New Zealand Marketing Academy Conference*. Dr Dann's research interests include political marketing, consumer behaviour, Internet marketing, marketing strategy and innovation adoption.

Dr José Augusto Giesbrecht da Silveira is an assistant professor in the Business Administration Department of the School of Economics, Administration, and Accounting at the University of São Paulo. He also serves as an associate professor at the Industrial Engineering School at the FEI University Center in São Bernardo do Campo. His academic interests include managerial economics and retailing. Dr da Silveira is the author or co-author of several articles in both Brazilian and foreign journals and the co-editor of a book series entitled *Varejo Competitivo* (*Competitive Retailing*), already in its twelfth edition. The series presents recent research papers on Brazilian retailing.

Dr Kirsti Dautzenberg is a senior researcher at the Centre of Entrepreneurship and Innovation at the University of Potsdam. She received her PhD from Martin Luther University Halle-Wittenberg. She has published in *Energy Policy*, the *Journal on Chain and Network Science*, the *Journal of Retailing and Consumer Services* and *Outlook on Agriculture*, among others. Her research interests include strategic and supply chain management, management teams, gender-related research and financing aspects of new technology-based firms.

Dr Ernest Cyril de Run is Associate Professor of Marketing at the Universiti Malaysia Sarawak. He received his PhD from the University of Otago. Dr De Run has published in the *International Journal of Business and Society*, the *Journal of Asia Entrepreneurship and Sustainability*, the *Journal of Asia Pacific Marketing and Logistics* and the *Journal of International Business and Entrepreneurship*, among others. His research interests include cross-cultural studies, promotions, the effect of cues in advertisements (e.g. language, colour and symbols) and marketing research, particularly invariance. Dr de Run serves on the board of the *Annamalai Business Review, International Journal of Business and Society* and *Scientific Journals International*, among others.

Dr Emma Dresler-Hawke is a lecturer in marketing at Massey University. She earned a PhD in psychology and has worked as a cross-cultural psychologist in Germany, England, and New Zealand prior to joining the Department of Marketing. Dr Dresler-Hawke is particularly interested in social and cultural influences on buyer behaviour. In addition to research on the nutritional value of packed lunches for primary school children, she has investigated the cost of a healthy diet. These research projects link together within her interest in the cultural implications and politics of food.

Dr Johan Fischer is an associate professor in the Department of Society and Globalization at Roskilde University. His work focuses on modern Islam and consumer culture in South-east Asia and Europe. A central focus in his research is the theoretical and empirical investigation of the proliferation of halal commodities on a global scale. Dr Fischer is presently working on a monograph with the provisional title *On the Halal Frontier: Consuming Malays in London* that explores ways in which modern halal is formative for emerging Islamic identities, the fusion of religion and consumption, novel approaches to an anthropology of the state, diasporic material culture and forms of capitalism in the new millennium.

Dr Vanessa Fonseca is Professor of Advertising and Cultural studies at the University of Costa Rica. She received her PhD from the University of Texas at Austin and has published articles and papers in various journals and books, including *Consumption, Markets, and Cultures* and *Signo y Pensamiento* (*The Encyclopedia of Advertising*). Her research interests include Hispanic marketing and advertising, e-commerce, e-learning, virtual worlds and communities for education and collaboration.

Dr Janaina de Moura Engracia Giraldi is Professor of Marketing and Management at University of São Paulo from where she received her MA and PhD degrees. Professor Giraldi also obtained a MSc degree from the Catholic University of Leuven. Her research interests include the country-of-origin effect, country image, consumers' personal values, retail store image, retail private labels and strategic marketing.

Kuldip Gujral is a business development manager of the Asian Business Forum of the Birmingham Chamber of Commerce and Industry, a strategic organization whose aim is to improve the performance of small businesses in general and Asian businesses in particular. Mr Gujral has been championing the cause of small businesses and shops for the past 11 years and has developed various innovative programmes like SHOPEASY. This award-winning retail programme is a best-practice model that has successfully supported retailers in Birmingham and other areas. He serves on the board of Midlands Mencap.

Dr Jon H. Hanf is a senior researcher at the Leibniz Institute of Agricultural Development in Central and Eastern Europe. Dr. Hanf received his PhD from Justus-Liebig-University Giessen. He has published in *Agribusiness*, *Energy Policy*, *International Food and Agribusiness Management Review*, the *International Journal of Cooperative Management* and the *Journal on Chain and Network Science*, among others. Dr Hanf's research interests include consumer behaviour studies, business-to-business marketing and strategic management.

Dr Siti Hasnah Hassan received her PhD in Marketing at the School of Management, Marketing and International Business at the Australian National University. Her thesis examines the influences on the consumption of functional food within a multicultural society. She has presented her research at the *Australian and New Zealand Marketing Academy Conference*.

Dr Ana Akemi Ikeda is an associate professor at the University of São Paulo. She has published *European Business Review*, *Qualitative Market Research* and *The Qualitative Report*, among others. Dr Ikeda is an active participant in international fora such as those hosted by the Academy of Marketing Science and the American Marketing Association. Her research interests pertain to consumer behaviour, services marketing, marketing research techniques and marketing planning.

Mr Kharil Annuar Mohd Kamal is a PhD student in International Business in the School of Management, Marketing, and International Business at the Australian National University. His thesis examines the effects of business group affiliations in Indonesia.

Adriana Beatriz Madeira is an assistant professor in the Business Administration Department of the Presbyterian University Mackenzie in São Paulo. She also lectures on retailing disciplines for professional postgraduate business courses. At the School of Economics, Administration and Accounting at the University of São Paulo, Ms Madeira is finishing her PhD thesis about the internationalization of Brazilian retail. She has published on packaging for single consumers and participated in international and national conferences. Her research interests include retailing, consumer behaviour, the internationalization of enterprises, and store locations.

Dr Juliana Mansvelt is a senior lecturer in geography at Massey University. She received her PhD from the University of Sheffield and has published in *Annals of Leisure Research*, *Area*, *Geography*, *New Zealand Geographer* and *Progress in Human Geography*, among others. She is the author of *Geographies of Consumption* (Sage, 2005) and has contributed chapters to books on her research interests, including qualitative research methods, teaching and pedagogy, and aging and consumption. In 2006 Dr Mansvelt was awarded a New Zealand National Tertiary Teaching Excellence Award; she recently completed a major research project for the New Zealand Ministry of Education on Professional Development and E-Learning.

Professor Sunita Mishra is professor and Dean at the School for Home Science, Babasaheb Bhimrao Ambedkar University, India. Her research interests include food safety and tribal women's health. She also studies the socio-psychological attributes of community and their relation to food systems. Dr Mishra has supervised several PhD students and she has published three books and various national and international papers in reputed journals.

Dr Des Nicholls is a professor at the School of Management, Marketing and International Business at the Australian National University, from which he also received his PhD. He has published over 50 research papers and two research monographs. His current research interests include the application and analysis of public policy issues to both the public and private sectors. Recent research has related to the detection and management of inappropriate practice in the medical profession; accounting for the impact of inflation in the defence industry; the development of a scorecard system for the measurement of defence contractor performance; and, as a result of the implementation of a National Competition Policy by the Australian Government, the restructuring and management of the taxi transport industry in Australia.

Dr Suresh H. Patel is Professor of Business and Enterprise at Birmingham City University. He received his PhD from the Open University and has published in several journals, including *Independent Grocer*, *Kingston University Working Paper Series*, *Management Review*, *New Community*, *New Life Publications*, *New Society*, *Open University Working Paper Series* and *Sundridge Park*. His textbook contributions include work with the Oxford University Press. Professor Patel's research interests focus on Asian retailing, ethnic minority businesses, insurance in inner cities, business support evaluation, entrepreneurship and ageing, and waste management. He has served on the board of a number of community-based business support and funding agencies.

Dr Eugenio Avila Pedrozo is Professor of Strategy, Interorganizational Relationships and Sustainable Innovation at the Federal University of Rio Grande do Sul, where he is

Director of the Center for Studies and Development in Agribusiness (CEPAN) and Leader of the Group of Studies in Organizations (GESTOR). Professor Pedrozo received his PhD from the Institut National Polytechnique de Lorraine. He has published in *International Food and Agribusiness Management Review, Management Decision, Management Internationale,* and the *SCMS Journal of Indian Management,* among others. Professor Pedrozo's research interests include interorganizational relationships, strategy, sustainable development, innovation, agribusiness, system analysis and complexity. He serves on the board of several journals.

Dr Hillary Shaw is a senior lecturer at Harper Adams University College. He received his PhD from the University of Leeds. Dr Shaw has published in *Geografiska Annaler,* the *International Journal of Baudrillard Studies* and *Social Responsibility Journal.* His research interests include consumer access to food, the psychology and economics of food purchasing, corporate social responsibility, and global and local developments in the food retailing sector. He has provided consultancy services on food access to a number of agencies, including local government, non-governmental organizations, national and local media, and the education sector.

Anamika Singh investigates the nutritional values of traditional foods. She has completed her M.Sc. thesis on *Adi Traditional Food Systems and Bio-cultural Knowledge* and has published four research articles in the *Journal of Traditional Knowledge.* She recently presented a paper about traditional foods and communication patterns in the traditional community of Arunachal Pradesh at a national conference in India. Currently, she is engaged in a project pertaining to the traditional foods of traditional communities of Arunachal Pradesh and entrepreneurship development.

Dr Ranjay K. Singh is Assistant Professor of Agricultural Extension at the Department of Extension Education and Rural Sociology, College of Horticulture and Forestry, Central Agricultural University. Dr Singh is an honorary associate scholar for the Centre of World Indigenous Studies, Olympia. He works at the interfaces of society and bio-cultural knowledge systems and has completed several projects and organized various workshops and seminars on the issues of bio-cultural knowledge, livelihood and sustainable development; he also studies the added value of traditional foods and bio-cultural knowledge for conservation and the protection of intellectual property among traditional communities of India. Dr Singh has presented many research papers at various national and international conferences and given seminars and keynote speeches. His research has aided many international and national agencies and appears in many books, research articles, inventories and short communications about traditional ecological knowledge systems and the conservation of bio-cultural knowledge systems.

Dr Ivo A. van der Lans is an assistant professor in the Marketing and Consumer Behaviour Group of Wageningen University. He received his PhD from Leiden University. Dr van der Lans has published in several journals, including *Appetite,* the *European Review of Agricultural Economics, Food Policy,* the *International Journal of Research in Marketing, Risk Analysis* and *Psychometrika.* His main research interest is in the application of more advanced data analysis techniques for studying consumer behaviour. He regularly acts as a reviewer for the *European Review of Agricultural Economics* and *Psychometrika.*

Reviews for *The New Cultures of Food*

"This book is very well timed. It casts an innovative and wider perspective on how global migrations are affecting the way we eat food, and the religious and cultural aspects of food which increasingly influence our daily lives."

Lord Haskins of Skidby,
Former CEO of Northern Foods, The United Kingdom

"Timely, insightful and commercially-relevant, The New Cultures of Food *is an excellent contribution to melting pot marketing theory and practice!"*

Emeritus Prof. David Hughes, Imperial College London, The United Kingdom

*"*The New Cultures of Food: Opportunities from Ethnic, Religious, and Cultural Diversities, *edited by professors Lindgreen and Hingley, is a rich source of thought for everyone who wants to get deeper insights in the marketing challenges and opportunities for the food and agribusiness industry induced by the fast changing landscape of ethnic, religious and cultural groups."*

Onno Omta, Prof. in Business Administration,
Wageningen University, The Netherlands

"Twenty-nine contributors including the two editors present their studies of marketing potentials based on various population groups in a number of countries. The book is divided into European, Latin American, and Asian parts with a majority of examples from the U.K. Over a long period, the U.K. has received a large number of immigrants from former Commonwealth territories, and in recent years Western Europe follows this same pattern. What can marketing learn and utilise from the buying behaviour of different groups? Can export be helped from studies of similar groups living overseas? The chapters vary from internet trade to fairly primitive conditions in India and is thereby giving thoughts to whether integration or segregation will dominate the global future. Figures for halal *marked products, exceeding US$150 billon annually in world trade, is of great importance to realize.*

The book should be read and studied carefully by marketing and sales department in all relevant countries and is highly recommended."

K.Porsdal Poulsen, Prof. h.c.,
Technical University of Denmark

Foreword and Acknowledgements

The world has always seen the migration of people, in search of the fruits of peace, freedom and trade. Some nations boast a melting pot of racial and ethnicity mixes that define their cultures. More commonly though, countries reflect the predominant faiths and homogeneity against which peoples from other cultures and diverse ethnicities may be defined, by either blending in or standing apart for reasons of either protection or ghettoization. In the modern age, the movement of people is rapid, determined not just by historic reasons but also by the creation of regional trade and community blocs, such as the enlargement of the European Union. New member states now are free to seek labour from other member nations of the European Union. Combined with the flight of peoples from war and conflict and the drive of those seeking a better life, these developments have created a climate of mobility on a global scale. Many host nations encourage new entrants because of their shortage of labour or admit people out of compassion for their circumstances. Thus, countries today contain large and diverse ethnic, religious and cultural populations, many of which continue to grow and expand relative to their respective "host" countries. Some populations have persisted for many generations, but new migration also has brought waves of new entrants. Research recognizes that some of these groups live isolated from the rest of the population, keeping their customs and traditions intact, whereas others assimilate, often abandoning their own customs and traditions. Moreover, when these different ethnic, religious and cultural groups interact, they may adopt some of the customs and traditions normally associated with another group.

From a business perspective, the changing landscape of ethnic, religious and cultural populations provides new and exciting opportunities that arise because of this diversity. Different groups demand different products and services; they also run business networks and undertake alternative ways of doing business. Tremendous challenges and opportunities relate to marketing to, within and across groups of different ethnicity, religion and culture. The overall objective of this book therefore is to provide a comprehensive collection of cutting-edge research on the opportunities induced by diversity, especially in terms of the consequences for businesses and appropriate marketing strategy plans. The book includes a number of issues that define, challenge and suggest new markets, products, and services created by the diverse ethnic, religious and cultural landscape. The setting is the international food and agribusiness marketing field.

This book's 17 chapters are organized in three Parts, covering European, Latin American, and Near and Far East perspectives. The chapters are briefly outlined here.

To begin, Chapter 1, by Sean Beer, explores the terminology associated with ethnic and ethnic foods within a multicultural United Kingdom. To explore definitions of ethnicity, the author questions whether white British ethnic groups with distinctive characteristics exist.

Chapter 2, by Hillary Shaw, describes and suggests some remedies for the problems of poor diet for ethnic minorities, especially with regard to the opportunities for healthy food retailing that the ethnic minority market presents.

The focus in Chapter 3 is welcome; here, Lorraine Brown addresses the challenges associated with adjusting to a new food culture, particularly for international students studying in the United Kingdom. She finds that willingness to adapt to foreign food increases with greater cultural similarity, as well as with a motivation to learn and an openness to new experiences. This study has significant implications for food businesses that cater for such market segments.

Chapter 4 (by Sean Beer, Martin Hingley and Adam Lindgreen) explores the approaches that innovative and entrepreneurial organizations take to respond to changing socio-ethnic circumstances. In examining two distinct UK regions (the South-West and the West Midlands), the authors find that evolving markets and regional and national gastronomies create product innovation, but that producers and markets can be hampered by channel and cultural disconnection.

According to Johan Fischer in Chapter 5, the proliferation of halal in a multitude of commoditized forms requires complex understandings and practices of certification. Set in the context of Malay Muslins living in London, this chapter confirms that certification and logos evoke a wide range of issues involved in modern forms of Islamic consumption.

Chapter 6, by Jon Hanf and Kirsti Dautzenberg, acknowledges that globalized markets and internationalization have initiated various structural changes in the food retail business by comparing the development and impact of globalization in the retail sectors of different Central and Eastern European countries.

In Chapter 7 Luis Aguiar focuses on the growing Brazilian diaspora in the United Kingdom. By consuming typical foods, people can reaffirm their ethnicity; the chapter suggests a typology based on consumption and reveals specific ethnicity indicators, including origin, culture and acculturation.

Chapter 8, by Marcia Dutros de Barcellos, Eugenio Pedrozo and Ivo van der Lans, summarizes Australian, Brazilian and Dutch consumers' attitudes to, involvement in and emotions about beef consumption. Effective marketing tools and knowledge about consumers can increase the competitiveness of global food chains and improve communication.

Brazilians also appear in Chapter 9, (by Adriana Madeira and José da Silveira), which explores the growth of single dwellers in big cities. These consumers have significant implications for marketing, retailing and manufacturing, among other fields.

Chapter 10, by Vanessa Fonseca, discusses how Hispanic remittances and e-commerce in the United States stimulate new retailing practices and consumer trends both in this country and in Latin America. Hispanic food portals help reproduce cultural practices and capitalize on nostalgic consumption – an important point for developing both marketing strategies and branding.

In Chapter 11 Janina de Moura Giraldi and Ana Ikeda consider how consumers' diverse personal values might influence country-of-origin effects. In the context of Chinese home appliances and Brazilian executives' perspectives, they identify personal values as a multidimensional construct, such that each dimension has a different influence on evaluations of foreign products.

The final section of the book begins with Chapter 12, by Sunita Mishra, Ranjay Singh and Anamika Singh, which examines the interrelationships of traditional foods with nutrition, knowledge, ecosystems and livelihoods among *Adi* women in the Indian province of Arunachal Pradesh. This innovative research identifies the importance of informal networks, formed by women, and social processes which pass knowledge about ways of integrating and domesticating wild ethnobotanicals into existing farming systems from one generation of women to the next.

Functional food consumption, according to Siti Hassan, Stephen Dann, Mohd Kamal and Des Nicholls in Chapter 13, depends on culture and value systems, and the role of ethnicity and the dynamics of cultural and value changes in traditional and emerging economies seem to be particularly important in terms of their influences on functional food consumption in multicultural societies. The chapter also outlines market lessons for business.

Chapter 14, by Siti Hassan, Stephen Dann, Mohd Kamal, and Ernest De Run, studies the influence of halal certification on consumer perceptions of food quality. Although the halal sign supports Muslim and non-Muslim markets, negative reactions are possible if the halal sign is closely associated with a specific region.

The authors of the next two chapters address the Asian industry in the United Kingdom. Chapter 15, by Suresh Patel and Kuldip Gujral, focuses on the change and renewal in the Asian food and drink industry in Handsworth, Birmingham, to determine why this industry has been so successful. Goad maps help identify the nature and dynamics of the Asian food industry, as well as conceptualize and reconstruct business journeys over time, which indicate the change, renewal, and stability of this sector.

In Chapter 16 the same authors investigate how independent Asian food retail businesses contribute to the regeneration of distressed areas, such as the UK West Midlands. These smaller, independent food retailers may regard such areas as an economic opportunity, and government initiatives could strengthen their contribution to community regeneration.

Finally, Chapter 17, by Emma Dressler-Hawke and Juliana Mansvelt, seeks to determine how authenticity is shaped in New Zealand supermarkets by exploring the availability, location and shelf position of ethnic foods. Foods aimed specifically at ethnic populations get separated into specialist ethnic sections, but most ethnic foods have been integrated into mainstream product lines. Interestingly, supermarkets that serve customers with higher socio-economic status have greater range of ethnic products.

The double-blind process for selecting entries for this volume required the assistance of many reviewers who dedicated time and effort to provide helpful feedback to the authors. We greatly appreciate their work, which helped improved the chapters herein. We extend a special thanks to Gower Publishing and its staff, which has been most helpful throughout the entire process. Equally, we warmly thank all of the authors who submitted their manuscripts for consideration for this book. They have exhibited the desire to share their knowledge and experience with the book's readers – and a willingness to put forward their views for possible challenge by their peers. Finally, we thank Harper Adams University College and Hull University Business School; it is a privilege working at universities that allow us to pursue our research interests. Special thanks go to Elisabeth Nevins Caswell, Jon Reast and Joëlle Vanhamme.

We are confident that the chapters in this book contribute to a greater understanding of the changing landscape of ethnic, religious and cultural mixes and of how this increasing diversity provides new and exciting opportunities. We hope these selected chapters continue to generate the kind of dialogue necessary to extend our understanding of this important area even further.

Professor, Dr Adam Lindgreen, Hull.
Reader, Dr Martin K. Hingley, Newport.

The European Perspective

1 *What is "Ethnic"? Reappraising Ethnic Food and Multiculturalism among the White British*

SEAN BEER*

Keywords

gastronomy, ethnic, ethnic food, Great Britain.

Abstract

This chapter explores some of the issues related to the nature of the terms "ethnic" and "ethnic food" within a multicultural Great Britain. The analysis focuses on definitions of ethnicity and whether white British ethnic groups exist with distinctive language, art, culture and gastronomy. Evidence in support of this distinction comes from an examination of popular interest in white British food and a regional case study of West Country cooking. The term "ethnic" is a complex one, but, the author concludes, must be used inclusively or possibly be eliminated altogether.

Introduction

The word "ethnic" seems to have varying applications. By its very nature, the term is a social construct that has been developed from an epistemological perspective, though based on ontological truth in terms of varying ethnicity. As such, it is used by many people in different ways, although in Great Britain, it is largely used in association with comparatively recently migrated, predominately non-white racial groups. The contributions of these groups to a dynamic food culture and the culture of the country cannot be underestimated, but what of white British ethnic groups and their food culture?

* Mr Sean Beer, School of Services Management, Bournemouth University, Dorset House, Talbot Campus, Fern Barrow, Poole, Dorset, BH12 5BB, UK. E-mail: sbeer@bournemouth.ac.uk. Telephone + 44 1202 965 109.

Do such groups exist? Are there distinctive gastronomies, and can the term "ethnic" be applied to these groupings, or are there different and more appropriate approaches?

This chapter explores some of the issues related to the nature of the terms "ethnic" and "ethnic food" within a multicultural Great Britain. It starts by considering definitions of ethnicity and how it is determined according to government classifications; definitions based on customs, language, dialect, food and geography; and the idea of self-determination. The discussion then moves to an examination of whether white British ethnic groups exist. The analysis focuses on ideas of localness, rurality, language, art, culture and gastronomy, which provide evidence in support of the concept of distinctive white British ethnic groups and gastronomies. An examination of popular interest in white British food and a regional case study of West Country cooking further supports this notion. The chapter concludes with concerns about the loss of heritage and authenticity and the nature of the term ethnic. The term is complex and must be used inclusively. If it continues to be used as it currently is, particularly in a pejorative way, it debases the culture of non-white British ethnic groups. If the term is used in a more positive way but to the exclusion of white British ethnic groups, it in effect denies the ethnic origin of white British and their cultural heritage. Possibly, it is best to stop using the term altogether.

Definitions

As a term, "ethnic" has been used in a variety of different ways. Generally, though, reference to the term in a British context describes groups of people connected by race, although the use of this term remains complex. When "ethnic" groups are referred to within the population, they tend to be minorities that have formed part of society comparatively recently. Thus, among many others, Great Britain contains Afro-Caribbean, Chinese, Indian and Pakistani ethnic groups that form parts of a modern multicultural society.

British society has always been in flux, having experienced past, often violent, migrations of Anglos, Danes, Romans and Normans. Thus, it is difficult to refer to a settled or homogenous cultural map at any one time. Further complications result because of the connection between the term "minority" and ethnic, which indicates that a particular group forms a minority of the total population. Yet, geographically, concentrations of particular groups might not represent a minority within a particular subregion or area, even if they do on a national basis.

These classifications have been formalized in several ways. Perhaps the most accepted is the National Statistics classification (identical to that used in the 2001 Census in England and Wales), which contains the groups indicated in Table 1.1.[1]

The general tendency has been to ascribe the term "ethnic" to more recently arrived groups in society. In Great Britain, these groups tend to be non-white, though there also are recent developments with regard to white European groups, such as Polish and Latvian migrants, as well as more established groups, such as Italians and Greeks. However, the term "ethnic" does not seem to be applied to subgroups of white British people, which in many ways represents an anomaly. When we look at ethnicity from a cultural or sociological perspective, a more reflective definition indicates that we refer to a group of people whose members identify with one another on the basis of a presumed common genealogy or ancestry.[2] Other common traits may include culture, language,

Table 1.1   Ethnic classifications used by the Office of National Statistics

Level 1	Level 2
WHITE	WHITE
	British
	Irish
	Other White background
	All White groups
MIXED	MIXED
	White and Black Caribbean
	White and Black African
	White and Asian
	Other Mixed background
	All Mixed groups
ASIAN or ASIAN BRITISH	ASIAN or ASIAN BRITISH
	Indian
	Pakistani
	Bangladeshi
	Other Asian background
	All Asian groups
BLACK or BLACK BRITISH	BLACK or BLACK BRITISH
	Caribbean
	African
	Other Black background
	All Black groups
CHINESE or OTHER ETHNIC GROUP	CHINESE or OTHER ETHNIC GROUP
	Chinese
	Other ethnic group

geography or even recognition by others. This term therefore may be contrasted with race, which tends to indicate common physical and genetic traits.

Race and ethnicity can be sensitive areas for discussion. In this context, the use of the term "ethnic" in relation to food is an interesting and complicated issue. For example, do people from non-white ethnic groups feel offended by having their gastronomy and themselves labelled as "ethnic" and do white people feel left out? Is "ethnic" the best term to use?

Are There White British Ethnic Groups?

So what of the ethnic white British and their subgroups? Do they exist? What of the lost tribes of the white British? Do they have distinctive gastronomies and gastronomic histories? Why do we not recognize them and celebrate them as we do other ethnic cuisines? It might be argued that the white population has become homogenized and that, as a result of migration, immigration and intermingling, ethnic diversity has declined. But is this really the case? Certainly there is evidence to suggest diversity in the white population. Customs, language, dialect and food all indicate potentially different ethnic groupings, often (though not necessarily) on a geographic basis, and differentiation on a geographical basis is one of Smith's criteria for ethnic identification.[3] Thus, Welsh, Scottish and English groups exist; the English category contains the Cornish, Cumbrians and Devonians.

At this juncture, two crucial points are necessary. The phrase "white British" does not exclude people of non-white backgrounds who belong to those groups. Rather, it is a term that recognizes antecedence, whether by blood or adoption, and the right of individuals to decide on their own ethnic background, just as individuals in Great Britain have the right to decide their own gender. As such, "white British" may be considered a clumsy term, but it is probably the best that we have. Second, for many white people, the act of trying to identify and tie down their ethnicity creates dissonance. It forces them to look at the past, consider injustices that may or may not have been committed by one ethnic group on another, and question motives. Billy Bragg, long the singing standard-bearer of the Left in Great Britain and a fervent campaigner against racism, has addressed these very issues in his book *The Progressive Patriot*.[4] His important, somewhat controversial stance explores the nature of what it means to be a white English man, a discussion that the Left is often uncomfortable with and that the Right seems, at times, fixated on. *The Progressive Patriot* offers an excellent account of Bragg's attempts to reconcile the many things that constitute his Englishness and, in many ways, review his own ethnicity. The account has been a long time coming; its roots can be seen, as he admits, in his most political album, *The Internationale*, as well as his 2002 album *England, Half English*. Further discussion in this chapter should be taken in this light. In the spirit of acknowledging the subjectivity of qualitative research, I also acknowledge that I have faced turmoil similar to that Bragg describes in looking at his past, which may emerge in the following analysis.

LOCALNESS

During the past decade, growing interest in food and where it comes from may have derived from insecurities about food as a result of problems such as *E. coli* infection, BSE (*bovine spongiform encephalopathy*), and foot and mouth disease. Changes in attitudes towards animal welfare, support for the natural environment and support for local economies and the British farming industry may also have had an effect. Food consumers are gradually experiencing more complex motivations and, theoretically, becoming more demanding in many ways, both collectively and as individuals. Yet it remains debatable whether this complexity really exists or whether there are considerable divergences within the population. In other words, consumers may look at food from a whole host of different perspectives,[5] as indicated in Figure 1.1.

In turn, it becomes valuable to consider in more detail the idea of localness. Considerable evidence suggests that localness has become very important for some consumers.[6] In this context, local may be a euphemism for ethnic white, but, then again, not all local food is of white British origin, although much is. All ethnic white food may be local (presuming that is it is being sold locally), but not all local food is ethnic white – just as a square is a rectangle but a rectangle is not a square.

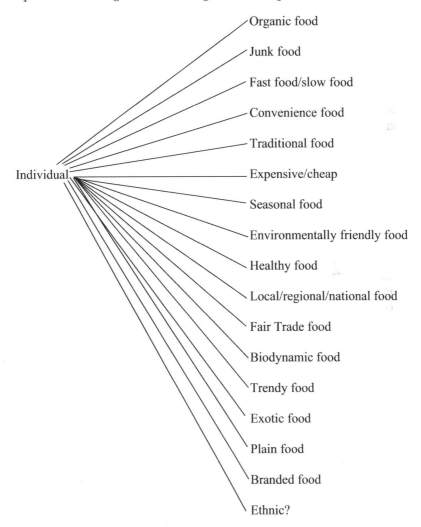

Figure 1.1   An impression of the range of perspectives with which British consumers may well view their food choices

Source: S. Beer (2008).

Organizations that try to promote and protect local distinctiveness include the Campaign for the Protection of Rural England (CPRE),[7] which has been involved in this sort of campaigning since 1926. A registered charity, with 60 000 members, the organization actively tries to support local food production and consumption. Various publications, including *Sustainable Local Foods,*[8] *Local Action for Local Foods,*[9] *Mapping Local Food Webs*[10] and *The Real Choice: How Local Food has Survived the Supermarket Onslaught,*[11] along with active campaigning, have aimed to support local food production and consumption. The organization Common Ground[12] has also worked hard to promote all aspects of localness. Its rules for local distinctiveness highlight the direction from which they, and a number of other organizations, are travelling. Some extracts appear in Table 1.2.

Table 1.2   Extracts from Common Ground's *Rules for Local Distinctiveness*

Fight for AUTHENTICITY and integrity. Keep places lived in, worked in and real. Demand the BEST of the new.

Value the COMMON place. Our Cultural Landscapes are our ordinary history and everyday nature intertwined.

Let the CHARACTER of the people and place express itself. Kill corporate identity before it kills our high streets. Give local shops precedence.

Local DIALECT should be spoken, heard and seen.

Get to know your GHOSTS. The hidden and unseen stories and legends are as important as the visible.

Don 't fossilize places. HISTORY is a continuing process, not just the past. Celebrate time, place and the seasons with Feasts and Festivals.

Our IMAGINATION needs diversity and variegation. We need standards not standardisation.

Work for local IDENTITY. Oppose monoculture in our fields, parks, gardens and buildings. Resist formulaic and automatic ordering from pattern books which homogenise and deplete.

Know your place. Facts and surveys are not the same as KNOWLEDGE and wisdom. Itinerant expertise needs to meet with aboriginal, place based knowledge so we can make the best of both worlds.

Buy things that are LOCALLY DISTINCTIVE and locally made – such as food and souvenirs. Resist the things that can be found anywhere.

The LAND is sacred in many cultures. Why have we put a protective noose around the spectacular and the special and left the rest? All of our surroundings are important to someone.

Bring the countryside to the town. Keep the fruit, vegetable and local produce MARKETS open and alive. We should be able to buy Norfolk Biffins in Norwich and James Grieves in Edinburgh.

Let NATURE in. Encourage the plants that want to grow in your locality. You'll find a succession of good and diverse neighbours that bring richness to your doorstep.

QUALITY cannot be quantified. You know when something is important to you – make subjective and emotional arguments. Don't be put off because the professionals have marginalised all the things they can't count. Make them listen and look.

REMEMBER the depth of people's attachment to places. Do not undermine local pride and rootedness with insensitive change.

VALUE your own values! Democracy thrives on discussion about things that matter to us. Let the experts in on your terms.

Exile XENOPHOBIA which fossilizes places and peoples. Welcome cultural diversity and vive la difference.

Source: Common Ground (2007), "Rules for Local Distinctiveness".

Note that the extracts quoted in Table 1.2 go beyond a specific focus on localness, and make reference to "exiling xenophobia"; Common Ground advocates a recognition of diversity and the need for communities to celebrate what has been, as well as the direction in which they are developing. Other organizations that support the development of local food culture include various Food Links organizations,[13] farmers' markets,[14] Sustain,[15] and the Soil Association.[16]

A RURAL CONNECTION

Many examples of "regional distinctiveness" and "localness" seem rurally based -a fact that demands some reflection. Urban areas tend to be more cosmopolitan than rural areas, and therefore rural populations may be slower to change. Considerable anecdotal evidence supports this claim. Their more insular nature may mean that rural areas maintain, rightly or wrongly, a more settled ethnic pattern that reflects older aspects of the ethnic white British population, which does not discount the very strong urban traditions. Rural areas may also experience a stronger connection to food, the land and landscape. Other social groups provide examples of how people survive or fragment between urban and rural settings. For example, the Aborigines in Australia or the Maori in New Zealand seem to have a much stronger tribal identity in their rural homelands than in urban areas.

LANGUAGE

Considerable evidence indicates varying white ethnicity in terms of the diversities of accents and languages within the white British population, the most obvious examples being the distinctive languages of Wales, Scotland, the Isle of Man and Cornwall. Moreover, many areas and regions have clearly different accents, words and phrases that, if not a different language, can be considered almost unintelligible by those from outside the area. The BBC has undertaken a project to capture much of this cultural richness, the results of which can be viewed at the Voices website.[17] Clifford and King's 2006 book *England in Particular* specifically addresses aspects of language and local distinctiveness.[18] Henry Ames's *Country Words* looks at language with reference to the countryside and the various regions of the British Isles.[19] This fantastically rich and scholarly book reveals the 26 different words for the smallest piglet of the litter used in different parts of rural Britain and multiple names for different crafts, tools, occupations, plants and animals. The listing of the various names for the bird commonly known as the lapwing sounds like an extract from a John Betjeman poem: "lapwing, corniwillen, flap-jack, happinch, horn-pie, lip-wingle, old maid, peesweep, piwipe, pute, teufit, wallop and wipe." Thus, there is ample evidence within the British language of ethnic diversity.

ART AND CULTURE

Popularist domains indicate much interest in what might be called "traditional British culture". A series of different magazines – *Best of British Magazine*,[20] *This England*,[21] *The Field*,[22] and *Country Life*[23] – aim to celebrate many aspects of "traditional British culture". *Country Life* recently ran an issue specifically focused on "Why the World Loves England. An Epic Celebration of All Things Local".[24] Articles examined areas such as the landscape, geology, houses, food and farming, arts, dialects, market towns, history, gardens, quirks and legends. Mark Hedges' editorial in that issue is also very interesting, in that it highlights the growth of interest in localness, its value and the need to protect and develop for the future:

> As if from nowhere, local suddenly became the buzzword of the Noughties (2000–2009). Now we all strive to buy local food, and that's got the supermarket chains falling over themselves to be the biggest and best local supplier. Local is suddenly the height of fashion. However, local distinctiveness isn't a new thing – it's something that we've lost and are only slowly beginning to rediscover, and it's about much more than food. It's about England itself. The French have been much better than us at celebrating a cherishing the local, or terroir as they call it, literally "the earth' … Local foods from Cromer Crabs to Dorset Knobs delight our pallets in a way a hamburger never will … In short we need to celebrate our glorious local distinctiveness so that we can pass on a country that our children and grandchildren can love and preserve too.

This trend is repeated on a more local and regional basis by a series of other magazines. South-west England, for example, hosts periodicals such as *Dorset Magazine*,[25] *Dorset Life*,[26] *Somerset Life*[27] and *Exmoor Magazine*.[28] These magazines cover a range of issues. but always make reference to food, cooking in the home and eating out. Amidst all this information, there is at times a certain feeling of unease; it would be very easy for xenophobia to creep into many of these discussions, both locally and nationally.

An article in *Country Life* by Kevin Jackson pays homage to localness, highlighting the connection of less popularist art and literature to specific areas.[29] Thus, we have John Constable's paintings featuring the countryside of East Anglia, Jane Austen's links to Devon (*Sense and Sensibility*), A.E. Housman and his connections to Shropshire, George Turner's connection to Derbyshire, and the Bronte sisters and Yorkshire. Henry Williamson wrote extensively not only about nature, but also about local south-west England communities in books such as *The Village Book*,[30] *The Labouring Life*[31] and *Tales of a Devon Village*.[32] The photographs of James Ravilious, published in *A Corner of England: North Devon Landscape and People*,[33] document the distinctive population of this area. In Dorset and further afield in south-west England, the classic poetry and novels of Thomas Hardy, such as *The Mayor of Casterbridge*[34] and *Far from the Madding Crowd*,[35] provide micro-studies of different populations during the late nineteenth century. In Wales, the poetry of R.S. Thomas vividly describes the lives of local men:[36]

> Iago Prytherchh his name, though, be it allowed,
> Just an ordinary man of the bald welsh hills.

Looking at art in a broad sense, the architecture of buildings provides a direct connection between the population and the land. Traditionally, buildings were built from earth and other locally obtainable materials; therefore, just as food was originally connected to the soils and rocks of the area, so were buildings, and so was the population.

Considerable evidence thus supports the existence of varying ethnic white British groups, based on aspects of geography, language, art and culture. This ethnicity might be considered simply a form of regionalism, but distinctive language, art and culture, as well as distinctive gastronomies, surely point to distinctive ethnicities. These ethnic groupings may not be as differentiated or distinctive as others, but they exist, and food and gastronomy might be used to highlight the experiences of these groups. It is also possible that much about these ethnic groups needs to be rediscovered and celebrated.

Evidence for a Distinctive White British Gastronomy

There is a tendency to misuse the word "gastronomy"; it does not refer solely to food. Rather, it connotes the relationship between food and culture, and involves various cultural dimensions, with food and drink as the central theme. Thus, all societies have a gastronomy, and British gastronomy reflects the broad relationship between culture and food within Great Britain as a whole. As such, all ethnic groups contribute to it as a result of different influences arriving in the islands, adding to what was already there. An analysis of this development would seem to indicate that this addition represents a process of assimilation. The "traditional" British cup of tea provides a good example. Tea initially arrived as a new ethnic influence. Initially, it maintained its original ethnic identity, but then gradually became Anglicized until it reached a point where it came to be viewed as quintessentially British. Today, the consumption of tea is considered a characteristic of British culture and gastronomy, and British gastronomy similarly can be seen as a composite of various ethnic traditions, in varying states of Anglicization. This combination forms a complex gastronomic mosaic, within which some traditions are clearer than others.

The question under discussion here is whether one tradition is distinctive to the ethnic white British. Previous arguments establish that distinctive traits mark the white population, which could be described as indicating distinct ethnic groups. In terms of this link between white British ethnic groups and food, much popular work has been done, including McFarlane's classic *The Dairy Book of British Food*[37] which outlines in some detail a regional gastronomy of Great Britain (see Table 1.3).

McFarlane's analysis is principally hierarchical in nature; he and many others highlight regional ingredients and dishes, yet the majority of McFarlane's recipes are not attributed to a specific region. Regional styles and techniques of cooking are less evident, possibly because they do not exist in the same way they might in other countries.

Recently, there has been a range of new attempts to produce gastronomic maps of Great Britain, including Fursdon's[38] Roll of Honour for British food products, as described in Table 1.4.

Another way of looking at regional differences and characteristics of food and gastronomy would be to address specific products, such as cheese. Possibly the most famous British cheese is Cheddar, originally produced in the Cheddar Gorge area of Somerset. The technique of Cheddaring, central to the production of Cheddar cheese, has been exported worldwide. At one time, British cheese production was considered in the doldrums and was compared unfavourably to French production. However, recently the British cheese industry has experienced a renaissance through the development of excellent local cheeses. A new map would therefore show a wide distribution of more than 700 different cheeses across the country, suggesting an emerging pattern of a varied and distinctive national, regional and subregional white British gastronomy, not based solely on cheese but, rather, on a diversity of products.

Table 1.3   A breakdown of McFarlane's analysis of British food

The West Country (36 recipes)
Tender young vegetables and fruits, fine fish and shellfish, refreshing ciders and, above all, superb cream and cheeses are typical West Country temptations.

The South-East (39 recipes)
Rich farmland stretched down to the coast, encompassing the Garden of England and making a cornucopia filled with soft fruits, vegetables, seafood, meat, milk and other good things.

Wales (15 recipes)
Sweet, tender lamb from the mountains; oats, wheat and barley; soft fruits in the warmer South; fish of all types, from cockles to sea trout; creamy milk and butter; carrots, cabbage and early potatoes. These are the good things of Wales, a country where the cooking is simple and wholesome.

Midlands (18 recipes)
From the fruit-laden orchards of the south to the lush Dairy pastures further north, the Midlands have much to offer. Famous cheeses, prime beef, abundant produce, as well as pies in plenty, cakes and ales, cider and pure mineral water all produced here in the heart of England.

The Eastern Counties (20 recipes)
Wheat and barley, potatoes and peas, salads and soft fruits, all thrive on the rich farmlands of England's Eastern counties. First-class fish and shellfish inhabit the coastal waters. Pigs and poultry are reared and there's an abundance of game. And the climate encourages a good harvest of grapes, which make light, white wines.

The North (28 recipes)
There is a wealth of good food to discover: choice lamb, celebrated cheeses, excellent fish, thirst quenching beers and mouth-watering home-baked cakes.

Scotland (26 recipes)
Succulent Highland beef and tender lamb, superb salmon, mouth-watering smoked fish, firm potatoes and juicy berries are second to none, as are the traditionally baked cakes, breads and biscuits, and the rich, mellow whiskies.

Northern Ireland (13 recipes)
Rivers and seas teeming with fish, creamy milk and butter, top-quality meat, and excellent ham and bacon give Northern Ireland its reputation for fine, simple food. The ubiquitous potato cooked in all manner of ways, is always mouth-wateringly good. And to savour afterwards, there is the incompatible smoothness of Irish whiskey.

Countrywide (191 recipes)
Recipes not attributed to a specific region

Table 1.4   Fursdon's Roll of Honour

Northumberland	Kipper And Berwick Cockles
Cumbria	Kendal Mint Cake, Damson and Cumberland Sausages
Durham	Stotty Cake
Tyne & Wear	Newcastle Brown Ale
North Yorkshire	Bakewell Tart and Yorkshire Tea Cakes (The author considers that Bakewell is in fact in Derbyshire)
Lancashire	Blackpool Rock, Chorley and Eccles Cakes, Fishermen's Friends and Hot Pot
Merseyside	Everton Mints
West Yorkshire	Parkin and Denby Dale Pie and Herdwick Sheep (The author considers that the Herdwick is really a sheep of Cumbria)
South Yorkshire	Henderson's relish
Greater Manchester	Tizer and Vimto
Cheshire	Cheshire Cheese
Derbyshire	Buxton Water
Nottinghamshire	Stilton (also made in Leicestershire and Derbyshire). (The author considers that the Stilton is primarily a cheese of Leicestershire)
Lincolnshire	Plum Loaf and Lincolnshire Sausages
Staffordshire	Branston Pickle and Marmite
Shropshire	Bread Cake, Shrewsbury Cake and Fidget Pie
Warwickshire	Tamworth Pig
Leicestershire	Melton Mowbray Pie
Northamptonshire	Haslet
Cambridgeshire	Gage Plum, Careless Gooseberry and Bronze Turkey
Norfolk	Norfolk Honey Cake, Coleman's Mustard and Cromer Crab
Suffolk	Suffolk Harvest Cake, Suffolk Ham and Cider Vinegar
Essex	Chelsea Buns
London	Jellied Eels
Hertfordshire	Cider (The author considers that Herefordshire my be more appropriate also Devon, Somerset and Cornwall)
Bedfordshire	Bedfordshire Clanger
Buckinghamshire	Cox's Orange Pippin, Double-Crust Cherry Pie
Oxfordshire	Oxford Fruit Cake
Worcestershire	Worcestershire Sauce
Gloucestershire	Double Gloucester Cheese and Gloucester Old Spot
Wiltshire	Wiltshire Bacon, Urchfont Chilli Mustard and Bradenham Ham
Berkshire	Wellington Cheese
Somerset	Mendip Wall Fish (snails) and Bath Oliver Biscuits
Hampshire	Watercress
Dorset	Dorset Blue Vinney Cheese, Dorset Knob Biscuits and Dorset Horn Sheep
Devon	Plymouth Gin
Cornwall	Black Cake and Clotted Cream and Cornish Pasty
Sussex	Southdown Sheep, Sussex Chicken and Sussex Cattle
Kent	Huffkin Roll

Popular Interest in White British Food

Magazines such as *Country Living*[39] and *Country Kitchen*[40] do not necessarily seek to highlight only one approach to food, but champion "traditional" cooking, which seems to translate as ethnic white British food of the preceding three or four generations. For example, books such as Pearce's *Exmoor Food and Cookery: A Moorland Heritage*[41] and *The Taste of Exmoor Cookery Book*[42] examine the gastronomy of Exmoor, a very specific area in north Devon and Somerset, with a specific history, geography and cultural heritage – much of which is covered in Pearce's book.

It remains debatable how much this interest might be linked to, or identify, specific ethnic groupings, considering the definitions of ethnicity already discussed. Similar studies appear for a multitude of British regions and areas. This approach is common in other countries too, as exemplified by books like *French Regional Cooking*.[43] Beer et al.[44] examine links between the regional gastronomies of south-west England and northern Portugal in developing their concept of the North Atlantic diet. This work also highlights the possibility that ethnic groups that are geographically separate develop similar gastronomies. Comparisons between Normandy in France and south-west England are also possible; the cheeses, milk, cream, cider and cider brandy represent very distinctive products.

Case Study: West Country Cooking

On a regional basis, different groups have tried to rediscover and celebrate distinctive gastronomies. In south-west England, the speciality food group, Taste of the West, has tried to highlight the distinctive gastronomies of the region.[45] The West Country Cooking Project examined this topic closely and produced a series of cookbooks as part of their output.[46] The following material consists of extracts from an interview with one of the leading members of the West Country Cooking Project, and it aims to get behind the project in order to determine any links between the project and other aspects of local culture and, possibly, ethnicity. The interviewee was a farmer who comes from generations of farmers, smallholders and farm workers in north Devon. The observations are interesting in that they present a clear case study of a distinctive gastronomy and an interplay of food, culture and ethnic origin.

In part, the West Country Cooking Project was established to take advantage of European Union money to promote West Country food, but it also was more. As indicated by the interviewee:

> It was more than stargazey pie [pilchard pie, with the heads staring up through the pastry] and pasties. The idea was that through the production of four cookery books, publicizing eating establishments and holding awards and competitions we could show how West Country Cooking could use West Country food and produce. This all reflected the past, when to a large extent it was the only produce that they had to use. What it was not was a project to highlight excellence in food and establishments achieved by using imported ingredients and styles.

The focus was very much on food and cookery from south-west England, its heritage and culture, as laid out, for example, in the books on cream and baking by Michael

Raphael and expressed and presented in Brian Pearce's *Exmoor Food and Cookery* book. The word "cuisine" was not used; the English word "cooking" was thought more appropriate. With regard to the distinctive gastronomy of the region, the patchwork of culinary traditions varied on a micro-level. When asked whether the Exmoor culinary tradition reflected the interviewee's own tradition – he was brought up in a lower-lying coastal area of north Devon – his response highlighted differences and the way in which traditional products were consumed by a range of social classes:

> South of the Taw [a river in North Devon] we didn't know much about Exmoor. We didn't know much about Venison and Whortleberries, the really characteristic foods of Exmoor. Wild Venison and Whortleberries though not unique to Exmoor are very characteristic. Cream yes, pies, pasties and tarts and clotted cream, very much so. These were characteristic foods of my area. The better off you were the more often you ate the better things. A farm worker might have a quarter [of a pound, or 114g] of cream on a Sunday, clotted cream. Farmers would have pans of cream all the time as they would be selling the cream and the butter made from the cream all the time.

Nevertheless, the situation was changing, with a decline in the production and consumption of traditional products. Farms now tend to specialize in terms of production, and orchards have been decimated. Farmers no longer produce eggs, and very few farm workers keep pigs, though local specialities could still be purchased. Having said that, it was interesting who purchased these products, the interviewee noted:

> … a lot of people wouldn't buy brawn [pig's head pate] or other pig products, even more chitterlings [pig's intestine] or hogs pudding [local white sausage], and a lot of people wouldn't know what they were. Some products are kept in the eye by specialist retailers. A classic example being Laver [a type of seaweed, Porphrya umbilicalis] in North Devon and Laver Bread in South Wales. It depends how much longer people are prepared to work the coastline picking seaweed to produce Laver. It probably relates to how much longer local boats will go out from ports such as Bideford, Appledore and Ilfracombe and other Severn Channel Ports to bring in the variety of local fish. How many ordinary run-of-the-mill family households have eaten Huss [rock salmon or dogfish]?

Some of these changes were attributed to a change in ethnicity as a result of immigration to the area by people who had no "local roots" – primarily migrants from other parts of England who are of white ethnic origin – as well as to a decline in cookery skills and changes in eating patterns, which potentially would lead to the demise of certain foodstuffs:

> There is a big interest in cooking in terms of the television programmes but this interest is totally different in the main to that which produced traditional farmhouse and cottage food. The other thing is the influence of eating out. Even at a pub counter people are more likely to order lasagne than steak and kidney pudding. Some of the foods will virtually disappear, for example, I couldn't guarantee that you could buy chitterlings in Barnstaple any more. I can't see a return to the collection of the wild foods of the countryside, rabbits, Whortleberries, Blackberries, all are much less likely to be used. As are other cultivated products such as damsons or even runner

beans. If you went back to the days of World War II the staple vegetable in the countryside community from mid-July until the frosts was the runner bean.

The farmer linked these changes to broader cultural change in the region. He indicated that the lack of public recognition for products such as Hogs pudding and the demise of the fish and chip shop were all part of this development and that the future consumption of these traditional food products and their contribution to local culture hung in the balance:

A lot of this is in the hands of the enthusiasts. In terms of core products such as quality beef and lamb, possibly from local and British breeds, there is hope as consumption of these products is linked to an increase in people's ability to pay, and they wish to pay for some quality and variety. Because there is such a wide range of products available consumers don't seek out products of a less than core nature. Having said that, with the fall in the percentage that people spend on food from 20 per cent 20 years ago to 9 per cent today, people should have more money to spend on food. Unfortunately they are more likely to spend it on other forms of leisure activity and living.

This particular case study highlights three specific findings: (1) the distinctive gastronomy of a rural area in southwest England; (2) its link to a perception of an individual's ethnic origin; and (3) the threat to this culture and the way in which this threat spurs on some individuals to act to conserve it.

Real Concerns

ANGST AT A LOSS OF HERITAGE

There is much discussion relating to a national angst about food, its quality, and the loss of traditional and other values across ethnic groupings. People face a proliferation of food choices and challenges, as indicated in Figure 1.1. Concerns about a move away from traditional values, whatever they may be, cross ethnic divides. It is not only white British parents and grandparents who bemoan the fact that their children and grandchildren are no longer eating "as we used to" and are not preparing meals in "the traditional way". Feelings amongst these white British can run high in certain quarters, as a recent article in the *Western Mail* indicates:[47]

"Junk-fed' teenagers shun traditional British dishes. Old favourites under threat from youthful indifference. Welsh specialities such as Caerphilly cheese and cawl could die out as teenagers increasingly shun traditional British food a survey by Sainsbury's warned.

AUTHENTICITY

If there are concerns about a loss of heritage, there are also concerns about authenticity. These concerns are highlighted in Common Ground's "Rules for Local Distinctiveness": "Fight for authenticity and integrity. Keep places lived in, worked in and real. Demand the BEST of the new."[48]

But what is authenticity? Common Ground offers no definition, and those groups that do contradict one another. This issue is important in its own right, but there are also economic considerations, because governments and other agencies encourage food producers to add value and revive or create distinctive products to aid their economic development. In turn, a range of initiatives standardises authenticity. For example, since 1993 organic production has been defined by EC Council Regulation 2092/91 and administered in Great Britain by the Advisory Committee on Organic Standards (ACOS).[49] Individual products such as Dorset Blue Vinney Cheese, Swaledale Ewes' Cheese and Traditional Farmfresh Turkey are covered by EU Certificates of Protected Geographical Indication (PGI), Protected Designation of Origin (PDO) and Specific Character (CSC), respectively. Retailers and those who run farmers' markets attempt to define "local" and sometimes end up in conflict when they do so.[50]

Academics have also worked on addressing authenticity and have ended up approaching it from a range of perspectives, including the idea of ditching authenticity as a concept altogether and replacing it with concepts related to objects being genuine, actual, accurate, real or true.[51] Although these efforts may seem to be no more than an exercise in semantics, as Wittgenstein maintained, philosophy may be a question of language.

Yet there are other ways of looking at the subject. All experience is ultimately personal. Far from making the subject area of authenticity academically redundant, this consideration opens it up to a focus on the personal nature of experience – that is, the relationship of the person who is having the experience to that which they are experiencing – and also recognizes that, however derived, concepts of authenticity will affect that experience.

THIS WORD "ETHNIC"

As indicated previously, the word "ethnic" in Great Britain is mostly used in association with comparatively recently migrated, non-white racial groups. The contribution of these groups to a dynamic food culture, and the culture of the country, cannot be underestimated, but what of white British ethnic groups and their food culture? There definitely seems to be a range of white British ethnic groups that have common characteristics in terms of their geography, language, food and gastronomy. Further work should be undertaken to define, explore and celebrate these groups, and geographical distinctions and reference to the concept of locality seems to be a useful place to start.

Here, however, is the central point of argument: if we have a complete range of ethnic groups, white and non-white, we cannot use the term exclusively for non-white groups. However we examine the issue, it does not hold. In using it solely for non-white groups, are we discriminating against white groups by excluding them? Or are we looking in a discriminatory way at non-white groups by labelling them? Does the use of the word "ethnic" serve a useful purpose?

Probably not. Great Britain cannot have a truly multi-ethnic and multicultural society until all groups accept and celebrate the multidimensional nature of British culture. If the use of the word and classification "ethnic" obstructs that celebration, it is probably time to stop using the term and move on.

Conclusions

At this chapter's heart lies a fundamental exploration of the term "ethnic". It examines the legitimacy of using this term within the context of the white British population, and it seems that this usage is reasonable at a variety of levels. If used as it currently is, particularly in a pejorative way, it debases the culture of non-white British ethnic groups. If the term is used in a more positive way but still excludes white British ethnic groups, it effectively denies the ethnic origin of the white British and their cultural heritage. Ultimately we must make a decision, and probably the best approach is to stop using the concept and replace it with more distinct terms, such as Indian, Chinese, British Chinese, West Country or whatever words that individuals from those groups wish to use. This approach seems more democratic and could contribute positively to modern multiculturalism in Great Britain.

References

1.   Office of National Statistics (2007), "The classification of ethnic groups", http://www.statistics.gov.uk/about/Classifications/ns_ethnic_classification.asp (accessed 10 September 2007).
2.   Smith, A.D. (1987), *The Ethnic Origin of Nations*. Blackwell, London.
3.   Ibid.
4.   Bragg, B. (2006), *The Progressive Patriot. A Search for Belonging*. Black Swan, London.
5.   Beer, S.C. (2008), "Authenticity and food experience – commercial and academic perspectives", *Journal of Foodservice*, Vol. 19, pp. 153–163.
6.   Beer, S.C., Spacey, J. and Perry, V. (2003), "An investigation into the market relationship that underpins the alternative food economy", in J.S.A. Edwards and I-B. Gustafsson (eds), *Culinary Arts and Sciences IV. Global and National Perspectives*, Proceedings of the Fourth International Conference on Culinary Arts and Sciences, Global and National Perspectives. Worshipful Company of Cooks Centre for Culinary Research, Bournemouth University and Orebro University, Sweden, pp. 381–391.
7.   CPRE (2008), http://www.cpre.org.uk/home (accessed 12 March 2008).
8.   CPRE (2001), *Sustainable Local Foods*. Campaign for the Protection of Rural England, London.
9.   CPRE (2002a), *Local Action for Local Foods*. Campaign for the Protection of Rural England, London.
10. CPRE (2002b), *Mapping Local Food Webs*. Campaign for the Protection of Rural England, London.
11. CPRE (2006), *The Real Choice: How Local Food has Survived the Supermarket Onslaught*. Campaign for the Protection of Rural England, London.
12. Common Ground (2007), "Rules for local distinctiveness", http://www.commonground.org.uk/distinctiveness/d-rules.html (accessed 12 September 2007).
13. Food Links (2008), http://www.foodlinks-uk.org/ (accessed 12 March 2008).
14. National Farmers' Retail and Markets Association (2008), http://www.farma.org.uk (accessed 12 March 2008).
15. Sustain (2008), http://www.sustainweb.org (accessed 12 March 2008).
16. Soil Association (2008), http://www.soilassociation.org (accessed 12 March 2008).
17. BBC (2008), "Voices project", www.bbc.co.uk/voices (accessed 12 March 2008).
18. Clifford, S. and King, A. (2006), *England in Particular*. Hodder and Stoughton, London.

19. Ames, H. (1999), *Country Words*. Christchurch Publishers, London.
20. *British Magazine* (2008), http://www.bestofbritishmag.co.uk (accessed 12 March 2008).
21. *This England* (2008), http://www.thisengland.co.uk (accessed 12 March 2008).
22. *The Field* (2008), http://www.thefield.co.uk (accessed 12 March 2008).
23. *Country Life* (2008), http://www.countrylife.co.uk (accessed 12 March 2008).
24. *Country Life* (2008), Special edition, 6 September 2007.
25. *Dorset Magazine* (2008), http://www.dorsetmagazine.co.uk/ (accessed 12 March 2008).
26. Ibid.
27. *Somerset Life* (2008), http://www.somerset-life.co.uk (accessed 12 March 2008).
28. *Exmoor Magazine* (2008), http://www.halsgrove.co.uk (accessed 12 March 2008).
29. Jackson, K. (2007), "From Wessex to Penny Lane", *Country Life*, Vol. 36 (6 September), pp. 148–150.
30. Williamson, H. (1930), *The Village Book*. E.P. Dutton and Co., New York.
31. Williamson, H. (1932), *The Labouring Life*. Jonathan Cape, London.
32. Williamson, H. (1944), *Tales of the Devon Village*. Faber & Faber Ltd., London.
33. Ravilious, J. (1995), *A Corner of England. North Devon Landscapes and People*. Devon Books, Tiverton.
34. Hardy, T. (1886), *The Mayor of Casterbridge*. Widely published in popular editions.
35. Hardy, T. (1874), *Far from the Madding Crowd*. Originally published in *Cornhill Magazine*, now widely published in popular editions.
36. Thomas, R.S., (1996), "A Peasant", Everyman, London.
37. McFarlane, Y. (1988), *The Dairy Book of British Food*. Ebury Press, London.
38. Fursdon, D. (2007), "A aste of England", *Country Life*, Vol. 36 (6 September), pp. 144–145.
39. *Country Living* (2008), http://www.countryliving.com/ (accessed 12 March 2008).
40. *Country Kitchen* (2008), http://www.countrykitchenmag.com/ (accessed 12 March 2008).
41. Pearce, B. (2000), *Exmoor Food and Cookery: A Moorland Heritage*. Exmoor Books, Dulverton.
42. Rundle, C. (1986), *The Taste of Exmoor Cookery Book*. English Tourist Board, London.
43. Willan, A. (1981), *French Regional Cooking*. Hutchinson and Co. (Publishers) Ltd, London.
44. Beer, S.C., Edwards, J.R., Fernandes, C. and Sampaio, F. (2002), "Regional food cultures: integral to the rural tourism product", in *Tourism and Gastronomy*, Hjalager, R. and Richards, G., eds. Routledge, London, pp. 207–223.
45. Taste of the West (2008), http://www.tasteofthewest.co.uk (accessed 12 March 2008).
46. See Raffael, M. (1997), *Cream*. Holsgrove, Taunton; Raffael, M. (1997), *Baking*. Holsgrove, Taunton; Molyneaux, J. and Yates, C. (1998), *Vegetables*. Holsgrove, Taunton; James, F. (2002), *Meat*. Iscanthus, Wellington, UK.
47. Williams, S. (2007), "'Junk-fed' teenagers shun traditional British dishes", *Western Mail*, 5 July 2007, p. 18.
48. Common Ground (2008), http://www.commonground.org.uk (accessed 12 March 2008).
49. ACOS (2008), http://www.defra.gov.uk/farm/organic/standards/acos/index.htm (accessed 12 March 2008).
50. *Sunday Times* (2007), "Waitrose sticks knife into rival", 29 July, p. 3.
51. Reisinger, Y. and Steiner, C.J. (2005), "Reconceptualizing object authenticity", *Annals of Tourism Research*, Vol. 33, No. 1, pp. 65–86.

2 Identifying and Overcoming Barriers to Healthy Eating Faced by Ethnic Minorities in the United Kingdom

HILLARY SHAW*

Keywords

diet, ethnic minority, migration, social deprivation, retailing.

Abstract

The UK has many ethnic minorities, each with its own set of food preferences. However, economic and cultural factors may create problems of poor diet within these communities. This chapter examines how such problems might be tackled and what opportunities for healthy food retailing are presented by the ethnic minority market.

Introduction

The UK has experienced a large rise in the incidence of obesity over the past few decades and a consequent increase in anxiety about the quality of the diet of British residents. During this period the UK also has seen a rise in ethnic diversity. Concerns about eating and health extend to all ethnic minority groups, but the diet of these groups varies greatly, modified by a wide range of factors, including cultural and religious heritage, socio-economic circumstances and experience of, and attitude towards, various foods.

This chapter draws on interviews with members of the Polish, Jewish, Arab, Pakistani, Indian, Bangladeshi, Chinese and Afro-Caribbean populations to elicit the primary causes

* Dr Hillary Shaw, Senior Lecturer, Harper Adams University College, Newport, Shropshire, TF10 8NB,UK. E-mail: hshaw@harper-adams.ac.uk. Telephone + 44 1952 815 296.

of poor diet in ethnic communities within Britain. It then examines some ways in which dietary problems within ethnic minority communities can be overcome, focusing on market-based solutions that raise demand for healthy foods or facilitate retailing of a more healthy food selection to ethnic minority consumers.

The overall findings note that lack of assets, in the form of not just low wages but also lack of transport and cooking facilities, coupled with the high prices for some foods, act as barriers to healthy eating. Lack of knowledge about which UK foods are healthy and poor English language skills also hinder access to a good diet, as do certain cultural norms. A range of non-commercial initiatives are in place to tackle these barriers. However, the commercial food retail sector is also set to facilitate dietary improvements as the size and spending power of ethnic minority communities grow.

Methodology

Semi-structured interviews were conducted in two UK urban locations (Birmingham and Leeds) and two rural locations (Lincolnshire and Norfolk). Between 2001 and 2007 members of ethnic minority communities in these four areas, as well as agencies involved in dietary improvement, such as dieticians and community cafe operators, were interviewed either in person or by telephone. The use of semi-structured interviews gave respondents the freedom to mention the presence and effect of a wide range of dietary influences that they might have considered significant for healthy eating. A total of 200 respondents were interviewed; approximately 100 of these respondents gave information relevant to the problems of, and solutions to, dietary problems among ethnic minority groups, and the remainder mentioned significant socio-economic barriers to a healthy diet encountered by less advantaged consumers generally.

Diet

Multiple factors promote the consumption of a poor diet. Poor knowledge of food nutrition and preparation, as well as demographic factors such as old age, widowhood and living alone or as part of a one-parent family are all significant. Also important are poverty-related factors such as lack of access to a car or subsisting on a low income, along with factors that affect physical access to food, such as disability or living far from a food retailer.[1] Members of ethnic minorities may be affected by several of these factors. In particular, they may be poor, lack private transport, live in substandard accommodations, live in areas remote from high-quality supermarkets, and be unable to work (perhaps for legal reasons, such as refugee status) or receive only the minimum wage. In addition, they may have poor English-language skills and a lack of knowledge about the health status of foods they encounter for the first time in the UK.

ETHNICITY AND DIET

Britain has a long record of ethnic diversity, although this racial variety has increased markedly since the 1950s. The modern era of diversity began with the arrival of Jamaicans on the *Empire Windrush* in 1948. The Commonwealth territories have been a source of immigrants to the UK from many parts of Africa, Asia and the Caribbean; Idi Amin's expulsion of the Ugandan Asians in 1972 added considerably to the ethnic minority population of Leicester and other cities. China and Indochina are other long-standing migrant sources. Since 1990, events connected with the fall of communism in Eastern Europe quickened the pace of ethnic diversification. The accession of ten mostly former Eastern bloc countries to the European Union in 2004 has greatly increased the numbers of Poles in Britain. By 2001 the country's ethnic minority population numbered 4.6 million. Indians and Pakistanis accounted for 1.8 million, and Afro-Caribbean blacks numbered a further 1 million.[2] Ethnic minority diets, as modified by living in Britain, often combine healthy and unhealthy elements. For example, the South Asian diet is high in vegetables but, especially in the UK, also often features fatty sauces. Poles prefer wholegrain breads to white bread but may consume too high a ratio of starch and meat to vegetables. The black African diet is rich in fruit and vegetables but may be short on protein. The challenge is to remedy the worst dietary features while retaining the best and to achieve this balance in a culturally appropriate manner.

Some factors appear to enhance the chances of members of ethnic minorities consuming a healthy diet. Newer ethnic minority members often cluster in inner urban areas where they have close (e.g. religious) ties with others of their ethnic group. They may be remote from out-of-town supermarkets but frequently have a discount supermarket such as Aldi or Lidl nearby. Ethnic minority areas often feature numerous independently owned grocery shops, specializing in local dietary preferences, as well as general "continental" stores offering a range of world foods. A higher birth rate and stronger marriage ties, along with a more youthful demographic profile, should ensure lower incidences of one-adult households, who tend to eat less healthily.

However, these health-promoting factors may not work as efficiently as expected or be outweighed by dietary risk factors. Research on Mexican women living in the USA found that their diet grew poorer the longer they lived in America, possibly because "their traditional cuisine is not well supported in their new country of residence".[3] The ethnic food situation in parts of the USA, such as Chicago, appears to be exacerbated by a spatial separation of ethnic minorities from retailers selling healthier foods.[4] The UK inner cities and ethnic-minority districts are better served by supermarkets,[5] and these areas host discount supermarkets and chains such as the Co-op and Somerfield, but physical proximity to a source of healthy foods is no guarantee that such foods will be consumed by all. Because UK ethnic minority groups are far from homogenous, they present many different dietary health challenges.

MONETARY FACTORS AND DIET

Food is more than a source of nutrients; it is "packed with social, cultural, and symbolic meaning".[6] Food has been described as noisy, because each dish contains different ingredients, and each ingredient "tells its own story" to the person eating it. Different people "hear" varying narratives from any one particular meal, depending on the person's cultural background and life history.[7] Dietary agencies may speak to ethnic minority consumers, but often the voice of their food, as part of a wider cultural heritage, may be louder. Thus any dietary message to ethnic minority communities must be in congruence with, not contrary to, their food culture.

Many religions include dietary stipulations, and, for ethnic minority communities, food constitutes an important link with their region of origin. When ethnic minorities try to purchase foods of cultural significance, they frequently face the dual problem of higher food prices and lower earnings. Small independent ethnic food shops may charge high prices because they lack the economies of scale enjoyed by supermarkets. These food shops also acquire food through a far less cost-efficient supply chain than do the supermarkets. Many Asian and Afro-Caribbean foodstuffs are imported through small wholesalers in the Manchester area[8] and then delivered to communities in Leeds and Birmingham. This supply chain results from industrial inertia, a relic of the days when Britain's colonial trade came mainly through Liverpool and Manchester.

Many ethnic minority arrivals to the UK enter low-wage occupations. The *Financial Times* suggests that, among recent arrivals, 60 per cent of Bangladeshis, 35 per cent of Pakistanis and 30 per cent of Jamaicans are in jobs paying less than £7,750 per annum, whereas only 21 per cent of those born in the UK earn below this wage.[9] For settled migrants, this low-wage percentage declines but is still 22 per cent for Pakistanis and 39 per cent for Bangladeshis. *The Guardian* further reports that the majority of migrants from the ten European Union accession states are working as factory process operatives, warehouse packers, farm workers and building labourers, or are in low-status service jobs such as cleaners, waiters or home care workers.[10] May et al. report on a preponderance of Eastern Europeans, Bangladeshis and Filipinos in the low-status care sector, in construction and in hotels and restaurants.[11] In addition, ethnic minority groups often send part of their UK earnings to family members in their country of origin. Migrant remittances are estimated to total £2.3 billion annually, with fees ranging from £3.50 to as high as £40 per £100 remitted.[12] According to *The Times,* the 2 million UK Muslims are "among the most deprived groups" of UK consumers.[13] Nevertheless, their total spending power was estimated as £20.5 billion per year, a figure also quoted by Lyons.[14] The British Muslim population is young, comprising 3 per cent of the UK population, and, although it earns below-average wages, it also contains "more than 5,000 Muslim millionaires, holding assets worth at least £3.6 billion".[15] With food requiring approximately 10 per cent of UK consumers' expenditures, and probably more for poorer households, there is a potential Muslim market for food that is worth in excess of £2 billion per annum and growing fast.

Low wages may push migrants towards unhealthy takeaway food. Fast food such as takeaway chicken at £1.25, provides "the easy option," and "chip shop specials" for the same price are described as "ridiculously cheap", which "negates the need to cook" according to community group leaders in less affluent parts of Birmingham.[16] Kebabs in Birmingham cost £1.20 (in 2007); the return bus fare to a supermarket was more than £2.00. The cost of food was also mentioned by a dietician in north Lincolnshire, who noted: "The Asian diet in Crosby [a poor part of Scunthorpe, with many Asian families] may have too much fat and too few vegetables. Asian vegetables are very expensive here in the UK, and they may not be aware of English alternatives, so although the home diet is good it has too much fat here in the U.K."[17]

Polish food was also perceived as expensive – a loaf of Polish bread cost approximately twice the price of its English equivalent, although it was valued for its quality in that it "[contains] no bleach." Polish food supply chains were much less geographically organized than the Asian routes through the Manchester area. Typically, the Polish supply chain would consist of a man and a van from a nearby city such as Nottingham. Other Poles made frequent trips back to Poland once the Warsaw Pact was dissolved, bringing Polish delicacies back via the Hull ferries.

The main problem with the cost of food was not simply its absolute price but, rather, the cost of such foods relative to many minority consumers' low wages.

OCCUPATION AND DIET

Lack of UK-recognized qualifications and relevant job experience may push many migrants into low-wage jobs. Some of these occupations may be predisposed to poor diet and poor health. Several Birmingham respondents reported that Yemeni and Pakistani men often worked as taxi drivers, because this work is easy to enter and driving skills are transferable to the UK. This job has deleterious effects on their health and diet, though, because it is a sedentary occupation and involves shift work, often in the evenings during unsocial hours. To compensate for the lack of exercise on the job, many spend time at gyms to keep fit, further eroding eating time with their families.† Therefore they eat "a lot of takeaways, kebabs and curries".[18] Housework is also often undervalued, and female house workers especially may skimp on meals to feed other household members.[19] Among some of the more patriarchal South Asian ethnic groups, intra-household dietary inequality may be a problem. In 2007 the Cradley Heath Community Centre (located in Birmingham) commented, "Yemeni women here don't eat breakfast, just a chapatti bread." Bread is not unhealthy per se, but the women were missing out on fruit and vegetables.

ASYLUM SEEKERS AND DIET

Asylum seekers represent an extreme version of the problem of poverty and poor diet. In 2001 a dietician in Norwich commented:[20]

> ... asylum seekers in Great Yarmouth in bed and breakfast have no cooking facilities, or they have to queue for hours to get on the cooker, over four hours in one bedsit. Or they have to leave the bed and breakfast for seven hours during the day, so nowhere to cook, so they eat crisps and fizzy drinks. Bosnian men, in their culture, don't cook. The poor here have no space for a freezer to bulk buy food, that would make food cheaper.

Similar comments mark the responses in 2007 in Birmingham.[21] A West Midlands refugee support centre indicated that "[m]en from the Middle East lack cooking skills, as there the women traditionally do all the cooking". Asylum seekers awaiting appeal or deportation exist on Section 4 support; they cannot access benefits and are not allowed to work. They get £35 per week in food vouchers, redeemable not at local independent ethnic grocers but at more remote supermarkets or at fast-food restaurants such as Burger King. Being among the more recent arrivals to the UK, asylum seekers have had little time

---

† This exercise and job factor was mentioned by several Birmingham respondents. It could be argued that office work is also sedentary, but office workers at least leave their desks from time to time, probably walking several miles a day in total. Compared to whites, minority workers may be poorer, work longer hours in lower-paid jobs, claim less in the way of meal breaks, and, due to poorer English in some cases, make fewer demands generally regarding work conditions and diet.

to improve their English or to become acquainted with indigenous British foods. This status makes them liable to eat unhealthily, perhaps unknowingly.

LENGTH OF TIME IN THE UK AND ETHNIC DIET

The length of time that a community has been present in the UK influences its culture and therefore its dietary preferences. The small Jewish community in Lincoln has a centuries-long history. Many Jews there have married non-Jews, and, apart from matzos at Tesco, they had to obtain kosher food, if required, from Leeds or Manchester. There is a larger Jewish community in Leeds, but even here "a lot of Jewish shops used to be on the Chapeltown Road but as the Jewish people have moved out so have they". Stricter Orthodox Jews have kosher shops in Moortown, further out of Leeds; others rely on food from a nearby Sainsbury's supermarket. Time and intermarriage have secularized many Jews' attitudes toward kosher food, especially in the less strict Liberal and Reform branches of Judaism, and often Jews have a similar diet to non-Jewish white people.

Like the Jews, the Muslim community in Britain can claim roots going back several centuries, but the modern Muslim community, mainly Pakistani or Bangladeshi, dates from the 1950s. The UK now hosts a mixture of original migrants and first- and second-generation descendants born here. Older Muslim women from Leeds and Scunthorpe tend to be chary of venturing out of their home area on their own, even by a few hundred metres to nearby discount supermarkets.[22] They prefer to use local shops, only going further when with their husbands or other Muslim women. They buy bulk packs of rice or chapattis to feed large, extended families living together. They often lack a car, which restricts their access to cheaper shops such as discount supermarkets until their husbands return from work. In 2007 the Birmingham Asian Resource Centre stated that some Bangladeshi women were unwilling to go out shopping on their own, and their inability to read English labels on food packs deterred them further.‡ Younger, British-born Pakistani Muslims have reached a dietary, cultural watershed. Their cultural tradition involves one large family meal or *handi* a day, but when out of the house they may eat, as well as dress and talk, in a more English way, consuming several smaller snacks or meals a day.[23] Eating snacks with friends outside the home and the *handi* with family in the home, two forms of social eating, may contribute to future obesity, unless this double-eating is compensated by, for example, more exercise; however, there was no evidence amongst the respondents of such compensation.

The longer an ethnic community has been in the UK, the less the diet of that group differs from the general UK diet. However, strong intra-community ties, such as those maintained by religion, can lessen this integration effect. Furthermore, the transition period between separateness from, and integration with, the host UK culture may feature very poor eating habits, because old cultural dietary good habits are abandoned, healthy British food has yet to be assimilated, and the spending power of households in the partly assimilated group has yet to reach average UK household levels.

---

‡   Lack of access to private cars was noted earlier as limiting refugees' capacity to transport food home. It appears that some Muslim women may face an additional constraints on their mobility rooted in their religious/cultural background.

COOKING SKILLS, FOOD KNOWLEDGE AND DIET

Poor choice of foods or lack of ability to cook healthy foods was mentioned as a factor exacerbating the poor diet by several ethnic minority community groups. The Muslim Community Centre in Tipton (Birmingham, 2007) noted, "People may be eating 5 a day, but if the vegetables are badly cooked they lose the nutrients anyway." A Bangladeshi centre in Birmingham (2007) also commented, "The Asian diet has a lot of spices and chillies, very rich and fatty food, not many fruit and vegetables." By contrast, another Birmingham community centre indicated that "[Asians] eat a mixed diet, fried and spicy foods along with lentils, fruit and vegetables. Pakistanis like meat a lot". The use of butter or ghee (a type of clarified butter with high saturated fat content) in many curry dishes was noted by many respondents as a negative dietary health factor.

A community centre in Smethwick, serving mainly the Afro-Caribbean community, commented on the high fat content of some African diets: "[T]each the African community how to remove palm oil, use olive oil instead, they won't eat English food." Palm oil is highly saturated and therefore very obesogenic.[24] Similar comments were made by a black community group in Leeds:[25]

> We have Afro-Caribbean shops here [Chapeltown]. They sell yams, green bananas, sweet potatoes, mangoes, star fruits. Yams and green bananas are carbohydrate foods, quite starchy, they are bulk foods that fill you up. It's proteins and the various meats we don't seem to get because they're quite expensive. We eat a lot of goatfish and monkfish, which are more expensive.

The black community in Leeds was less bound by religious dietary laws, but the cost of healthier foods was of concern.

LANGUAGE SKILLS AND DIET

Lack of English may also be a barrier to healthy eating that may function directly, in that some migrants cannot read nutrition labels and determine the healthiness or otherwise of unfamiliar foods. It also may function indirectly, by restricting the choice of shopping to more expensive local ethnic stores, in which their buying power declines. A Bengali community group leader also noted that some Muslims could not determine if supermarket foods were *halal*.[26] He wanted local supermarkets, such as ASDA and Morrisons, to put foreign-language labels on their foods based on local need. ASDA's head office responded, "In stores we have signs in the aisles in different languages in appropriate areas." However, Morrisons responded, "We don't put foreign languages labels on food, all our stores are standardized. Some of our staff will speak foreign languages." South Asians in Leeds travelled several kilometres to a supermarket, despite having independent Asian stores close by, suggesting that they value lower food prices. Individual store-based language labelling would probably threaten the economies of scale that facilitate these low prices in supermarkets. Meanwhile, local independent Asian stores may be better suited to selling non-food goods. In reporting on the transformation of the Belgrave shopping area of Leicester in the 1970s, Cordy notes that Belgrave went from no Asian shops in 1969 to 76 per cent of its shops, or 179 in total, Asian-owned by 1984.[27] Yet most of these shops were non-food–oriented; the Leicester city centre market remained an important food retailing venue for Leicester's Asians. Any language-based barriers to a healthy diet thus might best be tackled on the demand side rather than on the supply side.

The Polish community mentioned language problems among its older members. There have been two waves of Polish migration to the UK; the first was from 1939–45, as Poles fled the Nazis and then the Soviet occupation, and the second began in 2004 with the European Union enlargement. Members of the first wave are now well into their 80s. A Polish community leader in Scunthorpe (where many worked at the steelworks) said, "Some Poles' English is not very good; they regress to Polish as they get older."[28] This language habit placed a burden on the Polish community, although because it is quite close-knit, help for this group was available, which was fortunate because "it's hard to get Polish food in Scunthorpe".

Common factors leading to the consumption of a poor diet among ethnic minority members include high food prices, often coupled with low pay, poor accommodation, lack of English-language skills and barriers to travel, which may be either financially or culturally based.

Improving the Diet of Ethnic Minorities

A perceived need for better nutritional information marks many ethnic minority groups. Camden Primary Care Trust recently successfully used the Bengali Channel to promote its anti-smoking message. The Bangladeshi Centre in Smethwick (Birmingham, 2007) suggested using this channel to advertise which foods are high in salt, as well as leaving dietary advice booklets and posters at Asian-owned grocery stores and supermarkets. There are obvious opportunities for larger retailers here, perhaps by combining advertising with a health message. However, many smaller, independent, Asian grocery stores are quite cramped and very densely stocked; there might be no room for large posters, and booklets might be ignored by consumers. A multiplicity of languages would be needed; India alone has 24 languages with a million speakers each and an estimated 415 extant tongues. Small, independent, Asian retailers might not be able to bear the cost of such literature, although larger Asian chain stores might fund them as part of a corporate social responsibility initiative.[§] Alternatively, Asian food wholesalers might promote healthier foods through ethnic minority community centres, perhaps paying for this advertising by sponsoring facilities where such financial arrangements are appropriate.[29] The larger ethnic minority charities might contribute to the production and dissemination of dietary advice; Islamic Relief, for example, earned turnover in excess of £30 million in 2006.[30]

A centre in Smethwick held taste tester sessions, promoting healthier foods from different cultures.[31] On a wider scale, the Local Public Service Agreement team in Liverpool set up a scheme in 2000 whereby local doctors gave patients vouchers redeemable for fruit and vegetables from local Co-op stores.[32] Although certain households' fruit and vegetable consumption returned to pre-scheme levels once the vouchers had ended, there were improvements in the diet of some, especially schoolchildren. Again, there are opportunities for retailers and wholesalers regarding the promotion of healthier options. Schools with

---

[§]   Asian supermarkets have not yet grown to the sizes of Waitrose or Aldi in the UK. However, some Asian chain stores exist; Maumoniat has several branches in Leeds, one of which is a former Netto store, converted in 2003. The Pak chain is another large Asian food retailer.

high ethnic minority classes could be another venue for educational initiatives, either by retailers and wholesalers or by other agencies such as health or government bodies. Further research may be needed to determine which types of programme produce the most permanent improvements in diet.

Other schemes could tackle not only the more evident of lack of retail facilities, knowledge, or spending power, but also utiliZe the knowledge of ethnic minority communities themselves in order to achieve dietary improvements. In 1982 a pioneering project called Ashram Acres was set up in the inner-city Sparkbrook area of Birmingham.[33] By 1982 this district was already home to a considerable, and often impoverished, migrant community of Afro-Caribbeans, Bangladeshis, Indians, Irish and Pakistanis. Many of these migrants had learned farming skills from their childhood abroad. There were also large industrial wastelands resulting from deindustrialization. Putting these factors together and reclaiming the derelict land, the Ashram Acres project uses entirely voluntary labour and receives no outside grants. Participants pay a weekly subscription and work in exchange for produce. Ashram Acres has inspired similar projects in other UK cities with large ethnic minorities, including Bradford and Sheffield.[34] Most recently, a scheme in Shadwell, east London, has begun to convert underused communal gardens belonging to blocks of flats into productive vegetable plots.[35] Local women of all backgrounds take an active role in developing the plots, so this project has spin-off benefits in enhancing racial integration and empowering an often silenced section of the community.

Growing vegetables locally has other benefits, such as improvements in health and fitness: "Why run around a gym like a rodent on a wheel if your exertions can actually deliver your dinner."[36] Local schools can visit and learn about vegetable production and consumption. At school, children's learning experience also can be enhanced in areas such as biology, mathematics (e.g. output per square metre of produce), economics (costs of production in time, fertiliser inputs), geography (origin of vegetables) and media studies (how is this enterprise reported on in the local community).[¶] Surplus vegetables produced might even be sold commercially. The Ashram Acres scheme represents an opportunity for both local people, as vendors, and Birmingham retailers, who can adopt a corporate social responsibility-related policy of promoting local produce. The main threat to this idea is that in the current era of high house prices and scarce building land, former industrial sites are more valuable as residential developments than as allotments or urban farms. Many, albeit not all, inner-city areas have old industrial land left over from deindustrialization, including old railway land that, due to its long and narrow shape, is hard to redevelop for residential or commercial use. Some of this land will be polluted and unsuitable for small-scale vegetable growing. However, it only takes a few square metres of land to grow vegetables, and involving the community, especially children, in this effort might give them a taste for purchasing fruit and vegetables conventionally through shops.

Having described in this section me representative types of diet improvement initiatives from the broad and ever-changing range of schemes operating in Britain today, we now review the ethnic minority food situation in three key ethnic markets within the UK from the supply side.

¶   All subject to agreement among the school, the local education authority, the National Curriculum and other relevant parties, such as health agencies.

UK Ethnic Food Retailing

THE POLISH MARKET

The Polish food market is currently the fastest growing ethnic food sector in the UK;[37] in 2007 there were an estimated 600 000 Poles living there, and by 2006 the major UK supermarkets had already entered this market with Polish-style ready meals.[38] By 2007, 250 Tesco stores in Britain had a specialist Polish food range. In late 2006 Sainsbury's began selling carp, a traditional Polish Christmas meal. ASDA had introduced 350 Polish lines into 85 stores by mid-2007.[39] Food producers are also eyeing the Polish market. Heinz has introduced its specialist Polish brand, Pudliszki. Polish food, with its stews, sausages, tripe, eels, dumplings, cabbages and apple pies, bears some resemblance to traditional British country food, appealing to UK consumers who desire "retro" or traditional dishes. This appeal is being exploited by independent Polish food stores, such as The Polish Deli in Trowbridge, Somerset, where "40 per cent [of the customers] are English".[40]

THE HALAL/MUSLIM MARKET

The Muslim market constitutes another significant market for UK retailers. In 2001 there were 1.52 million Muslims, rising to an estimated 1.6 million in 2007.[41] Practising Muslims represent a unique market because the Koran sets out instructions in a wide range of areas of life, including what to eat and drink. There also may be a Muslim market for non-American versions of popular US brands such as Coca-Cola, and hence the emergence of the Mecca Cola brand.[42] An expansion of Muslim-specific brands seems likely; Sharia-compliant products, especially in the food sector, are much more commodity-based than brand-based, which implies an opportunity for a specialist brand to capture a large market share.

The supply of *halal* foods represents a considerable marketing opportunity. Manchester University's main campus canteen serves *halal* options to some 400 of the 2,500 daily customers.[43] For the approximately 90 000 Muslim students in the UK, the absence of *halal* menu options has meant that many students had to go off-campus to get hot lunches, possibly missing the start of afternoon lectures. To avoid this, some Muslim students would choose their university on the basis of whether *halal* food was provided on-campus – a crucial point for British universities in the era of top-up student fees. On a wider scale, *The Grocer* has reported[44] on the expansion of the Birmingham-based Pak supermarket chain, which in 2007 opened the UK's largest ethnic food supermarket. In addition to serving the large South Asian Muslim community, this store will cater to Somalis, Afro-Caribbeans and other ethnic minorities such as Eastern Europeans.

Traditionally, *halal* meat was bought from small independent butchers, but UK supermarkets are now penetrating the halal food market.[45] Second- and third-generation UK Muslims aim to purchase these foods from supermarkets along with the rest of their shopping purchases. ASDA therefore provides separate halal meat counters. As the Muslim community becomes more affluent, suppliers such as Abraham Natural Produce are supplying organic halal meats.[46] Other halal-based marketing opportunities include gelatine-free sweets, launched by Haribo in 2006.[47] Strong religious ties, combined with a higher than average birth rate and increasing wealth, make this sector very attractive in terms of retail expansion in a generally saturated UK food market.

THE WIDER ASIAN MARKET

Major retail chains are also entering other ethnic food markets in the UK, with a view to selling both to ethnic minorities and to white English consumers. As this food sector grows, splitting and specialization occurs in the market. For example, rather than generic Chinese food, often meaning food from South-east Asia generally, supermarkets such as Sainsbury's now sell Cantonese, Malaysian, Korean and Thai foods. Instead of just "Indian", UK consumers can now enjoy regional specialities, including Bengali, Gujerati and Punjabi foods.[48] In 2006 Waitrose introduced a range of curry sauces to facilitate the home preparation of Asian foods. Britain is the only European country where the ethnic food market accounts for more than 1 per cent of all packaged food sales, and the market continues to grow rapidly, with Indian-based food sales rising at a rate of 12 per cent per annum.[49]

The non-UK European ethnic food market is becoming more diverse,[50] particularly in Germany and Spain, where ethnic food sales are rising at a rate of 30 per cent per annum. The Netherlands is the fastest growing ethnic food market in Europe, with expansion in Italian, Mexican and Oriental dishes. The French food market also is becoming more ethnically diverse, with North African dishes, such as couscous, appearing more frequently.

With many supermarket chains being forced to look beyond their home territory for expansion, fast growing ethnic minority markets within other countries may represent a desirable prize in the global race among international supermarkets to grow and capture a wider market share. Yet within the UK there may still be unexploited ethnic markets to capture, such as the ethnic holiday and health markets.

Holiday and Health Market Opportunities

Religious and other holidays are areas from which major UK food retailers could reap dividends.[51] Indigenous UK festivals, such as Christmas and Easter, produce peaks in sales of certain foodstuffs, but retailers could gain a double benefit from considering a wider range of holidays. First, catering to ethnic minority holidays that fall at different times of the year to traditional UK holidays would help even out seasonal peaks and troughs in monthly food sales. Second, such diversification would insure against recent declines seen in the sales of foods associated with traditional UK holidays.**

Ethnic diversity means that there are many alternative festivals for giving gifts and consuming special foods. The Muslim festival of Eid is a traditional feast time, as is Mawlid, which marks the birthday of Mohammed. The Hindu Diwali festival and the Chinese New Year represent other points on the calendar when consumption peaks of various foods occur. The high level of ethnic diversity means UK food retailers are never far from a festival celebrated by a significant number of their customers. In the USA there are dates for Americans or Afro-Americans such as Kwanzaa, Sweetest Day and Grandparent's Day that are relatively unknown in the UK. Yet Halloween and Mischievous

---

** For example, in 2006 the retail website Food&drinkeurope.com and Bakeryinfo both reported falling Christmas pudding sales. Sales have since recovered, but diversification into growing ethnic markets could still strengthen retailers' trading positions. See "Retailers reveal Christmas trading performance", 13 January 2006, http://www.bakeryinfo.co.uk/news/fullstory.php/aid/684/Retailers_reveal_Christmas_trading_performance.html.

Night (Trick or Treat) are both recent additions to the UK calendar and now constitute major marketing opportunities for those selling pumpkins and face masks. The challenge for UK grocery retailers will be to identify foods associated with such festivals and market them effectively.

The ethnic food market may also present health-based marketing opportunities. As ethnic minority members become wealthier and experience increased concerns about fitness, nutrition and obesity, the demand for health-oriented ethnic minority foods is likely to grow. Lifeway Foods is promoting two yoghurt- or milk-based drinks – Kefir from the Caucasus region of Russia and Lassi from north India – as probiotic drinks for Western consumers with fast lifestyles.[52] Sales efforts initially targeted the Indian community, then white consumers. Lifeway hopes to emulate the example of Activia, whose yoghurt brand was launched in January 2006 and a year later had sold US$100 million.

Current Trends in the UK Ethnic Food Retailing Market

A continued move by the UK supermarket chains into smaller store formats and high street locations is likely, as is further penetration by these stores into the ethnic foods market. A study by the University of Southampton[53] showed that, rather than damaging other local retailers, the opening of Tesco Express stores in three affluent rural and one deprived inner-city location in Hampshire had created a clawback of trade effect, as well as reducing miles travelled to buy food and increasing fruit and vegetable consumption. The insertion of larger supermarkets into deprived areas has also been shown to improve local diet,[54] but, in practice, it might be difficult to find the sites or obtain planning permission for a large superstore in densely populated urban areas where less affluent ethnic minorities live. Nevertheless, improvements in store logistics mean smaller formats such as Tesco Express stores can efficiently supply fruit and vegetables at low prices.

The local clawback of trade effect and a gradual rise in the per capita income of migrant groups relative to the UK average could mean a positive outlook for small independent ethnic shops, as local spending power in ethnic minority neighbourhoods increases. Independent stores that specialize are best placed to compete against and therefore coexist with supermarket branches such as Tesco Express. It is the generalist stores, selling little in the way of fresh fruit and vegetables, and often located in poor white areas, that may have the most to fear from supermarket expansion. Stores such as The Polish Deli also worry about ASDA and Tesco stocking more Polish products; as the manager explains, "I have mixed feelings towards the competition we are facing."[55] Whether the outcome is positive or negative for independent ethnic food stores will depend on many individual store factors, such as location, the manager's business acumen and the demographic make-up of its local customers.

Conclusions

As the average wealth level of the UK's ethnic communities rises, some ethnic minority households will move to more affluent districts, although the strong community and religious ties within some communities may delay this spread to the suburbs and beyond. Increasing wealth, food knowledge and access to culturally preferred foods should help ameliorate some dietary problems in these communities. However, the UK society into which these groups are integrating is one that has shown signs of increasing polarization between rich and poor during the past decade. Individuals and families now suffering a poor diet due to lack of financial assets are likely to continue to face this situation. Worldwide, the economic system tends to polarize rather than equalize national wealth differentials, ensuring a steady source of migrants fleeing war zones, climate disasters or poverty for more amenable climes such as the UK. The identity of individual disadvantaged ethnic minorities may change, but there is always likely to be an ethnic minority section of the UK population facing dietary problems induced by factors such as deprivation, lack of English and cultural dissonances with the British food milieu.

References

1   National Consumer Council (2005), *Putting Food Access on the Radar*, report for Staffordshire County Council; Shaw, H. (2006), "Food deserts: Towards the development of a classification", *Geografiska Annaler,* Vol. 88B, No. 2, pp. 231–247

2   Marketing (2007), *Ethnic Britain*, 18 April 2007, pp. 31–33.

3   *Food Magazine* (2005), "Migrants suffer dietary decline", Vol. 69, April/June, p. 20.

4   Pierre, I., Bountje, Huang C., Lee, J. and Lin, B. (2005), "Dietary habits, demographics, and the development of overweight and obesity among children in the United States", *Food Policy*, Vol. 30, No. 2, pp. 115–128; Gallagher, M. (2006), *Examining the Impact of Food deserts on Public Health in Chicago*, Mari Gallagher Research and Consulting Group, Chicago, USA.

5   Maps of UK cities showing locations of main supermarkets are available at http://www.fooddeeserts.org.

6   Holloway, L. (2002), "Virtual vegetables and adopted sheep", *AREA*, Vol. 134, p. 71.

7   Smith, J. and Jehlicka, P. (2007), "Stories around food, politics and change in Poland and the Czech Republic", *Transactions*, Vol. 32, No. 3, pp.395–410.

8   Based on comments from Birmingham ethnic minority shop proprietors, 2002–05.

9   *Financial Times* (2005), "Half of population growth in past decade put down to immigrants", 8 August 2005, p. 2.

10   *The Guardian* (2006), "New in the UK: the 'guest' workforce who don't stay long", 23 August 2006, pp. 4–5.

11   May, J., Wills, J., Datta, K., Evans, Y., Herbert, J. and McIllwaine, C. (2007), "Keeping London working: global cities, the British state, and London's new migrant division of labour", *Transactions*, Vol. 32, No. 2, p. 155.

12   Department for International Development (2005), "New report launched into the the £2.7 billion UK remittance market", press release, notes to editors no. 6, 11 November, http://www.dfid.gov.uk/news/files/pressreleases/report-remittance.asp.

13   *The Times* (2007), "Business is urged to see opportunity in Muslim Community", 21 May 2007, http://business.timesonline.co.uk/tol/business/industry_sectors/retailing/article1816366.ece.

14   Lyons, T. (2007), "Pak superstore to tap ethnic food potential", *The Grocer*, 26 May 2007, p. 10.

15   *The Times*, "Business is urged to see opportunity", *op. cit.*

16   Comments from semi-structured interviews by author, 2007.

17   Author's research, Lincolnshire, 2002.

18   Interview with Birmingham NHS, 2007.

19   Harrison, M. (1997), *Running on Empty*, Demos Collection, December 1997, pp. 25–28.

20   Author's research, Norfolk, 2001.

21   Author's research, Birmingham, 2007.

22   Author's research, Leeds and Lincolnshire, 2002.

23   Jamal, A. (1998), "Food consumption among ethnic minorities: the case of British-Pakistanis in Bradford, UK", *British Food Journal*, Vol. 100, No. 5, pp. 221–227.

24   Critser, G. (2003), *Fat Land*, Penguin Books, London, pp. 13–16.

25   Author's research, Leeds, 2002.

26   Ibid.

27   Cordy, T. (1985), "Amazing growth of ethnic shopping", *Town and Country Planning*, Vol. 54, p. 225.

28   Author's research, Lincolnshire, 2002.

29   Shaw, H. (2007), "The role of CSR in re-empowering local communities", *Social Responsibility Journal*, Vol. 3, No. 2, pp. 11–21.

30   Islamic Relief website, http://www.islamic-relief.com (accessed January 2008).

31   Author's research, Birmingham, 2007.

32   Baines, C. (2006), *LPSA Life Expectancy Programme Interim Evaluation April 2004 – December 2005*, LPSA team, Liverpool and The Wirral.

33   Cressey, G. (1988), "Ashram Acres: where nothing is wasted", *Town and Country Planning*, Vol. 57, pp. 109–111.

34   Garnett, G. (1985), "Back to our roots", *Healthmatters*, Autumn 1985, pp. 10–11.

35   *Food Magazine* (2007), "Edible landscapes on housing estates", July–September 2007, p. 12.

36   Garnett, "Back to our roots", op. cit.

37   *Sunday Telegraph* (2007), "Polish becomes fastest growing ethnic cuisine", 15 April 2007, p. 12.

38   BBC News 24, (2006), "Supermarkets covet Polish spend", 10 September 2006, http://news.bbc.co.uk/1/hi/business/5332024.stm (accessed 25 July 2007).

39   *The Grocer* (2007), "Spotlight", 7 July 2007, p. 55.

40   *The Grocer* (2007), "Store visit – the Polish Deli, Trowbridge", 21 July 2007, pp. 34–35.

41   Muslim Council of Britain (2007), http://www.mcb.org.uk (accessed 5 September 2007).

42   Murphy, V. (2003), "Mecca Cola challenges US rival", BBC News Online, 8 January 2003.

43   *The Guardian* (2007), "Halal is hot", 30 January 2007, p. 12.

44   Lyons, "Pak superstore", *op. cit.*

45   *The Grocer*, "Spotlight", op. cit.

46   *The Grocer* (2007), "Multiples target potential of Halal", 5 May 2007, p. 63.

47   *The Grocer* (2007), "Asda pushes Halal and Polish ranges", 25 August 2007, p. 9.

48   *Mintel* (2002), "New product trends – ethnic, ambient ready meals", May 2002, p. 27.

49   Knowles, J. (2006), "Waitrose launches new authentic curry sauces", Food&drinkeurope.com, 18 October, http://www.foodanddrinkeurope.com/feature/news-by-month/10/2006.

50   Awbi, A. (2006), "UK suppliers urged to target European ethnic food demand", Food&drinkeurope.com, 2 March, http://www.foodanddrinkeurope.com/feature/news-by-month/03/2006.

51   Heller, L. (2006), "Ethnic, organic, could boost falling seasonal chocolate sales", 30 August, http://www.foodnavigator-usa.com/Financial-Industry/Ethnic-organic-could-boost-falling-seasonal-chocolate-sales-report.

52   Food&drinkeurope.com (2007), "Lifeway takes functional dairy further into ethnic market", 7 February 2007.

53   Wrigley, N. and Shaw, H. (2007), *Relocalising Food Shopping*, University of Southampton.

54   Wrigley, N. (2002), "Urban regeneration, social inclusion, and large store development: the Seacroft development in context", *Urban Studies*, Vol. 39, No. 11, pp. 2101–2114.

55   *The Grocer*, "Store visit", *op. cit.*

3 The Role of Food in the Adjustment Journey of International Students

LORRAINE BROWN*

Keywords

food, culture, cultural distance, interaction, adjustment.

Abstract

In an ethnographic study of the adaptation of international postgraduate students to life in England, food emerged as an issue of central importance to many participants. English food was rejected by many students, with criticisms of bland, fattening and unhealthy dishes, as well as poor-quality fresh food. These students reverted to the preparation of their home country dishes, exemplifying a segregation strategy towards food habits. Eating together was one of students' main leisure activities, and food of the origin country or region was the most popular cuisine. The greatest variable in the willingness to adapt to a foreign diet proved to be the degree of cultural similarity: Students whose daily diet was the least varied tended to come from an extremely dissimilar culture, such as China, Thailand, Indonesia, Malaysia or Taiwan. Nearly all of the South-east Asian students in the study adopted a rigidly mononational eating plan, often going to a great deal of trouble to emulate their national diet (including shipping ingredients from abroad and dedicating a lot of time to food preparation). Some students adopted a multicultural strategy towards food consumption, trying not only local food but also dishes prepared by their international friends. The two greatest variables in the decision to try different foods appear to be a motivation to learn and an openness to new experiences. Growing markets exist for the sale of foodstuffs from South-east Asia (the primary source of international students) and for higher-quality, more varied foods on university campuses.

*   Dr Lorraine Brown, School of Services Management, Bournemouth University, BH12 5BB, UK. E-mail: lbrown@ bournemouth.ac.uk. Telephone: + 44 1202 965 223.

Introduction

International education is a major export industry at university level, with fierce competition among the key markets of the United Kingdom, Canada, New Zealand and Australia.[1] Since 1997 the number of international students studying in the UK has soared, and their recruitment by British universities has steadily grown; UKCOSA statistics[2] show that, of 318 000 international students in British higher education (HE), 106,000 are postgraduates. Within the UK context, international students constitute 13 per cent of the total student population, although the percentage varies across institutions. In 2006 then-British Prime Minister Tony Blair announced the second phase of an initiative to promote British HE following the success of his 1999 programme, which set an original target of 75 000 additional international students and was comfortably exceeded.[3] The second initiative urged British universities to build partnerships overseas that would help them recruit 100 000 more international students by 2011.

The relationship between income generation and overseas recruitment in HE has been well documented; income from international students plays an important role in the financial health of the HE sector, representing almost one-third of the total income in fees for universities and HE colleges in the UK. The advent of full-cost fees means that most British HE institutions depend on income from international students.[4] In 2004 they earned £4 billion in fees, and students spent as much again on living costs; this level rose to £5 billion in 2006.[5]

Accompanying the steady rise in the number of international students in global HE has been growth in research dedicated to international sojourns, and cultural adjustment represents one of several research interests. The economic dependence of universities on fees from international students makes it critical to gain a clear understanding of the issues that face these institutions in their efforts to deliver optimum service and thereby improve student retention and positive word of mouth to increase recruitment.[6] If institutions do not consider international students' needs, their future recruitment may be endangered.[7]

The move to a new environment represents one of the most traumatic events a person can experience, and for most sojourners some degree of culture shock is inevitable.[8] Culture shock is defined as anxiety that results from losing the familiar signs and symbols of social intercourse and substituting them with other cues that are strange.[9] Many writers liken the shock to a period of mourning for the home world, characterized by feelings of grief and separation anxiety.[10] When a sojourner has completed his or her primary socialization process in one culture and then comes into contact with a new and unfamiliar culture, a process of adjustment takes place as the person adopts new behaviours.[11] In this context, adjustment is the process and outcome of change experienced during the international sojourn.[12] Berry distinguishes four adjustment strategies:[13]

- Assimilation: a renunciation of the heritage of the old culture and an adoption of the new culture.
- Segregation: the maintenance of ethnic identity, heritage, and traditions by the acculturating group.
- Integration: a willingness to adopt certain aspects of the new culture, such as cuisine, while maintaining some cultural identity.

- Marginalization: the renunciation of heritage and the refusal of a relationship with the dominant group.

A modification of the integration approach is multiculturalism, which is often put forward as the best approach[14] because it implies a willingness to both embrace other cultures and retain one's own ethnic identity and also has the possibility of producing mediating personalities, with positive implications for world peace and understanding.[15]

In a year-long, ethnographic study of a mixed-nationality group of postgraduate international students, one of the major themes that emerged was the importance of food in their lives and their adjustment journeys. Finkelstein [16] notes that food habits are inseparable from the culture that a person inhabits and that these habits vary from culture to culture; consequently, some degree of food shock is inevitable upon moving to a culturally dissimilar country, and it should come as no surprise that differences in food habits would be a preoccupation in this study. One of the most common symptoms of culture shock is an excessive preoccupation with food,[17] equated by Garza-Guerrero[18] with mourning for a love object left behind in the absent culture and a sense of grief for home. The study of food also is a major topic in anthropology and a growing topic area within academia.[19] Yet a recent literature search indicates that very little empirical research exists on the role of food in the academic sojourn of international students; food usually is mentioned only incidentally as one of the aspects of the sojourn that students find distressing.[20]

This chapter attempts to address this gap by reflecting on the role of food in the adaptive living experience and illuminating the adjustment strategy adopted by students in the area of food choice. As Hall[21] notes, food habits and practices represent a central element of culture; it is perhaps to be anticipated that sojourners struggle to break away from their habituated food choices. This chapter therefore exposes the challenges associated with adjusting to a new food culture and discusses the influence of HE over this area of international student life. It also offers some conclusions regarding the opportunity offered by increasing international student populations for local food suppliers.

Methodology

The aim of the qualitative study on which this chapter's findings are based is to obtain an insider perspective on the adjustment process; this aim is best fulfilled with an ethnographic approach, which offers the opportunity to study students in their natural setting over a long period using the twin methods of participant observation and in-depth interviews.[22] The setting chosen for this research, the graduate school of a university in the south of England, is the employer of the primary researcher, a lecturer in English for Academic Purposes (EAP). This setting puts the author "in the field" and provides direct access to students and ample opportunity for observation as an overt participant. The author does not grade these students' work or provide input in assessment, which is important to prevent any ethical issues. Of the 150 postgraduate international students attending the graduate school, most are from South-east Asia, which reflects the most common source of international students for UK universities.[23] Approximately one-third are from Europe, Africa or the Middle East.

Ethical approval to undertake this study came from the university's Research Ethics Committee, and the student subjects provided informed consent for observations of the 150-student cohort and for recording those observations on a daily basis; all students were assured confidentiality and anonymity. In addition, during induction week for volunteers, 13 students from 13 different nations volunteered to participate in regular interviews over a 12-month academic year (each prearranged, tape-recorded interview normally lasted two hours). Although no individual can represent an entire culture, culture clearly has a defining impact on an individual's perspective,[24] so these interviews offer access to the sojourn experience from many different perspectives. The interviewee profile in Table 3.1 details the various personalities noted in this chapter (all names are pseudonyms to protect confidentiality).

Various conversations that took place with the interviewees outside these formally arranged times complement and enrich the interview data. Ethnography is initially inductive, so the first interviews with students were informal and unstructured, and, as Spradley[25] recommends, grand tour (open) questions served to stimulate the conversations. Subsequent interviews used the topics and concepts that had emerged in previous interviews as guides, and new ideas and themes emerged throughout the academic year. An inductive approach to research requires researchers to suspend their preconceptions and avoid imposing their biases on the data collection process; the research findings are thus products of the participants' preoccupations, and the literature review does not precede, but rather is tied directly to, the themes that emerge from the data.[26] Specifically, the emergence of food as a major category of research reflects the importance of food in the adjustment experiences of international students.

The decision to study an institution at a particular time is significant. Students have particularly intense emotional experiences at the start of term, as they attempt to adapt not only to a new sociocultural environment but also to unfamiliar academic

Table 3.1   Respondent profiles

Kyoung: female, Korean, 40, Buddhist, married with two children.

Natalia: female, Slovenian, 32, cohabiting.

Xia: female, Taiwanese, 33, married.

Brigitte: female, German, 26, single.

Antonio: male, Brazilian, 30, single.

Mohamed: male, Jordanian, 26, single.

Ning: female, Chinese, 28, single.

Paranee: female, Thai, 28, single.

Rini: female, Indonesian, 27, single.

Panya: female, Malaysian, 22, single.

Kiana: female, Iranian, 32, married with one child.

Cecilia: female, South African, 34, married with two children.

Olga: female, Russian, 22, single.

situations. Thus, the research process initiated both interviews and observations at the beginning of the year, a choice of timing that helps counter common criticisms of studies of adjustment – namely, that they are hampered by sojourners' retrospective accounts.[27] Subsequent interviews took place every three months. The data collection finished at the end of the academic year; therefore, the data capture the total academic experience of these respondents.

In addition to formal interviews, participant observations (a key tool of ethnography)[28] occurred throughout the year to take the experience of the whole cohort of 150 students into account. Participant observing involves not only watching a scene, but also participating in it and recording events and conversations as they occur.[29] Examples of observation sites include the classroom, corridors, the library, coffee bars, the canteen, offices, as well as the induction and social events organized by the school, university or students themselves.

The first interviews and observation were followed by preliminary analysis involving coding the field and interview data. Coding entailed reading through notes and repeatedly listening to tapes and reading transcripts until specific themes or categories began to emerge in terms of certain phrases, events, activities or ideas that occurred repeatedly in the text. Transcripts, field notes and e-mail were also subject to scrutiny, and any recurring topics were highlighted for follow-up in subsequent interviews.

With regard to the generalizability of findings, qualitative researchers acknowledge that a small sample makes it difficult to assume general classifications.[30] Nevertheless, ethnographers often posit that similar settings should produce similar data, such that theory-based generalization, involving the transfer of theoretical concepts found in one situation to other settings and conditions, is possible.[31] The setting for this research explicitly enables the transfer of the findings to similar settings – namely, HE institutions in the UK that recruit international postgraduate students – as well as to similar actors, such as international postgraduates participating in one-year, intensive Master's programmes. Such students are likely to face experiences similar to those confronted by the students in this study, with modifications depending on external circumstances and personalities. Furthermore, this study establishes credibility, a criterion often preferred over generalizability in qualitative research,[32] by offering a thorough review of the literature on adjustment and the international student experience, which reflects many of this study's findings and points to common experiences among international sojourners.

Tasting the Difference: Perceptions of Local Food

During the first few weeks of their sojourn students tried local food, ranging from that provided by their host family to food bought from the university canteen, takeaway shops, local shops and supermarkets. Among those who were either tolerant of diversity or whose food culture was similar to that of the UK, no problems in adapting to an English diet emerge. Therefore, in line with this study's inductive approach, the comments excerpted in this section come from interviews with students who felt strongly enough about what they ate to raise the topic in interviews. Students whose food preferences were distinct from those of the local population experienced stress as a result of their exposure to a new food system. The experience of difference rests at the heart of this culture shock;[33]

the extent of difference between their home and local food meant that South-east Asian students, for example, experienced significant food shock, and eating became a focus of intense emotion.

"There is no Strong Taste to English Food": The Tastelessness of Local Food

During the first interviews, the students commonly stated that they were open to trying new food and broadening their eating experience. However, this willingness to expand their food repertoire was soon put to the test by their experience with bland and tasteless local food that stood in unpleasant contrast to the spiciness of their home country food:

> There is not strong taste to English food. I need spicy food. I mean it's not hot food but a lot of spice, more taste, more flavour than here. Here, there's not too much spice. (Rini)

> I like some taste, but the potato over here usually has no taste; we have to put on some salt or pepper: that's very strange for me. And I like vegetables but the vegetables here are only boiled, no spice at all. (Xia)

Local food was widely deemed "tasteless", "not spicy" and "boring". Key to students' experience was the extent of the dissimilarity, reflected in their repetition of the adjective "strange" and the adverb "here" to denote "not home". The more dissimilar the home and host cuisines, the greater was students' aversion to local food. The condemnation of bland local food by an overwhelming number of Asian students also suggests that their dislike of local food resulted from cultural differences in taste preferences, and this finding is echoed in other studies of migration and food choices.[34]

Not only did students manifest a negative reaction to their sensory experience, but they also expressed strong emotional reactions to eating unfamiliar food, as reflected in their exclamatory speech and their equation of adopting a local diet with grief:

> If I had to eat local food, I would be very sad because I cannot stand the food here. I cannot stand it! (Xia)

Food therefore influenced their mood, which probably explains the widespread intolerance of local food among South-east Asian students, because it signified loss to them. Locher et al.[35] explain that this emotional attachment to home food is predictable, because food holds the power to manipulate emotions. Removing flavourings associated with home also seemed to represent an attack on national identity, as reflected in repeated references to national heritage when the students talked about what they ate:

> I have to have chilli, everybody eats chilli in Malaysia. You're not a Malaysian if you don't eat chilli. (Panya)

The attachment to seasoning, especially notable in Malaysian cuisine, symbolizes a desire to maintain cultural identity as well as improve sensory pleasure. Reflecting the influence of programming in their own culture's approach to flavouring food, students spent money on importing seasonings and other cooking ingredients. Thus, their drive for frugality was outweighed by their need to re-create familiar and comforting objects associated with home.

The links between food and identity, and between food and emotion, are well documented,[36] which makes it all the more surprising that little of the literature considers the impact of diet on international students' well-being. Despite a growing body of research on food and migration, most international education researchers focus instead on other aspects of the academic sojourn. This study marks a departure from existing research by noting the importance of food tastes for international students.

Controlling the Body

Many female Asian students linked a local-food diet with weight gain; the second round of interviews revealed a common consensus that reverting to home country food had produced weight stabilization for them:

> *I put weight on especially in those first six weeks; now getting smaller now [that] I cook by myself. I can't eat too much, it'll make me fatter. (Paranee)*

Mindfulness of body size was a common theme and often cited as the reason for not adopting an English diet, perceived as fatty:

> *I heard from my friends that it's very oil [sic]. I don't like! I don't like that everything is fried; I like well-cooked food, so I think I might cook for myself. (Xia)*

Self-responsibility for ensuring physical well-being through healthy eating was important, but for those who lived with a host family there was little option but to eat what was offered. The emotional cost of this lack of choice is best revealed in Kyoung's reaction of frustrated tears to a diet that she considered not only tasteless, but also too high in carbohydrates and fat:

> *I have to have English food. It's one of the most terrible things I experience here! [Crying] Everyday they gave me potato, smashed potato, boiled potato, fried potato! Everyday the menu is different but always we get potato, and they pour some horrible sauce over it! So fat! So horrible!*

Kyoung clearly reveals the extent of her food shock in her exclamatory tone, as well as in the frequent use of negative superlatives ("horrible", "awful", "terrible"); the inescapability of her situation simply compounded her shock. Her English host family could not know that their efforts to introduce Kyoung to traditional English cuisine was meeting with such an extreme emotional reaction, which did not lessen until she moved, in January 2004, into accommodations that enabled her to choose her diet. Only then could she take control of what she put into her body. Ironically, according to Marshall,[37] "proper meals" consisting of meat, potatoes, vegetables and gravy are largely disappearing from English life and are increasingly being replaced by processed food and/or international cuisine, which indicates that Kyoung's experience was atypical.

However, in findings that replicate those of an older study of international students' food habits,[38] nearly all the interviewees commented disparagingly about the high fat, sugar and carbohydrate content of the English diet. Monneuse et al.[39] and Atkins and Bowler[40] state that preoccupation with health and body image is common among women in the West; following students' exposure to a Westernized diet, these issues become preoccupations, particularly for those with a propensity to gain weight. Western food (the students' term) was viewed with some trepidation; it was an unfamiliar and unnerving development in students' relationship with food. Moreover, recent scientific studies of health status in immigrants[41] appear to justify students' anxiety, in that deteriorated health (including a higher incidence of obesity and diabetes) is associated with an increased consumption of Western-style food.

Concern for their own health was matched by negative judgements that English people had lost the art of self-control:

> They eat too much fat. I think that's why it will make people to get weight. I don't know why they do that. They don't say no! (Xia)

> Eastern people care for health but Western people don't. If we eat hamburger we have one cheese, but here people like to order double. They don't care. (Chinese student)

A perception of overconsumption in England (usually generalized by students to the UK or the West) was commonplace, reflecting Gronow's[42] conceptualization of the modern Westerner as a self-indulgent hedonist. In contrast, self-deprivation of fattening and luxury foods, such as chocolate and cakes, became a common theme after only a few months of living in England; students used self-denying phrases such as "I daren't" or "I can't". These data reflect a tension between individual responsibility and environmental supply, between consumer freedom of choice and awareness of the dangers of overeating, that is widespread in contemporary Western society.[43] Students thus found themselves in the uncomfortable situation of exerting ongoing resistance to temptation.

The Fear of Contamination

The second interviews also revealed some concern about the quality of fresh fruit and vegetables in England compared with those in the home country, as Natalia's comment shows:

> I think the taste is less artificial in Slovenia because we can get more that is fresh, you know, than here. Here, for example, salad doesn't taste good, but in Slovenia when you buy something fresh, it tastes good.

A similar comment by Xia refers to chicken she bought locally to make Chinese dishes. Described as "boiling chicken", this meat would be used in Taiwan only to make stock, whereas she would use free-range chicken for main meals ("the chicken runs in the field, so the meat will taste different"). However, in England, free-range chicken was out of financial reach. As Blythman[44] notes, most people in the UK shop in supermarkets for reasons of cost and access; the students similarly bought the cheapest food available. Students had no control over the food supply, so they resigned themselves to deferring gratification in response to their perceptions of inferior food. In other words, the pleasure they could derive from eating high-quality, fresh food could be restored only upon their return home.

More important than perceptions of inferior taste were concerns about damage to their physical health due to chemical treatments of fresh produce. Olga was the most outspoken in her condemnation of the quality of the fruit and vegetables available in England, which she repeatedly described as "not real", with particular reference to their uniformity:

> Here I can't find good vegetables and fruits because all of them are specially treated, not really real. Umm, you know the apples are all the same size, the bananas are the same size, potatoes are the same size, especially selected, especially made, not really really real. It was growing specially selected. We have real food; we have good vegetables, not like here.

Food supply tends to vary both culturally and geographically, so it should not be surprising that Olga would be suspicious and apprehensive of fruit and vegetables that all looked the same, because this clashes with her experience in Russia. This uniformity probably results from the dominance of supermarkets over the UK food industry and their strict imposition of size, colour and shape standards. Farmers' markets offer a counterpoint, providing locally produced and often unstandardized food but, as Jamie Oliver[45] observes, they are not a traditional part of day-to-day life in England, which means they are also generally not accessible to international students. Olga found that eating food she did not trust was unavoidable, and this created dissatisfaction with, and alienation from, a significant part of her life. These findings regarding food choice support Giddens'[46] claims that alienation commonly results from a perception of powerlessness. Until control over their diet was restored, these students' feelings of life satisfaction suffered significantly.

Distrust of fresh food was also deepened by students' perception of differences in the perishability of fresh produce between the home and the new country:

> Here bananas can be fresh during the two weeks out of fridge, I think it's not real! I left a banana on a plate on a shelf and it's still good! I left it there two weeks ago; it couldn't be really really real! In Russia, if I left a banana like that it would become not fresh on a few dates [sic]! (Olga)

Suspicion about food safety was unsettling, yet research provides various reasons for this seemingly disconcerting discrepancy between the lengths of time fruit bought in different countries takes to decay. For example, the UK supermarket supply chain is quicker (that is, fruit arrives more quickly and has longer to ripen); Russia may use different banana suppliers that provide a different strain of banana; and bananas are shipped to UK supermarkets in protected atmospheres to arrest decay.[47] Unaware of these common food industry practices, Olga was left with an intense fear of the physical harm she might suffer from exposure to chemical additives. Ironically, Olga seemed unaware of health concerns regarding soil and water contamination in Russia as a result of intensive cotton farming.[48] This point highlights the observation that insight into a new culture's practices commonly appears sharper among newcomers than among those who are embedded in the culture;[49] it therefore seems understandable that students might be quicker to note objects of disquiet in a new, unfamiliar culture than they would at home.

Students' distrust of some foods also echoed a general lack of public confidence in food safety, a subject of much debate in contemporary food literature. For example, Atkins and Bowler[50] point to scientific evidence of poisoning through overexposure to chemically treated food, which lends some credence to the students' concerns. Townsend and Asthana[51] also attribute increased consumption of organic food to anxiety about food safety and the perception that organic food has healthful properties. However, the cost of such food is prohibitive to international students on a tight budget, and dissatisfaction and enduring suspicion continued to mar their enjoyment of eating food they could not avoid:

> *I have to eat vegetables, but I will eat it with sadness, because the taste is not really real. I will continue to eat because I have no choice, but I will eat without pleasure. (Olga)*

Feeling trapped in turn resulted in a reduced quality of life. As Tester[52] argues, it is beside the point to ask whether the risks associated with certain foods are real; what matters instead is the perception of danger, which has a profound impact on people's sense of ease. This unease is evident in Olga's dissatisfaction with the compulsion to eat food she not only disliked on the grounds of taste, but whose health implications she also feared.

In summary, distaste and distrust distinguished students' reactions to local food, which they criticized as fattening, bland and chemically treated. However, their access to local food mainly came through the university canteen and local stores, which were sources of high dissatisfaction in a recent survey of international students.[53] Students enjoyed very little contact with the local population, the best source of knowledge about the host culture.[54] If they had benefited from such interactions, they might have drawn different conclusions about the types of food eaten by local people, although variations in food habits and tastes would probably still have been evident, given the close link between food and culture.[55] Furthermore, many writers endorse the link that students made between a decline in health and an increased consumption of Western food, and the students might have embraced this link even if their daily food regimes had been more authentic.

Food Adjustment Strategies

During the academic sojourn, international students adapted to the new culture in different ways, using assimilation, segregation, integration, marginalization and multiculturalism. Students varied in their eating habits; many were willing to try different cuisines, but the majority demonstrated a strict determination to adhere to their country's eating habits. Three of the interviewees – Panya, Rini and Xia – even cited the desire to eat their home food as a reason to take a short trip home.

Re-creating a Taste of Home

A pattern of consumption of home country food emerges among all the South-east Asian students in this research, and this pattern exemplifies a segregation approach to food choice in which the students attempt to maintain their ethnic identity.[56] Describing her three-month experience with her English host family's food as "a very bad horrible experience", Kyoung cited her relief at resuming a Korean diet as the highlight of moving into a new flat. This relief was shared by Paranee, who moved in with fellow Asian students after just six weeks of living with a host family, for the sole reason of improving her diet:

I wanted to eat Thai noodles or something Asian like rice and oyster sauce and veggies. I thought, oh! I'm not going to die because of English food!

Restitution of access to home food signalled their release from intolerable living conditions. Such strength of feeling helps explain why students who did not live with a host family made the decision to cook their own national cuisine, usually within days of their arrival – a decision often explained in emotive language:

I am happy, I find I can buy rice here, buy noodles [the high proportion of students from South-east Asia prompted the growing proliferation of Asian food shops]. I cook quite simple, rice and vegetable, that's it. I'm glad I can do this still. (Ning)

I cannot eat local food!! I love cooking and eating Chinese food. I like the special taste of Chinese food. It is a familiar thing I do in Taiwan and it made me feel familiar with my home town, and made me feel more comfortable. (Xia)

Consuming familiar food was also about more than taste, because the students derived emotional sustenance from eating their home country's food. The word "comfort" repeatedly described the act of eating national dishes, which in turn often was credited with alleviating stress and loneliness. Locher and colleagues[57] explain that food can become a nostalgic object for sojourners, carrying the power to manipulate their emotional states and feelings. For example, a jar of pomegranate paste bought from a local Iranian food shop transported Kiana to the cosiness of home during an emotionally disturbing period of homesickness:

Kiana said she doesn't really miss Iranian food, but when she saw this she was comforted. When she cooked it she said it smells like her home: it had made her feel really happy. If her husband comes to live here, she won't miss these things so much, but while he is away, she misses everything about Iran that would bring her comfort. (Research notes, 21 June)

Students commonly imbued certain foods with the power to comfort during times of homesickness; food became a "love object" associated with home that reduced feelings of grief for home and significant others. In addition, the consumption of home food helped compensate for other unavoidable stressors (e.g. loneliness, language difficulties, study stress), offering the sojourners an opportunity to remember a happy past and forget an unhappy present.[58] Despite their time pressures, all of the South-east Asian interviewees dedicated significant time – sometimes up to two hours per day – to cooking home food. In recognition of the importance of food to emotional well-being, Kyoung even volunteered for a local organization of newly arrived Korean students whose members took turns cooking meals. The aim of this organization was to ease students' adjustment to life in

England by removing the extrinsic environmental stressor that local food can represent. For the younger students, who had to learn to cook for the first time in their lives, the desire to eat home food sparked a cultivation of independence that both challenged and frustrated them. A lack of cooking experience is common among both home and international students.[59]

An association between health and diet was prevalent among South-east Asian students, providing additional motivation for adopting a home culture diet. The medicinal use of food and drink (e.g. to aid digestion, alleviate stress, relieve a headache, or ease period pains) was noticeable, as Xia's reference to food and drink reveals:

> *In soup I cooked today, I put some dates. For woman, it's better for skin and you can have more comfortable during the periods. And this drink here [pointing to a flask she had brought to the interview], it's a kind of Chinese herbs to keep your health, you can just drink like tea. I drink this for years. It will make you feel clear and healthier. I cannot find those things here, so I brought them.*

South-east Asian students also remained attached to the belief that people can influence their own health through nutrition, and they obtained reassurance by using food to control their physical well-being. This norm replicates an observation made of many non-Western cultures.[60] Home food not only tasted better, but also offered physical and emotional sustenance.

Many students were surprised and baffled by their entrenched food preferences: indeed, for those who considered themselves to be cognitively flexible, the discovery of their dependence was shocking:

> *Most of my flatmates are Asian, so we eat a lot of rice. I have to have rice – what can I do? I don't know why, I just can't live without that! (Rini)*

> *I had to go without Chinese food for ten days, and I got upset, emotionally, all I could think about was rice. Me and my wife now cook separately from the English host family, we always cook Chinese. It is what we are used to. (Chinese student)*

Survival seemed to depend on access to the familiar, and deprivation of this access was a source of distress to students until they achieved relief through its reinstatement. For example, given that food preferences are often about more than nutritional value, consider what rice represents.[61] In these cases, did the loss of rice act as a reminder of the students' displacement? Was the consumption of rice so intrinsic to their emotional well-being that its sacrifice was intolerable? No South-east Asian student appeared willing to find out the answer. Previous studies echo this unforeseen inability among migrants to incorporate other national foods into their regime. During their transition, sojourners commonly realized the depths of their learned cultural habits and faced the choice of challenging various aspects of their behaviour.[62] The South-east Asian students in this research revealed a low acceptance of local food – that is, a lack of willingness to eat English food occasionally or develop some preferences for some English foods.[63] Perhaps the tendency towards resistance to change, common in cultures that score high on the uncertainty avoidance scale,[64] can help explain this reticence. However, food is not as open to individualizing tendencies as are other consumption fields,[65] as supported by a study of British university students showing that their food habits remained stable during a transition period.[66] This finding re-emerges among the South-east Asian students, who exhibited a segregation approach to diet following their initial encounters with culturally strange food.

Using Food as a Social Agent

Food also played a central role in both the construction and maintenance of social relationships, particularly for South-east Asian students who made frequent reference to communal eating. Anthropologists often highlight the social component of eating,[67] and this study confirms that daily food preparation and cooking (in pairs or small groups of students from the same country or region) and larger weekly parties were commonplace. Paranee's comment that cooking and eating together were her favourite social activities is typical:

> We always cook, we always have Asian dishes or Thai food, we always have three kinds of dishes, and because we always share, we have lots of food. It is the best thing we do.

When discussing their social lives, the South-east Asian students most frequently mention communal eating, in which the preparation of food was as important for the interaction it provided as was food consumption. Food thus became a vehicle for socializing, giving students a feeling of belonging and security and offering them the opportunity to eat the food they liked. This finding echoes Simmel's point that eating is both a personal and a social act:[68] The sensual pleasure of eating is subjectively experienced, but it is often undertaken in groups. This point is particularly relevant for collectivist cultures, which emphasize shared experiences and group interactions.[69] Therefore, it seems unlikely that these students would distinguish eating from interaction; in contrast, they perceived distance in English family life, as noted by a Vietnamese student staying with a host family:

> Here, they do things separately. They have a table, but they don't sit at it, they sit and eat alone!

Bafflement over the English approach to mealtimes was common, as was vindication of the South-east Asian link between togetherness and eating. Not only were these interactions familiar, but they offered comfort in an otherwise frequently unsettling environment. The perception that the family meal is not widely enjoyed in the UK is one that also offers contemporary significance; commentators increasingly call on consumers to reinstate communal dining as a route to improving their communication and emotional health.[70] The tendency towards shared experience among South-east Asian students in particular thus contrasts with the increasing isolation in British society, which carries critical implications for emotional and physical health.

Sitting with others during social eating also provided a contrasting phenomenon to the loneliness at mealtimes suffered by those who were the only representatives of their nationality. Envy of their Asian peers, whose group identity was clearly cemented through their interactions around their home food, was often expressed:

> They are always together: they always eat together and they cook only Asian food. (Olga)

Preparing intricate national dishes was time-consuming, and if the effort was not compensated for by companionship, it was usually abandoned by those who did not belong to a conational group:

> *I don't have patience because Iranian food take a long time, 5, 4 hours. That's why you have to waste your time, your gas, your electricity, so just I put [sic] fish, chicken. (Kiana)*

This move away from activities associated with communal life supports the negative link suggested between the motivation to cook and reduced social contact.[71] For socially isolated students, the association between food and interaction, between mealtimes and bonding with family, represented a shocking and saddening realization that often precipitated changes in both lifestyle and quality of life. Cecilia found that she seldom cooked in England because she could not find the motivation to cook just for herself, having spent years cooking for her family:

> *I'm not used to it. It's not easy to cook for yourself. Like sometimes I say "I want to cook" and I end up not cooking. I eat but maybe a sandwich, something like that. I'm not used to it. It's not easy.*

According to Atkins and Bowler,[72] a strong connection marks women and the domestic preparation of food; outside the domestic context, eating came to represent a substitution of familial roles and personal significance. For informants such as Kyoung and Xia, who had left behind husbands and children, mealtimes with conational friends provided solace and reminders of home, but for Cecilia they reinforced her isolation and provoked nostalgia for her place in her family and community in South Africa. The key difference lies in the friendship networks the students enjoyed.

Embracing Diversity

The multicultural strategy of adjustment involves retaining one's own culture but also learning several other cultures.[73] This strategy could influence students' diets, because they had access to a diverse range of cuisines offered by their peers, as well as local food. However, few students actually adopted this approach, and their behaviour often was influenced by other factors. For example, cultural similarity encourages a willingness to try local food, as Cecilia explained:

> *There is nothing I can say is strange. For me, to eat English food, in the end, it is the same in South Africa. We eat greens, roast chicken or chicken curry or beef; we eat pasta, or cottage pie. There is nothing much different.*

The lesser cultural distance between England and South Africa, at least in the food domain, accounts for Cecilia's feeling of ease, as well as her implicit assumption that relocation to an unfamiliar culture would be more difficult. This correlation, made by various writers, finds confirmation in this study. Because of her familiarity with English food, Cecilia displayed a high acceptance of local food, although the lack of sociability and her changed role often spoiled her enjoyment of eating and dictated her meal choices.

The motivation to experience something new and previous experience also prompted other students, including Antonio, Brigitte and Mohamed, to try different national foods. These drives universally appear as important variables for successful adjustment. The opportunity to try different national dishes resulted from sharing meals prepared by flatmates of various nationalities and attending food parties, to which students usually brought national dishes that they wanted others to sample, as Antonio's typical comment shows:

> In my flat most of them are Asians, and they cook beautiful food. I've never eaten so much, it's beautiful!

Pride in national cuisine was also common; approximately 60 of the 150 students brought homemade snacks or traditional sweets to the interviews to communicate affection or gratitude. The acceptance of such food gifts can demonstrate a willingness to establish or strengthen a bond.[74] In this sense, this study also reinforces the idea that ethnography findings often influence the researcher's behaviour and attitudes.[75] The central role occupied by food for communicating culture is now reflected in my own use of traditional English snacks during induction week to welcome students to England and invite them to be open, right from the beginning, to different foods. This activity carries symbolic power: The often hesitant act of eating unfamiliar food might assert an ongoing influence on students' openness to new experiences.

This study repeatedly shows that the example set by members of conational friendship groups cannot be underestimated in cross-cultural settings. Mohamed regularly cooked Arab food, but he saw it as his duty to try other dishes in his aim to learn about other cultures and insist on openness among his Arab friends, whom he described as rigid in their mononational food habits. In this and other aspects of life, Mohamed embodies the intercultural mediator who facilitates cultural learning and tolerance in others:[76]

> I do shopping, I buy lots of different food, and I try to suggest to them, "please this one you can cook this way, you make the sauce with this" to teach them about this.

Synthesizing his own and other food cultures meant that Mohamed became an example to his Arab friends, demonstrating to them how sojourners can embrace diversity without renouncing their culture of origin.

Yet embracing new cuisine does not always reflect openness to new cultural habits, but instead may signify withdrawal from a culture of origin. Food can be used to communicate difference, and, as Harris-Shapiro[77] states, wilful distinction from the dominant group produces a personalized identity – in this instance, developed through food choices. For Kiana, Iranian food negatively symbolized Islamic rule in Iran, from which she was keen to distance herself:

> I don't care if I never eat my food again! If she [her six-year-old daughter] doesn't want, I'm not going to cook. I never mind, I don't care if she said "I don't want Iranian food." If she said "I'm not Iranian" it's better. I don't like my nationality. Whatever she wants to do she's free. If she wants fish fingers every day, that's fine.

This declaration of freedom of choice refers not just to food, but also to the ability to control her own future; by welcoming her daughter's preference for what she defined as "English food" (e.g. burgers, chips, fish fingers, pizza), Kiana shows that the symbolic power she attached to Iranian food outweighed the health concerns she might have had about processed food. Consumption of food is thus highly meaningful, as reflected in Warde's claim that when people eat, they consume not just nutrients but also meanings and symbols.[78] Kiana rejected Iranian food because of its association with a disliked government and religious culture; by eating Western food, Kiana and her daughter declared their non-allegiance to the Iranian government and signalled the desire to be a part of British society. Conversely, by eating a variety of national dishes, students conveyed tolerance and openness, which are central to the success of cultural pluralism in both academic and wider communities.

Conclusions

This chapter opens a window on to the role of food in the adjustment of a sample of students who, as a result of living in a new culture, made many changes in their lives, except in the area of eating habits and practices. Only a minority of students embraced diversity in their eating habits. The decisive influence on the adjustment strategy they adopted for food consumption was cultural similarity; those from the most dissimilar cultures were the most rigid in their approaches. However, it would be wrong to assume that they avoided local food just because of taste differences, because the interviews indicate instead that food became a symbol of home and a means of bringing people together.

Anthropologists often present eating as a rite of passage and as a reflection of the importance of food to cultural identity.[79] The widespread avoidance of local and other national cuisines among the student respondents clearly suggests that many of them failed to embrace an important aspect of a new culture. However, new cultures often accept attachment to national symbols, such as cuisine, because this attachment does not interfere with the host society.[80] Therefore, a pertinent question with which to end this chapter is: does it matter what a sojourner eats during his or her stay, especially if it facilitates happiness by alleviating other stressors triggered by transition? The answer must be that eating habits do matter, especially considering the proven link between interaction and food. International students are often highly anxious about their language ability, which has important implications for their academic success, yet their interaction patterns deterred their linguistic progress, because native language predominated in interactions among conationals.

The role of the HE institution in this context is unclear; whether it can influence student behaviour in private spheres is debatable. However, this study might prompt a further debate about the role of food for international students, and it certainly signals the need for more dedicated research. A quantitative survey of international students' shopping and eating habits will follow this research, and additional research initiatives are being undertaken by the SOAS Food Studies Centre. A project with particular significance to international students pertains to on-campus food provision and suggests that HE institutions should provide food that is both nutritious and locally sourced. Access to such food might help international students overcome their concerns about the quality and freshness of local food, as well as offset their anxiety about gaining weight if they eat fast food. Furthermore, such a provision would provide an opportunity for interactions between domestic and international students, albeit mainly during the day. Further research findings will help inform these recommendations for managing HE institutions; in the meantime, local retailers should take advantage of the clear opportunity offered by the presence of increasing numbers of South-east Asian students by offering more products from their cultures of origin.

References

1   Cushner, K. and Karim, A. (2004), "Study abroad at university level" in D. Landis, J. Bennett and M. Bennett (eds), *Intercultural Training*, Sage, London.

2   UKCOSA (2006), "Student statistics", http://www.ukcosa.org.uk/student.

3   MacLeod, D. (2006), "International rescue", *The Guardian*, 18 April, available at: http://education.guardian.co.uk/egweekly/story/0,,1755401,00.html.

4   Leonard, D., Pelletier, C. and Morley, L. (2002), *The Experiences of International Students in UK Higher Education: A Review of Unpublished Research*, UKCOSA, London.

5   MacLeod, "International rescue", *op. cit.*

6   Ward, C. (2001), *The Impact of International Students on Domestic Students and Host Institutions*, New Zealand Ministry of Education, http://www.minedu.govt.nz/index.cfm?layout=index&indexID=2107&indexparentid=1000.

7   Ryan, J. and Carroll, J. (2005), "'Canaries in the coalmine': international students in Western universities" in J. Carroll and J. Ryan (eds), *Teaching International Students: Improving Learning for All*, Routledge, Abingdon.

8   Berry, J. (1994), "Acculturation and psychological adaptation: an overview" in A-M. Bouvy, F. van de Vijver, P. Boski and P. Schmitz (eds), *Journeys into Cross-Cultural Psychology*, S&Z, Amsterdam.

9   Hall, E. (1959), *The Silent Language*, Doubleday, New York.

10 Furnham, A. (1997), "The experience of being an overseas student" in D. McNamara and R. Harris (eds), *Overseas Students in HE: Issues in Teaching and Learning*, Routledge, London.

11 Kim, Y. (1988), *Communication and Cross-Cultural Adaptation*, Multilingual Matters, Clevedon.

12 French, J., Rodgers, W. and Cobb, S. (1974), "Adjustment as person-environment fit" in G. Coelho, D. Hamburg and J. Adams (eds), *Coping and Adaptation*, Basic Books, New York.

13 Berry, "Acculturation and psychological adaptation", *op. cit.*

14 Bochner, S. (1981), "The social psychology of cultural mediation" in S. Bochner (ed.), *The Mediating Person: Bridges Between Cultures*, Schenkman, Cambridge, MA.

15 Gudykunst, W. (1998), *Bridging Differences: Effective Intergroup Communication*, Sage, London.

16 Finkelstein, J. (1999), "Rich food: McDonald's and modern life" in B. Smart (ed.), *Resisting McDonaldisation*, Sage, London.

17 Okorocha, E. (1996), "The international student experience", *Journal of Graduate Education*, Vol. 2, No. 3, pp. 80–84.

18 Garza-Guerrero, A. (1974), "Culture shock: its mourning and the vicissitudes of identity", *Journal of the American Psychoanalytic Association*, Vol. 22, pp. 408-429.

19 Gosden, C. (1999), "Food: where biology meets culture" in C. Gosden and J. Hather (eds), *The Prehistory of Food: Appetites for Change*, Routledge, London.

20   Furukawa, T. (1997), "Cultural distance and its relationship to psychological adjustment of international exchange students", *Psychiatry and Clinical Neurosciences*, Vol. 51, No. 3, pp. 87–91; Okorocha, "The international student experience", *op. cit.*

21   Hall, J. (1995), "Food and dietary requirements for international students", *Journal of International Education*, Vol. 6, No. 1, pp. 53–60.

22   Fetterman, D. (1998), *Ethnography*, Sage, London.

23   UKCOSA, "Student statistics", *op. cit.*

24   Hofstede, G. (1991), *Cultures and Organisation: Software of the Mind*, HarperCollins, London.

25   Spradley, J. (1979), *The Ethnographic Interview*, Holt, Rinehart and Winston, New York.

26   Daymon, C. and Holloway, I. (2002), *Qualitative Research Methods in Public Relations and Marketing Communications*, Routledge, London.

27   Ward, "Impact of international students", *op. cit.*

28   Spradley, *The Ethnographic Interview*, *op. cit.*

29   Hammersley, M. and Atkinson, P. (1995), *Ethnography Principles in Practice*, Tavistock, London.

30   Mason, J. (2002), *Qualitative Researching*, Sage, London.

31   Daymon and Holloway, *Qualitative Research Methods*, *op. cit.*

32   Ibid.

33   Hall, "The silent language", *op. cit.*

34   Zwingmann, C. and Gunn, A. (1983), *Uprooting and Health: Psychosocial Problems of Students from Abroad*, WHO, Geneva; Smart, J., Huang, C., Pang, C., Kuah, K. and Smart, A. (2006), "Negotiating Chinese immigrant food", *Culture in a Global Setting*, ILAS newsletter online 19, http://www.iias.nl/iiasn/19/.

35   Locher, J., Yoels, W., Maurer, D.,and van Ells, J. (2005), "Comfort foods: an exploratory journey into the social and emotional significance of food", *Food and Foodways*, Vol. 13, No. 4, pp. 273–297.

36   Gosden, "Food", *op. cit.*

37   Marshall, D. (2000), "British meals and food choice" in H. Meiselman (ed.), *Dimensions of the Meal: The Science, Culture, Business and Art of Eating*, Aspen, Baltimore, MD.

38   Henry, C. and Wheeler, E. (1980), "Dietary patterns among overseas students in London", *The Nutrition Society*, Vol. 39, p. 2.

39   Monneuse, M., Bellisle, F. and Koppert, G. (1997), "Eating habits, food and health-related attitudes and beliefs reported by French students", *European Journal of Clinical Nutrition*, Vol. 51, No. 1, pp. 46–53.

40   Atkins, P. and Bowler, I. (2001), *Food in Society*, Arnold, London.

41   Burns, C. (2004), "Effect of migration on food habits of Somali women living as refugees in Australia", *Ecology of Food and Nutrition*, Vol. 43, No. 3, pp. 213–229; Himmelgreen, D., Bretnall, R., Peng, Y. and Bermudez, A. (2005), "Birthplace, length of time in the US, and language are associated with diet among inner-city Puerto Rican women", *Ecology of Food and Nutrition*, Vol. 44, No. 2, pp. 105–122; Kedia, S. (2004), "Changing food production strategies among Garhwali resettlers in the Himalayas", *Ecology of Food and Nutrition*, Vol. 43, No. 6, pp. 421–442; Saleh, A., Amanatidis, S. and Samman, S. (2002). "The effect of migration on dietary intake, type 2 diabetes and obesity: the Ghanaian health and nutrition analysis in Sydney, Australia", *Ecology of Food and Nutrition*, Vol. 41, No. 3, pp. 255–270.

42   Gronow, J. (1997), *The Sociology of Taste*, Routledge, London.

43   Schlosser, E. (2002), *Fast Food Nation: The Dark Side of the All-American Meal*, Perennial, New York.

44   Blythman, J. (2003), "Lords of the aisles", *The Guardian*, 17 May, available at http://www.guardian.co.uk/food/focus/story/0,,956562,00.html.

45   *Jamie's Great Escape*, Channel 4, 13 July 2006.

46   Giddens, A. (1991), *Modernity and Self-Identity: Self and Society in the Late Modern Age*, Polity Press, Cambridge.

47   Friends of the Earth (2004), *Real Food*. Available at: http://www.foe.co.uk.

48   Calder, J. (1995), "Aral Sea loss and environmental and economic repercussions", *The TED Case Studies*, Vol. 4, No. 1, available at: http://www.american.edu/TED/aral.htm.

49   Hofstede, *Cultures and Organisation*, *op. cit.*

50   Atkins and Bowler, *Food in Society*, *op. cit.*

51   Townsend, M. and Asthana, A. (2004), "Britain's organic appetite grows by£1.7m a week", *The Observer*, 4 July.

52   Tester, K. (1999), "The moral malaise of McDonaldisation: the values of vegetarianism" in B. Smart (ed.), *Resisting McDonaldisation*, Sage, London.

53   International Student Barometer. (2006), *International Students in the UK*, Bournemouth University.

54   Ward, *Impact of International Students*, *op. cit.*

55   Gosden, "Food", *op. cit.*

56   Berry, J. (1994), "Acculturation and psychological adaptation: an overview" in A-M. Bouvy, F. van de Vijver, P. Boski and P. Schmitz (eds), *Journeys into Cross-Cultural Psychology*, S&Z, Amsterdam.

57   Locher et al., "Comfort foods", *op. cit*

58   Zwingmann and Gunn, *Uprooting and Health*, *op. cit.*

59   Edwards, J.S.A. and Meiselman, H. (2003), "Changes in dietary habits during the first year at university", *British Nutrition Foundation Nutritional Bulletin*, Vol. 28, pp. 21–34.

60   Ikeda, J. (1999), "Culture, food, and nutrition in increasingly culturally diverse societies" in J. Germov and L. Williams, (eds), *A Sociology of Food and Nutrition: The Social Appetite*, Oxford University Press, Oxford.

61   Smart et al., "Negotiating Chinese immigrant food", *op. cit.*

62   Hall, "The silent language", *op. cit.*

63   Henry and Wheeler, "Dietary patterns", *op. cit.*

64   Hofstede, *Cultures and Organisation*, *op. cit.*

65   Warde, A. (1997), *Consumption, Food and Taste*, Sage, London.

66   Meiselman, H., Mastroianni, G., Buller, M. and Edwards, J.S.A. (1999), "Longitudinal measurement of three eating behaviour scales during a period of change", *Food Quality and Preference*, Vol. 10, pp. 1–8.

67   Counihan, C. and Van Esterik, P. (eds) (1997), *Food and Culture*, Routledge, New York.

68   Simmel, G. (1950), "The Stranger" in K. Wolff (ed.), *The Sociology of Georg Simmel*, The Free Press, London & New York.

69   Triandis, H., Bontempo, R. and Villareal, M. (1988), "Individualism and collectivism: cross-cultural perspectives on self-ingroup relationships", *Journal of Personality and Social Psychology*, Vol. 54, No. 2, pp. 323–338.

70   Marshall, "British meals and food choice", *op. cit.*

71   McIntosh, A. and Kubena, K. (1999), "Food and ageing" in J. Germov and L. Williams (eds), *A Sociology of Food and Nutrition: The Social Appetite*, Oxford University Press, Oxford.

72   Atkins and Bowler, *Food in Society*, *op. cit.*

73   Berry, "Acculturation and psychological adaptation", *op. cit.*

74   Beardsworth, A. and Keil, T. (1997), *Sociology on the Menu: An Invitation to the Study of Food and Society*, Routledge, London.

75   Spradley, *The Ethnographic Interview*, *op. cit.*

76   Bochner, "Social psychology of cultural mediation", *op. cit.*

77   Harris-Shapiro, C. (2006), "Bloody shank bones and braided bread: the food voice and the fashioning of American Jewish identities", *Food and Foodways*, Vol. 14, No. 2, pp. 67–90.

78   Warde, *Consumption, Food and Taste*, *op. cit.*

79   Smart et al., "Negotiating Chinese immigrant food", *op. cit.*

80   Boski, P. (1994), "Psychological acculturation via identity dynamics: consequences for subjective well-being" in A-M. Bouvy, F. van de Vijver, P. Boski and P. Schmitz (eds), *Journeys into Cross-Cultural Psychology*, S&Z, Amsterdam.

4 Ethnic Opportunities: The Emergence of New Supply Chains that Stimulate and Respond to the Need for "New" Ingredients

SEAN BEER,* MARTIN K. HINGLEY† AND
ADAM LINDGREEN‡

Keywords

ethnic markets, new food products, UK, supply and channel networks.

Abstract

This chapter considers the approach of innovative and entrepreneurial organizations that have responded to changing circumstances (e.g. socio-ethnic, market demand, even climatic) to develop new products for new markets. We discuss the agents for change against a background of evolving national and regional gastronomy. From this example, we address innovation and change in food developed in various regions of the UK. Producers from two distinct regions have very different food histories and socio-economic characteristics: the South West and the West Midlands. In the South West, producers draw on a rich food heritage to adapt products to meet the demands of ethnically diversifying UK consumers; in the West Midlands (one of the already most ethnically diverse areas of the UK), rural fresh produce growers are striving to meet the challenge of change in response to the major conurbation on their doorstep. The chapter concludes with the recognition that evolving markets and regional and national gastronomies create the

*   Mr Sean Beer, School of Services Management, Bournemouth University, Dorset House, Talbot Campus, Fern Barrow, Poole, Dorset, BH12 5BB, UK. E-mail: sbeer@bournmouth.ac.uk. Telephone: +44 1202 965 109.

†   Dr Martin Hingley, Department Business Management and Marketing, Harper Adams University College, Newport, Shropshire, TF10 8NB, UK. E-mail: mhingley@harper-adams.ac.uk. Telephone: + 44 1952 815 386.

‡   Professor Adam Lindgreen, Hull University Business School, Cottingham Road, Hull HU6 7RX, UK. E-mail: a.lindgreen@hull.ac.uk. Telephone: + 44 1482 463 096.

impetus for product innovation, but both producer and market can be hampered by channel and cultural disconnection. Actors in the processes and channels of production and supply must understand one another and unite in the service of new and emerging markets to best meet the burgeoning needs of ethnically diverse customers.

Introduction

Changes in national and international gastronomies create opportunities for individuals within the food supply chain. Gastronomies and supply chains develop in many ways. Suppliers may well be instrumental in these changes, helping create new products and, in effect, new demand. Alternatively, they may just respond to changes. Either way, there would seem to be significant opportunities for individuals to capitalize on change. This chapter examines how some such changes have taken place and, by looking at a series of case studies, how these opportunities can be exploited.

Gastronomic Change

Few can doubt that the gastronomic map of a country such as the UK has changed and that, during the early part of the twenty-first century, we are seeing enormous movement within the pattern and types of food consumed. Beer and Redman[1] have given an overview of this process during the latter half of the twentieth century; other commentators have also examined this area and the general subjects of food and culture, not only in the UK but around the world.[2] The whole subject of how we consume what we do, in the way that we do, and how it gets from field to fork, plough to plate, or seed to soul is indeed fascinating.

The debate about food consumption is diverse, as exemplified by the work of anthropological food researchers.[3] Gibson[4] explores the whole idea of food consumption on the move: Food, taste and eating are all implicated in differing motilities, whether corporeal, technological, imaginative or virtual. As such, she not only looks at E.M. Forster's experiences of a 1940 dining car but also the way in which food can take on greater symbolism. This theme is further taken up by Gibson in terms of culinary tourism: "culinary tourists are eating the Other (as something distinct from their own culture), but they are also eating the differences between various Others; differences that are often produced and consumed through mobility."[5] Molz identifies cultural links along the supply chain by way of a multi-site ethnographic study examining the relationship among commodity producers, consumers and those in between.[6] Primarily, two questions arise: why do these changes take place, and what or who are the drivers? Fundamentally, these are the questions regarding how we develop our food cultures.

Forces for Change

There are a range of theories that try to explain how and why our food culture develops in the way that it does; these theories develop as cultures develop. Figure 4.1 indicates how some of the main actors interact within this dynamic thing that we call food culture.

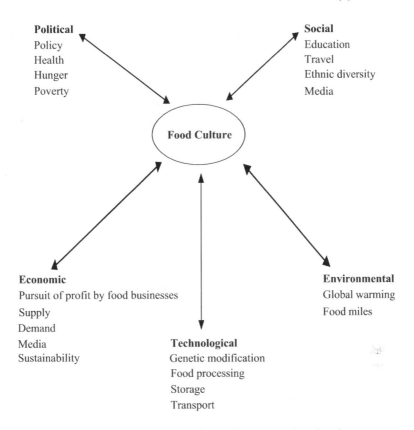

Figure 4.1   Model of forces for change that affect our food cultures

Cultural and social change is an enormous area to consider, but the importance of the media cannot be underestimated, nor can the role of food retailers in shaping the food culture. When questioned, large multiple food retailers often maintain that they are merely responding to the needs of their customers, which may well be the case, although at the same time it seems a little disingenuous, in that plenty of evidence indicates that retailers try to shape their customers' behaviour. In many ways, the media and retailers work together; most directly, this cooperation can be seen in reference to "the cult of the celebrity chef". The iconic figure of the celebrity chef appears in our living rooms, courtesy of the television, develops a relationship with viewers, and influences food culture and the food aspirations of the public. At the same time, these iconic figures advise us about our food during television commercials and reappear yet again in stores, still attempting to influence the way in which we behave and increase the profits of the retailer. The quaint term the "Delia effect" now appears in some dictionaries, in reference to the celebrity chef Delia Smith. Specific appearances by Delia on television supposedly led, the following day, to shelves cleared of cranberries and omelette pans, as consumers responded to what they had seen. However, other works provide further insight into how the supply chain works, particularly with reference to the retail sector and its power, structure and direction.[7]

With specific reference to ethnicity, considerable debate continues over what we mean with regard to the concept of ethnicity, ethnic groups and ethnic food. In this chapter we take it to mean a group of people whose members identify with one another on the basis of a presumed common genealogy or ancestry.[8] There also may be other common traits, such as culture, language, geography or even recognition by others. As such, it is almost self-evident for any observer of UK food culture that there has been a growth in interest in ethnic food as a result of the physical growth in numbers of individuals from various ethnic groups and the gradual evolution of a more multicultural society, along with travel and education. There have also been significant developments within the media that go back over a long period of time, as indicated by the work of Ken Hom for Chinese food[9] and Madhur Jaffrey for Indian cuisine.[10] A resurgence of interest in what might be called "white British" ethnic food is also evident, as indicated by Hugh Fearnley-Whittingstall, Rick Stein and many others.[11] All these developments have led to increased demands for specific ethnic foodstuffs from members of these particular ethnic groups, but also from other people who have been exposed in one way or another to this food and wish to purchase and cook dishes themselves.

How Do Producers Adapt?

Several commentators have suggested how food producers might change their practices or diversify to take advantage of other opportunities.[12] This approach has been a tenet of the whole process of farm and rural diversification. But how is this change actually accomplished? How do people diversify? Some ways are indicated in Figure 4.2. The actual nature of agricultural diversification varies from case to case, but the diagram illustrates

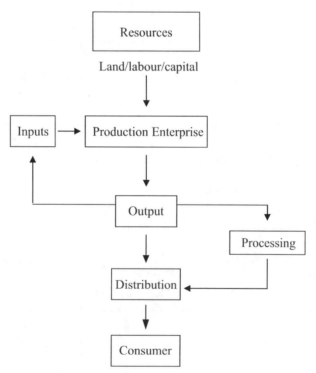

Figure 4.2   Systems model of a generic agricultural system

Source: S.C. Beer and M.R. Redman (1996).

a model of a generic agricultural production system. Thus we can see that resources are utilized in a production enterprise that produces an output which is then distributed to the consumer with or without processing.

We can then adapt this model to look at varying types of diversification. For example, if a farmer diversifies from a traditional crop to a new enterprise, the model may be amended as indicated in Figure 4.3. An example might be a producer changing from growing wheat to Chinese field vegetables in order to supply a local market.

Traditional enterprise B

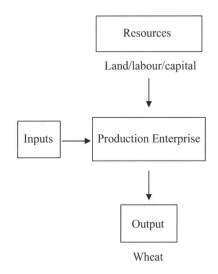

New enterprise C

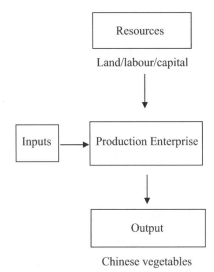

Figure 4.3   Diversification into a new agricultural enterprise

Source: S.C. Beer and M.R. Redman (1996).

Such movement may involve learning new skills or investing in new capital items, such as machinery or buildings. The new skills, however, will tend to build on those already used in primary production. There may be barriers to obtaining the skills. Capital may be limited or technology not commonplace. Or we could look at an example of vertical or structural diversification, as in the amended model in Figure 4.4, which indicates what might happen if the farmer in the preceding example moved into food processing, possibly to supply the demand for a specific type of foodstuff for which value is added through processing.

Diversification into an area such as food processing demands considerable changes in the producer's skill sets. The primary producer is moving away from the traditional area of agriculture into one that is much more service-orientated. He or she may also be moving away from a business that in the past has been highly supported by government subsidy to an area of the free market. In this context, concepts such as marketing take on a whole new dimension.

In terms of looking at how producers might take advantage of new/emerging markets for ethnic foodstuffs, various examples refer to situations in which producers have developed what might be called ethnic products that have directly or indirectly

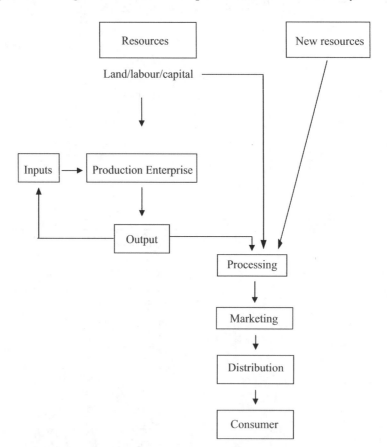

Figure 4.4   From agricultural production to production and processing[13]

Source: S.C. Beer and M.R. Redman (1996).

stimulated the marketplace, whereas other examples include producers who have responded to existing or growing demand to address consumer needs, although in many of these situations the needs remain largely unmet, particularly in terms of the volume of supply.

Examples from the South West of the UK

The UK South West is a very fertile and productive area in terms of product development, and there are some excellent examples of innovative products that have helped develop markets, as well as responding to changing markets. These examples form an interesting set of case studies. The region boasts one of the most successful speciality food groups, Taste of the West (see Case 1 in "Case Studies" below). This particular organization has helped develop an interesting range of producers in terms of their products and their marketing, aimed at diverse markets. Peppers by Post (see Case 2) is a long-standing Dorset-based company developed by the Michaud family that supplies a range of speciality vegetables, in particular capsicum peppers, by mail order. The company recently hit the headlines when it produced the world's hottest chilli pepper. Customers come from a wide range of backgrounds. An exciting new development in Cornwall relates to the production of Cornish tea by the Tregothnan Tea Company (see Case 3). Customers include retailers such as the renowned retailer Fortnum & Mason in London; the tea is also available on the Internet. The firm first started making tea in 1999 and was helped by Objective One, funded by the Cornish Horticulture Enterprise.[14] If we are considering traditional UK food and relating it to concepts of "white British" ethnic groups, Heal Farm (Case 4) is a good example of a company with an interesting history that produces authentic West Country produce.

The Developing Markets of the West Midlands

In many countries there are now large groups of diverse ethnic, racial and religious populations, many of which continue to grow and expand. The UK population in 2001, for example, included 1.8 million Indians and Pakistanis and 1 million black Africans and black Caribbean residents; in total, the black and minority ethnic group numbered 4.6 million, or 7.9 per cent of the total population.[15] This diversity has led to growing opportunities for organizations to market their products to ethnic, racial and religious groups. The influx of immigrants from different countries therefore presents many challenges and opportunities simultaneously. Businesses must ensure that they profit from this expanding marketplace, yet little attention focuses on the connection among burgeoning food markets, market demand created by fundamental shifts in ethnicity and ethnic mixes, and food production in the UK. Market demand is met by importing food, even though a greater understanding of new markets could benefit all channel members.

This point has particular significance for the West Midlands region of the UK, which, after London, contains the largest black and ethnic minority population. It also engages in significant food production. The 2001 Census reveals that the black and ethnic minority population constitutes 11.26 per cent of the West Midlands' regional population, of which Indians (Asian or Asian British) represent 3.39 per cent. Excluding white ethnic groups, more than half the region's black and minority ethnic group populations are Asian in origin: Indian (30.13 per cent), Pakistani (26.06 per cent), Bangladeshi (5.3 per cent) or other Asian (3.53 per cent). A further 17.5 per cent are black.

Moreover, religion influences food consumption – most Hindus, for example, are vegetarians. This distinction could have implications for future food requirements as various ethnic groups come to represent larger proportions of the region's population. Should the specialist food requirements of a changing population be met by importing food or can existing local and regional food channels adapt and reconnect to serve these markets?

The West Midlands has a culturally diverse population, and the implications of this population should be considered when developing a sustainable local and regional food chain. Ethnic foods clearly present an opportunity for growers and producers in the region. In particular, foods sought by Asian consumers appear to be in greatest demand. The cornerstone of the market is fresh produce, which has almost universal appeal across most consumer groups. Product differentiation can encourage growth and add value to the market – for example, differentiating foods as ethnic, local or regional might help producers market their produce and enable them to obtain premium prices. In the market for fresh herbs, for example, sales more than doubled between 2000 and 2005, such that fresh herbs now account for 20 per cent of all sales.[16] Because of the popularity of ethnic dishes, which often require specific fresh herbs, consumers are becoming more aware of the variety of herbs available, and coriander, widely used in ethnic cooking, has become the biggest seller. Herbs are generally not sold as branded products but are available instead through supermarkets in portion-controlled bundles. Greengrocers and independent convenience stores, particularly ethnic stores, usually offer bunched herbs and sell high volumes of this item of produce.

Supermarkets hold the largest market share for fresh fruit and vegetables, making up 84 per cent of all UK retail sales.[17] However, convenience stores and independent retailers have managed to increase their market shares. In the past, such retailers had a reputation for supplying lower-quality produce than supermarkets, often selling produce rejected by larger retailers; freshness was also an issue due to slower stock turnover. However, this image is now being directly challenged as more wholesaler groups and convenience store operators come to appreciate the importance of fresh produce among the portfolio of goods they offer and work to address concerns and increase their share in the fresh produce market. This trend is significant because many consumers from ethnic minority groups regularly use smaller stores within their locality, especially those specializing in ethnic foods and ingredients for their specific cuisines.

Local and regional food sales represent 6 per cent of all food and drinks sales in the UK. This dynamic market is currently experiencing growth and considerable change, although vegetables and fruit remain the most popular product categories.[18] Local growers might increase their market share by expanding their range to, include this increasingly popular ethnic produce, some of which is viable as a local crop.

One of the leading fresh food wholesaling markets, the Birmingham Wholesale Market, is located in the centre of the UK's second largest city and thus geographically well placed for producers in the West Midlands area. A recent article notes that 65–75 per cent of the trade at the horticulture wholesale market involves Asian business customers.[19] Furthermore, the majority of wholesalers are Asian in origin. The customers of this Birmingham market tend to be small businesses (often convenience stores or restaurants/ foodservice outlets), many of which are family-run.

Efforts to reconnect local suppliers of fresh produce with the growing demand from ethnic markets in the region have been hampered by the wholesale trade's dedication to imported produce, especially for specialist (herbs, vegetables, and fruits consumed by ethnic communities) and exotic (non-temperate) fresh produce. Few wholesalers sell produce grown in the West Midlands region, largely because of concerns about seasonality. Even when the local produce is in season, though, the market tends to focus on traditional (e.g. strawberries and potatoes) rather than specialist crops. From the wholesaler's perspective, it is far easier to deal with overseas agencies with which they often have long-term relationships or even family connections.

The Pakistani red carrot is a deeper red or purple in colour and sweeter than a traditional carrot. Introduced only in the last few years, this new item of produce helps illustrate the strength of family and trading ties between the UK Pakistani community and suppliers in Pakistan. The wholesale price for the new carrot is double that of domestically grown varieties, which may suggest a market gap for a home-grown variant.

As volume sales decline in staple items such as potatoes, West Midlands growers have a significant opportunity, emerging from the new ethnic markets, to enter growth areas for fresh produce in areas such as speciality herbs. Convenience stores and food-service firms are natural and expanding outlets for specialist produce (particularly among black and ethnic minority populations). However, supply-channel disconnection and the strength of the importer–wholesale channel continue to hamper this practical approach.

Nevertheless, one West Midlands (Shropshire) grower, JK Fresh Produce (see Case 5), has made considerable inroads into the specialist produce market by growing and marketing coriander, spinach, fenugreek (methi) and kale (saag).

As West Midlands growers identify demand for specialist fresh produce, they could grow them locally, although there are still barriers to overcome in making the leap from producing mainstream crops (e.g. potatoes) to growing niche and speciality ones. Growers need direction and guidance about the agronomy of these unfamiliar crops, as well as market knowledge. During the transition period, farmers' representatives (e.g. the National Farmers Union), agricultural universities, Asian business representatives and regional government should come together to generate more support for producing new crops and assist in increasing understanding and improving the targeting of new customers.

The UK fresh produce sector is growing moderately, but provides a major opening for developing markets that serve underdeveloped areas associated with specialist and convenience store retailing and food service. In these untapped business areas, supermarkets and multiple traders do not yet dominate. The black and ethnic minority population in the West Midlands is less reliant than most consumers on supermarkets, and thriving communities appear within retailing and food-service infrastructures.

West Midlands regional growers have attempted to form both horizontal grower collaborations and supply-chain and marketing hubs. However, to satisfy new market demand, they require further and ongoing interaction with other channel members and their representatives. Moreover, network members need considerable education if they are to overcome supply issues, preconceptions and cultural differences. Markets result not only from latent demand and inventiveness, but also access and smooth network integration.

Opportunities in these specialist subsectors develop as a result of increased demand from the large and growing population of black and ethnic minorities in the West Midlands. Progressive changes to the socio-economic demographics and mix of ethnicity in British society thus present new opportunities and challenges in the fresh produce industry.

Case Studies

CASE 1: TASTE OF THE WEST

Taste of the West (http://www.tasteofthewest.co.uk/) is a long-standing organization that promotes speciality food producers in the South West of England, principally from the six counties of Cornwall, Devon, Dorset, Somerset, Wiltshire and Gloucestershire. It is an extremely successful organization, if not the most successful of its type in the UK. The food producers promoted by Taste of the West promotes largely produce typical or innovative versions of the traditional white ethnic food of the region, such as clotted cream, pasties, Cheddar cheese and cider. A range of products also targets other ethnic markets, and interesting developments involve what might be called fusion cuisine. The analysis in Table 4.1 is based on membership listings (producers are not necessarily primary producers as well as processors, although many are), and there may be some cross-listings.

Table 4.1   Taste of the West: producer and product profile

Type of producer	Numbers of members listed	Notes on products
Cider, perry and mead	20	Very traditional products of the South West of England
Spirits and liqueurs	12	E.g. Somerset Cider Brandy
Beer	11	Long tradition of brewing in the region
Wine	15	Rapidly developing area of production
Mineral and spring water	7	
Tea, coffee and herbal teas	6	
Soft drinks	10	Often based on the fruit of the region, particularly apples
Fruit juices	15	Similar to soft drinks
Biscuits, cakes and confectionary	15	A diverse range of products above and beyond the famous cut rounds that are a constituent of a traditional cream tea
Chocolate confectionary	21	
Bread	16	
Cakes and tray bakes	44	
Grain and breakfast cereals	10	
Flour and cereals	3	
Dried herbs and spices	5	Includes a specialist company supplying materials for Indian food
Spices	10	Includes a specialist company supplying materials for Indian food and a specialist producer of chillies
Condiments	28	Includes a range of producers specializing in chutneys

Table 4.1   *Continued*

Type of producer	Numbers of members listed	Notes on products
Goat's milk and products	12	
Cow's milk and products	23	Purbeck Ice Cream's chilli ice cream
Sheep's milk and products	6	Includes a buffalo cheese producer
Cream, yogurt and ice cream	35	Again includes Purbeck Ice Cream's chilli ice cream
Dairy desserts	12	
Egg products	4	
Eggs	17	
Cheese	39	Traditionally a major product of the South West of England, e.g. Cheddar cheese, now showing developments in many different areas
Seafood and shellfish	12	
Freshwater fish	6	
Prepared fruit	6	Includes olive producer Olives Et Al., representing the growing number of olive processors in the region
Prepared vegetables	9	Includes a specialist curry producer
Fresh fruit	32	
Fresh vegetables	26	
Herbs	14	
Game	14	With the important problem of adding value to game, which is an important component of white ethnic cooking
Poultry	34	
Venison	16	
Lamb	36	Facing new initiatives to promote local breeds, such as the Exmoor Horn, and also mutton
Pork, ham, bacon	48	
Beef and veal	39	Home to possibly the finest of all beef breeds, the Devon or Devon Red Ruby, a cornerstone of the revival of traditional British beef
Wild boar, ostrich and other meat	9	Also includes buffalo
Savoury pastry	36	Much more than pasties; there are new innovations using different ethnic influences, vegetarian and vegan
Sweet pastry	36	
Other prepared meat products	20	
Smoked meat	11	

Table 4.1   *Concluded*

Type of producer	Numbers of members listed	Notes on products
Smoked fish	10	
Smoked cheese	7	
Ready meals	24	
Sources and marinades	20	Includes innovative companies such as Feeding Your Imagination Ltd, currently producing therapeutic chocolate infused with essential oils, super foods such as goji berries, and acai and gourmet seaweed sauces
Snacks and crisps	8	
Preserves	30	
James, marmalades and jellies	35	
Oils and dressings	24	
Chutneys and pickles	34	
Honey	16	
Pasta, rice and pulses	5	
Organic produce	6	Although the number of producers underrepresents the growth in organic producers and produce

CASE 2: PEPPERS BY POST

Peppers by Post (http://www.peppersbypost.biz), established in 1996 by Joy and Michael Michaud, specializes in the production of chilli peppers and their sale by mail order and attracted international attention with its breeding of the exceptionally hot Dorset Naga.

The enterprise, built on the Michauds' knowledge of horticulture, tropical agriculture and their wide interest in food, was originally based in a small horticulture unit with protected cropping overlooking the South Dorset coast. Gradually it has developed, with an expanded range of crops to include tomatillos, sometimes known as Mexican green tomatoes. They have a distinctive tart flavour typical of Mexican cooking. Epazote is a pungent South American herb traditionally used with black beans, but also used to season quesadillas, sopes, tamales and enchiladas.

The Michauds have also diversified their business by offering open days and visits. They regularly attend food festivals and now sell seeds through Really Cool Seeds (http://www.reallycoolseeds.co.uk). In response to demand, they run a series of courses on food and cooking under titles such as "What's hot, what's not," "Fusion Thai," and "Asian Roots" (http://www.growandcook.biz).

The development of the Dorset Naga chilli was a major news story that drew international attention to the business. The Dorset Naga (http://www.dorsetnaga.com/) is a very hot relative of the Scotch Bonnet pepper. When tested in 2005 and 2006, samples earned Scoville heat ratings of 923 000–960 000 SHU (Scoville heat units§). The BBC measured them as even hotter.

---

§   Other SHU ratings are as follows: pure capsaicin: 15–16 million, U.S. police-grade pepper spray: 5 million, Scotch bonnet: 100 000–325 000, Jamaican hot pepper: 100 000–200 000, Cayenne pepper: 30 000–50 000,

CASE 3: TREGOTHNAN TEA COMPANY

Tregothnan is a Cornish estate that has been in the same family since 1335. As with many land-based businesses, it has diversified interests based on its resources and collective skills. The estate enterprises include the production of English estate tea, charcoal, bespoke joinery, essential oils, bouquets, garlands, wreaths and large plants, as well as private garden visits. The cultivation of tea is of specific interest. In terms of diversification into an "ethnic" product, tea poses some interesting questions. Can it, for example, be considered an ethnic product for a tea-drinking country? Certainly tea has been consumed for a long time, such that it has in some way become naturalized, but has it been cultivated? The Tregothnan tea comes from a special variety of *Camellia sinensis*, which grew outdoors ornamentally at Tregothnan 200 years ago. The estate proved that it could grow high-quality tea in Cornwall and embarked on setting up a commercial operation. It currently produces four blended teas:

- Classic Tea – a blend of Assam and China-type leaf with Tregothnan leaves
- Afternoon Tea – a blend of Darjeeling tea and estate leaves
- Green Tea – a blend of Chinese green tea and Tregothnan green tea
- Earl Grey – *Citrus bergamia* blended with the Classic Tea to create a new version of Earl Grey.

The teas sell at a considerable premium, approximately 1600 per cent higher in price than supermarket tea. The Afternoon Tea is £16.62 for 100g. However, compared with other connoisseur teas, this price is not necessarily all that expensive. In this specific context, tea production is part of the wider operations of the estate, including tourist attractions. The estate hopes to develop an international tea centre, with tea gardens, galleries and tastings, and intends to "champion the growers and the diversity of tea produced" and seek "to develop 'beyond fair-trade' relationships with growers around the world". In this effort, the company is not attempting to take on mainstream suppliers, but rather targets a niche market, so whether this effort represents a mainstream form of producer diversification is debatable. However, it clearly offers a good example of an integrated approach that makes good use of existing resources and expertise.

CASE 4: HEAL FARM

Heal Farm is a food business based in North Devon that specializes in the production and retailing of a variety of products associated with "traditional English fare". The business was developed by Anne Petch on a small farm, where the family tried to produce as much of their own food as possible in response to stories about intensive farming methods and industrial food processing. An interest in traditional breeds of livestock, initially of pigs, and work with The Rare Breeds Survival Trust (http://www.rbst.org.uk) led to the foundation of pig breeds within an overall herd – something Petch calls genetic conservation. In turn, she concluded that the only way to ensure the future of the breeds was to develop sustainable supply chains. Many rare breeds, when fed, slaughtered,

Tabasco sauce: 2500, Pimento: 100–500, Bell pepper: 0. Source: BBC (2008), "Gardeners' World's hottest chilies", http://www.bbc.co.uk/gardening/tv_and_radio/factsheets/pages/46.shtml.

butchered and cooked properly, produce excellent meat with a traditional feel and taste. In other words, Heal Farm proposes conserving animals by eating them! Its proposition has benefited from the simultaneous increase in interest in "white British" ethnic food – food produced in sympathy with the environment.

Production and sales began in the late 1970s with the establishment of an on-farm butchery and more formal farm sales. Demand for beef and lamb led to supply arrangements with likeminded producers. Beef came from Devon cattle (colloquially known as the Devon Red Ruby) and lambs from "old fashioned British breeds". The business maintains an ethical buying policy, with prices linked to costs of production. The isolated nature of the business limits most sales to mail or online orders. However, an article about the farm in *The Telegraph* in 1981 resulted in 1500 enquiries in just ten days. It appears that Petch was supplying the early stages of a niche market while also developing it, responding to a market, and shaping it.

The business has moved to a modern production facility, built on the farm using private capital and EU funding. Heal Farm produces a full menu, including desserts and a range of oven-ready products. Further opportunities to expand have been discarded; Petch no longer raises the livestock herself, but she remains in control of the business and in contact with the customers, and she believes she would lose these positions if the company were to increase in size. She maintains that the underlying business philosophy remains the same: "What we are offering is wholesome food made with the best of fresh ingredients, many of them organic. What our customers get is super food they can trust, that is fully traceable and made individually for them without additives or industrial processing."

CASE 5: JK FRESH PRODUCE

JK Fresh Produce is unusual for a UK firm, in that the company was established by an Asian grower, Surindar Pal, who now farms 1200 acres in Shropshire after establishing himself as a grower only ten years ago. In some ways, this Asian entrepreneur offers a distinct advantage to customers, many of whom come from similar ethnic origins. Wholesalers maintain overseas ties based on ethnicity; similarly, UK supply channels might involve Asian growers supplying caterers and retailers directly and thus achieve a similar advantage. In particular, Pal provided a potential solution to the cultural disconnect problem faced by growers, because he could bridge the Asian culturally bound dominance of the fresh produce wholesale markets through his links to growers. Pal now offers wholesale access to other local growers (including producers of specialist crops, such as coriander and fenugreek, destined for Asian end users) by providing his packing and marketing facilities, which then serve as a produce hub. In this way, JK Fresh Produce is a significant market channel innovator and acts as a language and cultural bridge. JK Fresh Produce supplies produce all over the UK through a wholesale market network. In addition, the company has invested in value-adding (e.g. grading, prepacking, cool storage) facilities. The market for specialist fresh produce is growing fast, and this hub-and-spoke approach should provide an excellent means to bring to market the produce of small growers, who may be producing only small acreages.

Conclusions

More diverse gastronomy gives rise to some very specific opportunities for food producers to develop opportunities by stimulating demand and responding to new and existing supply chains and the demand for a greater diversity of products. This realization creates benefits for food consumers and local food producers, as exemplified by the entrepreneurial producers of the South West of England. In the West Midlands the growing and underserved demand from black and ethnic minority retailers and food-service providers has stimulated producers to think about reconnecting town and country and producing new crops that reflect the nature of a changing customer base. But all the cases detailed in the Appendix reinforce the fact that individual producers cannot act alone; they need support in terms of networks and skills development to help realize their potential and engender true market-oriented network collaboration.

Assumptions are often made about the nature of markets that feature considerable latent demand, as is apparent in the enthusiasm for and movement in local, regional and specialist products. However, amidst this enthusiasm for market-making and market satisfaction, it is too easy to ignore the issues of market power and the role of channel leaders or gatekeepers. Wholesalers are the gatekeepers of the fresh produce industry, but their possible lack of understanding and lack of flexibility towards home-grown production and producers bars the entry of regional and specialist products and produce, as identified in prior studies on business-to-business markets in the food sector.[22] Such considerations often conspire to confound new market channels or simply act to maintain the status quo. Other barriers,, such as language and culture, also require consideration if the smooth integration of food channels is to be made possible.

References

1.   Beer, S.C. and Redman, M.R. (1996), "The relationship between post war cultural shift, consumer perspectives and farming policy" in J.S.A. Edwards (ed.), *Culinary Arts and Sciences: Global and National Perspectives*, Proceedings of the First International Conference on Culinary Arts and Sciences: Global and National Perspectives, Computational Mechanics Publications, Southampton.

2.   Atkins P. and Bowler, I. (2001), *Food in Society: Economy, Culture and Geography*, Hodder Headline, London; Beardsworth, A. and Keil, T. (1997), *Sociology on the Menu: An Invitation to the Study of Food and Society*, Routledge, London; Blythman, J. (2006), *Bad Food Britain: How a Nation Ruined its Appetite*, London: Fourth Estate; Civitello, L. (2003), *Cuisine and Culture: A History of Food and People*, New York and Chichester, Wiley; Fieldhouse, P. (1998), *Food and Nutrition: Customs and Culture*, Stanley Thornes, Cheltenham; Germov, J. and Williams, L. (1999), *A Sociology of Food and Nutrition*. Oxford University Press, Oxford; Gillespie, C. (2001), *European Gastronomy into the 21st Century*, Butterworth-Heinemann, London; Macbeth, H. (ed.) (1997), *Food Preferences and Taste: Continuity and Change (The Anthropology of Food and Nutrition)*, Berghahn Books, Oxford; Mennell, S. (1992), *Sociology of Food and Eating: Eating, Diet and Culture*, Sage Publications, Newbury Park, CA; Rebora, G. (2001), *Culture of the Fork: A Brief History of Food in Europe*, Columbia University Press, New York; Spencer, C. (2002), *British Food: An Extraordinary Thousand Years of History*, Grub Street, London; Tansey, G. and Worsley, T.

(1995), *The Food System: A Guide*, Earthscan, London; Warde, A. (1997), *Consumption, Food and Taste: Culinary Antinomies and Commodity Culture*, Sage, London.

3.   Watson, J. and Caldwell, M. (eds) (2004), *The Cultural Politics of Food and Eating: A Reader*, Blackwell Publishers, Oxford; Molz, J.G. (2007), "'Eating difference', The cosmopolitan mobilities of culinary tourism", Space and Culture, Vol. 10, No. 1, pp. 77–93; Cook, I. and Harrison, M. (2007), "Follow the thing: West Indian hot pepper sauce", Space and Culture, Vol. 10, No. 1, pp. 40–63.

4.   Gibson, S. (2007), "Food mobilities: Travelling, dwelling, and eating cultures", *Space and Culture*, Vol. 10, No. 1, pp. 4–21.

5.   Ibid.

6.   Molz, "Eating difference", *op. cit.*

7.   Hingley, M. (2005), "Power imbalance in UK agri-food supply channels: Learning to live with the supermarkets?", *Journal of Marketing Management*, Vol. 21, No. 1–2, pp. 63–68; Fearne, A., Hughes, D. and Duffy, R. (2001), "Concepts of collaboration: supply chain management in a global food industry" in J. Eastham, L. Sharples and S. Ball (eds), *Food Supply Chain Management. Issues for the Hospitality and Retail Sectors*, Butterworth-Heinemann, Oxford.

8.   Smith, A.D. (1987), *The Ethnic Origin of Nations*, Blackwell, Oxford.

9.   Hom, K. (1985), *Chinese Cookery*, BBC Worldwide, London.

10. Jaffrey, M. (1986), *A Taste of India,* Athenaeum, New York.

11. Fearnley-Whittingstall, H. (1997), *A Cook on the Wild Side*, Boxtree: London; Stein, R. (2003), *Guide to the Food Heroes of Britain*, BBC Worldwide, London; Stein, R. (2004), *Food Heroes: Another Helping*, BBC Worldwide.

12. Slee, B. (1987), *Alternative Farm Enterprises*, Farming Press: Ipswich; Beer, S.C., Edwards, J.R., Fernandes, C. and Sampaio, F. (2002), "Regional food cultures: integral to the rural tourism product" in A-M. Hjalager and G. Richards (eds), *Tourism and Gastronomy*, Routledge, London, pp. 207–223.

13. Mintel (2005), *Seasonings: UK*, April, Mintel International Group, London.

14. BBC (2005), "Company plans Cornish tea centre", http://news.bbc.co.uk/1/hi/england/devon/4112272.stm [accessed 11 July 2007].

15. Anonymous (2007), "Demographics: Ethnic Britain", *Marketing*, 18 April, pp. 31–33.

16. Mintel (2007), *Fresh Fruit and Vegetables: UK*, May, Mintel International Group, London.

17. Institute of Grocery Distribution (2005), *The Local and Regional Food Opportunity*, March, IGD, Watford.

18. Anon. (2005), "Relocation, relocation, relocation", *Fresh Produce Journal*, 29 July, pp. 18–26.

19. Hingley, M. (2005), "Power to all our friends? Learning to live with imbalance in UK supplier–retailer relationships", *Industrial Marketing Management*, Vol. 34, No. 8, pp. 848–858.

5 *The Other Side of the Logo: The Global* Halal *Market in London*

JOHAN FISCHER*

Keywords

halal, UK, Malaysia, types of certification, logos, Malays.

Abstract

This chapter argues that the proliferation of *halal* in a multitude of commoditized forms is premised on complex understandings and practices of certification. Discussing empirical material gathered among Malay Muslims living in London, the author shows how certification and logos evoke a wide range of issues involved in modern forms of Islamic consumption.

Introduction

A Canadian government study reveals that the value of global *halal* trade amounts to $150 billion per year, and it is growing amongst the world's approximately 1.6 billion Muslims.[1] Concern over *halal* is more pronounced in some South-east Asian countries, such as Malaysia, Indonesia, Brunei and Singapore, than in much of the Middle East and South Asia. The reasons are many, but the proliferation of *halal* in a country such as Malaysia cannot be divorced from the country's steady economic growth, the emergence of large groups of Malay Muslim middle-class consumers, and centralized state incentives to strengthen *halal* production, trade, and consumption during the past three decades. In addition, Europe, the USA, Canada and Australia are emerging as centres with large and growing Muslim populations and major markets for *halal*.

In their book, *Halal Food Production*, Riaz and Chaudry provide the most comprehensive guide to promoting, marketing and producing *halal* foods for professionals in an

*   Dr Johan Fischer, Department of Society and Globalisation, Roskilde University, Postbox 260, 4000 Roskilde, Denmark. E-mail: johanf@ruc.dk. Telephone: + 45 4674 2781.

expanding global food market.[2] To my knowledge, it is also the only book of its kind and is widely used by companies worldwide that try to understand and comply with the current transformation of *halal*. This study, however, does not explore how *halal* is understood and practised among consumers in the marketplace. For broader discussions of the origin and nature of *halal* as a food taboo, readers should consult Frederick J. Simoons's book, *Eat Not This Flesh: Food Avoidances from Prehistory to the Present*.[3]

During my fieldwork-based research on the understanding and practice of *halal* in London in 2006, I met a Malay Muslim imam from Malaysia who had lived in London since 2002. In our discussions of *halal* in London, the question of proper *halal* certification and logos on commodities frequently emerged. First, the imam argued that, in Britain, most types of *halal* certification were quite unreliable, because producers, traders and certifying bodies did not really understand the definition of *halal* and proper certification – unlike those in Malaysia, where the state has standardized, certified and institutionalized *halal* since the 1980s. The imam further maintained that because the state has no authority to carry out inspections in Britain, the unregulated market was open to fraud. Conversely, he trusted the Department of Islamic Development Malaysia's (JAKIM) state certification of *halal* and its distinctive logo. Because of EU restrictions on meat imported from Malaysia, such *halal*-certified products are unavailable in Britain, so Malays in London must look for *halal* alternatives. Exploring *halal* in Malaysia and among Malays in London may reveal something about more general tendencies in the global *halal* market.

Second, the imam complained that it was unconvincing when London restaurants advertised themselves as *halal* when in fact only the chicken, for example, probably was *halal*-certified. He did not recognize a restaurant as *halal* if it sold alcohol, much in the same way that a pizzeria could not claim to be *halal* if it used and stored ham together with *halal* meat or allowed the same utensils to be used uncritically for all types of food.

This chapter explores Malay Muslims' everyday understanding and practice of *halal* certification in London. The first part of its title, "The Other Side of the Logo", indicates two points subject to empirical substantiation. First, although more and more types of *halal* certification, and thus logos on *halal* products, appear in the *halal* market in London, in the eyes of many Muslim consumers, this marking tells them relatively little about the actual or intrinsic "*halal*ness" of the product. Second, I will show how certification and logos are contingent on the context in which they are produced, displayed and sold.

The second part of the title, "The Global *Halal* Market in London", suggests that in contemporary London *halal* is no longer an expression of esoteric forms of production, trade and consumption but, rather, part of a huge and expanding globalized market.

The initial stage of six months' research in London was quantitative in method and outlook. The selection of informants relied on a survey that covered 100 mainly Malay respondents, designed primarily to map migration trajectories, broader *halal* consumption patterns and informants' understanding and practice of divergent types of *halal* certification in London.

On the basis of the survey, I selected 12 Malay informants for interviews and participant observations. Background interviews and participant observations carried out with *halal* producers and traders, Islamic organizations and food authorities provide additional data. Although the proliferation of *halal*, understood as changing Muslim dietary preferences and sensibilities, highlights several broader issues, including health, identity, risk and ethnicity, I limit the present exploration to the question of certification.

What is *Halal*?

Halal literally means lawful or permitted. The Koran and the Sunna (the life, actions and teachings of the Prophet Muhammad) exhort Muslims to eat the good and lawful food God has provided for them, but with various conditions and prohibitions. Muslims are expressly forbidden from consuming carrion, spurting blood, pork and foods that have been consecrated to any being other than God himself. These substances are *haram* and thus forbidden.

The lawfulness of meat depends on how it is obtained. Ritual slaughtering requires that the animal is killed in God's name and by making a fatal incision across the throat. In this process, the blood should be drained as fully as possible. Another significant Islamic prohibition relates to wine and any other alcoholic drink or substance; all such are *haram* in any quantity or substance.[4]

In addition, doubtful items should be avoided, which suggests a grey area between clearly lawful and unlawful.[5] This doubtful or questionable property is expressed by the word *mashbooh*,[6] which can be evoked by divergences in religious scholars' opinions or suspicion about undetermined or prohibited ingredients in a commodity. Hence, far more abstract, individual and fuzzy aspects of context and handling also determine the "*halal*ness" of a product.

In the modern food industry many Muslim requirements have taken effect, including the injunction to avoid any substances that may be contaminated with porcine residues or alcohol, such as gelatine, glycerine, emulsifiers, enzymes, flavours and flavourings.[7] For example, an article in *The Guardian* (2006)[8] demonstrated that, in some cases, gelatine and other products are "snuck" into a variety of foods. The problem associated with certifying that food and other products do not contain these substances is that they are extremely difficult to discover.

Apparently, a growing number of Muslim consumers are becoming concerned with not only traditional *halal* food requirements, but also contamination from *haram* sources in products such as toiletries and medication. Moreover, for some Muslims, *halal* sensibilities necessitate that *halal* products be produced by Muslims only and that production be kept strictly separate from non-*halal* production.

Muslim dietary rules have assumed new significance in the twenty-first century as some Muslims strive to demonstrate how such rules conform to modern reason and the findings of scientific research. Another common theme in the revival and renewal of these dietary rules seems to be the search for alternatives to perceived Western values, ideologies and lifestyles. These re-evaluations of requirements and prohibitions are prominent primarily in postcolonial Islamic cultures, such as Malaysia, as well as among migrant groups for whom *halal* can serve as a focal point for Islamic movements and identities.

To use *halal* labels or logos on products, a certifier must inspect all related enterprises and organizations. This certifier "guarantees that the enterprise respects a set of predetermined criteria. Any label supposes inspection of the technical process and/or the management methods."[9] *Halal* certification of products thus provides a way of branding at two concurrent levels: in the sphere of institutional relations and in material objects. In summary, the certification of *halal* products and marking them with logos are essential in Muslim consumption, because the "*halal*ness" of products is not easily verifiable; smell, texture or taste cannot determine whether a product is *halal* or not.

Halal in Malaysia and Britain

My exploration of *halal* among Malay Muslim migrants in London elaborates and continues a study of what I refer to as proper Islamic consumption in Malaysia.[10] Building on ten months of anthropological fieldwork in suburban Malaysia during 2001–2002, I argue in this study that, as cultures of consumption increasingly assert themselves, controversies over what Islam is, or ought to be, intensify. As new consumer practices emerge, they give rise to new discursive fields within which the meaning of Islam and Islamic practice get debated. One key effect of these transformations is the deepening and widening concern for *halal* commodities among Malay Muslims, which I label "*halal*ization". *Halal*ization signifies a major preoccupation with the proliferation of the concept of *halal* in a multitude of commoditized forms. Out of *halal*ization have emerged new forms of Malay aesthetic communities based on different taste preferences in various middle-class fractions. This proliferation of *halal*ization has also incited a range of elaborate ideas about the boundaries and authenticity of *halal* purity versus *haram* impurity. My informants for the present study are middle-class Malays who migrated to London to study or work.

Since Malaysia gained independence from Britain in 1957, constitutionally people may be Malay only if they are Muslims. Malaysia is not an Islamic state, but Islam is Malaysia's official religion, professed by more than 50 per cent of the population. In the Malaysian population of around 23 million, 65.1 per cent are indigenous Malays (virtually all Muslims) and tribal groups, 26 per cent are Chinese, and 7.7 per cent are Indians.[11]

In Malaysia, institutions such as JAKIM regulate the proliferation of *halal* and concentrate certification in the realm of the state. The proliferation of *halal* in a country such as Malaysia cannot be divorced from developments in the country over the past three decades, including its steady economic growth, the emergence of large groups of Malay Muslim middle-class consumers, and centralized state incentives that attempt to strengthen *halal* production, trade and consumption. Moreover, the rise of resurgent Islam in Malaysia in the 1970s challenged the foundation of the Malaysian state, which has tried to promote a modern and moderate form of Islam. To pre-empt this resurgence, the state started to express its dedication to Islam and introduce Islamic education, finance and the institutionalization of *halal* in Malaysia.[12]

In 2004 Malaysia launched its first Malaysia International *Halal* Showcase (MIHAS) in the capital, Kuala Lumpur. The Malaysian prime minister, Abdullah Haji Ahmad Badawi, argued in his opening speech that establishing Malaysia as a global "*halal* hub" was a major priority of the government and that MIHAS was the largest *halal* trade expo to be held anywhere in the world[13].

The main motive for focusing on Malays in multi-ethnic London results from the Malaysian state's vision of, and commitment to, promoting *halal*, which specifically identifies London as a centre for *halal* production, trade, and consumption. In addition, London is home to a substantial number of Malays and Malaysian organizations. As we shall see, most of my Malay informants are younger people who have migrated to London to study or work. Furthermore, the institutionalization and certification of *halal* in Malaysia contrasts with the more fragmented and complex *halal* market in Britain, in which a plethora of groups, organizations and individuals have divergent ideas about *halal*. Hence, distinctions between *halal* in Malaysia and Britain identify a range of contestations in the context of modern forms of *halal* understanding and practice.

Thus far, scholarly attention to *halal* in Britain has, for the most part, focused on conflicts over the provision of *halal* in schools[14] and the politics of religious slaughter.[15] In many parts of London, such as Finsbury Park and Whitechapel Road, *halal* is a distinctive presence on signs and in butchers' shops and restaurants. Lately, more and more types of *halal*-certified products are appearing in supermarkets such as Tesco and ASDA.

Claiming Authority through *Halal* Certification

Halal and its certification remain highly contested issues in London. Dr Yunes Teinaz, Health Advisor to the Director General at the Islamic Cultural Centre in London, has worked on illegal food and brought cases to court for approximately ten years. He explained that "You can easily buy certification if you pay for it. And they get away with it because there is no control, regulation or inspection from the state."

As *halal* and the aspect of religious slaughter increasingly infused Muslim identity in Britain, the need to establish a body of *halal* butchers' shops became clear. Consequently, in 1994 the Halal Food Authority (HFA), with encouragement from the Muslim parliament, established a network of approved abattoirs and shops to provide the community with independently certified *halal* meat.[16]

The initial goal of the HFA, a "voluntary, non-profit making organisation",[17] was to license slaughterhouses, distribution centres, retailers and providers of meat and poultry for human consumption. These licences are granted on an annual and contractual basis. HFA inspectors audit and monitor compliance with Islamic laws as well as MAFF (Ministry of Agriculture, Fisheries and Food) and EU regulations of slaughter. The HFA is also assiduously engaged in regulating, endorsing and authenticating foodstuffs, pharmaceuticals, confectionary, toiletries, flavourings, emulsifiers, colourings (including E-numbered additives etc.) for Muslim usage. In an increasingly complex food market, these activities seem ambitious for a voluntary organization.

Another organization that certifies *halal* in Britain is the Halal Monitoring Committee (HMC),[18] established in 2003 in Leicester. In contrast with HFA, it takes a stance against stunning animals before slaughter. These two organizations can be seen as competitors with overlapping interests and claims for authority in the *halal* market.

When I attended the Halal Exhibition at the World Food Market (WFM) in London in 2006, a former director of environmental health and consumer affairs services, who was also an advisor to the London Central Mosque at WFM, critiqued products being promoted as not properly certified. In front of a large audience at the WFM seminar, he identified a large market for fraud and corruption within the *halal* trade, as well as in the local certifying bodies such as HFA and HMC – both represented in the audience at the seminar. He called for the Muslim community to "wake up" and "clean up their act" and declared that state authorities may be willing to "take somebody to court" and "take enforcement action", but that these bodies "feel that the Muslim community has not decided yet what the definition of *halal* is in the first place". As it was, so-called expert certifiers (e.g. imams without any real knowledge of *halal*) were issuing certificates "as long as the money is sent first". Consequently, to standardize this "totally unregulated" market, he asked the government and the Food Standards Agency[†] "to give us a hand so that we can come up with something like standards against which *halal* food can be inspected".

Most research into *halal* in the UK has been conducted by market research companies such as Mintel[19] and Ethnic Focus[20] that are starting to recognize the commercial aspect of *halal*. Supermarkets in London, such as Tesco and ASDA, require products that are *halal*-certified by recognized bodies such as HFA and HMC. In this way, *halal* is being lifted out of its traditional base in *halal* butchers' shops to become part of "world food" product ranges in major supermarkets.

Advising Muslim consumers about *halal* in London has become an industry in its own right, as demonstrated in the handbook *Halal Food: A Guide to Good Eating – London*[21] by a Malaysian publishing company. As we shall discover, several informants use such *halal* guidebooks or websites that advise Muslims on *halal*. In general, a lively debate continues about *halal* on many Muslim websites.

The huge Tesco Extra store in Slough, outside London, boasts that it offers the widest world food product range, including *halal*, in Britain. In November 2006 I found Maggi chilli sauce produced in Malaysia and certified by JAKIM, a *halal* "Curry Special" butter chicken with no certification/logo on it, and a more traditional *halal* butcher's shop, operating as a concession and selling fresh meat in this store. Anecdotal evidence from fieldwork suggests that Tesco is using this store to enter the *halal* market, which has reduced sales among *halal* butchers in the surrounding area. Around the same time, in an ASDA supermarket in North London, I found HFA-certified chilled chicken and mutton.

Supermarkets such as Tesco and ASDA also have introduced a *halal* chocolate bar[22] that uses advertising slogans such as "Community & chocolate close to your heart? Isn't it time your chocolate bar did something more than just taste good?". Furthermore, the label of the chocolate bar states that "10% of net Profit goes to Charity". I could not identify any certifier of this product. While *halal* in Malaysia expands to cover more and more products that are either state-certified or certified by Islamic organizations recognized by the state, in many cases new *halal* products in Britain are not properly certified in the eyes of some Muslim consumers.

Before discussing Malays' understanding and practice of *halal* certification, I will briefly discuss my survey data pertaining to divergent types of *halal* certification in London. In this survey I asked 100 mainly Malay respondents about *halal* certification. Virtually all these Malay respondents were familiar with JAKIM state certification, and most of them preferred it for various reasons. Respondents also indicated that, after JAKIM certification, certifiers such as HFA and HMC were reliable and trustworthy. Conversely, they considered certifiers such as Islamic Food and Nutrition Council of America (IFANCA)[23] and the Central Islamic Committee of Thailand (CICT) the most unreliable, followed by local certification by an imam or food expert. In summary, Malaysian state certification by JAKIM is preferred to other competing forms of *halal* certification in this rapidly expanding market.

---

†   The Food Standards Agency (www.food.gov.uk) is an independent government department established in 2000 to protect the public's health and consumer interests in relation to food.

"Anyone Could Have Put Up That *Halal* Sign"

The empirical material suggests two registers of understanding and practice of *halal* certification among Malays in London. The first group is relatively strict or purist about *halal* certification, whereas the second group tends towards a more pragmatic approach to these contested questions. Selected informants in each group represent diverse approaches to *halal* certification. In other words, these informants are exemplars of the scale of strategies involved in everyday *halal* consumption.

The heading to this section, a quotation from the informant Yasir,‡ illustrates the sentiments towards *halal* certification among the first group of informants. When we discussed the state of *halal* certification in London, Yasir complained that, as a general tendency, shops and butchers' shops simply put up a sign displaying the Arabic word for *halal*. In the eyes of these Muslims, marking such products and premises lacks proper certification by a trustworthy certifying body that can be held accountable for the "*halal*ness" of products. Yasir also argued that anyone could put up a sign in Arabic that indicated *halal*: "I worry about local *halal* certification sometimes because you can see people we don't even know creating their own *halal* signs and putting them up." More specifically, Yasir referred to Chinese shops, restaurants and takeaways in London that displayed a wide variety of *halal* signs. In Bayswater, for example, Yasir could identify several such Chinese establishments. Conversely, Yasir found that *halal* certification by HMC or HFA was more reliable and trustworthy. At the same time, he acknowledged that *halal* in the UK and elsewhere was increasingly about politics, power and business – and not so much about religious beliefs and injunctions.

Yasir hoped to see more shops and restaurants selling properly certified *halal* products; as long as the certification process was ensured by a dependable certifier, he did not take the trouble to look at labels that could reveal if products contained alcohol or gelatine. To Yasir, proper *halal* certification with a convincing logo was sufficient proof that the products were fit for Muslim consumption.

As in the case of most other informants, Yasir patronized a local *halal* butcher's shop for meat; this requires trust in the Muslim butcher because, in most cases, there is no visible certification in such facilities. Local *halal* butchers were favoured by many Malay consumers in London, because the meat is affordable compared with *halal* meat in supermarkets. However, the meat in these *halal* butchers' shops often appeared to lack proper certification. Conversely, *halal* in supermarkets was normally certified by HFA, HMC or another Islamic organization. Consequently, to consumers, the proper "branding" of *halal* commodities may represent a luxury that is not always affordable.

Like Yasir, most informants observed the atmosphere, ethnic affiliation and appearance of the *halal* butcher in order to judge the reliability of the meat. To most informants, asking about certification in a *halal* butcher's shop in London means questioning the authority of the butcher.

---

‡   Yasir is a single man in his 20s who came to London in 2001 from Kuala Lumpur to study. He is also a councillor with an Islamic student organization. His monthly income was less than £1,000 gross (hereafter, income statements refer to gross income), and he lived with 15 other students in a hall of residence. Yasir normally shopped for groceries at ASDA, *halal* butchers and a local grocery store, noting that his main *halal* concerns involved meat and intestines. Yasir also was dissatisfied with the current availability of *halal* in London and felt that the labelling of products was unsatisfactory.

The informant Siti[§] looked for two things when buying food in London: proper *halal* certification by a reliable certifier or vegetarian food, even though she was not a vegetarian. None of the respondents or informants was vegetarian, despite the fact that becoming a vegetarian would solve many problems for Muslims, who are fastidious about *halal* certification. Siti would only accept certification by a local imam or food expert if this person were familiar to her. Thus, she often used websites as consumer guides for *halal* in London:

> *I usually refer to the London Central Mosque website. Because when I came to London to study it was on this website I learned about where to get* halal *food. So, if I'm familiar with a local Mosque or Imam I trust it's* halal.

This sentiment shows that trust and personal relationships are essential in the understanding and practice of *halal* certification. Normally, however, Siti would go to Green Valley supermarket, because it sold *halal* meat certified by trustworthy authorities, the meat was fresh, and in general the quality standard was high, she felt. Thus, *halal* and *halal* certification have much to do with the context in which it is displayed and sold: it is not just a matter of "*halal*ness" as an intrinsic quality that complies with a particular religious injunction.

Another informant, Izura,[¶] had an extensive understanding of *halal* certification and practised it in London through JAKIM certification in Malaysia. According to Izura, Malay concerns about *halal* can be ascribed to the relatively strict *Shafi'i* school of jurisprudence[24] within the Sunni division of Islam dominant in Malaysia. She argued:

> *I would always say that Malays are stricter. It is just the way that we were taught, I think. We are Sunni, Shafi'i school of thought, we are the strictest. Even if you go to Mecca there is a lot of people who pray differently, or eat differently, they say that this is considered* halal, *but for us it is not* halal. *I have Pakistani friends here in London and they still go to KFC and eat the chicken, they don't care. I guess to them if you have been in a country for a long time you can eat whatever in that country whether it's* halal *or not.*

This point is important in two respects. First, it reflects the particular way in which *halal* and *halal* certification have been institutionalized in Malaysia and thus have become an essential part of everyday life for Malays. Izura was outraged that, in London, she could find false *halal* signs in Arabic that pretended to represent proper certification.

---

§   Siti is a single woman in her early 20s, who lived with two flatmates in London. She moved to London in 2005 to study, and she also worked for a phone company. The monthly income of the household was £4,500–5,000. Normally Siti shopped for groceries in supermarkets, such as Tesco, Sainsbury's, Waitrose and Green Valley, and tried to find not only *halal* food and drink, but also pharmaceuticals and toiletries. On the whole, Siti considered the availability of *halal* products in London satisfactory, but she often asked friends to bring back *halal* products from Malaysia.

¶   Izura is a woman in her 20s who moved to London in 2005 to complete her postgraduate studies in international marketing. At the same time, Izura worked part-time with an insurance company. Izura was married to Yusof. The monthly income of the household was between £2,000 and £2,500. Normally, Izura shopped for groceries in London's Chinatown – e.g. in Loon Fung and Loon Moon markets – but she also went to supermarkets such as Sainsbury's and local *halal* butchers. Izura used Muslim websites to access information about *halal* and *haram* products, and she considered the current availability of *halal* products in London unsatisfactory. In much the same vein, she was not satisfied with product labelling. Yusof is about the same age as Izura; he accompanied her to London in 2005 and was working for a mobile phone company before starting a Master's degree. Yusof did much of the couple's shopping in convenience stores, supermarkets, hypermarkets, local *halal* butchers and the Loon Fung market in Chinatown. Unlike Izura, Yusof found the current availability of *halal* products in London satisfactory.

Izura described this as "private" or "shop" certification. Second, this quotation shows that many Muslims see other groups of Muslims as "others", whether they are very pragmatic, individualistic and relaxed about their religion or very strict and dogmatic. For instance, several informants referred to Brunei and Bruneians as being extremely purist about *halal*.

When asked about this distinction between groups or individuals of divergent orientations with regard to *halal*, most informants would refer to schooling, upbringing and gender as generating difference. Most informants hold as a general fact that women are more concerned about *halal* and *halal* certification; the empirical data in this study support this claim.

When discussing *halal* with Yusof, the issue of thrift dominated:

> *On weekends I go to Tesco. On weekdays, normally I buy* halal *food in a* halal *butcher shop near my place and I go to Lidl because it's cheap. They also have* halal *meat in Lidl, but in terms of certification I'm not so sure about this meat. I have never seen a logo. That is why I go to the proper* halal *butcher shop in ASDA, for example. I think they have a* Halal Food Authority *logo stamped on it.*

The price level of properly certified *halal* conditions a range of shopping practices in everyday life. Yusof explained that, as a Malay in London, he was used to the reliability of JAKIM certification and that all other types of certification would be second to that. As a consequence, *halal* certification and logos are important for everyday shopping, during which he compared these types of certification with the unachievable JAKIM standard.

Nur** was aware that, although McDonald's and KFC are not *halal*-certified, more and more proper alternatives for Muslims in London are emerging. She reasoned:

> *The thing in London is that McDonald's and KFC are not* halal, *so if I like to go to a* halal *fast-food place I go to the Chicken Cottage or any other fast-food place that is* halal-*certified,* halal *logos at their doors.*

Nur had chosen Chicken Cottage after checking on the Internet and noticing the *halal* logo on the façade of a Chicken Cottage outlet. In general, Nur acknowledged that she would "take all of the authorities as long as it is a body, a well-known and big organization that has undergone certain processes of the law". When I was out shopping for *halal* with Nur and her flatmate in *halal* butchers' shops near their home in South London one day, I noticed that logos of certification were rare and not overtly displayed. Nur reasoned that, even though she felt that enquiring about certification in some of the butchers' shops was embarrassing, she would do it anyway as many of these establishments simply "put a sign on the door when they don't have a certificate. In other butcher shops the certificate is put up so far away I can't see if it's Halal Food Authority or ..."

** Nur is a single woman in her 20s. She moved from Kuala Lumpur to London in 2005 to start her education at the London School of Economics. Her monthly income was £1,000–1,500. She lived with three flatmates in South London and normally shopped for *halal* meat in Somerfield supermarket and local *halal* butchers. Her main concerns about *halal* pertained to meat, ice cream, cakes and fish. Nur used Muslim magazines as guides for her *halal* shopping. She found the current availability of *halal* products satisfactory and was content with labelling on the products.

The last informants in this register are Henny[††] and Murni,[‡‡] who are flatmates. These women are confused about the state of *halal* certification in London to such an extent that when going about their daily shopping, they explore the labelling of products for any *haram* substances such as alcohol or gelatine. They scrutinize the ingredients of *halal*-certified products as well, because they perceive that the certifying bodies in Britain lack credibility and authority and are only involved in certification for financial gain. As Henny noted. "We look at logos, signs, labelling, ingredients and then we decide. It's just that we are more familiar with the JAKIM logo." Because Henny and Murni often look at labels on food, they are not really familiar with the wide range of *halal* logos in the London market.

This group of Malays is relatively strict about *halal* as a modern food taboo that requires proper certification. They are often interested in the certification of not only meat, but also a whole range of other products. In this way, they support the current proliferation of *halal*. Furthermore, among this register of modern Muslim consumers, *halal* is not an individualized choice in everyday life but a religious injunction that should inspire a particular form of Muslim lifestyle.

"In Our Belief If Someone Says It's *Halal*, We Just Take It"

The heading to this section is a quotation from an informant called Udzir.[§§] Compared with the more purist Malays in the first group, Udzir and the other Malay informants in this second group are more pragmatic and relaxed about their understanding and practice of *halal* certification. As an expression of this type of sentiment, Udzir explained to me that basically he trusted producers to live up to *halal* requirements and that it was not his responsibility as a Muslim consumer to mistrust the intentions of producers. Pragmatically, he also argued that there were no significant difference between various types of certification, such as JAKIM and local certification in London: "I would take both, JAKIM and local certification in London, there's not too much of a difference anyway." Udzir trusted the signs in Arabic stating that a product, butcher's shop or restaurant was *halal*. He concluded that "[i]n our belief if someone says it's *halal*, we just take it. So if anything is wrong, we just blame the producer or trader." To Udzir, certification by an imam or food expert would be "at the bottom of the list, but I wouldn't say I wouldn't take it. When you are living outside Malaysia you just have to shut one eye."

---

††   Henny is a 21-year-old single woman. She moved from Kuala Lumpur to London in 2005 to study economics at University College London. Her monthly income was £1,000–1,500. She shared a flat with a friend, Murni. Henny normally shopped for groceries at Tesco. In London, she tried to find *halal* meat, drinks and intestines in, for example, the Bloomsbury Halal Food Store. On the whole, she was content with the availability of *halal* in London, but considered labelling on products unsatisfactory.

‡‡   Murni is 21 years old and single. She also moved from Kuala Lumpur to London to study economics at University College, London. Murni's monthly income was between £1,000 and £1,500. Henny and Murni shop for groceries and *halal* at the same places. According to Murni, the current availability of *halal* products in London is unsatisfactory, as is the labelling on many products.

§§   Udzir is a single man, 30 years old, who had lived in London since 1995. He moved from Kuala Lumpur to study and now worked as an architect. His monthly income was £1,500–2,000. He lived with a friend in a flat and normally shopped for groceries in Sainsbury's, a corner store, the Chinese supermarket Wing Yip, and the Portobello Road Market. Udzir was mainly interested in *halal*-certified meat and margarine. In general, he was satisfied with the current availability of *halal* products, but he felt that labelling on products in London left much to be desired for Muslims.

Udzir's friend Binsar⁶⁶ reflects similar sentiments. Binsar put it plainly that, in terms of *halal* and *halal* certification in London, "I'm just not too concerned. I couldn't be bothered. I am a bit ignorant, so if I see a *halal* sign I wouldn't do more research." Consequently, Binsar, like Udzir, trusted the *halal* butchers' shops he visited around Bayswater and Notting Hill. Ultimately, he felt that *halal* was an issue for the individual and not a religious injunction that should dominate his family's everyday life in London. Even though Binsar was familiar with JAKIM certification, he did not necessarily prefer this type of certification. Indeed, in general he was not really concerned about *halal* certification at all.

Unlike these young Malay men, the informant Sardi,*** who had been living outside Malaysia for a longer period of time, had not been widely exposed to Malaysian state *halal* certification. Sardi was the only informant not familiar with JAKIM certification, which had not been institutionalized at the time he left Malaysia. In terms of *halal* reliability, Sardi preferred local authorities such as HFA or HMC. In the 1970s *halal* in Malaysia mainly meant trusting the authority of the local *halal* butcher's shop, he told me. His story about shopping for *halal* in Malaysia in the 1970s is comparable to younger Malays' accounts of contemporary shopping for *halal* meat in local butchers' shops in London. More pragmatically inclined informants such as Sardi simply trust the authority of these butchers' shops, which for the most part are not certified by any organization. Sardi made clear to me that "[t]here are times when you don't know whether it's *halal* or not so you just say a Muslim prayer before you eat." Sardi described himself as a "flexible Muslim" who was not overly subjected to religious injunctions, as was clearly demonstrated by his attitude towards *halal* and *halal* certification.

Whereas Izura and Yusof were preoccupied with proper *halal* certification in London, another Malay couple, Ahmad and Altaf,††† were more pragmatic. Ahmad admitted, "We are not very particular in terms of *halal* food, we are only particular if there is pork in it." However, Ahmad and Altaf were concerned when "[w]e buy gifts for visiting other people's places. Then we do pay particular attention to it and go to a supermarket and select proper *halal* certification." This point reflects the social significance of *halal* certification among some Muslim groups and individuals.

When asked why some Muslims are more fastidious about the understanding of *halal* and its practice, most informants indicated that a preoccupation with *halal* depends on the forceful impact of schooling, and thus the state, which provided information about *halal* as part of the Malaysian education system. Most informants asserted that their

---

¶¶   Binsar is 29 years old and lives with his wife and their child in London. He moved to Britain in 1996 to study accountancy and was now working as an accountant. The monthly income of the household was between £5,500 and £6,000. Binsar normally shopped for groceries in Tesco and ASDA hypermarkets. His main concern was *halal* meat, not so much other *halal* products. Binsar was content with the current availability of *halal* products in London and thought that labelling on products was adequate.

***   Sardi is a single man in his 50s who left Malaysia in the 1970s to study engineering in Singapore. Sardi's monthly income was £1,500–2,000. He travelled extensively in many parts of Asia and Europe and lived permanently in London, where he worked for engineering companies. He normally shopped for groceries in Sainsbury's, Tesco, and *halal* butchers' shops around Earl's Court. In general, Sardi found that the availability of *halal* was satisfactory in London, whereas labelling on products left much to be desired.

†††   Ahmad, a man in his 20s, is married to Altaf, who is about the same age; the couple moved from Kuala Lumpur to London in 1998 to study, and they both worked in the financial sector. The monthly income of the household was £4,000–4,500. The couple normally shopped for groceries in a local Co-op near their home in Walthamstow and in ASDA and Tesco. In London, they looked for *halal* meat, biscuits, dairy products, and chips. The couple felt that both the availability of *halal* in London and the labelling of products were unsatisfactory.

knowledge of *halal*, whether basic or extensive, derived from their school experience. As might be expected, *halal* knowledge and practice was also generated within families, but *halal* within the school system was far more pronounced in informants' accounts. Malay informants referred to this type of knowledge as a natural part of "a national curriculum", "a common understanding", "general knowledge" or "a syllabus".

Although most informants were equally exposed to this type of knowledge in the Malaysian school system, everybody also acknowledged that individuals and groups have divergent understandings and practices of *halal*. Therefore, bringing food to other people's homes or as gifts is a sensitive issue, and the best thing to do, as a Muslim, was to ensure that what they brought was as properly certified as possible, as in the case of Ahmad and Altaf.

With regard to the couple's personal *halal* food consumption, they were fairly pragmatic, although for non-food products like shoes, Altaf contended that she would never, for example, buy a pair of shoes without enquiring whether they were made out of pigskin: "We can't touch pigs and if we do we have to wash in a certain way, so that might be why some non-food products are certified *halal*." Thus, Altaf would prefer more certification on leather products.

This second group of Malay consumers either reluctantly accepted the imposition of *halal* and its certification or simply rejected it as a material, and therefore shallow, display of belief that was unnecessary in their everyday lives. However, the understanding and practice of *halal* among these more pragmatic Muslims cannot be separated from the fact that *halal* production, trade and consumption are undergoing drastic changes.

Managerial Implications

Producers and traders should consider the following recommendations in their efforts to meet rising demands among Muslim consumers in Britain for proper *halal* certification (see Table 5.1).

IDENTIFY WELL-DEFINED TARGET GROUPS ACCORDING TO SOCIO-ECONOMIC STRATIFICATION

This analysis shows that ethnicity and country of origin are essential determinants of everyday *halal* consumption. Different Muslim groups understand and practise *halal* differently from other ethnic and Muslim groups in the marketplace and often perceive other groups as overly pragmatic or purist about *halal*. In this way, *halal* can distinguish divergent groups of Muslims. Moreover, the length of stay in Britain plays a significant role in patterns of *halal* consumption. The empirical data suggest that Malays in London tend to be more relaxed about *halal* the longer they have lived outside Malaysia. However, women appear more focused on *halal* than men.

DESIGN "AESTHETICIZE" *HALAL* LOGOS TO MAKE THEM DISTINCTIVE, VISIBLE AND RECOGNIZABLE

Modern consumers are accustomed to a wide range of logos on products. Unlike *halal* meat in butchers' shops, *halal* products in supermarkets are packaged, so customers

Table 5.1   Identified areas, empirical examples and suggested marketing actions

Identified areas	Sample quotation	Marketing actions suggested
Certification by a trustworthy religious authority is essential.	"I worry about local *halal* certification sometimes because you can see people we don't even know creating their own *halal* signs and putting them up."	Clearly display the name, history, and details of the *halal* producer and certifier on products. A distinctive and recognizable logo should embody this information.
Familiarity with *halal* certifiers increases consumers' trust in *halal* certification.	"I usually refer to the London Central Mosque website. Because when I came to London to study it was on this website I learned about where to get *halal* food. So, if I'm familiar with a local Mosque or Imam I trust it's *halal*."	The *halal* industry should identify the reasons why consumers consider some certifiers trustworthy.
Ethnicity, country of origin and religious self-identity distinctions condition *halal* understanding and practice.	"I would always say that Malays are stricter. It is just the way that we were taught, I think."	Identify well-defined target groups according to socio-economic stratification and religious self-understanding.
The relationship between availability, certification procedures and price shape *halal* shopping practices in everyday life.	"On weekends I go to Tesco. On weekdays, normally I buy *halal* food in a *halal* butcher shop near my place and I go to Lidl because it's cheap. They also have *halal* meat in Lidl, but in terms of certification I'm not so sure about this meat. I have never seen a logo. That is why I go to the proper *halal* butcher shop in ASDA, for example. I think they have a *Halal* Food Authority logo stamped on it."	It should be clear how proper certification influences price levels of *halal*.
New consumer alternatives for Muslims pose new challenges for well-established producers and companies.	"The thing in London is that McDonald's and KFC are not *halal*, so if I like to go to a *halal* fast-food place I go to the Chicken Cottage or any other fast-food place that is *halal*-certified, *halal* logos at their doors."	The industry should recognise that *halal* can be part of mainstream forms of production and trade, such as selling a limited number of *halal* products in an otherwise non-*halal* restaurant. Or *halal* can be an alternative promoted as distinctive in its own right.
The relationship between the authority of the certifier, labelling and ingredients is significant for *halal* understanding and practice.	"We look at logos, signs, labelling, ingredients and then we decide."	Producers and certifiers must ensure that their declared *halal* standards correspond to actual ingredients in products.
Halal certification of non-food products is becoming important to some Muslim consumers.	"We can't touch pigs and if we do we have to wash in a certain way, so that might be why some non-food products are certified *halal*."	The industry should consider mapping the rising interest in *halal* non-food products.

look for recognizable and proper logos on packaging among the expanding world food ranges.

CLEARLY DISPLAY THE NAME, HISTORY AND DETAILS OF THE *HALAL* PRODUCER AND CERTIFIER ON PRODUCTS

Logos should clearly indicate who the producer is and that certification has been carried out by an accountable organization. Additional information about available Websites, the definition of *halal*, and the organizational structure and mission and ethical position of the producer and certifier contribute to increased transparency in what many Muslim consumers often find to be a confusing market.

MAKE THE RELATIONSHIP BETWEEN COMMERCIAL AND RELIGIOUS INTERESTS IN *HALAL* CLEAR

Some informants indicated that *halal* in Britain was being overcommercialized and that this had led to unhealthy competition and fragmentation among Muslims. Producers, traders, certifiers and consumers alike understand *halal* products as commodities that are marked as religious. Consequently, the relationship between commercial and religious interests in *halal* should be as explicit as possible.

ENSURE THAT ACTUAL INGREDIENTS IN PRODUCTS ARE FULLY COMPATIBLE WITH THE CERTIFIER'S *HALAL* REQUIREMENTS AND STANDARDS

Some Muslim consumers rely on what they consider proper *halal* certification expressed with a logo. If the certification is considered unreliable, consumers scrutinize labels for any substances that may be contaminated with porcine residues or alcohol, such as gelatine, glycerine, emulsifiers, enzymes, flavours and flavourings. Thus, producers and certifiers must ensure that their declared *halal* standards correspond to actual ingredients in products.

CONSIDER AND MAKE CLEAR THE RELATIONSHIP BETWEEN PROPER CERTIFICATION (INSPECTION, ADMINISTRATION AND CONTROL) AND THE PRICE LEVEL OF PRODUCTS

In general, this study indicates that *halal* meat in supermarkets is more expensive than in *halal* butchers' shops. Ideally, producers and certifiers should detail the costs involved in proper *halal* certification and how they affect the price – that is, how certain types of products and certification processes may affect price levels.

INFORM CONSUMERS ABOUT THE RELATIONSHIP BETWEEN TRACEABILITY AND CERTIFICATION

Halal is increasingly being subjected to requirements that are not directly related to the intrinsic qualities of products but rather to their handling and storage. Hence, traceability is becoming important to convince consumers that producers, certifiers and carriers are aware of the increasing requirements in this market.

Conclusions

This empirical exploration of *halal* demonstrates that proper certification is a question that even the most pragmatic Muslims must relate to and negotiate in their everyday lives. In my discussion I have not included other ethnic or Muslim groups, because this research effort is based mainly on Malays who embody a particular trajectory of *halal*. However, research I have done with other groups, such as Pakistanis, Bangladeshis and Indians, suggests that, between and within these groups, purism and pragmatism represent powerful distinctions. In other words, difference between the self and the other is often manifested in being fastidious versus relaxed about *halal* as a moral register or category.

Informants far preferred JAKIM-certified products if they were readily available. State-certified *halal* in Malaysia was described as "familiar", "trustworthy", "reliable" and "convincing". In much the same way, the challenge for producers, traders and certifiers in the British *halal* market is to develop trustworthy and recognizable forms of *halal* certification that follow uniform or national standards. The way in which *halal* has developed in countries such as Malaysia will probably affect future tendencies in the global *halal* market. Thus, the Malay Muslim consumers interviewed for this research can be seen as representative of trends that may prove significant in this global market.

Many Muslim consumers are confused about the moral implications of an expanding *halal* market, as exemplified by the introduction of *halal* chocolate and toothpaste. The industry should be aware that some Muslim groups and individuals find this seemingly boundless expansion of *halal* and certification into ever more commodities excessive and unnecessary.

References

1   http://ats-sea.agr.gc.ca/asean/4282_e.htm.
2   Riaz, M.N. and Chaudry, M.M. (2004), *Halal Food Production*, CRC Press, Boca Raton, FL, pp. 22–25.
3   Simoons, F.J. (1994), *Eat Not This Flesh. Food Avoidances from Prehistory to the Present*, The University of Wisconsin Press, Madison and London.
4   Denny, F.M. (2006), *An Introduction to Islam. Third Edition*, Pearson Prentice Hall, Upper Saddle River, NJ, p. 279.
5   Riaz, M.N. and Muhammad, M.C. (2004), *Halal Food Production*, CRC Press, Boca Raton, FL, pp. 6–7.
6   Ibid., p. 7.
7   Riaz and Chaudry, *Halal Food Production*, op. cit.
8   "Something fishy in your pasta?", *The Guardian*, 26 October 2006, p. 26.
9   Daviron, B. and Ponte, S. (2005), *The Coffee Paradox. Global Markets, Commodity Trade and the Elusive Promise of Development*, Zed Books, London and New York, p. 42.
10 Fischer, J. (2008), *Proper Islamic Consumption: Shopping among the Malays in Modern Malaysia*, NIAS Press, Copenhagen.
11 http://www.statistics.gov.my.
12 Fischer, *Proper Islamic Consumption*, op. cit.
13 See http:www.pmo.gov.my.

14   Abbas, T. (2005), *Muslim Britain: Communities under Pressure*, Zed Books, London and New York.

15   Bergeaud-Blackler, F. (2007), "New challenges for Islamic ritual slaughter: a European perspective", *Journal of Ethnic and Migration Studies*, Vol. 33, No. 6, pp. 965–980; Charlton, R. and Kaye, R. (1985), "The politics of religious slaughter: an ethno-religious case study", *New Community*, Vol. 12, No. 3, pp. 490–502; Kaye, R. (1993), "The politics of religious slaughter of animals: strategies for ethno-religious political action", *New Community*, Vol. 19, pp. 235–250.

16   Ansari, H. (2004), *The Infidel Within. Muslims in Britain since 1800*, Hurst & Company, London, p. 355.

17   http://www.halalfoodauthority.co.uk.

18   http://www.halalmc.co.uk.

19   http://www.mintel.com.

20   http://www.ethnicfocus.com.

21   Azmi, J. (2003), *Halal Food: A Guide to Good Eating – London*, KasehDia Sdn. Bhd, Kuala Lumpur.

22   http://www.ummahfoods.com.

23   See http://www.ifanca.org.

24   Esposito, J. (1995), *The Oxford Encyclopedia of the Modern Islamic World*, Oxford University Press, Oxford, pp. 460–61.

6 Retail Internationalization as a Driver of Global Developments: The Example of Central and Eastern Europe

JON HANF* AND KIRSTI DAUTZENBERG†

Keywords

agrifood business, Central and Eastern Europe, retail internationalization, structural change.

Abstract

Increasingly globalized markets and internationalization have initiated various structural changes in the food retail business. Formerly nationally-oriented retailers have suddenly become global. In the retail sector this process also affects new structures across agribusiness, most notably as general retailers export their business models. A comparison of the development and impact of globalization in the retail sectors of different Central and Eastern European countries reveals varied opportunities and threats for participants in agribusiness.

Introduction

Because growth possibilities in their domestic markets are largely exhausted, Western retailers are expanding internationally. In most cases, retailers export their entire business model. The CIES (International Committee of Food Retail Chains) Food Business Forum

*   Dr Jon H. Hanf, Leibniz Institute of Agricultural Development in Central and Eastern Europe, Theodor-Lieser-Str. 2, 06120 Halle (Saale), Germany. E-mail: hanf@iamo.de. Telephone: + 49 345 2928 246.

†   Dr Kirsti Dautzenberg, Centre for Entrepreneurship and Innovation, University of Potsdam, Am Park Babelsberg 14, 14482 Potsdam, Germany. E-mail: kirsti.dautzenberg@uni-potsdam.de. Telephone: + 49 331 977 4641.

surveys top managers from the food industry about which economic topic is most likely to dominate professional discussions; according to almost 70 per cent of these managerial respondents, the answer is "the internationalization of food retail business". If most businesspeople in the food industry agree that the internationalization of the retailing system is a critical topic for discussion and reflection, it seems logical to assume that firm managers similarly believe that development in this context must entail either a dangerous and general threat or a great and promising opportunity.

The aim of this chapter is threefold. First, using different theories of internationalization, we determine why the retailers internationalize. For the actual degree of internationalization, we rely on an analysis of secondary data and recognize that exhausted growth possibilities in domestic markets, at least with respect to growth through merger and acquisition, certainly drive internationalization. However, the effects of internationalization go beyond further growth of leading retail firms to offer new or improved opportunities for food retail corporations. These new opportunities apply to both the demand side and the supply side.

Second, using theories of new institutional economics and strategic management, we elaborate on the consequences of internationalization for participants in the agrifood business.

Third, we discuss the contributions of internationalization to the development in Central and Eastern Europe (CEE), including a detailed analysis of the current situation and an outlook for future developments in general, with particular reference to different CEE countries.

Internationalization of Food Retailers

As early as 1905 the Swiss food processor Nestlé owned production sites in Germany, France, the UK and the USA. By 1908 the German food-processing firm Dr Oetker had established its first foreign base; by 1924 the company had production plants in seven countries. Unilever had operations in more than 40 countries in 1930. However, less than 20 years ago, almost all the world's retail firms remained pure national firms with a negligible share in foreign markets. Wal-Mart opened its first retail outlet outside the USA in Mexico City in 1991, Carrefour started its international business in Taiwan in 1989 and Rewe began its internationalization with the acquisition of Billa in 1996.[1] That scenario has changed dramatically. Among the top 200 global retailers, almost all the players except those in the USA operate in numerous countries, having established noteworthy business capacities in foreign markets.[2] For example, Metro increased its foreign sales volume from 5 per cent in 1997 to 39 per cent in 1999; today the share is approximately 55 per cent. In general, retail firms start with a geographical expansion across their national borders but shortly thereafter move into more distant countries.[3]

The most important reason for internationalization remains stagnating domestic food markets and the resulting enforced competition.[4,‡] Such internationalization

---

‡   Because further national-level concentration through mergers and acquisitions appeared impossible considering the already realized degree of concentration, a jump over the border seemed the easiest way to avoid legal persecution by the Monopolies and Merger Commission.[7] In the first half of the 1990s the national market share of the largest three retailers in almost all Western European countries clearly surpassed 50 per cent, but if Western Europe represents a single market, the aggregated market share of the five biggest retail firms did not exceed 15 per cent. In many cases,

has been effective in almost all Western countries, although remarkable differences occur in the degree of market saturation and exhaustion of food demand among countries. The internationalization of companies did not include a synchronized concentration process across different national systems, so these factors could not be solely responsible for the simultaneous and explosive internationalization of retailing in several countries.

Rather, the international retail market penetration also depends on at least four pull factors:

- Financially strong retailers can disrupt the structure of any foreign market and successfully install their own business ideas in new market environments, as did Wal-Mart in the UK and Lidl in France.[5]
- The collapse of the socialist central planning system in Central and East Europe left behind an economic vacuum that offered the unique opportunity to establish an entirely new retail system modelled on Western ideas. Western retail firms took this opportunity and established subsidiaries in various countries.[6]
- An additional investment possibility arose from the financial crises in South-east Asia. In particular, French and German retail firms took advantage of the temporary shortage in money that afflicted Asian countries, in the hope of taking advantage of this presence when China began opening its markets.[8]
- The international retail sector profits from considerable progress in WTO negotiations regarding quality and safety standards that facilitate the trade of intermediate and convenience food products across borders.[9]

However, internationalization is not without dangers. Some retail firms have already begun to rearrange their spheres of influence by building regional clusters.[10] The most prominent example is Wal-Mart, which has withdrawn from several foreign markets after suffering high financial losses. Retailers often do not adopt their business system to the new business environment at all.[11] Furthermore, increasing profits are not guaranteed with an expansion into a new market, but may be attained through adequate adjustment to country characteristics and positive synergy effects. Such synergetic effects are more likely if emerging trends in retail business strategies intensify through globalization. Three such development tendencies offer outstanding opportunities for more efficient retailing use in combination with globalization: enhancement of global sourcing,[§] sophisticated usage of supply chain management[¶] and augmented use of retail brands.[**]

---

the foreign retailer was really a newcomer in the entered market, so that antitrust departments had no reason to prevent acquisitions.

§   Global sourcing means that the process of recruiting production factors and trade goods takes into consideration available global products.

¶   Supply chain management refers to the management of materials, information and financial flows in a network that consists of suppliers, manufacturers, distributors and customers.

**   The surge of retail branding is characterized by not only an increased number of brands and market share, but also a considerable augmentation of standard quality.

Consequences of Retail Internationalization on the Processing Industry

These organizational and strategic changes in the retail sector, to be expected with ongoing internationalization, have effects both upstream and downstream. However, we confine our analysis to the expected impacts on the food-processing industry. To facilitate this discussion, we subdivide the food-processing -industry into five firm categories. This categorization is somewhat crude and imprecise but sufficient for our purposes:[††]

- very large multinational food-processing firms that traditionally maintain many subsidiary companies, distributed throughout the world, and are engaged in many different food branches;
- firms that are more or less strictly concentrated on their core competences but also produce and supply globally.[12] These firms possess remarkable market power based not on their size but on consumers' appreciation;
- medium-sized firms that produce diverse food for a national or regional market. Most of their products are marketed as retail brands or no-name products;
- small and medium-sized, specialized food processors that mainly produce according to orders from retail firms;
- all small food-processing firms that serve local markets or provide special niches in regional or national markets.

If retail procurement alternates between predominantly national sourcing and global sourcing, and if retail firms internationally centralize and reorganize their supply chain network, serious consequences will result for food-processing industries. Such changes notably increase the competitive pressure on suppliers, because each firm must compete with not only its national antagonists, but also firms from several countries. If we consider the different firm categories, we note remarkable differences within the food-processing industry. Firms of the first category are only marginally affected by the concentration of retail procurement, because multinationals distribute strong brands in almost all relevant national markets, so increasing their international retail procurement will not cause a substantial effect on the quantity of their sales. Hence, their relative position also does not change significantly.

Firms of the second category also retain more or less the same status. The volume of their sales is probably not seriously affected by the international pooling of retail procurement, assuming that they adjust their sales organization appropriately.

The most important effects of the change in retail procurement will probably ensue in the third category. Some food-processing firms will achieve success in the altered situation, but many firms will suffer drastically. We first address those firms that represent national cost leaders and lack strong producer brands. If national retail procurement systems prevail, their strong cost leadership protects these firms from competitive threats, because they possess the necessary experience and know-how to undercut competitors' cost levels and counter any price wars. In contrast, if the retailers unify their national

---

[††]   The purpose of this discussion is to demonstrate that the consequences of retail internationalization affect different types of suppliers differently. Thus, we must discuss the results for each type separately; we orient this discussion according to Hanf's and Hanf's (2004) categorization.[13]

procurement divisions and form a multinational division, national processors with cost leadership will lose control over the competition, because they must confront cost leaders from other countries with the same skills. As a result, the market power and the price margin of national cost leaders radically shrink, and at least some of these former national cost leaders will be forced out of the market. The survivors retain a relatively positive situation: although they have forfeited some market power, in return, they win sales and turnover victories. The situation differs significantly, though, if we consider processing firms that use product differentiation to compete with their business rivals on the national market. In a unified international procurement market, the number of competitors increases with the number of countries involved, but very few, if any, of them represent direct substitutes because they have rather similar products. In the event that the product differentiation is narrowly based on national consumer habits and preferences, there is no reason to assume that any fundamental and abrupt displacements in demand will arise from changing the procurement process.

Small and medium-sized food processors in the fourth category that produce retail brands by contract with a retailer usually benefit from the internationalization of the retail firm. Every time the retail firm invades a new country or expands its engagement in a country, it needs additional quantities of the retail branded products, which it purchases from the primary supplier. For example, when Lidl entered the Swedish market in 2003 it was importing milk from Germany. Hanf and Maurer argue that this advantage becomes particularly important when the retailer enters economically and politically unstable regions.[14] This context allows food processors to follow the growth path of the retailer, without making any of their own investments in market development.

Finally, the small firms within the last category have little concern about the mode of procurement. Regardless of whether retail procurement is internationally bundled or predominately organized nationally, a certain share of retail supply must be of local origin and locally purchased.‡‡ The same is true for regional and national niche products. However, in some cases, a niche may become larger through retail internationalization, in which case the small processor can use this larger niche in a piggyback process with the retail firm. In other cases, a foreign competitor gets introduced into a niche through the same piggyback process.

A forced introduction of supply management tools also should result from retail internationalization. This development trend absolutely favours large, globalized firms within our first and second categories. The installation of necessary coordination instruments, such as efficient consumer response (ECR) and collaborative planning, forecasting and replenishment (CPFR) systems, are expensive and require significant organizational expenditures. Small and medium-sized firms (category 5) are usually not willing, and perhaps not able, to raise the necessary money,[15] especially because most of the costs are fixed and the investment in human capital is indivisible and has a sunk-cost character.

Because the installation of such a coordination instrument also implies fixed costs on the retail side of the system, the retail firm should do as much business as possible with

---

‡‡   Consumers demand local food; a number of smaller but independent retailers still function under the umbrella of cooperative retail chains such as Edeka, Rewe and the purchasing association, Spar.

partners that have installed the same coordination system or that are willing to do so.[§§] Such close and trusting relations may arise from a multitude of successful transactions over a long time. Multinational food producers with a broad product portfolios (category 1) and global specialists with a worldwide reputation (category 2) are natural candidates that are likely to be preferred by retailers. Food processors that produce retail brands under contract (category 4) are more or less obliged to introduce such a supply management system if required by the retailer. The investment costs thereby incurred are relatively small, because most firms produce a very limited range of products for a single retailer. The same is true for knowledge of IT. However, many smaller contracting producers will have considerable difficulties fulfilling the increasing logistical demands that result from the implementation of the supply management system and the regional enlargement of the delivery duties in several countries.

Food processors of category 3 are among the likely losers of the increased supply management requirements incurred by retail internationalization: They are unlikely to be able to afford the additional financial obligations, and they lack a large enough labour force with sufficient training. In addition, they may have difficulties persuading retailers of their trustworthiness, their capability to innovate and their flexibility to respond to sudden changes in demand. Particularly significant difficulties may occur if a domestic supplier must negotiate with a globally-oriented bulk purchaser.

Retail Internationalization in CEEC

Having outlined the coherence between retail internationalization and its impact on suppliers in general, we now draw attention to a more concrete setting. Because many recent studies of management consultancies highlight the potentials for retailers in the former states of the Soviet Union, we address this geographical area. For example, analysing variables such as country risk, market attractiveness, market saturation and time pressure, the consultancy A.T. Kearney states that five of the most attractive countries for retailers are Central and Eastern European countries (CEEC).[16] Using slightly different variables, KPMG developed a similar picture. In both studies, Russia represents the second most attractive country.[17,¶¶]

In the context of retail internationalization, verticalization can be a major force that drives structural change. Swinnen shows that vertical coordination in agrifood chains is an important and growing phenomenon in transitional countries in Europe and Central Asia. He also indicates that, in these countries, vertical coordination is even more widespread in scope and complexity than it is in Western economies.[18] Verticalization enables private contractual initiatives to form, and thereby overcome, supply disruptions. Traders, agribusinesses and food companies have contracted with farms and provided input and assistance in return for guaranteed and high-quality supplies.[19] Quality probably provides the main catalyst for this development.[20] Reardon further states that retailers and foreign

---

§§   This competitive advantage becomes stronger because ECR and CPFR systems require close and trusting relations between food suppliers and retailers.

¶¶   KPMG points out that hypermarkets have particularly great potential. For example, within the first year of operations, the southern Moscow outlet of the German retailer AVA, valued at €40 million, attracted 120,000 customers per week and earned an annual sales volume of €55 million, reaching break-even point almost immediately.

direct investments provide more powerful impetuses of structural changes in transitional countries than do the World Trade Organization or trade policies.[21]

Noting differences in the degree of verticaliztion in transition countries, Dries et al.[22] refer to the concept of retail waves. They characterize "first-wave" countries as those whose supermarket sector went from a tiny niche of around 5 per cent of total food retailing in the mid-1990s to 40–50 per cent by the mid-2000s; examples include Hungary, Poland and the Czech Republic. In the "second-wave" countries, such as Bulgaria and Croatia, the sector grew to a share of 20–30 per cent. Finally, in "third-wave" countries, the share remained steady as a luxury niche of 5 per cent, such as in Russia.

The transition process of the retail sector from state-run retail shops, cooperatives and farmers' markets to Western-style, large-format retailers occurred along with heavy foreign investments and therefore with changes in the procurement systems. Six major shifts are key:[23]

- from local store-by-store procurement to (nationally centralized) large and modern distribution centres;
- to regionalization of procurement across countries;
- from traditional brokers to specialized wholesalers;
- towards increasing use of global logistic firms;
- to preferred-supplier systems;
- towards higher private standards of quality and safety.

Four of these general trends are associated with retail internationalization and are applicable to the CEEC. Because of the significant differences between first- and third-wave countries, we analyse and focus on the consequences of these changes in the procurement systems in individual countries.

First-wave Countries

In the context of first wave countries, we focus on Hungary, because it has modernized its retail sector, starting from the 1990s, faster and more successfully than any other CEECs. Today, Hungary is home to one of the best developed retail sectors among CEEC.[24] As Table 6.1 reveals, in 2002, modern retail formats already had gained an approximately 50 per cent market share.

The rapid development of modern retailers was accompanied by heavy investments by Western retailers in Hungary. In 2005 foreign retailers dominated the Hungarian retail market, as Table 6.2 shows.

However, not only are the major players are foreign-owned, but the first round of consolidation is also taking place. Table 6.6 in the Appendix to this chapter indicates a similar development in Poland. Due to its heterogeneous market and loosely structured retail landscape, first movers such as the German Dohle Group succeeded in Poland with hypermarkets. However, despite its strong market position, Dohle decided to sell the business to Tesco due to intense competition demanding higher financial expenditures.[25]

Because the big players in first-wave retail markets are more or less identical to those in Western Europe, we posit that there are no significant differences with regard to

Table 6.1   Number of retail formats in Hungary

Retail format	2000	2001	2002
Hypermarket	13	17	19
Supermarket	15	14	14
Discount store	16	16	15
Supretten	35	35	36
Market and street vendors	5	4	5
Other	16	14	11
Total	**100**	**100**	**100**

Source: BBE (2006).

Table 6.2   Sales volume in billion Euro: Different retail formats in Hungary

Rank	Company	Sales 2005 in billion Euro	Number of outlets
1	Tesco-Global Aruhazak Rt.	1.89	89
2	Metspa Supply and Trade Co. Ltd.	1.83	181
3	CO-OP Hungary Rt.	1.50	4970
4	Reál Hungária Élemiszer Rt.	1.10	2290
5	Provera	0.80	213
6	Auchun Magyarország Kft.	0.70	10
7	PennyMarket Kft.	0.50	148
8	Plus Elemiszer Diszkont Kft.	0.40	165
9	Honiker Kft.	0.23	1970
10	Interfruct Kft.	0.20	22

Source: LZ online (2006).

procurement systems and quality demands, and thereby vertical coordination, between these markets.

Assuming that the general implications for the food sector are applicable without major modifications, we note several other points that demand some discussion, notably the Pan-European competition of cost leaders and the integration of farmers into vertically coordinated chains. According to several interviews, German product managers of retail brands are beginning to include food processors from first-wave countries in their tenders for retail branded products, such as pasta and sausages. As long as the food quality meets their demands, retailers will give the bid to the most cost-competitive processors. In turn, the cost structures for basic products that do not demand high-quality requirements give the advantage to processors from CEEC.

The agricultural sector in CEECs remains a mixture of small-scale – even household – production and large-scale farming. Retailers and processors favour large-scale production to reduce the complexity of their supply chains, yet Dries and Swinnen[26] show that small-scale farmers can find a place in vertically coordinated chains. Nevertheless, several international retailers indicate that they require small-scale farmers to build horizontal cooperation to provide products that meet their qualitative and quantitative demands. If they cannot meet these demands, the farmers get excluded from the procurement systems.

Second-wave Countries

Bulgaria, a second-wave country, is about five to six years behind Hungary. Modern retail formats have been introduced but mainly by small local retail chains. Furthermore, the vast majority (97 per cent) of the 102 000 stores consist of less than 120 m^2 and only 0.2 per cent have more than 1000 m^2.[27] In the course of its EU accession, international retailers have made inroads into Bulgaria, including Metro, the largest foreign retailer, as well as other international retailers. The increasing attractiveness of the Bulgarian retail sector is represented by Bulgaria's ranking (13) on the AT Kearney Global Retail Development Index.[28] However, most foreign investments in Bulgaria go to the capital city, Sofia. International retailers locate mainly in urban areas, although local retail chains exist in rural areas.

Third-wave Countries

Because of its economic importance, we have selected Russia as an example of third-wave countries. The weight of organized retail is increasing, but street vendors, small shops and markets still dominate the sector. Supra-regional and regional chains may be slightly gaining in importance, yet, as Table 6.3 shows, in comparison with other CEECs the percentage in Russia remains rather low.

Table 6.3   Comparison of the importance of different retail formats: Russia versus Hungary

Retail format	Russia %	Hungary %
Hypermarkets	1	21
Supermarkets	6	14
Discounters	6	15
Cash & CArry	1	4
Small shops	26	34
Street vendors/markets	32	4
Other	28	8

Source: BBE (2006).

In Moscow retail chains constitute 16–17 per cent of the market, and in St Petersburg they account for 18–20 per cent.[29] No retail chains operate throughout Russia, although some of the larger Moscow and St Petersburg chains are expanding to other regions; some are even moving into neighbouring countries such as Ukraine. The development of organized retail also has intensified since international retailers, including Metro, Auchan and Rewe, entered Russia in 2000; Carrefour, Wal-Mart and even some German discounters are expected to enter soon. Thus, even though Metro remains the top retailer in Russia, as Table 6.4 shows, Russian retailers continue to make the majority of sales. This situation, in which modern retail formats constitute only a small portion of the Russian retail sector, leaves space for the expansion of all retailers, even in metropolitan areas. However, we assume that competition among the retailers will increase and that retailers will therefore seek to differentiate from one another.

Russian retailers will probably continue to improve the quality and lower the prices of their goods. Changes in retailer–supplier relationships are already emerging: for example, in the past, Russian suppliers dictated the rules of the exchange to domestic retailers[30] and these suppliers were so powerful that they could afford to keep retailers waiting 72 hours for goods that they ordered.[31] However, Western retailers demand that suppliers accommodate their original business models when entering a new market.[32] By applying global sourcing strategies and providing interesting new markets, international retailers have been able gain market power.[33] As a result, retailers expect suppliers to meet their global requirements for food quality, safety and delivery. For example, since entering the country five years ago, the Metro Group Russia has already installed Metro Asset Management, Metro Buying Group, Metro Advertising, Metro Group Logistics and Metro Group IT.

The 140 000 items carried by the 26 cash and carry markets and the three supercentres come from 2500 suppliers. Only 5 per cent are foreign manufacturers, and 20 per cent of the items are specific to the region. Thus, the Metro group has a strong influence on the Russian agrifood business in general, particularly in the Moscow region where most markets are located. This example shows that different quality and process management styles and requirements are applied in the short and medium term. In the long run,

Table 6.4   Ranking of food retailers in Russia according to turnover in 2005

Rank	Name of retailer	Format	Turnover, $ mio Euro
1	Metro Cash & Carry	Cash & Carry	1815
2	Magnit	Discounter	1553
3	Payaterochka	Discounter	1359
4	Auchen	Hypermarket	1350
5	Perekrestok	Multi-format	1015
6	Diksi, Megamart	Multi-format	860
7	Sedmoy Kontinent	Multi-format	713
8	Lenta	Hypermarket	649
9	Kopeyka	Multi-format	646
10	Viktoria C & C	Multi-format	608

Source: S. Malkov (2005).

however, suppliers must meet the retailers' home-country standards. Meeting these requirements moves competition away from a one-way street; suppliers can enlarge their sales volumes by exporting goods in old member states.

Consequences for the Different Waves

From this review of the scenarios it becomes evident that modifications are necessary among first-, second- and third-wave countries. With regard to global sourcing and retail branding,*** we differentiate between suppliers from the home country and suppliers of second- and third-wave countries. Retailers often take their suppliers into new markets. For example, when Metro entered Russia, Hochland AG followed and has built a dairy plant near Moscow. In its early years it received competitive protection, but over time local producers improved their quality and process management standards to equal those of Hochland AG and now compete effectively with the company.

As outlined previously, suppliers (both branded and retail brand suppliers) can grow through retail internationalization. A well-known German retailer has recently begun to consider retail brand suppliers on a grand scale. When the retailer began its internationalization, it used country-specific retail brands to differentiate itself from its retail competitors. Today, the German retailer has changed from regional retail brands to a single (the former German) retail brand, which enables it to apply a single global food quality and safety standard. Thus, every supplier must meet the same process and product standards, and German suppliers may be exchanged for foreign ones, or vice versa. However, in the medium term we anticipate that processors from second- and third-wave countries will begin to compete with processors in first-wave countries, because production costs will increase in these countries while the quality standards will remain slightly lower than in Western European countries. Nevertheless, in the long term the quest for global cost leadership is underway.†††

These examples indicate that the consequences are rather mixed. Multinationals (category 1) likely will expand their sales because, with rising discretionary income, consumers are willing to spend more money on well-known "Western" brands, forcing retailers to carry them. Furthermore, multinationals' stronger knowledge of SCM and ECR offers a further argument to list them. Big processors that produce nationwide brands (category 2) experience pressure from global brands and due to the rising quality standards set by the retail brands. Thus, we posit that major structural changes are forthcoming.

Firms in category 3 face fierce competition from other cost leaders, but their favourable cost structures give them good chances to win in this cost-cutting game. We predict that innovative and modern cost leaders will prosper, while those that fail to emphasize adequate food quality and safety standards or efficient production processes will fall out of competition. The same applies to firms of category 4. However, due to their small structure, they risk losing control over firm growth.‡‡‡ Niche suppliers and speciality

---

*** Although we separate these aspects, we combine them in this more applied discussion, because the most important question regarding retail brands pertains to securing a supply of goods of comparable quality to that in home countries.

††† Because logistic/distribution costs are very important in the context of food products, all supply decisions allow for them. Thus, quests generally focus on pan-European cost leadership rather than global leadership.

‡‡‡ In Germany, the bottled-water supplier of a well-known southern German discounter grew enormously as a result of the vast German and global expansion of the discounter. However, because of the investments required, the supplier

suppliers are generally not affected; retailers may use them in their home countries to complete a particular category. For example, Real (the hypermarket subsidiary of Metro Group) carries a "Russian category" in Germany that consists mainly of major Russian brands, but provides some shelf space for niche products and Russian specialties.

Conclusions

The retail industry has been undergoing immense structural changes for approximately two decades. Formerly nationally-oriented players have suddenly become global players. In many cases, these global giants still act like agglomerates of national tycoons, but that status is likely to change drastically in the near future. Some organizational adjustments are already visible, although most of the organizational measures are yet to be implemented. For example, the structural development of the food-processing industry will respond to the ongoing globalization process of the retail sector. The distinct firm groups will experience very different effects. Large multinational food producers with wide supply portfolios and worldwide and specialized premium food processors can easily adjust to the changing requirements of globalized retailers. Of course, individual winners and losers will emerge, but the group as a whole will not be affected seriously. The large group of national and regional food-processing firms will experience the most significant impact. A few firms will profit from the international retail development, perhaps by asserting themselves as multinational cost leaders. Others will survive by becoming accepted as differentiated brand producers in one or several national markets. However, the majority of firms in this category will eventually vanish.

Some small and medium-sized contract processors will disappear because they cannot extend their delivery adequately to foreign countries. However, most of these firms will evolve along with the international growth of their contract-granting retail firm. In the future more, rather than fewer, of these firms are likely to be required, because retail brands will gain additional market share. Hence, the competitive situation of specialized food contractors appears rather promising, assuming that the firms are capable of adjusting to changing business obligations. Finally, small producers that deliver to local or niche markets should not be directly affected by retail internationalization. Demand for local and niche products requires that they be offered, regardless of whether the retailer is nationally or internationally positioned.

Since the structures of the agrifood business first began to undergo dramatic changes at the beginning of the 1990s the impact of retailers' internationalization has been even more striking. Rapid changes have taken place in the retail markets themselves, as well as in the supplier structures. However, it is becoming obvious that Western retailers are exporting their business models, such that the structure of the agrifood business is becoming comparable to those in old member states.

In addition to these general findings, we distinguish among different developing stages of the retail sectors in the different countries. A three-wave model introduced in previous literature and applied to CEECs makes these differences even more obvious. We use three countries to exemplify these differences: Hungary as a first-wave country; Bulgaria as a second-wave country; and Russia as a third-wave country. In Hungary most

eventually ran out of equity and cash, and the discounter had to take over the supplier in order to secure its supply.

of the general implications apply, but in the other two countries modern retail has not yet made such inroads, particularly in rural areas.

Two particular findings are crucial. First, we argue that national cost leaders will face much stronger (global) competition due to retail internationalization. Second, farmers from around the world should form horizontal collaborations to satisfy the qualitative and quantitative demands of international retailers.

References

1. Rudolph, T. and Einhorn, M. (2001), "Herausforderung im europäischen Einzelhandel", *Thexis*, Vol. 3, pp. 2–7.
2. Deloitte (2006), "2006 Global Powers of Retailing", http://www.deloitte.com (accessed 10 September 2007).
3. Fernie, J., Hahn, B., Gerhard, U., Pioch, E. and Arnold, S.J. (2006), "The impact of Wal-Mart's entry into the German and UK grocery markets", *Agribusiness: An International Journal*, Vol. 22, No. 2, pp. 247–266.
4. A.T. Kearney (2006), "Emerging market priorities for global retailers – Global Retail Development Index", Consulting Study; Burt, S.L. (1993), "Temporal trends in the internationalization of British retailing", *International Review of Retail, Distribution and Consumer Research*, Vol. 3, No. 4, pp. 391–410; Davies, R. and Finney, M. (1998), "The future of retailing", *Financial Times*, Retail and Consumer, London; Fernie et al., 'The impact of Wal-Mart's entry", *op. cit.*; Robinson, T. and Clark-Hill, C.M. (1990), "Directional growth by European retailers", *International Journal of Retail and Distribution Management*, Vol. 18, No. 5, pp. 3–14.
5. Fernie et al., "The impact of Wal-Mart's entry", *op. cit.*; George, G. and Diller, H. (1993), "Internationalisierung als Wachstumsstrategie des Einzelhandels", in V. Trommsdorff (ed.), *Handelsforschung 1992/93*, Gabler, Wiesbaden; Wrigley, N. (2002), "The landscape of Pan-European food retail consolidation", *International Journal of Retail and Distribution Management*, Vol. 30, No. 2, pp. 81–91.
6. Rapp, S. (1995), "Internationalisierung von Einzelhandelsunternehmungen nach Ostmitteleuropa", dissertation, Zurich.
7. George, G. (1997), *Internationalisierung im Einzelhandel: strategische Optionen und Erzielung von Wettbewerbsvorteilen*, Duncker und Humblot, Berlin.
8. Lingenfelder, M. (1996), *Die Internationalisierung im europäischen Einzelhandel: Ursachen, Formen und Wirkungen im Lichte einer theoretischen Analyse und empirischen Bestandsaufnahme* Schriften zum Marketing, 42, Duncker und Humblot, Berlin.
9. Fieten, R., Friedrich, W. and Lagemann, B. (1997), Globalisierung der Märkte. Schriften zur Mittelstandsforschung, Nr. 73 NF, Stuttgart, Schäffer-Poeschel.
10. KPMG (2004), *Internationalisierung im Lebensmitteleinzelhandel*, published Consulting Study; Moore, C.M., Fernie, J. and Burt, S.L. (2000), "Brands without boundaries: the internationalization of the design retailer's brand", *European Journal of Marketing*, Vol. 34, No. 8, pp. 919–937.
11. Hurt, J. (2003), "Von der Notwendigkeit des Scheiterns – Wal-Mart Germany", *Wirtschaftswissenschaftliches Studium*, Vol. 11, pp. 688–692.
12. Simon, H. (1996), "The world's best unknown companies", *The Wall Street Journal*, 20 May 1996.

13. Hanf, C-H. and Hanf, J.H. (2004), "Internationalization of food retail firms and its impact on food suppliers", paper presented at the 88th EAAE Seminar, Paris, France.

14. Hanf, C-H. and Maurer, O. (1994), "Performance of the domestic food sector and internationalization" in Agricultural University in Prague, Economic Faculty (ed.), *Agrarian Prospects III*, pp. 57–69.

15. Hanf, J.H. and Kühl, R. (2002), "Consumer values vs. economic efficiency in food chains and networks" in J.H Triekens and S.W.F. Omta (eds), *Paradoxes in the Food Chain and Networks*, Wageningen Academic Publishers, pp. 35–43.

16. A.T. Kearney, "Emerging market priorities", *op. cit.*

17. KPMG, *Internationalisierung im Lebensmitteleinzelhandel*, *op. cit.*

18. Swinnen, J. (2005), "When the market comes to you – or not. The dynamics of vertical coordination in agri-food chains in transition", *Dynamics of Vertical Coordination in ECA Agri-Food Chains: Implications for Policy and Bank Operations*, World Bank, Rome and Washington.

19. Dries L. and Swinnen J.F.M. (2005), "Globalisation, quality management and vertical coordination in food chains of transition countries", paper prepared for the 92nd EAAE seminar on Quality Management and Quality Assurance in Food Chains, 2–4 March, Göttingen; Swinnen, "When the market comes to you", *op. cit.*

20. Gorton, M., Dumitrashko, M. and White, J. (2006), "Overcoming supply chain failure in the agri-food sector: a case study from Moldova", *Food Policy*, Vol. 31, pp. 90–103.

21. Quoted in Swinnen, "When the market comes to you", *op. cit.*

22. Dries, L., Reardon, T. and Swinnen J.F.M. (2004), "The rapid rise of supermarkets in Central and Eastern Europe: implications for the agrifood sector and rural development", *Development Policy Review*, Vol. 22, No. 5, pp. 525–556.

23. Ibid.

24. BBE (2006), "Retail-expansion osteuropa", Consulting Study.

25. KPMG, op. cit.

26. Dries, L. and Swinnen J.F.M. (2004), "Foreign direct investment, vertical integration, and local suppliers: evidence from the Polish dairy sector", *World Development*, Vol. 32, No. 9, pp. 1525–1544.

27. BBE, "Retail-expansion osteuropa", *op. cit.*

28. A.T. Kearney, "Emerging market priorities", *op. cit.*

29. BBE, "Retail-expansion osteuropa", *op. cit.*

30. Roberts, G.H. (2005), "Auchan's entry into Russia: prospects and research implications", *International Journal of Retail & Distribution Management*, Vol. 33, No. 1, pp. 49–68.

31. Corstjens, J. and Corstjens, M. (1995), *Store Wars: The Battle for Mindspace and Shelfspace*, Wiley, Chichester.

32. Roberts, "Auchan's entry into Russia", *op. cit.*

33. BBE, "Retail-expansion osteuropa", *op. cit.*

Appendix

Table 6.5   Degree of internationalization of German retailers

Retailer	Netto-sales 2003 in billion Euro	Percentage of sales in foreign countries	Countries of operation
Metro-Group	53.6	47.2	Austria, Belgium, Bulgaria, China, Croatia, Czech Rep., Denmark, France, Germany, Greece, Hungary, Italy, Japan, Luxembourg, Morocco, Netherlands, Poland, Portugal, Romania, Russia, Slovakia, Spain, Switzerland, Turkey, UK, Vietnam
Aldi	39.3	33.3	Australia, Austria, Belgium, Luxembourg, Netherlands, Rep. of Ireland, Spain, UK, US
Rewe	39.2	25.6	Austria, Bulgaria, Croatia, Czech Rep., France, Germany, Hungary, Italy, Poland, Romania, Slovakia, Ukraine
Edeka	31.3	5.3	Austria, Czech Rep., Denmark, France, Germany, Poland
Schwarz-Group (Lidl. Kaufland)	24.7	34.8	Austria, Belgium, Croatia, Czech Rep., Finland, France, Germany, Greece, Rep. of Ireland, Italy, Netherlands, Poland, Portugal, Slovakia, Spain
Tengelmann	24.1	52.1	Austria, Canada, China, Czech Rep., Germany, Hungary, Italy, Poland, Portugal, Slovakia, Slovenia, Spain, Switzerland, US

Source: Deloitte (2004).

Table 6.6   Retail market in Poland

Rank	Company	Sales 2005 in billion Euro	Formats
1	Metro Polska S.A.	2.9	Makro Cash & Carry, Real, Media Markt, Satum
2	Jerónimo Martins Dvstrvbucia Polska S.A.	1.3	Biedronki
3	Tesco Polska Sp.z.o.o.	1.3	Tesco, Savia
4	Carrefour Polska Sp.z.o.o.	1.2	Carrefour, Champion
5	Auchan Polska Sp.z.o.o.	1.1	Auchan, Schiever, Elea
6	Ruch S.A.	1.0	Ruch
7	Géant Polska Sp.z.o.o.	0.9	Geant, Leader Price
8	Eurocash S.A.	0.8	Eurocash, KDWT
9	Schwarz-Gruppe	0.7	Lidl, Kaufland
10	Rewe Sp.z.o.o.	0.7	Minimal, Selgros

Source: LZ online (2006).

The Latin American Perspective

7 *The Expanding Demand for Brazilian Groceries: The Case of Cachaça, a too Ethnically Charged Product?*

LUÍS KLUWE AGUIAR*

Keywords

ethnicity indicators, ethnic food consumption, cultural adoption, diaspora, assimilation, *cachaça*.

Abstract

In this chapter, a rapid appraisal of the growing Brazilian diaspora in the UK reveals how ethnicity is reaffirmed by means of consumption of typical foods. Using a typology based on ethnic origin consumption,[1] traits of demand reveal ethnicity indicators such as origin, culture and acculturation.

This chapter will:

- explore the motives behind migration of Lusophone groups, especially the Brazilians;
- map the dispersion of Brazilian in diaspora and food outlets in the UK;
- address issues of consumption and ethnicity;
- provide an understanding of Brazilians' ethnic food consumption and preferences while in diaspora;
- gain an insight into the likely acceptance of *cachaça* by British drinkers;
- propose the argument that the demand for ethnic Brazilian foodstuffs could be too ethnically charged.

* Mr Luís Kluwe Aguiar, Senior Lecturer, School of Business, Royal Agricultural College, Stroud Road, Cirencester, GL7 6JS, UK. E-mail: luis.aguiar@rac.ac.uk. Telephone: + 44 1285 652 531.

Introduction and Background to the Research.

The aims of this study are threefold. First, it attempts to characterize ethnic consumption following a typology[2] about consumption based on ethnic origin. Second, it addresses issues regarding migration and how communities of Brazilian expatriates now occupy a market which was initially held by the Portuguese. Finally, it tests the possible market acceptance of an exotic beverage, *cachaça*: a Brazilian alcoholic rum-like drink.

This study addresses the expansion of ethnic grocery outlets which specifically cater for the Brazilian expatriate community in the UK. This is a unique study as there has been little research in the UK with regard to specific demand for foodstuffs from an ethnic minority's perspective. A previous study concerning this topic was carried out by Ahmad Jamal,[3] who investigated the food consumption of British Pakistanis in Bradford. In that study he explored how British-born Pakistanis perceived a typically Pakistani diet and also investigated their perceptions towards English food. The results from that study reveal that the first-generation British Pakistanis had increasingly adopted mainstream English foods. Jamal also found that respondents felt that traditional Pakistani foods, despite being tasty, were "oily". The higher fat content in traditional Pakistani foods was considered problematic for respondents. Conversely, English foods were perceived by the same group as being foreign and bland, despite being healthier. The study revealed that the younger British Pakistani generation's attitude towards food consumption clearly indicated a growing assimilation of not only the host cuisine, but also, quite frequently, other British cultural traits.

A more recent study[4] researched a sample of Latin Americans living in Belgium. The findings suggested that barriers to maintaining Latin-American food habits in Belgium were mostly affected by both the availability of ethnic food ingredients and the limitation imposed by time constraints. The latter is due to the fact that some Latin American dishes demand elaborate food preparation and cooking time. The Latin Americans studied considered their food of origin as better tasting, despite an overall perception of Belgian food being more than just satisfactory.

When investigating how the Brazilian expatriate community in the UK has adapted to the local food culture or resisted embracing it, it was important to explore the motivations behind such consumption. The Brazilian minority community is dissimilar to that studied by Jamal as it is more numerous and widespread. In Europe, eating and drinking have increasingly determined the creation and reproduction of local, regional and national cultures and identities.[5] Therefore, the eating and drinking habits of ethnic groups (specifically, in this case, Brazilians), upon emigrating to a foreign country, is likely to reproduce and reinforce their original culture.

How such a cultural dimension expressed through ethnic food consumption could be relevant in determining and differentiating a specific consumer segment will be addressed in this chapter. Consumption is largely dictated by ethnicity and is therefore primarily a cultural phenomenon.[6] In this sense, Brazilians are expected to have attempted to reproduce their original food habits through the consumption of food staples that are sometimes not easily available in the host country – Britain. Therefore, any resistance by the Brazilians towards adoption of British foods could be interpreted as a means of reaffirming their culture and ethnic origin through maintaining a preference for their original national food habits.

Ethnicity and Consumption

Ethnic foods may be described as those considered different from the ones typical of the host country. When ethnic consumption is considered, it should be understood as a characteristic set of dietary practices. These are often strongly linked to cultural and faith beliefs which are reflected in traditions that represent an important role in one's diet. Cultural identity established by food ethnicity preference and consumption is "formed by complex configurations of one's awareness of one's own culture and a recognition of the social group to which one belongs in practice".[7]

In their work on consumption based on ethnic origin and media usage, Hui, Laroche and Kim[8] were interested in typifying ethnicity consumption. They proposed some ethnicity indicators relating to aspects of consumption, which were fixed, hence remaining unchanged, even after a prolonged contact period with another ethnic group. Ethnic origin is reflected in fixed ethnic indicators, where cultural behaviour is identified by a further set of ethnicity indicators. These are partly influenced by a person's own choice and preference in addition to being further influenced by the extent and duration of the contact with another ethnic group. The complex relationships between ethnicity and consumption are also acknowledged in these indicators, which involve levels of ethnicity inclination: "slightly ethnic" or "strongly ethnic". Whilst "slightly ethnic inclinations" are determined by cultural traits, "strongly ethnic inclinations" have roots in origin. Nevertheless, Wang and Lo,[9] when referring to investigations into culturally distinct immigrant groups, have mentioned that such a study should consist of an intriguing but more complex inquiry, which is not the purpose of this chapter.

Nonetheless, an immigrant's rate of adoption of different aspects of a new culture – for example, products and services – deserves special attention. On the one hand, Glock and Nicosia[10] have mentioned that some consumption behaviours tended to relate more closely to key cultural values of an ethnic group and were therefore more resistant to pressures of acculturation. On the other hand, some consumption behaviours may undergo changes even after minimal contacts with another ethnic group. This is what Andreasen[11] called "cultural interpenetration" or the exposure of members of one culture to another through either direct or indirect experience. However, aspects of the mainstream culture of the host country are generally expected to be adopted less rapidly by a minority group. Acculturation,[12] indicated that ethnic foods end up contributing to the diversity of traditional or host cuisine.

Resistance to adoption expressed by minorities will occur if the corresponding behaviour is predicted by a reflective, rather than formative, ethnicity indicator. When a distinction between reflective and formative ethnicity indicators is interpreted, the former may be identified with common origin, whilst the latter may be identified with shared cultural traits. Common origin is expressed as a reflective attribute and it is, in effect, a characteristic that cannot be changed. Yet, cultural traits are a combination of one's cultural background and levels of acculturation resulting from contacts with other ethnic groups.[13] Hence, it is suggested[14] that ethnicity should not be explained in the light of racial and biological characteristics since it may be regarded as a behavioural attribute.

Some ethnicity indicators, such as a language used for social communication implies family, religion and school interactions. Nevertheless, ethnic self-labelling relates to the degree of identification an individual may feel to a particular group. Language may be understood as being an objective indicator whilst ethnic self-labelling a subjective indicator. However, language proficiency and heritage may be considered as integral parts of cultural traits, thus, determining ethnicity. Sook-Lee.[15] when investigating second-generation Koreans in the USA, established links between the level of heritage language proficiency, language use and food preferences. The second-generation Koreans showed that 63 per cent of males and 37 per cent females liked eating Korean foods. Conversely, adoption of typically American foods was low, at 30 per cent for males and 20 per cent for females respectively. By preserving language as an identity of a distinct ethnic group, the second-generation Koreans also related more to their food ethnicity. Furthermore, in an article about American Jewish ethnicity it was linked[16] to one belonging or not belonging to an ethnic group. It is argued that individuals may relate towards an ethnic group in degrees. That author also stated that "the degree of a person's ethnic identification should largely determine the level of commitment the person experiences regarding the norms of the group and, thus, the degree of influence the group has on the person's behaviour and attitudes."[17]

As a result of the different viewpoints outlined above, it may be possible to identify the typology[18] used here as being a function of reflective and formative indicators, as well as acculturation patterns. Such a typology can be seen in Table 7.1.

Table 7.1   A typology for ethnicity indicators of consumption

A. Reflective Indicators	
	Ethnic origin (Fixed)
	a.1 Ethnicity – common origin, cannot be changed.
B. Formative Indicators	
	Cultural Traits Cultural background, preference ad duration of contact leading to acculturation.
	b.1 Language – an objective indicator for social communication.
	b.2 Ethnic Self-labelling – a subjective indicator used for identification.
	b.3 Religion Affiliation.
C. Acculturation Patterns	Based on Mendoza (1989)
	c.1 Cultural Resistance.
	c.2 Cultural Incorporation (adoption).
	c.3 Cultural Shift (substitution).
	c.4 Cultural Transmutation (alteration).
	c.5 Cultural Ethnic Affirmation.
	c.6 Cultural Ethnic Overshooting.

Source: M.K. Hui, M. Laroche and C. Kim (1998).

Whilst ethnicity is now widely accepted as multifaceted in nature, little attention has been given to the differences between various ethnicity indicators commonly employed by marketing researchers. It is conceivable that some consumption behaviours exhibited by a member of an ethnic minority could be more ingrained in the minority culture and could, therefore, be less likely to change regardless of the extent and duration contacts with the host group. In contrast, some other consumption behaviours are more amenable to acculturative pressures, and assimilation may occur as a result of prolonged contact with such a host group.

Moreover, a migrant's duration of residence could have either significant impact on changing behaviour for some aspects of consumption or little effect at all.[19] In his study Ahmad Jamal[20] found that the Pakistani group sampled showed signs of adopting British food. If food consumption behaviour has not changed in the host country, this may reflect that food consumption is associated with activities which were highly relevant to culture of origin, such as the celebration of traditional or ethnic festivals. This concurs with Lisa Peñaloza's article concerning Mexican migrants' consumer acculturation when crossing the border into the USA.[21] Peñaloza found that acculturation would more readily occur with culture-irrelevant activities rather than with more culture-relevant activities such as celebrating ethnic festivals.

Methodology

A review of the literature regarding issues of consumption and ethnicity was carried out. Consumption and ethnicity served as the theoretical background for testing the argument that perhaps Brazilian-branded products might be too ethnically charged and thus not appeal to the general British population. In order to ascertain Brazilian consumption behaviour, Hui et al.'s typology of consumption based on ethnic origin[22] was used. Due to the limited existence of similar studies about ethnic group food consumption and, with a view to characterizing and identifying the Brazilian expatriate community in Britain, Rapid Rural Appraisal methodology was used.

This type of methodology originated in rural development projects and is used to assess communities.[23] Rapid Rural Appraisal is also widely applied in urban areas as such a methodology is considered a creative and reliable way of assessing a situation, topic, problem or sector. Since the methodology falls midway between a formal survey and non-structured interviewing, and, owing to the short-term nature of the project and the non-existence of previous data on the topic, the possibility of creating a dialogue with respondents was valuable. Interview-type conversations were used to assess the market arrangement regarding the trading of Luso-Brazilian ethnic foodstuffs. The respondents formed a sample of seven Brazilians and two Portuguese owners of grocery outlets, one Brazilian diplomatic official, one NGO representative, one bar owner, as well as two wholesale importers in the London area. The sample was chosen from a list of establishments furnished by the Commercial Section at the Brazilian Embassy in London.

Following this, pure *cachaça* and *caipirinha* cocktails were tasted during a focus group session with 15 British nationals in order to collect information on the participants' preference for, or possible dislike of, the product. The reasons for non-consumption would reveal likely barriers to, and challenges for, the adoption of such a product. The group consisted of volunteers drawn from lecturing, administration and support staff from both Cirencester College and the Royal Agricultural College, who had shown interest in the topic by replying to a general e-mail invitation. The tasting session took place in October 2007. The make-up of the focus group can be seen in Table 7.3 in the Appendix.

The Lusitanian Foundation

To understand the Brazilian ethnic market in the UK it is necessary to first understand another ethnic group: the Portuguese. Brazil, despite gaining its independence from Portugal in the early nineteenth century, still shares much of its heritage, language, culture and customs with the once great colonial power.

The force behind emigration is mainly determined by economic imbalances,[24] which, in Portugal, was reflected in wage differentials. Post-World War II, Portuguese emigration was not only determined by economic problems, but also by political motivations. The salazar's dictatorship also forced many to flee the country on account of their political views. Until the 1960s the typical Portuguese emigrant was single, male, from a rural area and with little or no skills. Following this, a second wave of emigration consisted of families joining those who had emigrated earlier.[25] This second wave of emigration is important in determining how communities of immigrants, now with their families, became established not only in the UK, but also in the USA and France.

A growing community gathered around a central focus of interest, either related to work opportunities or affordable accommodation, fulfils a basic condition of demand in which ethnic products can be supplied. A community of expatriates would then generate a volume of food sufficient to meet the needs of such a specific population. Hence, with a guaranteed constant and consistent demand, groceries may be imported from the country of origin. In response to demand, grocery outlets will in turn be established to satisfy specific ethnic food needs. Such a phenomenon can be seen in many examples of substantial minority communities worldwide. More remarkable, and the focus of some attention, is the present case of Polish workers in the UK. As a result of a consistent demand for Polish groceries, an ever-expanding presence of businesses catering for Polish needs may now be seen in high streets across the country.

Until the 1990s the UK played a marginal role as a country of destination for the Portuguese. However, once they gained EU citizenship status, they began to settle more in the UK. Then, building on an already existing network of expatriates, the new settlers opened small businesses, such as cafes, bars, restaurants and delicatessens in areas where there was a greater concentration of Portuguese-speaking groups. Such a phenomenon helped establish communities, which have now become traditionally Portuguese.

Nonetheless, the motivations to emigrate have remained practically identical, as confirmed by research carried out by Beswick[26] who identified the contemporary migratory profile of Portuguese speakers, which, in the case of her research, also included migrants from Lusophone† Africa and Brazil. As before, the typical emigrant profile is that of someone in search of economic stability. Yet, in the 2000s a new group of young and relatively more affluent Portuguese emigrants may be perceived specifically targeting the UK. These emigrants arrive in the UK with the main motivation of learning English

---

† The author prefers to use the term "Lusophone" to "Portuguese-speaking".

while working in the hotel or catering businesses. Hence, the emigrants' motivations are satisfied both economically and in the acquiring of skills that will eventually be employed on returning home.

In the UK the Portuguese initially settled in London, notably in two main areas. The first of these consisted of neighbourhoods south of the river Thames along the Vauxhall–Stockwell axis. The other was located west of London along the length of Harrow Road that cuts through the districts of Bayswater, Notting Hill, Maida Vale and Kensal Green. Portuguese immigrants, despite choosing to live in the proximity of other fellow expatriates concentrated around the Lusitanian community, could not be described as being as cohesive as some other ethnic groups. Moreover, the Lusitanian community has also geographically spread to other regions in the UK such as the South East (Brighton), the Midlands (Birmingham), Merseyside and the East of England. East Anglia, in particular, has been one of the major settlement zones outside London.[27] Nevertheless, those Portuguese immigrants in the Thetford region differed from those who settled in London. In East Anglia the immigrants were still typically working in low-wage agribusiness-related activities, whereas in London the resident Portuguese tended to be more skilled.[28]

In general, in the quest to emigrate, Brazilians have been affected by similar economic and political conditions as the Portuguese. Since the mid-1970s, but with increased intensity in the 1980s, vast numbers of the young population, faced with limited future prospects of developing a career in Brazil, migrated to the USA, Japan and, in the later 1980s, to Europe. The 1980s represents a watershed for emigration. After a long military dictatorship Brazil endured successive economic crises, which resulted in hyperinflation, general unemployment and many failed government attempts to stabilize the economy. However, the European Union posed fewer obstacles than the USA in terms of entry requirements and ease of obtaining a work permit – the equivalent to the green card in the USA. Some Brazilians have taken advantage of their European ancestry, which entitles them to an EU passport. Nevertheless, among the Brazilians emigrants it is common to find those who have married EU nationals, students in their gap year, those studying English and others who had usually overstayed or possessed the wrong visa and were thereby designated as illegal.[29]

Locating the Market Segment

According to Gordon and Travers,[30] some 50 per cent of the UK's total immigration was absorbed by London. Recent data has revealed that in 2004 London saw the highest level of net immigration influx ever. This is confirmed by demographic statistics indicating that, from 6.7 million in the mid-1980s, the population in London rose to 7.5 million in 2006.[31] The 1991 census showed that some 9301 Brazilian citizens were living in the UK, with the figure jumping to 14 555 in 2001. In the 2001 census, Brazilian immigrants corresponded officially to 0.908 per cent of total migrants. However, it was difficult to obtain an exact figure for the Brazilian expatriate population in the UK. In a mapping exercise the International Organization for Migration (IOM)[32] carried out a study in which it identified the geographical dispersion of the Brazilian community in the UK (see Table 7.2).

Brazilian expatriates tended to concentrate in the London area,[33] but smaller groups may be also found in the Midlands, Merseyside, Dorset and Oxfordshire. Seventy-two per cent of Brazilians are spread all over London, and like the Portuguese (as mentioned above), do

Table 7.2   Estimated distribution of Brazilians in the UK (2005)

Location	Population
London	50 000
Midlands (Birmingham mainly)	20 000
Norfolk (Norwich and King's Lynn)	15 000
Manchester, Liverpool, Merseyside	10 000
Brighton and East Sussex	10 000

Source: IOM (2005).

not form a cohesively concentrated group. The general picture of the Brazilian expatriate community is that it is expanding. In 2000, officials in the Brazilian Embassy in London estimated that the number of Brazilians residing in the UK was around 80 000. Following this, the Brazilian consulate-general in London estimated that, in 2005, some 105 000 Brazilians were residing in the UK, increasing to 120 000 in 2007. Two things are evident: first, the number of Brazilians in the UK has steadily increased each year and, second, the authorities do not have accurate data on such a population group. The IOM estimates that more Brazilians will soon be arriving in the UK, particularly those with EU passports arriving from other ports of entry in the European Union.[34]

All those interviewed as part of this research felt that, in the period from 2005 to 2007, the influx of Brazilians into the UK has intensified, a feeling also shared by the Brazilian consulate-general whose officials are now attending more cases than ever. Those respondents who had been residing in the UK for over ten years confirmed the growing presence of a thriving Brazilian expatriate community, since Portuguese, with all its variations in accent, is now commonly heard in the London Underground, in buses, restaurants, bars and shops. Anecdotal evidence from members of the Brazilian Association in London have estimated that Brazilians could number 300 000 in the UK, with some claiming that there could be even more.

In the UK, the Brazilians initially settled in London in close proximity to the original Portuguese migrants. Abreu[35] has suggested an explanation for this. In her research she mentions that, in the transition from being full members of one community to being a new arrival in a host country, immigrants have to engage in new social interactions in order to successfully adapt. In the case of Brazilians, by opting to be close to the already established Portuguese community, social interactions were initially facilitated by language and shared heritage. Consequently, Brazilians are also notably concentrated in the west of London, around the postcode districts W2, W9 and NW10, typically following the Harrow Road axis around Bayswater, Notting Hill, Maida Vale, Kensal Green and Shepherds Bush. However, the area in south London along the Vauxhall–Stockwell axis, although predominantly more Portuguese, is less sought after by Brazilians. More recently, owing to the cheaper cost of accommodation, the east end of London has been attracting an increasing number of Brazilians. The area delineated by the districts of Finsbury Park, Stamford Hill, Clapton, Hackney and Dalston has seen a surge of Brazilians who have moved from their original north and south London boroughs.

Data was collected on the location of Portuguese and Brazilian establishments such as grocers, bars and restaurants to ascertain their spatial distribution. When it was organized by postcode district and fed into a Geographical Information System (GIS) computer package it was possible to obtain a map of the Luso-Brazilian outlets. The map in Figure 7.1 shows the plotting of all the postcode district data with the resulting spatial distribution. The distribution of establishments reveals correspondences to the population distribution proposed by the IOM[36] as a result of its original research into the key areas of dispersion of the Brazilian community in the UK. The most important concentration was in London, followed by the Midlands, Norfolk, the south-east coast, Manchester and Merseyside. However, what is striking in the map is the non-existence of a large number of Luso-Brazilian grocers, bars or restaurants outside the London area. Postcode district sizes reflect overall population density and, given that grocers, bars and restaurants would presumably cater for a concentration of an ethnic population, the map confirms that the Luso-Brazilian population is concentrated in the London area.

The Expansion of Portuguese Grocery and Brazilian Outlets

Until recently, grocery outlets owned by the Portuguese served the relatively small Brazilian expatriate community in the UK. These used to cater mainly for the aforementioned

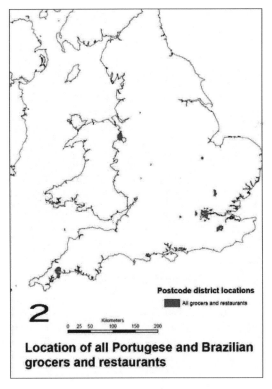

Figure 7.1   Geographical dispersion of Brazilian and Portuguese grocers and restaurants by postcode district data

Source: Proposed by the author.

Portuguese community which was keen on consuming, among other things, the famous dried cod (*bacalhau*) and charcuterie products. The Brazilians, on the other hand, were eager to buy dried grocery foodstuffs such as cassava flour, black beans, guava marmalade and *guaraná*.[‡] As preferences have changed, the relationship within the Portuguese–Brazilian network has shifted.

At present, the Brazilian expatriate community constitutes a strong niche market for processed foodstuffs that cater specifically for Brazilian needs. The owners of Brazilian grocery outlets are moving away from more traditional products such as olives, olive oil and *bacalhau* that also appeal to other Lusophone consumers to a different product mix. Brazilians look for processed products of established Brazilian brands. Brazilian grocery outlet owners trade in products which attract relatively low profit margins and are bulky in nature (e.g. flour, beans, carbonated drinks and fruit preserves). Moreover, evidence from interviews has suggested that this ethnic[§] market segment has little appeal for consumers other than Portuguese-speaking ones. Thus, products stocked and sold by Brazilian groceries could perhaps be considered too ethnically charged. This would mean that Brazilian-branded products are unlikely to attract the interest of a British consumer.

A growing expatriate population has led to a rise in demand; Brazilians have taken over market opportunities which the Portuguese might have failed to perceive or, as the respondents observed, did not react to early enough. This has also had an impact on the channels of distribution of ethnic Brazilian groceries. Brazilian-owned outlets are now importing Brazilian groceries, which were originally carried by Portuguese traders. Initially the reason for relying on the Portuguese marketing channel was to do with the size of a shipment. In order to make an import consignment viable, the minimum requirement would be one container load or the equivalent to 20 tonnes of cargo shipment from Brazil.

Portuguese traders had the advantage of being able to ship greater volumes because of their considerable trading links with Brazil and because ships destined for the UK would usually visit a Portuguese port. A greater demand for Brazilian groceries made it possible to set up specialist Brazilian wholesalers/importers that could contract shipments direct to the UK, bypassing the Portuguese traditional trade route. As a result of importing foodstuffs directly into the UK the supply chain has been rearranged, and despite this arrangement being still in its early stages, it is clear that the Portuguese are losing their previous dominance. In contrast, the Brazilian supply chain for traditional branded food staples is now being extended and is becoming more international.

The net effect of the restructuring of the ethnic food supply chain is a reduction in average prices. The reason for this is twofold. First, importing larger volumes directly to the UK has reduced transaction costs and the larger scale has allowed per-unit costs to be reduced. Second, establishments selling Brazilian groceries have displaced Portuguese outlets, thereby increasing their market segment. In addition, Brazilian entrepreneurs now provide a greater range of outlet formats – for example, mini-markets, butchers, bars, cafés, bistros, restaurants and fast-food restaurants – where typical branded foods can be consumed, either directly or indirectly. The Brazilian consumer has benefited from such restructuring as choice increases and the prices charged are less exorbitant than

---

‡   *Guaraná* is a fizzy drink, typically Brazilian, made from an Amazon berry.

§   Here, an ethnic food is considered as a food that is typical of a group of people due to language, cultural heritage, folklore and tradition, means of preparation and use of ingredients not commonly available in the host country.

before. Nevertheless, the interviews indicated that the UK might still not be sufficiently attractive to a Brazilian food manufacturer to justify targeting the market directly: a typical Brazilian branded staple food manufacturer might not yet perceive enough UK market opportunities. The UK market is currently supplied with Brazilian goods by importers/wholesalers that distribute the groceries to the numerous grocery outlets. This has important implications in the case of one particular beverage, *cachaça*, as is discussed later in this chapter.

Increase in the use of the Internet has led to virtual grocery stores selling Brazilian foods, giving access to those living outside London. The advent of the Internet, according to one respondent, the owner of São Paulo Imports, has meant that customers living outside London who used to regularly replenish their larders with Brazilian specialities by personally visiting specialist shops, no longer do so, preferring to continue purchasing groceries online. The São Paulo Imports online side of the business is thriving, and the company now supplies groceries by post to Brazilian consumers in the Midlands and Merseyside, for example. It could therefore be argued that clearly outside the London area there could be a significant market gap, which could be filled to cater for Brazilian expatriate needs, However, the costs associated with online shopping would justify, and more than compensate for, the effort and risk of setting up a business outside the London area. As we have seen in Figure 7.1 there is a lack of Brazilian and Portuguese groceries, bars or restaurants outside the London area, despite some evidence of expatriate densities.

The Consumer

Beswick[37] uses the notion of "being and becoming" with respect to ethnic groups. She explores how assimilation and anti-assimilation into a new society plays an important role in defining how ethnic groups relate to their new environment. In her paper Beswick mentions that "immersion within the host society does not always imply integration" and subsequently "does not challenge group and intra-group identification practices".[38] This is confirmed by Wang and Lo[39] and is in line with ethnicity indicators of consumption.[40] In this sense it is relevant to address issues on how personal or group assimilation, "being", "becoming" and "belonging" relates to, for example, food neophobia.[¶] Migrants' acceptance and rejection of new food offerings they are exposed to in a host country and how they regard and relate to their foods of origin play an important role in determining consumer behaviour.

Brazilians in the UK have a characteristically transient nature. Many stay for up to three to four years working in jobs where English-language skills are not essential, such as casual labouring, cleaning and washing up in restaurants and bars. As seen from Sook-Lee's investigation on second-generation Koreans,[42] language for social communication is important for establishing or preserving cultural and ethnicity identity. In groups of Brazilians where English is not frequently spoken, respondents often felt that they relied more heavily on their ethnic food staples. However, the UK Brazilian community is more complex than this. In addition to those economic migrants in menial jobs, it also

---

¶   According to Cooke et al.,[41] food neophobia is defined as avoidance of, and reluctance to taste, unfamiliar foods. It might be assumed that such a behaviour pattern would have negative dietary consequences in terms of the variety of foods consumed.

encompasses teenagers on their gap year, university students, students learning English while working, diplomats, those who have married British citizens, representatives of companies and bankers, as well as officials of international organizations. Furthermore, social class, disposable income and level of education would also impose differences in consumer behaviour for ethnic foods. Consequently, the community that constitutes a market segment is, in essence, not homogeneous. In respect of the shared ethnicity traits with the Portuguese, Brazilian food preferences, despite some overlap, should also be considered as more distinct from the Lusitanian.

The transience of the Brazilian community means that it is very slow to adopt new food groups and assimilate a new culture's food habits. Young and temporary residents also face the effects of psychological disruption[43] because of their inability to easily access familiar foodstuffs and preparations. In such an alien environment, they quite frequently express feelings of homesickness in terms of the urge to consume specific foods. Following Mendoza's acculturation patterns[44] with reference to the Brazilian expatriate community there are four major foods that were identified by interviewees as being dominant: black bean stew (*feijoada*), a cocktail made of sugarcane spirit (*caipirinha*), *pão de queijo*,** and *churrasco*.†† These are the four major food and drink items that make Brazilians long for their typical food and therefore seek and consume imported products from Brazilian-owned outlets.

The interviews revealed that the consumption of Brazilian foodstuffs in the UK is clearly a function of being isolated from the cultural and nationality references of origin. Quite often, elements of nationalism and patriotism are reflected in the proposition that Brazilian food tastes better or is of higher quality. Such an affirmation is important when Brazilians reject foods from the host country. This is in line with studies undertaken in Belgium.[45] Anecdotal evidence reveals that sometimes Brazilians more frequently consume typical Brazilian foods in the UK than in Brazil itself. This would be the case with, for example, black bean stew, *feijoada*, which is prepared with different pork cuts and sausages. *Feijoada*, a characteristic Brazilian dish, is very heavy to digest. Whereas in Brazil *feijoada completa*‡‡ is consumed on Saturdays with much less frequency than before, Brazilian expatriates in the UK eat it regularly, accompanied by some *caipirinha*. Owners of grocery outlets have recognized this market demand and now sell *feijoada* kits consisting of all the ingredients required for its preparation and cooking. Relatives, especially mothers visiting their children, buy sufficient quantities of the ingredients and prepare *feijoada* to be frozen for consumption in the months to come after they have returned home.

As referred to previously, Hui et al.[46] mention that some aspects of the host country's mainstream culture are generally expected to be adopted less rapidly by a minority of migrants. In view of this, acculturative pressures on a transient population are expected to be less important with respect to the Brazilian adoption of the host's foods. The fact that the Brazilians relate more to their own culture's foods, confirms other studies[47] where it

---

**   The direct translation of *pão de queijo* is "cheese bread"; however, they consist of small round buns made of extra-fine cassava starch (*polvilho*) and *queijo de minas*.

††   *Churrasco* is the Portuguese word for barbequed beef, but in this case it refers to a *rodízi*- style barbeque where different meats and cuts of meat are offered to the consumer for a set price.

‡‡   *Feijoada completa* refers to a dish of black beans with many pork cuts and charcuterie products accompanied by white boiled rice, Portuguese cabbage, oranges, cassava flour (*farofa*), pepper sauce, a drink that could be either *caipirinha* or coconut cocktail, followed by either beer or red wine.

is stated that the presence of both Brazilian and Portuguese outlets has meant that ethnic foods have also ended up contributing to the diversity of the host country's cuisine.

Following Mendoza's Acculturation Patterns[48] (as seen in Table 7.1), cultural resistance amongst the Brazilians to adopting British food could be said to be strong. Brazilian expatriates, due to their short period of stay, could then be characterized in terms of the Acculturation Patterns as being culturally resistant. With an increasing number of years' permanence residence in the host country Brazilians would demonstrate some incorporation (adoption) of the host country's food habits. When asked about the extent to which Brazilians adopted British foods, the respondents promptly used as an example the adoption of the potato as a food staple. As rice is the staple starchy food in Brazil, the frequent consumption of potato as a staple food is considered "unappealing", "boring" and "unimaginative". Many Brazilians find the various ways of cooking potatoes – that is, boiled, mashed or roasted – unappealing. The only exception to this are chips which, in Brazil, are generally prepared in much thinner cuts. Thick potato chips are a common source of complaints such as "how unskilled the British can be in making chips". Hence, those Brazilians who had succumbed to the British habit of eating potatoes were regarded by the members of the community as "going native": a symbol of acculturation. Therefore, in terms of Hui et al.'s the typology,[49] Brazilian immigrants are expressing their ethnicity and cultural traits through the limited consumption of foods, thus expressing resistance from the host country. The levels of adoption or resistance are, in turn, also reflected in the pattern of acculturation to UK society.

Cachaça: A Symbol of Brazilian Ethnicity

Cachaça is a spirit resembling rum but, whereas rum is made from the fermentation of molasses (treacle syrup) made from sugarcane juice, which is distilled and then aged in oak barrels, *cachaça* originated as a result of the Portuguese colonial exploitation of sugarcane plantation in Brazil in the mid-1500s and was created as a byproduct of sugar production. The beverage is a product of the fermentation and distillation of sugarcane juice whose final alcohol content varies between 38 and 48 per cent in volume. In Brazil some 1.3 billion litres of *cachaça* are produced annually,[50] of which 1.9 per cent is exported.[51] It is expected that by 2010 some 50 million litres will be exported to the EU (Germany, Portugal and the UK), and the USA.

Cachaça is consumed pure or in a lime, sugar and ice cocktail mixture known as *caipirinha*. Here, I make a distinction between *caipirinha*, which follows a set preparation formula, and other *cachaça* with lime preparations. As it is such a popular drink in Brazil, various organizations have made attempts over the years to introduce it into the UK market. In the 1990s *cachaça* could be found in supermarkets such as Tesco. During the 2002 football World Cup, backed up by a promotional campaign, a *caipirinha* type of Alcopop was available in off-licences and also in some supermarkets. However, without a continuous promotional effort, the product has failed to be accepted by the general British public. More recently, an article in *The Guardian*[52] highlighted how one *cachaça* brand company, Sagatiba, has endeavoured to make *cachaça* as famous as tequila in bars and pubs in London. For those who have come across the *caipirinha* cocktail, and, *cachaça*'s connoisseurs, the beverage can only be found in exclusive bars, specialist food retailers such as Waitrose, restaurants and off-licences.

Amongst the many other high-alcohol-content beverages such as vodka, tequila, rum, moutai, bourbon, gin and whisky, all of which can be drunk in a pure form, *cachaça* is more accepted as cocktail: *caipirinha*. In Brazil, however, only people on very low incomes regularly drink pure *cachaça*. Such behaviour is determined not only by lack of income; high-income groups avoid it as a matter of maintaining social status, rather than because of its taste or palatability. The middle and upper classes would only consider drinking *cachaça* in its pure state provided it was of extremely good quality and provenance. Price is a key determinant of product acceptance by the wealthier classes in Brazil, and one litre of a popular brand of *cachaça* retailing at between £0.87 and £1.20 is reasonably affordable. Moreover, in Brazil, beer is the preferred drink in bars and whisky is *de rigueur* at private parties, with *caipirinha* being less in demand. *Caipirinha* is well accepted as an aperitif at barbecues or while eating *feijoada completa*.

Nonetheless, interview respondents believed that the Brazilian diaspora, who would not usually drink *cachaça* or *caipirinha* in Brazil, are eager to do so in the UK. This could be explained by the expatriate's eagerness to express ethnicity through labelling themselves as being proud of their cultural origin, as identified by the Hui et al.'s typology.[53] Preparing a *caipirinha* cocktail would impress new friends and would affirm ethnicity. Respondents also mentioned that the Brazilians' expressions of self-labelling, through the consumption of ethnic products, have been the driving force for increased sales of the beverage.

Hence, it could be argued that *cachaça* could be a too ethnically-specific product, suited only to the Brazilian taste. The consumption of *cachaça* represents more than simply consuming an alcoholic drink as it encompasses ethnicity, origin, culture, as well as a sense of identity and nationality.

In order to gain initial insights about whether the average British person would adopt *cachaça*, a group of 15 British nationals were asked to taste the beverage, first in its pure state and then prepared as a *caipirinha* cocktail. Prior to the tasting, the respondents were asked to express their willingness to try different foods in a questionnaire using a Food Neophobia Scale (FNS)[54] which measures the extent to which a person is reluctant to eat or avoid new foods. The reason for applying the FNS scale to the group was to ascertain the sample's validity – to find out if it included anyone who was either extremely reluctant or too accepting in regard to the product, which could bias the results.

The results from the tasting session revealed a positive acceptance of the *caipirinha* cocktail. However, in its pure form, *cachaça* is considered too strong. The likely barriers to, and challenges for, the adoption of such a product reside in the fact that mixing such a cocktail requires some preparation. When preparing *caipirinha* is compared to, for example, mixing a gin and tonic, some female respondents expressed their opinion that chopping limes, crushing ice and adding sugar in preparing the cocktail could mess up a kitchen surface. Following an exact recipe was also considered a difficulty whereas preparing a gin and tonic was considered easy. No respondent stated that they would certainly purchase the beverage should they see it on a supermarket shelf. Nevertheless, when next in a bar they would look at the menu and would be prepared to order *caipirinha*.

Some UK bars already sell *cachaça,* at least in its cocktail preparation. Bar Guanabara, which specializes in Brazilian drinks, music and food in London's West End, claims to sell more *caipirinhas* than any bar in Brazil itself. In Bar Guanabara typical ethnic self-labelling behaviour can be observed when homesick Brazilian customers are induced to drink *cachaça* more by impulse than anything else when "*cachaça* girls" – waitresses wearing a belt with two bottles of *cachaça* – circulate amongst the customers, selling shots.

Despite the drink's acceptance, *cachaça* sales in the UK are still limited to a niche market segment. This segment could be characterized as being representative of Brazilian expatriates, their friends, either of British or other nationality, partners who have been exposed to the cocktail or the beverage, those who have already visited Brazil or are planning to do so, and a small number of British nationals looking for novelty in the West End scene.

Conclusions

This chapter, far from exhausting the theme, has provided an insight into a marketing topic that is multifaceted and little explored. As the segment grows, other aspects of the Brazilian ethnic food and drink market ought to be studied. Examples of these include relationships in the supply chain, the diversification and specialization of the internationalization of such a supply chain and aspects of governance and trust, amongst others. In respect of the ethnic migrant consumer behaviour, more synergy with experts from the field of social sciences could lead to a rich form of collaboration towards understanding not only the Brazilian case, but also many other emerging niche markets in the UK, such as those from Eastern Europe.

Understanding ethnicity typology would help managers in the food and drink industry better target and explore the deeper psychological determinants of buying behaviour. At present, ethnicity typology is rarely used in food marketing studies, but is an approach that would be of great interest in the future for researchers, marketers and decision-makers in the sector. In the case of the migrant who is physically, culturally and psychologically removed from familiar surroundings, effective marketing communication strategies should be targeting elements of being, belonging and becoming. Large food retailers are generally slow to capture these trends. Asian foods are now widely available in the major food retail chains. In areas of strong Polish presence, typical foodstuffs have also been made available. Asian and Polish food offerings in retail outlets demonstrate characteristic cultural transmutation[55] when tastes are adapted to cater for a British palate as part of the acculturation of the ethnic groups. If growth margins are found in niche segments, studies on food-buying behaviour and ethnicity typology would provide an opportunity that is currently eluding managers.

As the title of this book proposes, as ethnic diversity expands in the UK, traditional core British food offerings undergo a process of fragmentation and fusion with the new ethnic cuisines and are incorporated into society. Likewise, evidence shows that the traditional Portuguese control of the supply of ethnic food products for the Lusophone community is slowly fragmenting in the light of a growing presence of Brazilian expatriates who are becoming established and providing more alternatives and more choice. However, the increased presence of Brazilian restaurants and bars in London also adds to the dissemination[56] of the Brazilian culture.

Brazilian *cachaça*-producing companies, either individually or in consortium, have to make explicit choices with regard to seriously entering the European market. In the case of *cachaça*, it could be argued that, without serious investment in marketing communication campaigns, the penetration of such a beverage will remain restricted to its adoption by a niche market. *Cachaça* would not meet with the same success that tequila had in the 1990s as it could be considered an ethnically charged product. Despite the fact that some 1.3 billion litres of the beverage are produced annually of which 98.1 per cent is consumed domestically, there may not be enough justification for Brazilian *cachaça*-producing companies to attempt to break into the British market. Nevertheless, the total sales revenue is low when compared to the price that could be achieved overseas. Sales of *cachaça* will be restricted to specialist restaurants, ethnic bars and some off-licences. If nothing changes, consumption will be restricted to Brazilians in diaspora and those few seeking to evoke either past or present exotic tropical experiences. However, the competition amongst other more established beverages, such as vodka, tequila and rum, is, and will continue to be, fierce.

References

1. Hui, M.K., Laroche, M. and Kim, C. (1998), "A typology of consumption based on ethnic origin and media usage", *The European Journal of Marketing*, Vol. 32, Nos 9–10, pp. 868–883.
2. Ibid.
3. Jamal, A. (1998), "Food consumption among ethnic minorities: the case of British-Pakistanis in Bradford, UK", *British Food Journal*, Vol. 100, No. 5, pp. 221–227.
4. Verbeke, W. and López, G.P. (2005), "Ethnic food attitudes and behaviour among Belgians and Hispanics living in Belgium", *British Food Journal*, Vol. 107, No. 11, pp. 823–840.
5. Wilson, T.M. (2006), "Food, drink and identity in Europe: consumption and the construction of local national and cosmopolitan culture", *European Studies*, Vol. 22, pp. 11–19.
6. Hui et al., "A typology of consumption", *op. cit.*
7. Sook-Lee, J. (2002), *The Korean Language in America: The Role of Cultural Identity in Heritage Language Learning*, Rutgers University, http://www.multilingual-matters.net/lcc/015/0117/lcc0150117.pdf (accessed: 22 October 2007).
8. Hui et al., "A typology of consumption", *op, cit.*
9. Wang, L. and Lo, L. (2007), "Immigrant grocery-shopping behaviour: ethnic identity versus accessibility", *Environment and Planning*, Vol. 39, No. 3, pp. 689–699.
10. Glock, C. and Nicosia, F.M. (1964), "Use of sociology in studying consumption behaviour", cited in Hui, et al., "A typology of consumption", *op. cit.*
11. Andreasen, A.R. (1990), "Cultural interpenetration: a critical consumer research issue for the 1990s", *Advances in Consumer Research*, Vol. 17, Association for Consumer Research, Provo, pp. 847–849.
12. Hamid, F. and Sarwar, T. (2004), *Global Nutrition: A Multicultural Pack* cited in European Food Information Resources (EUROFIR) (2007), *Ethnic Foods*, http://www.eurofir.net/public.asp?id=4291 (accessed 14 December 2007); European Food Information Resources, *Ethnic Foods* (accessed: 14 December 2007).
13. Greeley, A.M. (1971), "Why can't they be like us?" cited in Hui et al., "A typology of consumption", *op. cit.*
14. Hirschman, E.C. (1981), "American Jewish ethnicity: its relationship to some selected aspects of consumer behaviour", *Journal of Marketing*, Vol. 45, No. 3, Summer, pp. 102–110.
15. Sook-Lee, *The Korean Language in America*, *op. cit.*
16. Hirschman, "American Jewish ethnicity", *op. cit.*
17. Hui et al., "A typology of consumption", *op. cit.*, p. 871.
18. Hui et al., "A typology of food consumption", *op. cit.*
19. Ibid.

20. Jamal, "Food consumption among ethnic minorities", *op. cit.*

21. Peñaloza, L. (1994), "Atravesando fronteras/border crossings: a critical ethnographic exploration of the consumer acculturation of Mexican immigrants", *Journal of Consumer Research*, Vol. 21, pp. 32–54.

22. Hui et al., "A typology of food consumption", *op. cit.*

23. McCracken, A., Pretty, W. and Conway, G.R. (1988), *An Introduction to Rapid Rural Appraisal For Agricultural Development*, International Institute For Environment and Development, London.

24. Baganha, M.I.B. (2003), "From Closed Doors to Open Doors", *e-Journal of Portuguese History*, Summer Vol. 1, No. 1 available at: http://www.brown.edu/Departments/Portuguese_Brazilian_Studies/ejph/.

25. Ibid.

26. Beswick, J. (2005), "The Portuguese diaspora in Jersey" in B. Preisler, A. Fabricius, H. Haberland, S. Kjaerbeck aand K. Risager (eds), *The Consequences of Mobility: Linguistic and Socio-cultural Contact Zones*, Department of Language and Culture, Roskilde University, Roskilde, Denmark.

27. Corkill, D. and Almeida, J.C. (2007), "The 3Ps: Portuguese migrant labour in East Anglia", *Conference Proceedings of the Portuguese-speaking Diaspora in the UK*, June, Manchester Metropolitan University, Manchester.

28. Ibid.

29. International Organization for Migration (IOM) (2005), *Mapping Exercise: Brazil*, December, IOM, London, available at: http://www.iomlondon.org/publications.htm; Téchio, K. (2007), "I am not dog, no: experiências de vida e formas de integraçao de imigrantes brasileiros indocumentados em Manchester", *Conference Proceedings of the Portuguese-speaking Diaspora in the UK,*June, Manchester Metropolitan University, Manchester.

30. Gordon, I. and Travers, T. (2006), *Race, Immigration and Community Relations in Contemporary London*, April, London School of Economics, London, pp. 1–10.

31. Ibid.

32. IOM, *Mapping Exercise: Brazil, op. cit.*

33. Ibid.

34. Ibid.

35. Abreu, G. (2007), "Self and other imposed withdrawing in social interactions at school: experiences of Portuguese students in British schools", *Conference Proceedings of the Portuguese-speaking Diaspora in the UK*, June, Manchester Metropolitan University, Manchester.

36. IOM, *Mapping Exercise: Brazil, op. cit.*

37. Beswick, "The Portuguese diaspora in Jersey", *op. cit.*

38. Ibid., p. 100.

39. Wang and Lo, "Immigrant grocery-shopping behaviour", *op. cit.*

40. Hui et al., "A typology of food consumption", *op. cit.*

41. Cooke, L., Carnell, S. and Wardle, J. (2006), "Food neophobia and mealtime food consumption in 4–5 year old children", *International Journal of Behavioural Nutrition and Physical Activity*, Vol. 3, No. 14. Available online.

42. Sook-Lee, *The Korean Language in America, op. cit.*

43. Hui et al., "A typology of food consumption", *op. cit.*

44. Ibid.

45. Verbeke and López, "Ethnic food attitudes", *op. cit.*

46. Hui et al., "A typology of food consumption", *op. cit.*

47. Hamid and Sarwar, *Global Nutrition*, *op. cit.*; European Food Information Resources, *Ethnic Foods*, *op. cit.*
48. Hui et al., "A typology of food consumption", *op. cit.*
49. Ibid.
50. Brazilian Drinks Association ABRABE (2007), *A cachaça*, http://www.abrabe.org.br. (accessed 13 May 2007).
51. Instituto Brasiliero da Cachaça (IBRAC) (2007), *Dados estatísticos*,http://www.ibrac.net. (accessed 28 April 2007).
52. *The Guardian* (2007), "Exporting the spirit of Brazil: make mine a caipirinha", 19 February, http://www.guardian.co.uk/business/2007/feb/19/brazil (accessed: 23 March 2007).
53. Hui et al., "A typology of consumption, *op. cit.*
54. Pliner, P. and Hobden, K. (1992), "Development of a scale to measure the trait food neophobia", *Appetite*, Vol. 19, pp. 105–120.
55. Hui et al., "A typology of consumption", *op. cit.*
56. Wilson, T.M. (2006), "Food, drink and identity in Europe: consumption and the construction of local, national and cosmopolitan culture", *European Studies*, Vol. 22, pp. 11–29.

Appendix

Table 7.3   *Cachaça* **tasting focus group**

Gender		Occupation	
Females	8	Lecturing	5
Males	7	Admin/clerical	4
		Support (kitchen/housekeeping/maintenance)	3
Age		Student	3
18 -29	4		
30 – 39	5		
40 – 49	3	**Shopping habits**	
50 – 59	3	I shop at a supermarket everyday	2
60 +	0	I shop at a supermarket 3 times a week	3
		I shop at a supermarket twice a week	4
Educational level		I shop at a supermarket once a week	3
CGSE	4	I shop at a supermarket 3 times a month	1
A level	1	I shop at a supermarket once a month	2
Undergraduate	3	I never shop at a supermarket	0
Degree	3	I do all my shopping online	0
Postgraduate	4		

Household situation	
Live alone	5
Live with both parents	1
Live with partner/spouse	4
Live with a friend	2
Live in hall of residence	0
Live with my children (single parent)	3

8

"Beef Lovers": A Cross-cultural Study of Beef Consumption

MARCIA DUTRA DE BARCELLOS,* EUGENIO AVILA PEDROZO† AND IVO A. VAN DER LANS‡

Keywords

consumers, beef consumption, cross-cultural research, Brazil, Australia, the Netherlands.

Abstract

In this chapter we will explore beef consumption behaviour from a cross-cultural perspective. Data collected in Brazil, Australia and the Netherlands supports the main objectives of identifying consumers' anticipated emotions, degree of involvement, attitudes and main concerns towards beef consumption.

Attitudes, Involvement and Emotions towards Beef: What do Brazilian, Australian and Dutch Consumers Have in Common?

Identifying how consumers view, and behave during, their consumption experiences provides a better understanding of their attitudes and preferences, especially if they live in various countries. This information in turn can be used to customize new marketing initiatives that better fulfil consumer expectations. However, until recently, food was regarded as a commodity, and research studies on food consumers' behavioural intentions were scarce. The worldwide expansion of markets and new consumption patterns

---

*   Dr Marcia Dutra de Barcellos, Faculty of Economics, Business Administration and Accounting (FACE), Pontifical Catholic University of Rio Grande do Sul (PUCRS). Av. Ipiranga 6681, Prédio 50, room 1101. Porto Alegre, RS, Brazil, ZIP code 90619-900. E-mail: marcia.barcellos@pucrs.br. Telephone: + 55 51 3320 3524.

†   Professor Eugenio Avila Pedrozo, Centre for Study and Research in Agribusiness (CEPAN), Federal University of Rio Grande do Sul (UFRGS). Av. Washington Luis 855, Room 412. Porto Alegre, RS, Brazil, ZIP code 90010-460. E-mail: eapedrozo@ea.ufrgs.

‡   Dr Ivo A. van der Lans, Marketing and Consumer Behaviour Group, Wageningen University, Hollandseweg 1, 6706 KN Wageningen, The Netherlands. E-mail: ivo.vanderlans@wur.nl. Telephone: + 31 317 484 353.

creates an even greater need to understand consumer behaviour and its implications for developing marketing strategies.

The new world dynamics have strongly affected agrifood chains and their members. Cultural interchanges, better access to transportation and communication, increases in income levels, new household situations (e.g. more women in the labour force, single households, ageing populations) and environmental and animal welfare issues have continuously influenced agrifood consumers.

The new global reality also indicates that market-oriented firms have greater chances of success in competitive environments.[1] In this regard, understanding consumers and fulfilling their needs and desires becomes a strategic issue, because more satisfied consumers will spend more time and financial resources with firms that better support them. More satisfied consumers also tend to engage in long-term and more committed relationships with firms, prompting brand loyalty and fidelity.[2] Hence, firms and productive chains that can understand and respond to consumers' wishes in a sustainable way add value to their products and ensure customer satisfaction.

Consumer behaviour is influenced not only by their own psychological, personal, social and cultural characteristics, but also by environmental stimuli to which they are constantly exposed. They are continuously bombarded with products, services and ideas that may induce them to purchase and consume. In engaging in such behaviours, consumers may experience satisfaction or frustration in relation to their expectations, which increases the complexity of the process. Therefore, understanding this process remains one of the great challenges that agrifood managers face as they attempt to increase the competitiveness of their product ranges.

People and food are inextricably connected through tradition, marketing, culture, education, learning, economy, religion, society and affect – and this has been the case since the prehistoric hunter-gatherer period to the modern era of *cuisine gourmet*. In this regard, involvement represents a key issue, because it entails a fundamental construct that clarifies how consumers become attached to the products and food they consume.

This means that of the various ways in which consumers may be attached to products, their degree of involvement and their emotional expectation about the consumption experience may be critical. Their degree of involvement enables consumers to increase their perceptions about the differences in attributes among products, increase their sense of its importance and demonstrate more commitment in their brand choices. Involvement also prompts more detailed searches for information and more time dedicated to choosing products.[3] Finally, the degree of involvement with food varies from person to person,[4] indicating that a measurable continuum describes degrees of involvement.

Yet few academic studies analyse the role of involvement with food products,[5] and no cross-cultural studies assess a single product in different countries or cultures. Contemporary marketing studies relating emotions to food consumption also remain scarce.[6] Most studies in this area focus on consumption behaviour pertaining to luxury goods, such as automobiles, shoes or jewellry.[7] However, some anthropological and sociological studies discuss existing relationships between food, (mostly negative) emotions, attitudes and behaviour.[8]

From a marketing perspective, anticipated emotions might provide an important framework, because they may regulate the performance of a determinant behaviour. In other words, the expected consequences (positive or negative outcomes) may influence consumers to take some action or not.[9] In turn, attitude relates directly related to affect. According to Ajzen, an attitude is "a disposition to respond favourably or unfavourably to an object, person, institution or event".[10] Therefore, attitudes have an evaluative nature, but because they cannot be observed directly, they must be inferred from measurable responses that reflect consumers' positive or negative evaluations of a selected object. Rosenberg and Hovland also find that attitude is a multidimensional construct that consists of cognition (beliefs), affect (evaluations and feelings), and conation (intentions and actions).[11] If attitudes, emotions and behaviours are interconnected, an understanding of this relationship is fundamental for marketers, especially in the context of a broader and more systemic marketing orientation.

Our goal is to assess the degree of involvement, identify the anticipated emotions experienced during special occasions when beef is consumed, and determine attitudes towards the product and other behavioural issues (e.g. concerns) in an attempt to contribute to not only consumer behaviour theory, but also the strategic marketing management of the beef production chain.

We present descriptive data for each set of constructs we study. In a future study we will describe the structural equation modelling analysis we conducted to test the proposed theoretical relations proposed, but, for this chapter, we focus on investigating the link between attitudes and beef consumption by inserting emotions, involvement and culture into our exploratory analysis – that is, we investigate whether consumers from different cultures feel the same way about a product. Food marketers need to take into account consumers' feelings and cultural backgrounds, because such knowledge has great practical relevance for the agribusiness food chain.

The relevant results of this study reveal that consumer behaviour researchers continue to ignore the importance of emotions for experiences of consuming products traditionally considered as entailing low involvement – such as beef – as well as the influence of culture. Nevertheless, the multidisciplinary character of consumer behaviour research and the systemic and interdisciplinary focus inherent in agribusiness makes this theme undeniably significant. As a theoretical contribution, we also offer some modifications of the theory of planned behaviour[12] that include constructs which seem very relevant to the understanding of beef consumption.

In addition, we consider the effective use of marketing tools and knowledge about consumers as a means of increasing the competitiveness of global food chains and improving communication and market-driven strategies. Therefore, we selected three countries for this study – Brazil, Australia and the Netherlands – representing two of the main beef exporters in the world (Brazil and Australia) and one of the main beef importers in Europe (the Netherlands). Given the economic and social importance of the beef trade in these countries, it might be thought that their populations would be equally involved with the product. Yet, the average consumption of beef is much higher in Brazil and Australia (36.4 and 37 kg per person per year respectively) than in the Netherlands (17.9 kg), which prompts our investigation of possible reasons for such differences.

In the following sections we present an overview of the beef chain in a multicultural context, the research method used, the main findings and a discussion of the results, and, finally, the conclusions drawn.

The Importance of Beef in the Ethnically Diverse Agrifood Context

Among the significant agrifood products in the world market, beef may be one of the most important. For strong exporters like Brazil and Australia and importers like the Netherlands, the study of beef holds a particular interest. Since 2003 Brazil has ranked as the world's leading beef exporter, surpassing the United States and Australia,[13] two traditionally strong beef suppliers to the world market. Australia remains the second-ranking beef exporter in volume, but it earns first place in value per ton exported, largely because it has commercialized an added-value product that offers high quality and safety.

Medium-term forecasts for the global beef market suggest increases in production, consumption and trade. An increase in consumption appears likely because of the favourable macro-economic environment, sustained by increasing income, particularly in emerging countries in Asia and Latin America, as well as changing dietetic patterns in many regions, especially Asia.[14]

Meat has long been an important element in the European, Brazilian and Australian diet, providing a high-quality source of protein. Data published by the European Commission[14] indicates that beef and veal consumption in the European Union has rapidly recovered since the "mad cow disease" crisis, and, for the first time in the past decade, consumption has now outpaced production. Production is also expected to decrease in coming years in response to structural reductions of bovine herds and reforms in the EU Common Agricultural Policy (CAP) (namely, reductions in subsidies). Thus, steady demand and a tight domestic supply should result in an increasing level of imports – notably, high-quality beef cuts from South America and other European suppliers (such as Ireland and Eastern European countries, for instance).

According to the US Department of Agriculture,[15] on average, a European consumes 17.9 kg of beef per year, and Brazilians and Australians consume 36–37 kg per year. Despite the huge geographic distance and different population origins, consumers from these different cultures (nationalities) seem to engage in similar beef consumption patterns. Various political, socio-economic and environmental factors affect each country's population, which might have more or less influence on their similarity. In this sense, nationality as the dominant paradigm provides a unit of analysis, because national groups tend to be relatively homogeneous.[16] However, we also acknowledge that an *a priori* classification of the consumers, whether by nationality or social or ethnic group, can provide only partial insights into behaviour. For this reason, we identify nationality as a unit of analysis, but also recognize that we must understand, in a broad sense, the consumption context and food habits of consumers. According to Braga, "food habits are part of a cultural system, full of symbols, meanings and classifications, in a way that no food is free from the cultural associations that a given society attributes to them".[17]

Overall, Australians' food habits are quite similar to those of Brazilians in terms of the volume of beef consumed and frequency, as well as in their explicit preference for beef over other meat options. Beef meals, such as barbeques, feature in both food cultures and bear a close relationship to the importance of the beef industry in both countries.[18] Brazil has the world's largest commercial beef herd (200 million head), and its production system is a very specialized activity based on pasture, which makes it extremely cost-efficient. The national herd contains approximately 80 per cent *Bos indicus* (zebu), but herds in the southern region also include British and Continental breeds (e.g. Angus, Hereford, Limousin). In general, consumers prefer beef cuts, such as steaks for roasting or cooking.

The beef cattle industry remains one of Australia's major agricultural industries. It is extremely diverse, ranging from intensively managed smallholdings in south-east Australia, where more fertile soils and plentiful water supplies allow high stocking rates, to extensive, large-scale, unfenced cattle stations where cattle rarely see a human being.[19] Australia maintains only 2.5 per cent of the world's cattle population (20 million head) and suffers environmental limitations (e.g. drought), but is still the world's second largest beef exporter. Approximately 35 per cent of its production is based on the feedlot system. Australian beef is renowned for its safety and high quality.

The Dutch beef production system differs significantly from those of Brazil and Australia. According to the Product Boards for Livestock, Meat and Eggs,[20] beef production is based on the dairy herd, kept indoors for most of the year. The country's 80 000 specialized beef cattle account for less than 1 per cent of the total EU beef herd. This small beef herd grazes in nature reserves,[21] for the purpose of conservation management organized between farmers and nature conservation bodies. According to producers, retailers and consumers, beef from nature reserves constitutes a high-quality product on account of its superior taste and structure resulting from the production method – slow growth rates, type of vegetation consumed, characteristics of the cattle (sex and breed), and meat processing (ageing). Also important to consumers are its extrinsic quality aspects, such as the emotional value of "nature", known origins and reliable production processes, contact with the producer, price, ease of stocking beef in the freezer and so forth.

Approximately 200 000 young bulls are fattened annually on regular beef farms on a diet of maize silage plus concentrate and co-products from the feedstuff industry. Artificial insemination is used to help poorly productive dairy cows produce beef crosses (e.g. Piemontese, Belgian Blue, Blonde d'Aquitaine). Dutch consumers tend to prefer minced beef, probably due to its convenience and low price.

Finally, beef constitutes an interesting topic for study, because of the diversity in its production systems and the influence of so many factors – such as price, brand, country of origin, intrinsic characteristics – on consumption behaviour, which in turn affects the whole food chain.

Methodology

To gain preliminary insights into consumers' behaviour, we collected exploratory data through in-depth interviews with beef chain members (consumers, retailers, abattoirs and producers) in Brazil, Australia and the Netherlands. In addition, we conducted a quantitative, cross-cultural consumer survey during 2005–2006 in Brazil (Porto Alegre and São Paulo), Australia (Sydney) and the Netherlands (Amersfoort). The data pertain to a larger research project that uses structural equation modelling to test the proposed concepts (attitudes, anticipated emotions, involvement, consumption behaviour) and contribute to the theory of planned behaviour. This chapter offers the main descriptive findings pertaining to each concept and thus brings to light the field of cross-cultural research and opportunities related to ethnic diversity.

The data collection process used a quota sampling procedure, with age and gender as representative control variables. Most respondents were interviewed face-to-face, but in the Netherlands data were collected by means of a self-administered postal questionnaire. This process provided a total of 816 valid questionnaires (Porto Alegre = 202, São Paulo = 400, Australia = 143, Netherlands = 71). Despite the low response rate (12.5 per cent) in the Netherlands, due to the data collection procedure (postal) and the complexity of the questionnaire, the quality of the obtained data and scale validation justify their inclusion in the data analysis.

The initial questionnaire, developed in Portuguese, was translated into English and Dutch using back-translations procedures and pre-tests to confirm its equivalence. The questionnaire measured a wide variety of constructs, as discussed below.

INVOLVEMENT

To assess the degree of involvement, the new involvement profile (NIP) scale was selected, as proposed by Jain and Srinivasan.[22] We used 15 observable variables from the NIP scale, adapted to beef consumption, plus another variable derived from the exploratory stage of this research – namely, "My choice of beef can be used by others to judge my origin". The five-point semantic differential scale is multidimensional and consists of five factors: *relevance, pleasure, symbolic value, risk importance* and *risk probability*. Table 8.1 presents the results related to these factors.

ANTICIPATED EMOTIONS

To measure anticipated emotions, we used the consumption emotion set (CES).[23] The CES consists of a set of descriptors that represent the range of emotions that consumers most frequently experience in consumption situations. Emotions may be either positive or negative. Furthermore, on the basis of interviews with experts, we considered only those emotions that the experts considered relevant for beef consumption. Consumers thus assessed the frequency at which they expected to feel each emotion during a special beef consumption situation, ranging from never (1) to always (5). Table 8.2 presents the results pertaining to positive anticipated emotions; Table 8.3 offers those related to negative anticipated emotions.

ATTITUDE

The measure of attitude toward beef uses the evaluative semantic differential scale proposed by Ajzen,[24] who cites it as the most frequently employed multi-item scale to measure attitude directly. Using a set of five-point, bipolar adjective scales, we uncovered the evaluative reactions (that is, attitudes) that capture the most important dimension of an object's connotative meaning. Consequently, we obtained a measure of attitude by asking respondents to rate each construct on a set of bipolar evaluative adjective scales, such as good–bad or harmful–beneficial. Specifically, respondents compared the variables *safety, taste, price, quality* and *tenderness* on a bipolar evaluative scale ranging from poor to excellent.[25] We present the results in Table 8.4.

CONCERNS

People are increasingly concerned about their diet and health, especially in response to worldwide discussions about obesity, salt, sugar and cholesterol levels. In addition, recent food scares,[26] such as the dioxin crisis in Belgium, "mad cow disease" across Europe and North America and bird flu in Asia, have modified consumer's perceptions of food consumption. We investigated possible similarities or differences in consumers' food concerns across Brazil, Australia and the Netherlands with eight items: four aimed at measuring specific beef-related concerns and four that measure general food concerns. The response format for each item consists of a five-point Likert scale, and we provide the results in Table 8.5.

With regard to the accuracy and reliability of the constructs, we confirm statistically significant findings at a 95 per cent confidence level ($p < 0.05$). In addition, Cronbach's alphas assess any correlations between items in the attitudes, anticipated emotions and concern scales, and coefficient measures test the internal consistency (reliability) of the scale, such that values greater than 0.7 are satisfactory.[27]

Empirical Findings and Discussion

The exploratory data obtained from beef chain experts and consumers enabled us to investigate perceptions about beef consumption. We considered each cultural context as an opportunity to investigate the multicultural traits of the respondents. The results show that beef is considered a special food product by Brazilians and Australians. Dutch consumers show interest in, but a lack of knowledge about, beef. Thus, Dutch consumers have yet to explore beef fully and still need to find different ways to cook it. Diverse involvement levels and attitudes toward beef also emerge. Concerns about beef consumption issues appear quite important for consumers in Porto Alegre, whereas Dutch consumers indicate a high level of trust in food safety. The quantitative stage of the research provides the data to fulfil our research objectives.

INVOLVEMENT

As we show in Table 8.1, the degrees of involvement with beef differ across cultures. Involvement exists when a product relates to the important values, needs or self-concepts of consumers.[28] On the five-point differential semantic scale, values greater than 3 indicate high involvement and those below 3 indicate low involvement.

Jain and Srinivasan[29] propose that involvement is a multidimensional construct; in Table 8.1 the first three variables represent the *relevance* factor (shaded), the next three are the *pleasure* factor, followed by four *symbolic value* (shaded) variables, three *risk importance* variables and three *risk probability* (shaded) items. The results reveal that factors 1, 2 and 4 achieve the highest involvement averages in all cultures, yet important differences also emerge. Interviewees from Porto Alegre and Australia characterize themselves with the highest means, indicating a higher degree of involvement with beef, though for different reasons.

Risk importance represents the potential negative consequences associated with a bad beef choice; it is the most important involvement factor for consumers from Porto Alegre

Table 8.1   Degree of involvement with beef: Porto Alegre, São Paulo, Australia and the Netherlands

Involvement	Porto Alegre n = 202		São Paulo n = 400		Australia n = 143		Netherlands n = 71	
	Mean	SD	Mean	SD	Mean	SD	Mean	SD
Beef is important for me	3.54	1.38	4.07	0.86	4.43	0.84	3.76	1.08
I believe beef is beneficial to me	3.38	1.36	3.12	1.31	4.74	0.55	3.99	1.15
I do need beef (RI)	3.56	1.27	3.60	0.93	4.37	1.15	3.14	1.51
I consider beef pleasurable (RI)	3.97	1.13	4.25	0.72	4.82	0.58	4.41	1.13
For me, beef is exciting (RI)	3.55	1.22	2.93	1.20	4.01	1.18	2.34	1.59
I think beef is fun	3.20	1.46	3.33	1.23	3.50	1.26	2.64	1.85
My choice of beef tells others something about me	2.64	1.42	1.76	1.20	3.13	1.49	2.10	1.44
The kind of beef I consume can be used by others to judge me	2.48	1.40	1.34	0.71	2.77	1.72	1.85	1.42
My choice of beef can be used by others to judge where I come from	2.89	1.56	1.58	0.96	2.51	1.65	1.67	1.22
My choice of beef does portray an image of me to other people (RI)	2.90	1.44	1.80	1.23	2.90	1.76	1.84	1.43
It is really annoying to make an unsuitable purchase of beef	4.71	0.52	4.11	1.15	4.36	1.17	3.73	1.43
A poor beef choice would upset me	4.71	0.49	4.11	1.07	4.51	0.71	2.65	1.49
I have much to lose by choosing beef poorly (RI)	4.06	1.33	3.88	1.44	4.2	1.11	2.75	1.53
In purchasing beef, I'm not certain of my choice (RI)	1.88	1.14	1.77	0.85	1.65	0.98	2.11	1.58
I never know if I am making the right beef purchase	2.27	1.44	2.15	1.35	2.01	1.36	2.21	1.36
I feel a bit at a loss in choosing the right beef	2.45	1.52	2.50	1.37	2.10	1.50	1.76	1.21

Note: Means are based on a five-point semantic differential scale. Reverse items (RI) from the original scale were inverted for better comprehension.

and São Paulo – that is, at the moment of purchase these consumers consider a poor choice as problematic. For Australians, relevance, or personal interest in beef, emerges as the most important factor, as it does for Dutch consumers. Comparing these main results, it appears that, for Brazilians, beef choice, purchase and consequent outcomes are very important, whereas for consumers in Australia and the Netherlands, although this process is important, the product itself is more critical.

Pleasure or hedonic value, which refers to beef's ability to provide pleasure and satisfaction, ranks second in importance for consumers in Porto Alegre and the Netherlands and third for consumers in São Paulo and Australia. According to its average score on the five-point scale, symbolic value or symbolism ranks below average in all cultures, which indicates that consumers do not become involved with beef because of its symbolic value – that is, they do not believe that beef can influence their concepts of self.

Risk probability, or the probability that consumers may make a bad choice at the moment of purchase, receives the lowest involvement scores – below 3. The interviewees do not have doubts about the beef they are acquiring, so they consider the probability of making a poor choice rather low.

Finally, the results generally are consistent and positive in terms of the similarities. The high degree of involvement with the relevance, pleasure and risk importance factors signals the strong relation of consumers from Brazil, Australia and the Netherlands to beef. In that sense, beef supply chain members must ensure satisfaction and quality in order to fulfil consumers' needs and desires.

POSITIVE ANTICIPATED EMOTIONS

Table 8.2 summarizes the positive emotions interviewees expect to feel when consuming beef on special occasions.

Consumers generally expect to feel positive emotions when consuming beef, although the frequency differs according to the culture and emotion analysed. Specifically, they expect to feel fulfilment frequently during special occasions, but rarely anticipate feeling homesickness. Pleasantness also ranks highly. Therefore, independent of ethnicity, beef consumption is associated with fulfilment and pleasure, which is strategically important from the point of view of marketing communications.

In São Paulo and Australia happiness also ranks highly, and in the Netherlands interest is among the three positive emotions most frequently expected. Curiosity also reveals strong means in all studied cultures. In that sense, marketing strategists should note that

Table 8.2 Positive anticipated emotions experienced by beef consumers: Porto Alegre, São Paulo, Australia and the Netherlands

Positive anticipated emotions	Porto Alegre n = 202		São Paulo n = 400		Australia n = 143		Netherlands n = 71	
	Mean	SD	Mean	SD	Mean	SD	Mean	SD
Excitement	2.48	1.30	1.08	0.29	2.07	1.15	1.72	0.87
Fulfilment	**3.56**	1.38	**3.15**	1.27	**3.21**	1.05	**3.28**	1.08
Pleasantness	**3.20**	1.49	**3.49**	1.10	**3.20**	0.97	**3.05**	1.22
Pride	**3.43**	1.53	1.20	0.55	2.21	1.35	2.27	1.25
Happiness	2.91	1.71	**2.20**	1.28	**2.61**	1.24	2.59	1.21
Homesickness	1.40	0.80	1.26	0.58	1.54	0.88	1.39	0.66
Interest	1.93	1.21	2.08	1.23	2.17	1.25	**2.81**	1.31
Curiosity	1.97	1.28	1.91	1.13	1.98	1.23	2.64	1.31
Cronbach's alpha	0.79		0.75		0.84		0.88	

Note: Means based on a five-point frequency scale (never to always). The three highest means of each culture are shaded. $p < 0.05$.

consumers are generally willing to learn more about the product (that is, beef stimulates the curiosity and interest of the respondents).

In Porto Alegre, consumers frequently expect to experience pride, whereas others expect it less frequently. Pride thus reveals the highest cross-cultural discrepancy rate among the interviewees. Specifically in Porto Alegre, this emotion seems strongly related to the *gaucho* culture through barbeque preparation. In Rio Grande do Sul state (of which Porto Alegre is the state capital), the barbeque is considered a special occasion for beef consumption[30] that involves many ritualized stages of preparation. In addition, the preparation of "high-quality" barbeques is associated with *gauchos* (mainly male) in Brazil, which may help explain the pride felt by the Porto Alegre respondents.

Consumers from Australia and Porto Alegre also expect to feel excitement more frequently than others, probably because of their high degree of involvement with the product. Homesickness is inadequate to characterize the affective expectations of beef consumption.

NEGATIVE ANTICIPATED EMOTIONS

Table 8.3 illustrates the results pertaining to negative anticipated emotions. One of the first findings that draws our attention is the relatively lower expectation of feeling negative emotions, regardless of the culture, compared with the results obtained for positive anticipated emotions. Most respondents answered that they never or rarely expected to feel the negative emotions described when consuming beef (all means are less than 3).

However, interviewees from Porto Alegre indicated that they expected to experience some negative emotions, such as dissatisfaction and worry, rarely or sometimes..

Table 8.3   Negative anticipated emotions experienced by beef consumers: Porto Alegre, São Paulo, Australia and the Netherlands

Negative anticipated emotions	Porto Alegre n = 202		São Paulo n = 400		Australia n = 143		Netherlands n = 71	
	Mean	SD	Mean	SD	Mean	SD	Mean	SD
Anger	1.95	1.16	1.00	0.07	1.55	0.87	1.64	0.72
Dissatisfaction	2.52	1.43	1.33	0.60	2.19	0.93	1.88	0.91
Disgust	1.36	0.75	1.04	0.19	1.43	0.82	1.41	0.68
Guilt	2.65	1.61	1.14	0.33	1.42	0.87	1.39	0.64
Fear	1.62	0.97	1.07	0.24	1.14	0.36	1.42	0.68
Shame	1.41	0.80	1.20	0.50	1.12	0.39	1.45	0.65
Worry	3.24	1.49	1.95	1.04	1.33	0.67	1.97	0.93
Disappointment	1.52	0.93	1.18	0.38	2.15	0.95	2.00	0.88
Anxiety	1.76	1.04	1.32	0.62	1.17	0.45	2.05	1.04
Cronbach's alpha	*0.72*		*0.72*		*0.75*		*0.85*	

Note: Means are based on a five-point frequency scale (never to always). The three highest means of each culture are shaded.

Anticipated emotions relate to attitudes,[31] so we can interpret this result as a strong indication of the affective relationship these consumers have with beef consumption. Negative anticipated emotions interfere with their attitude towards beef and therefore with their consumption behaviour.

In Porto Alegre, worry, guilt, and dissatisfaction are the negative anticipated emotions most frequently associated with beef consumption during special occasions. Guilt and worry could reflect the high frequency of beef consumption among these consumers (more than six times per week). High consumption rates are usually associated with high cholesterol and fatty acids levels, despite the beneficial nutrients (iron, zinc, B vitamins) beef has.

To Australians, dissatisfaction is important, followed by anger and disappointment. These results confirm the importance of quality to Australians.

In São Paulo, the means are generally low, but worry, dissatisfaction and anxiety are the most relevant emotions. Finally, in the Netherlands, the rare negative anticipated emotions include anxiety, disappointment and worry, a triplet that appears related to risk issues associated with consuming beef. Mad cow disease scares might still be associated with this perception; further studies should investigate these issues.

ATTITUDE TOWARDS BEEF

Table 8.4 presents the results regarding consumers' attitudes towards beef. A person's attitude influences the way he or she perceives, experiences and thinks about things. Therefore, respondents evaluate quality, tenderness, taste, safety and price according to a favourable or unfavourable perspective.

The different samples display different attitudes towards overall beef quality. Brazilian consumers evince more favourable attitudes towards beef with regard to quality, tenderness, taste and safety.

Table 8.4   Attitude towards beef: Porto Alegre, São Paulo, Australia and the Netherlands

Attitudes towards beef	Porto Alegre n = 202		São Paulo n = 400		Australia n = 143		Netherlands n = 71	
	Mean	SD	Mean	SD	Mean	SD	Mean	SD
Quality	4.35	0.98	4.31	0.71	3.82	0.98	2.72	0.88
Tenderness	4.14	1.17	4.24	0.78	3.62	1.08	2.60	0.97
Taste	4.37	1.14	4.43	0.63	3.73	1.01	2.67	0.88
Safety	3.93	1.23	4.29	0.73	3.93	1.07	3.05	1.00
Price	2.38	1.37	1.39	0.65	2.97	1.26	2.01	0.90
Cronbach's alpha	0.70		0.82		0.89		0.76	

Note: Means based on a five-point semantic differential scale (poor to excellent). The three highest means of each culture are shaded. $p < 0.05$.

Australians provide the highest mean for safety, despite their moderate attitude on the other variables compared with the Brazilian response. Conversely, Australians indicate a better attitude towards beef prices, even though the overall attitude is negative (median = 3).

In the Netherlands, beef quality, taste and price also rank below average, which suggests a negative attitude that probably influences Dutch consumers' purchase and consumption behaviour. However, for Dutch consumers, the highest mean applies to beef safety, which signals that EU efforts to control "mad cow disease" and re-establish consumer confidence have been largely successful among these consumers. In addition, Dutch consumers seem more conscious of the risks involved in food consumption. Their attitudes towards beef generally are the lowest of the cultures we consider, especially on those attributes related to quality (taste, tenderness and overall quality). A beef production system that depends on dairy, rather than specialized, herds might contribute to this perception of a lack of quality.

Other respondents provide positive evaluations of beef safety, especially those in São Paulo, followed by Porto Alegre and Australia. The fact that Brazil and Australia have been free from "mad cow disease" might contribute to this result.

Attitudes towards price are negative, independent of culture. In São Paulo, sample characteristics might help explain this response (respondents have lower education and income levels than do the other samples). In the Netherlands, the negative cost–benefit comparison (low quality, tenderness and taste plus high prices) appears to affect consumption behaviour. For Australians and Brazilians (higher involvement), the attitude towards price, though negative, is still more favourable than that of the others.

CONCERNS

Recent food scares and growing health consciousness are driving consumers to make dramatic changes in their food consumption patterns and increasing their concerns. The term "food scare" describes contemporary anxiety about the consumption of genetically modified (GM) food[32] or food that could harm consumers (because it contains contaminants such as prions or bacteria). These issues have become global media events – a constant bombardment of scandals and food crisis news. In addition, global climate change, nutrition labelling, environmental pressures and fashion (e.g. the obsession with thinness) expand consumers' concerns. We therefore investigate this issue from an ethnic-diversity perspective, and the results in Table 8.5 highlight some interesting differences and key similarities among the cultures.

The quality of purchased beef is the main concern for respondents in Porto Alegre, São Paulo and Australia, indicating high expectations for the product. In Porto Alegre, concerns with beef safety attain the second highest mean, which suggests that *gaucho* consumers are aware of the possible risks related to beef consumption. In Australia, the same indicator achieved the lowest mean value, which may derive from the privileged, sanitary status of the Australian herd, which has been well communicated to consumers. Dutch consumers confirm their confidence in beef safety.

In the Netherlands, the main concern relates to the protection of the environment – an unsurprising result given that previous studies have indicated that this issue is one of the most important in the European Union.[33] Dutch consumers also reveal high levels of

Table 8.5 Consumers' degree of concern with food consumption issues: Porto Alegre, São Paulo, Australia and the Netherlands

Concerns	Porto Alegre n = 202		São Paulo n = 400		Australia n = 143		Netherlands n = 71	
	Mean	SD	Mean	SD	Mean	SD	Mean	SD
I am concerned about whether I get value for the money when I buy beef	**4.49**	0.79	**3.87**	1.46	**4.20**	1.27	2.68	1.42
I am concerned about beef safety	**4.68**	0.57	3.00	1.57	3.18	1.74	2.86	1.43
I am concerned about animal welfare in beef production	4.05	1.10	2.83	1.55	3.37	1.71	3.46	1.49
I am concerned about the quality of the beef I buy	**4.85**	0.35	**4.28**	1.18	**4.72**	0.73	2.94	1.56
I am concerned about getting a lot of cholesterol in my food	3.92	1.32	3.58	1.56	3.79	1.54	3.55	1.38
I am concerned about gaining weight	3.71	1.41	3.33	1.62	3.59	1.63	**3.79**	1.36
I am concern about the protection of the environment	4.45	0.80	**4.20**	1.17	**4.26**	1.20	**4.03**	0.97
I am concerned about eating food with Genetic Modified Organisms (GMO)	4.01	1.35	3.84	1.33	4.19	1.28	**4.01**	1.18
Cronbach's alpha	0.67		0.68		0.50		0.69	

Note: Means based on a five-point Likert scale. The three highest means of each culture are shaded.

concern with food produced with GM organisms. European consumers, in general, adopt negative attitudes towards GM food.[34]

Concern about weight gain is the third item noted by Dutch consumers, although it is one of the least worrisome for consumers in Porto Alegre. Yet this issue might be expected to be concern there, because 40 per cent of the Brazilian population is overweight and 10 per cent is considered obese. The population of the Netherlands reveals similar percentages, according to statistical data published by official sources.[35]

Value for money is very important for consumers in Porto Alegre, São Paulo and Australia, which reaffirms previous research findings that indicate price is a significant factor for purchases.[36] This means that the difference between what is being offered and how much consumers will pay deserves attention. This finding probably applies not only to expensive, high-quality products, but also to a cheap, undifferentiated ones, which consumers weigh at the moment of purchase. For Dutch consumers, value for money is not a significant concern, which suggests that the few differentiated products on the shelf (retail beef products are similar in quality and price) fail to stimulate consumers into analysing cost–benefit ratios more deeply.

The reduced concern with animal welfare in São Paulo and Australia seems quite surprising, considering the ongoing global discussion about this theme.[37] Further research should investigate the factors associated with such behaviour, including perhaps the income, education level and age of the respondents. Similarly, concerns about cholesterol levels are minimal across samples, which seems unusual considering media efforts to raise awareness about health issues.

Finally, we note the internal consistency of the scale is suboptimal, because Cronbach's alpha values range between 0.5 and 0.7. Cronbach's alpha measures how well a set of items (or variables) measures a single unidimensional latent construct. When data have a multidimensional structure, Cronbach's alpha will usually be low. We consider these results reasonable however, in that we actually find a two-factor solution (one factor related to beef and another related to food issues in general), which could justify the low values overall.

Conclusions

In this research we investigate beef consumers' behaviour according to their involvement, emotions, attitudes and concerns about the product. The results provide a better understanding of important issues related to ethnic diversity in beef consumption. From a managerial perspective, Brazilian, European and Australian beef sectors can benefit from the results, because they suggest ways in which marketing campaigns and global sales efforts should target specific groups of consumers according to their behavioural trends. The entire beef supply chain could improve its competitive advantage if it undertook consumer-driven or market-oriented actions.

The results also confirm the many similarities in beef consumption behaviour among Australian and Brazilian consumers. Consumers from Porto Alegre (Brazil) and Australia declared their strong positive attitudes towards beef and high degrees of involvement with beef consumption, especially compared with consumers from São Paulo (Brazil) and the Netherlands. Measures of anticipated emotions also indicated that consumers from Brazil and Australia experienced more frequent positive emotions during special beef consumption occasions. In addition, Brazilian and Australian consumers were more concerned with beef quality issues, whereas Dutch consumers expressed more concerns with the environmental aspects of beef production.

In this regard, consumers from Porto Alegre and Australia might be considered the real "beef lovers" in light of the strong relationship they indicate between beef and their own culture.

With regard to marketing strategies, in the Netherlands, marketers should improve beef quality and communicate product differences to consumers. Beef is considered an important product, and consumers show interest in and curiosity about it, indicating that they are open to changes and improvements in the beef production chain. Quality improvements might increase consumption, which would benefit the beef trade and enhance overall consumer satisfaction.

In addition, especially in Brazil, quality assurance schemes should be implemented, because consumers do not perceive consistency in beef quality. In Australia, however, classification schemes like the Meat Standard Australia (MSA) guarantee the desired eating quality. In this regard, benchmarking this system could provide an alternative means for beef chains to improve overall beef quality and, hence, consumer satisfaction.

Finally, cross-cultural differences and similarities offer an important avenue for research. Culture represents an important determinant of consumers' behaviour[38] and one of the driving forces of consumers' food choices. This fundamental topic can help researchers understand different food consumption patterns among consumers worldwide; studies in this area started to appear in the beginning of the 2000s.[39] The widely accepted definition of the concept is based on Boas's anthropological view,[40] which postulates that culture represents a system of shared beliefs, values, customs, behaviours and artefacts that the members of a society use to cope with their world and with one another and that are transmitted from generation to generation through learning. Boas also argues that specific cultural traits – behaviours, beliefs and symbols – must be understood in terms of their local context. As such, he offers a major contribution to the anthropological concept of cultural relativism, which assumes that "good and bad are culture specific and cannot be imposed in cultural analysis. The reason for this view is, of course, that what is good in one culture may not be bad in another. This indicates that every culture determines its own ethical judgments to regulate the proper behaviour of its members."[41]

When taking into account cultural traits related to food, barbeque provides a good illustration of local differences. Even within the USA, the differences surrounding this traditional food are significant. In countries like Argentina, *Parrilla* is the traditional method: beef is prepared on a grill (metal frame), directly over the live coals (usually made of wood or coal, but not flames alone). The most common cuts are entrecote, ribs and striploin (*entrecote*, *asado de tiras* and *bife de chorizo*). In Uruguay, barbeques feature a huge variety of fancy meat, like lamb kidney (*rinhõn*), tripe (*chinchulin* and *choto*), and others (*molleja*, *matambre*, *morcillas*). In the south of Brazil, the traditional *Churrasco* is prepared on a fireplace, and the beef cuts are usually placed on a metal skewer, then grilled directly over live coals and mild flames (also made of coal or wood). The preferred cuts are beef ribs *gaucho*-style, rump cap, rump tail with the fat on, and flank steak (*costela Gaúcha*, *picanha*, *maminha* and *vazio*), with fresh sausages (*salsichão*) and chicken heart (*coração de galinha*) included as appetizers. In the USA, barbeques take place on backyard grills or gas grills, with the beef grilled directly over the flames. Hamburger, sausages and pork chops are usually preferred, eaten with different kind of sauces. In each of these locations, the rituals of barbeque preparation and the choice of beef require expertise from local inhabitants. Even the architecture of houses is often adapted to this kind of food.

Moreover, assuming that consumers from different cultures make different choices, food chain marketers must be aware of these differences if they are to identify and understand consumers' preferences and habits. Such knowledge can contribute to effective marketing that enables the generalization of ideas across cultures while also respecting their particular differences.

Even though national culture can serve as an excellent predictor of most behaviours and values in a certain society, it does not represent an absolute and unalterable truth. Inside the same state or province, regional culture still characterizes consumers according to their self-identity, inserted into a broader national cultural context.

In addition, international market segmentation should be considered when developing, positioning and selling products across national borders.[42] Such segments reflect geographic or individual groupings consisting of potential consumers who are likely to exhibit similar responses to marketing efforts. Additional research should address such issues and fill the gap that exists in the current literature. Furthermore, studies investigating the relationship between the degree of involvement and other factors, such as extrinsic and intrinsic cues,[43] will be important.

Finally, the similarities and significant differences among beef consumers that we have found should provide beef chain producers and members a better understanding of this market and enable them to create new opportunities based on ethnic diversity.

References

1. Narver, J.C. and Slater, S.F. (1990), "The effect of a market orientation on business profitability", *Journal of Marketing*, Vol. 54, No. 4, pp. 20–35; Kohli, A.K. and Jaworski, B.J. (1990), "Market orientation: the construct, research propositions, and managerial implications", *Journal of Marketing*, Vol. 54, No. 2, pp. 1–8.

2. Bloch, P.H. and Richins, M.L. (1983), "A theoretical model for the study of product importance perceptions", *Journal of Marketing*, Vol. 47, No. 3, pp. 69–81.

3. Bolfing, C.P. and Woodruff, R.B. (1988), "Effects of situational involvement on consumers' use of standards in satisfaction/dissatisfaction processes", *Journal of Consumer Satisfaction, Dissatisfaction and Complaining Behavior*, Vol. 1, pp. 16–24; Howard, J.A. and Sheth, J.N. (1969), *The Theory of Buyer Behavior*, John Wiley, New York.

4. Bell, R. and Marshall, D. (2003), "The construct of food involvement in behavioral research: scale development and validation", *Appetite*, Vol. 40, No. 3, pp. 235–244.

5. Verbeke, W. and Vackier, I. (2004), "Profile and effects of consumer involvement in fresh meat", *Meat Science*, Vol. 67, pp. 159–68; Marshall, D. and Bell, R. (2004), "Relating the food involvement scale to demographic variables, food choice and other constructs", *Food Quality and Preference*, Vol. 15, pp. 871–879.

6. Costa, A.I.A. and van der Lans, I. (2004), "Impact of emotions, moral standards and social norms on ready meals' use", *2nd International MAPP workshop on Consumer Behaviour and Food Marketing, Denmark. Proceedings*, Middelfart, Denmark, 26–27 April; Laros, F. and Steenkamp, J-B.E.M. (2005), "Emotions in consumer behavior: a hierarchical approach", *Journal of Business Research*, Vol. 58, No. 10, pp. 1437–45; Verhoef, P.C. (2005), "Explaining purchases of organic meat by Dutch consumers", *European Review of Agricultural Economics*, Vol. 32, No. 2, pp. 245–267.

7.   Celsi, R.L. and Olson, J.C. (1988), "The role of involvement in attention and comprehension processes", *Journal of Consumer Research*, Vol. 15, pp. 210–224; Bloch and Richins, "A theoretical model", *op. cit.*

8.   Fessler, D.M.T., Arguello, A.P., Mekdara, J.M. and Macias, R. (2003), "Disgust sensitivity and meat consumption: a test of an emotivist account of moral vegetarianism", *Appetite,* Vol. 41, No. 1, pp. 31–41. Available at http://www.sscnet.ucla.edu/anthro/ faculty/fessler/reprints.htm (accessed 7 July 2006); Harvey, T., Troop, N., Treasure, J. and Murphy, T. (2002), "Fear, disgust and abnormal eating attitudes: a preliminary study", *International Journal of Eating Disorders*, Vol. 32, pp. 213–218.

9.   Perugini, M. and Bagozzi, R.P. (2001), "The role of desires and anticipated emotions in goal-directed behaviours: broadening and deepening the theory of planned behaviour", *British Journal of Social Psychology*, Vol. 40, pp. 79–98.

10.   Ajzen, I. (1988), *Attitudes, Personality, and Behavior* ,Open University Press, Milton Keynes.

11.   Rosenberg, M.J. and Hovland, C.I. (1960), "Cognitive, affective, and behavioral components of attitudes" in C.I. Hovland. and M.J. Rosenberg (eds), *Attitude, Organization and Change: An Analysis of Consistency among Attitude Components*, Yale University, New Haven, CT, pp. 1–14.

12.   Ajzen, *Attitudes, Personality, and Behavior, op. cit.*; Ajzen, I. (1991), "The theory of planned behavior", *Organizational Behavior and Human Decision Processes*, Vol. 50, pp. 179–211.

13.   Food and Agriculture Organization of the United Nations (2006), *Food Outlook Global Market Analysis: Meat and Meat Products*", No. 2, December, http://www.fao.org/docrep/009/j8126e/ j8126e10.htm (accessed 18 January 2007).

14.   European Commission (2004), *Prospects for Agricultural Markets and Income 2000–2011*, European Commission, Brussels.

15.   US Department of Agriculture Foreign Agricultural Service (2006), *Livestock and Poultry World Markets and Trade*, Circular Series DL&P 2-06, October, http://www.fas.usda.gov/dlp/Annual/ Livestock&Poultry.pdf (accessed 14 October 2006).

16.   Davis, A. and Fitchett, J.A. (2004), "Crossing culture: a multi-method enquiry into consumer behaviour and the experience of cultural transition", *Journal of Consumer Behaviour*, Vol. 3, No. 4, pp. 315–330; Steenkamp, J-B.E.M and Ter Hofstede, F. (2002), "International market segmentation: issues and perspectives", *International Journal of Research in Marketing*, Vol. 19, pp. 185–213.

17.   Braga, V. (1994), "Cultura Alimentar: contribuições da antropologia da alimentação", Piracicaba, *Saúde Rev*, Vol. 6, No. 3, pp. 37–44.

18.   Barcellos, M. D. de (2002), *Processo decisório de compra de carne bovina na cidade de Porto Alegre*, Dissertação (Mestrado em Agronegócios), Programa de Pós-Graduação em Agronegócios, Universidade Federal do Rio Grande do Sul, Porto Alegre; Pettigrew, S. (2003), "Australians and their leisure time", *Journal of Research for Consumers,* Vol. 6, http://web.biz.uwa.edu.au/ research/jrconsumers/consumer/cons_article.asp?ArticleID=36 (accessed 13 May 2007).

19.   Australian Bureau of Statistics (2005), *Yearbook 2005*, http://www.abs.gov.au/Ausstats/abs@. nsf/Previousproducts/1301.0Feature Article232005?opendocument&tabname=Summary&pr odno=1301.0&issue=2005&num=&view= (accessed 21 December 2005).

20.   Productschappen Eieren Vee Vlees (2006), *Livestock, Meat and Eggs in the Netherlands*, http:// www.pve.nl (accessed 12 January 2007).

21.   European Commission (2001), *The Welfare of Cattle Kept for Beef Production*, http://ec.europa. eu/food/fs/sc/scah/out54_en.pdf (accessed 14 December 2007); Kuit, G. and van der Meulen, H. (2007), *Marketing Beef from Nature Reserves in Holland*, http://www.macaulay.ac.uk/ livestocksystems/faunus/faunus2/kuit.htm (accessed 17 November 2007).

22. Jain, K. and Srinivasan, N. (1990), "An empirical assessment of multiple operationalizations of involvement" in M. Goldberg, G. Gorn and R. Pollay (eds), *Advances in Consumer Research*, Vol. 17, Association for Consumer Research, Provo, UT, pp. 594–602.

23. Richins, M.L. (1997), "Measuring emotions in the consumption experience", *Journal of Consumer Research*, Vol. 24, pp. 127–146.

24. Ajzen, I. (2002), *Constructing a TPB Questionnaire: Conceptual and Methodological Considerations*, http://www-unix.oit.umass.edu/~aizen/ tpb.html (revised January 2006, "Brief description of the theory of planned behavior" (accessed 15 May 2006).

25. Verbeke, W. and Vackier, I. (2005), "Individual determinants of fish consumption: application of the theory of planned behaviour", *Appetite,* Vol. 44, pp. 67–82; Barcellos, *Processo decisório, op. cit.*

26. Bernard, A. and Fierens, S. (2002), "The Belgian PCB/dioxin incident: a critical review of health risks evaluations", *International Journal of Toxicology*, Vol. 21, No. 5, pp. 333–40; World Health Organization (2007), *Bovine Spongiform Encephalopathy*, Factsheet 113, http://www.who.int/mediacentre/factsheets/fs113/en/ (accessed 14 January 2007); Center for Disease Control and Prevention (2007), *Avian Influenza (Bird Flu)*, http://www.cdc.gov/flu/avian/ (accessed 15 January 2007).

27. Hair, J.F. Jr, Black, W., Babin, B.J.C., Anderson, R. E. and Tatham, R.L. (2006), *Multivariate Data Analysis* (6th edn), Prentice-Hall, Upper Saddle River, NJ.

28. Houston, M. and Rothschild, M. (1978), "Conceptual and methodological perspectives on involvement" in S.C. Jain (ed.), *Research Frontiers in Marketing: Dialogues and Directions*, American Marketing Association, Chicago, pp. 184–187.

29. Jain and Srinivasan, "An empirical assessment", *op. cit.*

30. Barcellos, *Processo decisório, op. cit.*

31. Perugini and Bagozzi, "The role of desires and anticipated emotions", *op. cit.*

32. Fitzgerald, R. and Campbell, H. (2001), "Food scares and GM: movement on the nature/culture faultline", *The Drawing Board: An Australian Journal of Public Affairs*, http://www.australianreview.net/digest/2001/10/fitzgerald campbell.html. 120 (accessed 25 December 2006).

33. Saba, A. (2001), "Cross-cultural differences in food choice" in L.J. Frewer, E. Risvik, H.N.J. Schifferstein and R. von Alvensleben (eds), *Food, People and Society. A European Perspective of Consumer Food Choices*, Springer, London, pp. 233–246; Grieger, K. and Trapp, S. (2006), "Pesticide residues in drinking water versus other beverages: a case of unjustified discrepancy?" in M. Kaiser and M. Lien (eds), *Ethics and the Politics of Food: Preprints of the 6th Congress of European Society for Agricultural and Food Ethics*, Oslo, Norway, 22–24 June, Wageningen Academic Publishers, The Netherlands, pp. 569–71.

34. Eurobarometer (2001), *Europeans, Science and Technology*, European Commission, Report 55.2, http://ec.europa.eu/research/press/2001/ pr0612en-report.pdf (accessed 6 March 2005).

35. IBGE (2004), *Pesquisa de Orçamentos Familiares–POF 2002–2003 Excesso de peso atinge 38,8 milhões de brasileiros adultos*, http://www.ibge.gov.br/home/presidencia/noticias/noticia_impressao.php?id_noticia=278 (accessed 9 May 2007); Raad Voor de Volksgezondheid & Zorg (2006), *Health and Behavior 2007*, http://www.rvz.net/cgi-bin/rvz_p.pl?id=69 (accessed 12 June 2007).

36. Buso, G. (2000), *Análise do perfil do consumidor de carne bovina na cidade de São Paulo*, Dissertação (Mestrado em Administração), Departamento de Engenharia de Produção, Universidade Federal de São Carlos, São Carlos; Barcellos, *Processo Decisório, op. cit.*; Saab, M.S. (1998), "Changes in consumer demands in the beef agribusiness system in Brazil: consequences to the whole

chain", *Proceedings of the Third International Conference on Chain Management in Agribusiness and the Food Industry*, Vol. 1. Wageningen, the Netherlands.

37. Kaiser, M. and Lien, M. (eds) (2006), "Ethics and the politics of food", *Preprints of the 6th Congress of European Society for Agricultural and Food Ethics*, Oslo, Norway, 22-24 June. Wageningen Academic Publishers, the Netherlands.

38. Steenkamp, J-B.E.M. (2001), "The role of national culture in international marketing research", *International Marketing Review*, Vol. 18, No. 1, pp. 30–44.

39. Valli, C. and Traill, B.W. (2005), "Culture and food: a model of yoghurt consumption in the EU", *Food Quality and Preference*, Vol. 16, No. 4, pp. 291–304; Cervellon, M-C. and Dubé, L. (2004), "Cultural influences in the origins of food likings and dislikes", *Food Quality and Preference*, Vol. 15, Nos 7–8, pp. 611–911; Barnués, A., Olaizola, A. and Corcoran, K. (2003), "Extrinsic attributes of red meat as indicators of quality in Europe: an application for market segmentation", *Food Quality and Preference*, Vol. 14, pp. 265–276; Bech-Larsen, T. and Grunert, K. (2003), "The perceived healthiness of functional foods: a conjoint study of Danish, Finnish and American consumers' perception of functional foods", *Appetite*, Vol. 40, No. 1, pp. 9–14; Verbeke, W. (2005), "Consumer acceptance of functional foods: socio-demographic, cognitive and attitudinal determinants", *Food Quality and Preference*, Vol. 16, pp. 45–57.

40. Boas, F. (1920), "The methods of ethnology", *American Anthropologist New Series*, Vol. 22, No. 4, pp. 311–321.

41. Glazer, M. (1994), *Cultural Relativism*, http://www.utpa.edu/faculty/mglazer/Theory/cultural_relativism.htm (accessed 17 June 2007).

42. Steenkamp and Ter Hofstede, "International market segmentation", *op. cit.*

43. Grunert, K., Bredahl, L. and Brunsø, K. (2004), "Consumer perception of meat quality and implications for product development in the meat sector – a review", *Meat Science*, Vol. 66, pp. 259–272.

9 *Challenges of Marketing to Brazilian Single Consumers*

ADRIANA BEATRIZ MADEIRA* AND JOSÉ AUGUSTO
GIESBRECHT DA SILVEIRA†

Keywords

market segmentation, single consumer, Brazil.

Abstract

This chapter presents the main characteristics, and their implications for marketing decisions, of a growing Brazilian demographic minority – namely, single dwellers in big cities. Brazil has one of the highest rates of people living alone, relative to the total population. However, analysis of this phenomenon has been only recent and lacks research based on large samples. The eight largest Brazilian state capitals in terms of population provide the focal point of this study which suggests that the characteristics of this growing and heterogeneous group of people must be taken into account with regard to issues related to the consumption and production of consumer goods and services.

Introduction

Do Brazilian industrialists and retailers recognize the characteristics of the people who live alone? Do they know the extent to which this group of people could represent sales for their firms? For several years, Brazilian companies have been delivering special-sized food portions, as well as manufactured gadgets, tourism packages and real-estate items

* Ms Adriana Beatriz Madeira, Department of Administration, CCSA, University Presbyterian Mackenzie, Rua da Consolação, 930 – Cep 01302-907 – Consolação – São Paulo – SP – Brazil. E-mail: adri.madeira@mackenzie.br; adri.madeira@usp.br. Telephone: 55 1121 148 140.

† Dr José Augusto Giesbrecht da Silveira, Department of Administration, School of Economics, Administration, and Accounting, University of São Paulo, Professor Luciano Gualberto, 908, CEP 05508-010, São Paulo, Brazil. E-mail: jags@usp.br. Telephone: 55-11-30916045.

designed to please the wealthy portion of this minority. However, not all the members of this group are rich.

The percentage of single dwellers in the Brazilian population has grown faster than the population as a whole. Nevertheless, the conception that the entire group or its majority consist of well-to-do people is false. This study shows that people who live alone in Brazil are a very heterogeneous group, of whom only a small portion are prosperous men and women.

Until a few years ago, few people lived alone. Families were normally large and included various close relatives. However, families have been shrinking, marriages are taking place later, the number of divorces is rising, and many unmarried and divorced people now live alone.

Brazil is one of the ten countries with the highest incidence of people living alone as a percentage of the total population. However, investigations into this phenomenon have been recent and lack details. The scarcity of in-depth information therefore has driven Brazilian planners and managers to rely mainly on geographic segmentation when dealing with single consumers.

The sources of the data analysed herein include several editions of the Brazilian Demographic Censuses, with a focus on the eight largest capitals in terms of total population: São Paulo, Rio de Janeiro, Salvador, Belo Horizonte, Fortaleza, Curitiba, Recife and Porto Alegre. The period for the study spans 30 years, covering the censuses of 1970, 1980, 1991 and 2000, the latter being the most recent. Finally, the segmentation variables investigated include gender, age, income, literacy, retirement and type of domicile.

The Research Problem

Overall statistics can mask significant changes in the number of inhabitants per home, as well as the effects of these changes. For example, they influence consumption per capita. In Brazil the number of homes has been rising significantly beyond demographic growth. This study therefore investigates two main research questions: what is the impact of this changing dynamic on the production of consumer goods and services? And what are the impacts on consumption habits?

STUDY OBJECTIVES

This study attempts to, first, supply socio-economic data about Brazilian single dwellers and show the growth and diversity of this portion of the population, with a particular focus on the implications of the phenomenon, especially for decision-making about marketing, retailing, manufacturing, urbanism, architecture, public administration and the environment. Second, it classifies and describes sub-segments of the segment of persons who live alone, in terms of geo-demographic and socio-economic profiles. Third, and finally, it calculates the growth rate of single dwellers during the past three decades in São Paulo, Rio de Janeiro, Salvador, Belo Horizonte, Fortaleza, Curitiba, Porto Alegre and Recife.

STUDY JUSTIFICATION

The population of people who live in single dwellings has major marketing potential not only because of its consumption profile but also because of the actual number of people it comprises. According to the Brazilian Institute of Geography and Statistics (IBGE), in 1991, 5.7 per cent of all Brazilian homes had only one inhabitant,[1] whereas by 2000[2] this share had risen to 9.1 per cent.[3]

Also according to the IBGE, 4 million homes contained only one inhabitant in 2000,[4] and more than 4.6 million homes were added to the total number of domiciles in Brazil between 1991 and 2000, due to the falling number of persons per home. Even in countries in which total population has been dropping, the number of homes is continuing to rise.[5] Such data confirm that it is relevant to investigate this phenomenon, improve understanding of the trend and eventually model the same.

The profile and behaviour of consumers at the beginning of this century exhibited new tendencies, leading to substantial changes in consumption habits. Thus, before undertaking any entrepreneurial activity in relation to the market niche represented by the segment of single dwellers, entrepreneurs must take several variables into account, not just the total number of individuals who form a segment.

Market Segmentation

Market segmentation was first recognized in an article published in 1956 by Wendell R. Smith.[6] Historically, three types of segmentation have gained momentum.[7] The first was geographical segmentation; small manufacturing concerns that wanted to limit their investments segmented or "divided" markets and sold their products only in certain specific geographical areas. This type of segmentation became especially popular among manufacturers, retailers, banks and service providers. The second type of segmentation – demographic – arose out of the need to service both national and dispersed markets; it relies, among other things, on variables such as age, gender, income, occupation and race, which can be very useful for defining general objectives. The third wave of market segmentation was based on behavioural variables (e.g. buying habits). Finally, psychographic segmentation (e.g., based on lifestyles) has emerged.

Analyses of demographic trends associated with economic characteristics, such as income or purchasing power, can help forecast demand and consumption over time,[8] as well as inform the development of products, brands, media distribution and communication, among other applications.[9] Geo-demographic analysis, in turn, enhances demographic studies with an evaluation of where people live, how they make money and how they spend it. A key structure in such evaluations is the city.

Singles in the World

A study by Liu et al.[10] provides ratios of single dwellers to the total population for 76 countries. Brazil ranks among the top ten in highest ratios.

The number of domiciles influences per capita consumption and consequently the environment through fuel consumption, the construction of high-rise buildings or energy consumption.[11] Even if the size of the population declines, the number of homes can rise substantially. The difference between the growth of the population and the growth in the number of homes suggests that it is crucial to take into account the number of dwellings for economic evaluations. A larger number of homes generally means higher demand for construction material and reduced efficiency in resource use, because resources are no longer shared by a large number of people. In addition, reasons for the falling number of people per home include lower fertility rates, higher per capita income, growing divorce rates, ageing populations and the declining frequency of families that include various generations.

According to the Applied Economic Research Institute (IPEA),[12] the increasing trend towards one-person homes started after World War II and intensified during the 1980s, when a sort of individualistic ideology arose. It is based on a new lifestyle that has become increasingly popular and is associated with new family situations, a growing number of broken marriages, people choosing to remain single and those with stable marital relations who live in separate households.[13]

Divorce rates have been rising since 1960, whereas birth and marriage rates have been falling.[14] Drastic changes since the Industrial Revolution mean that a large family is no longer the norm. In the pre-industrial era, the family generated economic stability and helped ensure well-being, and the home was the primary production unit. Work and family life were integrated. People, who often worked from home, plus friends and relatives made up the household, and families expanded across communities.[15]

With the advent of the industrial society, the family changed and became smaller, and the extended family lost its position to the core family. The rules for each gender became sharply set: men worked away from home, whereas women stayed at home and looked after the children. This family model provided the basis for developments after 1945, characterized by employer paternalism and improved standards of living, work and financial security.[16]

Presently, family structures are shrinking, whereas the segment comprising individuals living alone is growing.[17] This single-dweller segment is broad and combines many profiles, such as young people who want to get married later, people who have divorced, widows and widowers, and part of the GLS (gay, lesbian, bisexual and transgender) public.[18]

Singles in Brazil

In Brazil more than 4.6 million homes appeared between 1991 and 2000, largely as a result of a reduction in the number of people per home.[19] The 4 million single-person homes in Brazil in 2000 became the target of specific food, beverage, personal care and household cleaning product industries.[20] The IBGE census shows that people marry less and later, especially those in wealthier strata, while formal separations (divorces) occur sooner and more often every year.[21] The number of weddings appears inverse to population growth, whereas the number of separations mirrors such growth.[22]

By assessing and analysing population and census data, this study attempts to identify and understand predictive factors and infer projections. On the basis of these projections, we generate information for the industrial and retail sectors (e.g. inputs for developing appropriate products, services and commercial strategies), the public sector (e.g. managing administrative issues, guidance about urban matters) and the environmental sector (e.g. structuring ecological issues).

Methodology

This study analyses secondary data from the Brazilian censuses of 1970, 1980, 1991 and 2000 for eight state capitals: São Paulo, Rio de Janeiro, Salvador, Belo Horizonte, Fortaleza, Curitiba, Recife and Porto Alegre. These cities represent the largest capitals in terms of the total number of inhabitants.[23] The data supply geo-demographic and socio-economic information pertaining to people residing in homes researched by the Brazilian censuses.

According to Curry,[24] because censuses are geo-demographic in nature, they provide aggregate data about the researched homes within a geographic unit. This aggregation of geo-demographic data may identify groups or segments (clusters) of people with similar standing. For example, people who live in groups of similar areas generally share many socio-economic and demographic characteristics and consequently should have similar purchasing and usage habits and media preferences.

In turn, we project that an analysis based on the statistical treatment of census data for these eight cities can classify and describe the segment of individuals who live alone. To this end, we adhere to methodological and scientific requirements to ensure that the study is both scientifically acceptable and methodologically valid.

Statistical Methods and Techniques

A key step for guaranteeing the reliability and validity of scientific research is ensuring the proper treatment of the analysed data, which includes making necessary adjustments to render comparisons and inferences both possible and fair.

We first undertook a detailed analysis of the organization of the databases for the 1970, 1980, 1991 and 2000 censuses. These databases contain a sample equal to 25 per cent of the population, with the total numbers obtained by applying an expansion factor that is an integral part of the structure of each census. The databases are heterogeneous in terms of their internal organization, the quantity and characteristics of the variables they investigate, and the concepts that they adopt. The methodology used to interview the population changed during the period covered by these four censuses, reflecting the point in time each census was taken and the changes in society. Therefore, any immediate comparison is unfair.

These different methods dictated that we build a new database with compatible data. The new database contains only those variables that could be compared across the four censuses. However, these comparisons often required adjustments as well, because the variables were not identical in terms of their organization, content or categories. We therefore applied database trimming procedures to the original databases and adjusted the variables and categories, but without affecting the original concepts that underlie the construction of the Brazilian Demographic Censuses.

After building the new database, we calculated descriptive statistics, such as the frequency, mean, mode and median, and deployed the crosstabs technique for crossing variables. Conglomerate analysis[25] also enabled us to place elements into groups that are internally homogeneous but heterogeneous in comparison with other groups, as well as mutually exclusive. In other words, we grouped individuals whose characteristics are shared but differ from those of different groups that we identified. Conglomerate analysis is exploratory rather than conclusive, so we are leaving an evaluation of the results to a subsequent phase in which we will analyse the meaning and significance of the derived conglomerates.

Specifically, we employ the K-means technique[26] and express measures of distance or similarity according to Euclidean distance. The chi-squared test indicates the quality of the indicated results. We applied these procedures both by city and by census, and then evaluated the results by organizing them in an attempt to identify any regularities over time, such as identical sub-segments across several decades for a given city. Another comparison also identifies cities with the same sub-segments of people living alone.

Main Results

The collected, statistically treated, analysed data refer to permanent private dwellings – that is, buildings used exclusively as homes which, as of the reference date, housed one or more people. For simplicity, we refer to these dwellings as "homes" in this analysis.[27]

Table 9.1 shows the total number of one-person homes and their percentage share of the total number of people for the four censuses, in the eight cities studied. A clear increase marks the number of people living alone as a percentage of the total population, such that the average percentage for the eight cities combined stood at 1.34 per cent in 1970, 1.79 per cent in 1980, 2.27 per cent in 1991 and 3.24 per cent in 2000 (all general population averages in this study are weighted averages). The yearly growth rate (geometric rate) of the population living alone for the 1970–2000 period is 5.13 per cent.

Table 9.1   Total number of one-person homes and their percentage share of the total population people

Total people in permanent private homes					
	1970			1980	
Cities	One-person	%	Total	One-person	%	Total
São Paulo	64 674	1.18	5 498 631	140 910	1.70	8 306 388
Rio de Janeiro	75 823	1.93	3 931 993	124 115	2.48	4 996 785
Salvador	11 537	1.23	936 721	20 890	1.42	1 473 844
Belo Horizonte	12 599	1.08	1 170 741	23 073	1.31	1 756 827
Fortaleza	5410	0.68	800 883	11 187	0.86	1 296 683
Curitiba	4642	0.82	564 569	12 955	1.29	1 004 451
Recife	11 148	1.13	987 992	16 614	1.40	1 187 172
Porto Alegre	11 177	1.39	805 799	28 322	2.57	1 099 967

Table 9.1 *Concluded*

Total people in permanent private homes

Cities	1991			2000		
	One-person	%	Total	One-person	%	Total
São Paulo	203 077	2.13	9 528 774	308 121	2.98	10 340 047
Rio de Janeiro	164 657	3.03	5 29 554	242 000	4.17	5 807 228
Salvador	386 56	1.88	2 058 336	69 707	2.87	2 428 487
Belo Horizonte	37 909	1.89	2 004 265	67 975	3.05	2 226 076
Fortaleza	17 786	1.01	1 760 074	34 047	1.60	2 132 078
Curitiba	27 274	2.10	1 301 669	52 515	3.33	1 576 199
Recife	21 226	1.64	1 291 133	33 806	2.39	1 413 351
Porto Alegre	48 644	3.89	1 248 951	76 253	5.66	1 346 477

Total single-person homes, as a percentage of total homes in the eight cities combined, accounted for 5.97 per cent in 1970, 7.43 per cent in 1980, 8.60 per cent in 1991 and 11.22 per cent in 2000. Therefore, people who live alone represent a substantial segment of consumers (see Table 9.2). The yearly growth rate of single-person homes for 1970–2000 was 5.13 per cent, whereas the growth rate of total homes was 2.95 per cent. Table 9.3 reveals a derived drop in the number of people per home.

These initial figures alone would suffice to suggest that producers of consumer goods should turn their attention to the segment of consumers living alone. However, the study also discloses several curious elements, which we discuss next in an attempt to develop a more in-depth understanding of the specific characteristics of this group. Such an understanding can help marketers avoid falling into traps during the course of their strategy definition and market planning.

Table 9.2   Single-person homes as a percentage of total homes

Cities	1970			1980		
	One-person	%	Total	One-person	%	Total
São Paulo	64 674	5.08	1272 279	140 910	6.83	2 062 196
Rio de Janeiro	75 823	7.95	953 883	124 115	9.54	1 301 073
Salvador	11 537	6.45	178 881	20 890	6.99	299 025
Belo Horizonte	12 599	5.49	229 571	23 073	6.01	383 973
Fortaleza	5410	3.66	147 640	11 187	4.39	255 088
Curitiba	4642	3.69	125 653	12 955	5.38	240 932
Recife	11 148	5.76	193 609	16 614	6.73	246 727
Porto Alegre	11 177	5.65	197 728	28 322	9.46	299 368

Table 9.2 *Concluded*

Cities	1991			2000		
	One-person	%	Total	One-person	%	Total
São Paulo	203 077	7.99	2 540 656	308 121	10.32	2 985 977
Rio de Janeiro	164 657	10.55	1 560 691	242 000	13.43	1 802 347
Salvador	38 656	8.08	478 128	69 707	10.70	651 293
Belo Horizonte	37 909	7.58	500 062	67 975	10.82	628 447
Fortaleza	17 786	4.61	386 053	34 047	6.47	526 079
Curitiba	27 274	7.78	350 699	52 515	11.15	471 163
Recife	21 226	6.93	306 071	33 806	8.99	376 022
Porto Alegre	48 644	12.81	379 855	76 253	17.31	440 557

Table 9.3 **Average number of people per home**

Cities	1970	1980	1991	2000
São Paulo	4.65	4.11	3.80	3.49
Rio de Janeiro	4.46	3.91	3.51	3.25
Salvador	5.74	5.02	4.34	3.75
Belo Horizonte	5.46	4.63	4.03	3.56
Fortaleza	5.91	5.12	4.58	4.07
Curitiba	4.97	4.25	3.74	3.37
Recife	5.60	4.88	4.24	3.78
Porto Alegre	4.57	3.76	3.33	3.09

Single-city Analysis

At the beginning of the study we imagined a certain amount of homogeneity in the composition of the segment of consumers living alone across the cities, because these cities are among the eight largest capitals in terms of population. The first major surprise consisted of finding an altogether different reality.[28]

The highest growth rates from 1991 to 2000 do not relate directly to cities with the largest ratio of single-person homes. Crossing these data suggests that this outlook will probably be inverted over time (see Table 9.4).

Dividing the segment into two classes – single homes inhabited by a retired person and single homes inhabited by a non-retired person – sheds more light on the dynamics of the growth phenomenon (Table 9.5). In the first decade (1970–1980), retired people provided more important drivers of the growth in single-dweller homes, whereas during the 1990s (1991–2000), non-retired people replaced them as the most important catalyst for segment growth.

Table 9.4 Share and growth of single-person homes

Cities	Singles-person vs total homes in 2000 (%)	Yearly growth rate of single-person homes in 1991–2000(%)
Porto Alegre	17.31	5.12
Rio de Janeiro	13.43	4.37
Curitiba	11.15	7.55
Belo Horizonte	10.82	6.70
Salvador	10.70	6.77
São Paulo	10.32	4.74
Recife	8.99	5.31
Fortaleza	6.47	7.48

Table 9.5 Retiree versus non-retiree growth

	Average yearly growth rate %	
	Non-retirees	
Cities	From 1970–1980	From 1991–2000
Curitiba	6.92	9.62
Fortaleza	4.27	8.94
Belo Horizonte	3.50	8.41
Salvador	4.85	7.34
Porto Alegre	5.45	6.88
Rio de Janeiro	1.66	6.68
Recife	1.39	6.50
Sao Paulo	3.83	6.23

	Average yearly growth rate %	
	Retirees	
Cities	From 1970–1980	From 1991–2000
Salvador	12.83	4.86
Curitiba	14.63	3.67
Fortaleza	14.58	3.54
Belo Horizonte	12.08	3.47
Recife	10.53	2.83
Porto Alegre	11.98	2.19
Sao Paulo	11.91	1.82
Rio de Janeiro	9.42	0.94

Curitiba, though not the segment's largest city in terms of the rate of single-person homes, posts one of the highest yearly growth rates for both retired and non-retired segments throughout the 1970–2000 period. The retirees segment tends to consist of literate women aged 60 years and older, with an annual income of US$422.45–1,689.79. Among non-retired people, however, literate women are predominant in 1970, 1980 and 2000, whereas in 1991, men take precedence. In 2000, non-retired people appear distributed across age brackets between 20 and 59 years of age, with income ranging from US$422.45 to more than US$1,689.79.

The city with the greatest retiree growth is Salvador, although it ranked only fifth in terms of the share of single-person homes, which mostly belonged to men, in 1970. From 1980 to 2000 these single-person homes instead were inhabited mainly by women. In 1980, 48.19 per cent of this segment was illiterate, aged 60 years and above, with income ranging from US$43.25–84.49. As of 1991, although the age bracket remained unchanged, they had become literate. In 2000 the segment consisted primarily of literate women aged 60 years and older, with earnings centred in one of two income brackets: US$253.47–422.45 or more than US$1,689.79. The non-retired group consists predominantly of men, distributed over several age and income brackets.

The capital with the second highest non-retiree rate and the third highest retiree rate is Fortaleza, but it ranks last in the ratio of single-person to total homes. From 1970 to 2000, non-retirees were largely literate men, aged 30 to 39 years, earning either up to US$168.98 or between US$422.45 and US$844.90. Retirees in 1970 were mostly men aged 60 years or older, but by 1980 and 2000, the composition changed, becoming predominantly older women, distributed across two income brackets of up to US$253.47 and US$422.45–844.90.

Belo Horizonte has been characterized from 1970 to 2000 by a predominance of literate, retired women, aged 60 years and above, with a varied range of income. They tend to be concentrated in the income brackets of up to US$168.98 and from US$1,267.35 to US$1,689.79. In contrast, non-retirees in this city have been mainly men throughout the 1970–2000 censuses, in the age group 30 to 39 years, literate, and earning up to US$168.98, from US$422.45 to US$844.90 or more than US$1,689.79.

The city of Recife is marked by the predominance of retired women aged 60 years and above, literate, and earning up to US$168.98 or between US$422.45 and US$844.90 across the entire time span analysed. The non-retired group also consists mainly of women from 1970 to 1980, but of men from 1991 to 2000. Between 1991 and 2000 this male population concentrates in the 30 to 39 year age bracket. These men also are literate and earn either up to US$168.98 or more than US$844.90.

Porto Alegre contains the largest share of single-person homes relative to total domiciles. Across all four censuses, its single retirees were largely women, mainly over 50 years of age, and literate, who earned up to US$168.98 or between US$422.45 and US$844.90. In 1970, 1980 and 2000 the non-retiree portion of the segment was also predominantly female, whereas in 1991 it was male. In 2000 the female segment of the group spread over several age and income brackets.

São Paulo is the most significant capital city in terms of the absolute number of people who live alone. The most populous Brazilian city, and one of the most populous in the world (more than 10 million inhabitants in 2000), the city is characterized by a predominance of retired, female single dwellers, aged 60 and above, literate, and distributed over the income brackets from US$21.12 to US$844.90. Non-retired single dwellers are largely men, aged 30 to 49 years, literate, and distributed over the income brackets from US$422.45 to US$1,689.79.

Rio de Janeiro is the second most populous city in Brazil (more than 5.8 million people in 2000) and ranks second in terms of the ratio of single-person homes to total domiciles. Retired single dwellers here are mainly women throughout the 1970–2000 censuses; they are mostly over 60, literate, and earn incomes in all brackets between US$21.12 and US$1,689.79. In the earlier years most non-retirees were men, but from 1991 to 2000 the population was balanced between men and women. In the female segment of this population, the group older than 50 years stands out: They are literate, and their income falls within two brackets, either up to US$168.98 or more than US$1,689.79. The male population consists of people aged 30 to 49 years, who are literate and fall within three different income brackets. The first goes up to US$168.98; the second ranges from US$422.45 to US$844.90; and the third falls between US$844.90 and US$1,267.35.

What do these cities have in common in terms of single dwellers? Clearly, diversity is easy to perceive, but it also is possible to identify some main directions or major trends.

Trends

The composition of the population that lives alone reflects a rising retiree participation curve prior to 1991. At that point, it peaks, with an overall average of 39.33 per cent of the total of the segment for the eight cities. In 2000 the level drops to 29.74 per cent. Possible reasons for this trend include increased life expectancy or the need to continue working into old age. Nonetheless, retirees still account for almost one-third of the total segment of single dwellers. In 2000 Salvador and Fortaleza contained the largest shares of non-retirees in terms of the composition of the population living alone, at 79.13 per cent and 77.75 per cent, respectively.[29]

Women come to predominate in the population in almost all cities. In 1970 men stood out, but in Curitiba, Recife and Porto Alegre, the male segment already accounted for less than half of the population. In just one city, Salvador, women remained a minority (45 per cent) continuously from 1970 to 2000. In the last census, Fortaleza had achieved a balance between men and women, whereas elsewhere the female population tend to comprise more than 55 per cent of the entire segment.

The population that lives alone is also concentrated mainly in the over-30 years age brackets, and its largest portion – more than one-third – consists of people who are 60 years or older. The 20–29 age bracket appears to be declining, dropping to 12.61 per cent of the total segment of people who live alone in 2000 compared with 18.07 per cent in 1970. Among people older than 60 years, the share rose between 1970 and 2000, such that they accounted for more than one-third of the segment by 2000 (36.73 per cent). The median age brackets – 30 to 39, 40 to 49, and 50 to 59 – combined accounted for almost half (49.68 per cent) the segment in 2000, with average shares of 17.73 per cent, 16.56 per cent, and 15.39 per cent, respectively, of the population across all eight cities.

As late as 2000 illiteracy remained a factor in all cities included in our study. The percentage of illiterate single dwellers in Salvador was 11.20 per cent; that in Fortaleza was 17.66 per cent. Recife suffered the highest rate of illiteracy across the entire period: In 1970 illiterate single dwellers accounted for 41.17 per cent of the total population, and even in 2000 this figure stood at 17.64 per cent. In 2000 illiterate people still accounted for

7.72 per cent of the total single-dweller segment for the eight cities, although Curitiba and Porto Alegre exhibited the lowest rates at 5.28 per cent and 4.02 per cent, respectively.

With regard to income, there is a polarization of dominant brackets: a low-income group on one hand and the highest-income group on the other. However, the percentage of people with an annual income between US$42.24 and US$844.90 is dropping, while the percentage of people with higher incomes (US$844.90–1,267.35, US$1,267.35–1,689.79, and more than US$1,689.79) is rising. This constant trend marks the entire 1970–2000 period.

Despite this trend towards higher incomes, a significant share of people lack income in 2000, especially in Salvador, Fortaleza and Recife (more than 10 per cent). The lowest percentages appear in Belo Horizonte, Curitiba and Porto Alegre (less than 5.50 per cent). In 2000 Salvador, Fortaleza and Recife posted the largest shares of people without incomes within the total segment (respectively, 11.59 per cent, 10.35 per cent and 10.58 per cent). For Belo Horizonte, Curitiba and Porto Alegre, this category reached the lowest share in terms of the composition of the population living alone (respectively, 4.80 per cent, 5.27 per cent and 3.89 per cent).

Finally, when we evaluate the ownership of the single-person homes, we find that in 2000 they were mostly the property of those who dwell in them (average for eight cities: 66.95 per cent) or rented (24.99 per cent).

Conclusions and Recommendations

Meeting the needs and requirements of the segment of consumers who live alone means working with more than 10 per cent of Brazil's entire population! This segment must be significant for most companies and cannot be disregarded by the various spheres of government. This high percentage also implies significant implications of this phenomenon for marketing, corporate planning, urban planning, public administration and the environment. Business and government officials must remember that this segment encompasses groups with very different characteristics in terms of income, age, literacy, retirement conditions and residence, and some of these socio-economic conditions appear diametrically opposed.

Growth of this segment, coupled with its intrinsic diversity, will have a substantial impact on the production of consumer goods and services, consumption habits, urban equipment needs, and domestic and industrial waste treatment. This study provides a means of evaluating these impacts and addressing the business potential offered by a proper recognition of the segment's diversity.

Although we describe and classify the demographic characteristics of the population that lives alone, as well as its socio-economic characteristics, in the cities of São Paulo, Rio de Janeiro, Salvador, Belo Horizonte, Fortaleza, Curitiba, Recife and Porto Alegre, this study also raises additional questions related to the theories addressed, the research methodology employed and the results obtained. These questions serve as directions for further research, which might address:

- the behaviour of the segment of people who live by themselves in the capitals of other Brazilian states;
- the behaviour of this segment in other urban centres with different population sizes;

- possible reasons for the existence of specific sub-segments of individuals who live alone in some cities but not in others;
- a model that can enable quantitative projections.

These suggestions represent just a few of the study possibilities suggested by this research area. The interpretation and analysis of the data, and the results recorded herein, should also generate further questions, propositions and possibilities for research. With this attempt to establish certain statistical bases regarding the phenomenon of single dwellers, we provide a path for others to enhance our understanding of the specificities of the segment of people who live alone.

References

1. Nigro, Soraia (2001), "¿Sozinho? Supermercado Moderno. São Paulo", http://www.google.com (accessed 11 March 2003).
2. Pacheco, Paula (2003), "¿A lucrativa diversidade ?", *Carta Capital*, http://www.cartacapital.com.br (accessed 9 April 2003).
3. Mariz, Juliana and Boccia, Sandra (2003), "¿O Rei da Cocada? Estampa", *Valor Econômico*, February.
4. Ferreira, Vivaldo (2002), "Single: o grande mercado do consumo individual", http://www.google.com (accessed 9 April 2003).
5. Liu, Jianguo, Daily, Gretchen C., Ehrlich, Paul R. and Luck, Gary W. (2003), "Effects of household dynamics on resource consumption and biodiversity", *Nature*, No. 421, pp. 530–533.
6. Smith, Wendell R. (1956), "Product differentiation and market segmentation as alternative marketing strategies", *Journal of Marketing*, Vol. 21, No. 4, pp. 3–8.
7. Boone, Louis E. and Kurtz, David L. (1998), *Marketing Contemporâneo* (8th edn), Livros Técnicos and Científicos Editora SA, Rio de Janeiro; Czinkota, Michael R., Kotabe, Masaaki and Mercer, David (1972), *Marketing Management: Text and Cases*, Blackwell, Oxford; Green, Paul E. and Tull, Donald S. (1970), *Research for Marketing Decisions*, Prentice Hall, Englewood Cliffs, NJ; Haley, Russell I. (1985), *Developing Effective Communications Strategy. A Benefit Segmentation Approach*, John Wiley & Sons, New York; Hunt, Shelby D. (1995), *Marketing Theory: The Philosophy of Marketing Science*, Richard Irwin, Homewood, IL; Kotler, Philip (1995), *Administração de marketing – análise, planejamento, implementação e controle* (4th edn), trans. Ailton Bomfim Brandão, Atlas, São Paulo; Kotler, Philip and Armstrong, Gary (1999), *Princípios de marketing* (7th edn), trans. Vera Whately, Livros Técnicos and Científicos Editora, Rio de Janeiro; Lambin, Jean-Jacques (1989), *Le marketing strategique – fondements, méthodes et applications* (2nd edn), McGraw-Hill, Paris; Lambin, Jean-Jacques (2000), *Marketing estratégico* (4th edn), trans. Domingos Silva. McGraw-Hill, Portugal; Toledo, Geraldo Luciano (1972), "Segmentação de mercado e estratégia de marketing", doctoral thesis, School of Economics, Business Administration and Accounting, University of São Paulo; Weinstein, Art (1995), *Segmentação de mercado*, trans. Celso A. Rimoli, Atlas, São Paulo.
8. Blackwell, Roger D., Miniard, Paul W. and Engel, James F (2001), *Consumer Behavior* (9th edn), South-Western–Thomson Learning, Columbus, OH; Britt, Stewart Henderson (1966), *Consumer Behavior and the Behavioral Sciences*, John Wiley & Sons, New York; Grisi, Celso Cláudio de Hildebrand e (1986), "Contribuições ao estudo das técnicas de segmentação de

mercado – uma análise de dados sobre apostadores da Loteria Federal", master's dissertation, School of Economics, Business Administration and Accounting, University of São Paulo.

9.　Siqueira, Antonio Carlos Barroso de (1997), "Contribuições ao estudo de segmentação de mercado industrial: caso da indústria brasileira de elevadores", doctoral thesis, School of Economics, Business Administration and Accounting, University of São Paulo.

10.　Liu et al., "Effects of household dynamics", *op. cit.*

11.　Ibid.

12.　Instituto de Pesquisa Econômica Aplicada (IPEA) (2005), http://www.ipea.gov.br (accessed 23 February 2005).

13.　"Alone in America" (1995), *The Futurist*, Vol. 29 (October), http://www.wfs.org/ (accessed 21 February 2005); Althaus, F. (1991), "Young adults choose alternatives to marriage, remain single longer", *Family Planning Perspectives*, Vol. 23, No. 1, pp. 45–46. Available at http://trial.ep.net.com (accessed 21 February 2005); Darko, Kendra L. (1999), "A home of their own", *American Demographics*, http://proquest.umi.com (accessed 2 May 2003); Hall, Ray and Ogden, Philip E. (2003), "The rise of living alone in inner London: trends among the population of working age", *Environment and Planning*, Vol. 35, No. 5, pp. 871–888. Available at http://trial.ep.net.com (accessed 21 February 2005); Hasson, Larry (2004), "Monitoring social change", *Journal of the Market Research Society*, No. 37, pp. 69–80. Available at http://trial.ep.net.com (accessed 21 February 2005); Jancsurak, Joe (1999), "Small could be big", *Appliance Manufacturer*, http://proquest.umi.com (accessed 2 May 2003); "More Americans live alone" (2003), *The Futurist*, Vol. 37, No. 4. Available at http://www.wfs.org/ (accessed 21 February 2005); Ogden, Philip and Hall, Ray (2000), "Households, reurbanisation and the rise of living alone in the principal French cities, 1975–90", *Urban Studies*, Vol. 37, No. 2, pp. 367–390. Available at http://trial.ep.net.com (accessed 21 February 2005); "Rise of singles" (2000), *The Futurist*, Vol. 34. Available at http://proquest.umi.com (accessed 2 May 2003); Thornton, Arland and Young-Demarco, Linda (2001), "Four decades of trends in attitudes toward family issues in the United States: the 1960s through the 1990s", *Journal of Marriage and the Family*, Vol. 63, No. 4. Available at http://trial.ep.net.com (accessed 21 February 2005); "The Bridget Jones economy – singles and the city" (2001), *The Economist*, http://proquest.umi.com (accessed 2 May 2003); Wellner, Alison Stein (2001), "The American family in the 21st century", *American Demographics*, Vol. 23, No. 8. Available at http://trial.ep.net.com (accessed 21 February 2005); Wellner, Alison Stein (2002), "The census report", *American Demographics*, Vol. 24, No. 1. Available at http://trial.ep.net.com (accessed 21 February 2005); Wilkinson, Helen (1999), "Celebrate the new family", *New Statesman*, Vol. 128, No. 4448, pp. 21–23. Available at http://trial.ep.net.com (accessed 21 February 2005); Zinn, Laura (1991), "Home alone – with \$660 billion", *BusinessWeek*, No. 3224, p. 76. Available at http://proquest.umi.com (accessed 5 May 2003).

14.　Ibid.

15.　Mariz and Boccia, "¿O Reid a Cocada?", *op. cit.*

16.　Hasson, "Monitoring social change", *op. cit.*

17.　Wilkinson, "Celebrate the new family", *op. cit.*

18.　Pacheco, "¿A lucrative diversidade?", *op. cit.*

19.　Ber, Alessandra (2002), "Solteiros e cobiçados. Pelo Mercado", *Jornal da Tarde*, http://www.jt.estadao.com.br (accessed 9 April 2003); Borges, Robinson (2003), "O impacto do homem só", *Jornal Valor Econômico*, June, pp. 10–12; Madeira, Adriana Beatriz, Garcia, Alex, Ferraz, Cleber P., Silva, Danilo N.L. and Vianna, Paulo Roberto B. (2003), *Influência das embalagens dos produtos no hábito de compra do público single no distrito de Moema, na cidade de São Paulo*, FIA/

FEA, University of São Paulo; Estatísticas do Século XX (2003), Rio de Janeiro, IBGE, CD-ROM; *Manual do Recenseador* [Demographic Census] (2000), Rio de Janeiro, IGBE, CD-ROM.

20. Madeira et al., *Influência das embalagens dos produtos, op. cit.*
21. Ferreira, "Single", *op. cit.*
22. *Censos Demográficos Brasil – 1970, 1980, 1991, 2000 – Microdata*, Rio de Janeiro, IBGE, CD-ROM.
23. Curry, David J. (1993), *The New Marketing Research Systems. How to Use Strategic Database Information for Better Marketing Decisions*, John Wiley & Sons, New York.
24. Hair, Joseph F. Jr, Anderson, Rolph E., Tatham, Ronald L. and Black, William C. (1998), *Multivariate Data Analysis* (5th edn), Prentice Hall, Englewood Cliffs, NJ; Hair, Joseph F. Jr, Anderson, Rolph E., Tatham, Ronald L. and Black, William C. (2005), *Análise multivariada de dados* (5th edn), trans. Adonai Schlup Sant`Ana and Anselmo Chaves Neto Bookman, Porto Alegre.
25. Hair et al., *Análise multivariada, op. cit.*
26. Madeira, Adriana Beatriz (2005), "Estudo e caracterização do perfil da população que vive sozinha em centros urbanos brasileiros", master's dissertation. School of Economics, Administration and Accounting, University of São Paulo.
27. Ibid.
28. Ibid.

10 *Targeting Hispanics/ Latinos Beyond Locality: Food, Social Networks and Nostalgia in Online Shopping*

VANESSA FONSECA*

Keywords

e-commerce, Hispanic/Latino food, nostalgic consumption, transnational communities.

Abstract

This chapter studies two examples that illustrate how Hispanic/Latino online purchases may reterritorialize food practices and communities in the frame of migration and globalization processes. It further discusses marketing and retailing practices that can capitalize on the psychological dimensions of ethnic food consumption and e-commerce among transnational communities.

Introduction

The twenty-first century has inaugurated an era of simultaneous integration and fragmentation. On the one hand, globalization increases the flow of commodities, services and people as it reconfigures markets and retailing practices. On the other hand, technological convergence transforms media landscapes, and the development of communication infrastructures reshapes consumer behaviour. As a consequence, the current delivery of media content and its articulation for conventional marketing and advertising formats is changing today faster than ever before.

* Professor Vanessa Fonseca, Department of Communications, The University of Costa Rica, San Pedro de Montes de Oca, San José, Costa Rica. E-mail: vafons@gmail.com. Telephone: (506) 22 07 51 61.

Food artefacts and practices also enter this flow. The relocation of migrants, exiles or refugees generates complex cultural processes that go beyond the suggestions of traditional acculturation and assimilation theory. Modernity has witnessed the emergence of national communities and identities located at specific territories. Conversely, current migration and globalization processes, along with technological convergence, result in the rise of transnational and virtual communities all over the world. As a result, food artefacts, rituals and cultural meanings travel and change within transnational communities, which experience and reproduce their cultural heritage far from their homeland.

Transnational communities forge and sustain multiple social relations that link societies of origin and settlement.[1] For many, the World Wide Web constitutes an imagined territory[2] that helps connect former social networks with current relatives and friends. For transnational persons, food production, distribution and consumption through the Web constitute key factors in the reproduction of their cultural identities. This chapter studies two examples that illustrate the role of online ethnic food consumption among transnational communities of Hispanic/Latino consumers. First, it analyses how US Hispanic remittances and e-commerce stimulate new retailing practices and consumer trends in Latin America and the USA. Second, it discusses the role of Hispanic food portals in the reproduction of cultural practices that capitalize on nostalgic consumption. As a result of globalization, territories are reworked and reconfigured by consumers and retailers, who experience them beyond a traditional, physically bounded space. Marketers should acknowledge the importance of identifying and assessing these virtual territories to develop branding and marketing strategies that benefit both consumers and retailers.

Methodology

Ethnic food consumption as a research field claims an interdisciplinary, multi-methodological approach, encompassing anthropological concerns with a particular focus on food artefacts, meanings, practices and rituals that characterize a specific ethnic identity and its culinary and gastronomic habits.

This chapter aligns with Kozinets's netnography[3] and uses a cyber-ethnography to study communities located mainly in the World Wide Web. This method combines traditional anthropological techniques, such as participant observation and interviews, with field notes to investigate social dynamics, artefacts and meanings used by a specific online community.

I first documented the location and characteristics of the websites and portals pertinent to this study. A case study of Grupo Supermercados Wong, a site located in Peru, illustrates marketing and retailing strategies exhibited by similar retailers throughout Latin America. An initial personal contact with an EWong consumer in Los Angeles, California, provided data about 11 additional participants. Telephone interviews with six participants located in Austin and San Antonio, Texas, increased the study validity. In addition, one of these participants referred to a former Texas resident who currently lives in Utah. Face-to-face and telephone in-depth interviews took place between September 2005 and May 2006

The selection of participants from California and Texas relied on a snowball technique, in view of the difficulties of finding this specific population in the USA. The final number of participants reflects the principle of saturation, such that the findings had begun to show increasing consistency and frequency. Contacts with ethnic food marketers and consumers were either personal (face-to-face in-depth interviews) or electronic (via e-mail, Yahoo messenger or Google chat). I then triangulated and compared these findings with data gathered from articles and reports on US Hispanic/Latino online consumption trends.

The most representative ethnic food portals in Costa Rica, La Carretica.com and Ticoshopping.com, indicate high user traffic and offer a convenient sample. In-depth interviews with retailers provided information about marketing strategies and access to consumer databases that included requests, e-mails and complaints. A snowball technique again gathered data about 12 consumers, contacted electronically (e-mail or Yahoo messenger). Discourse and semiotic analysis helped analyse the e-mails, requests and other documents that consumers sent to retailers, as well as consumers' reviews posted on both portals. Ethnic food blogs and other ethnic portals also helped clarify the use and cultural meanings that encompass ethnic food consumption. In-depth interviews with retailers and correspondence with consumers began in January 2006 and ended by October 2006.

Shopping for Groceries Online, Consumer Empowerment and Social Networks

Inter-American Dialogue,[4] a Washington-based research centre, predicts that US remittances to Latin America will total $45.9 billion in 2008. Banks and companies such as Western Union remain the preferred means used to send such remittances, which provide a significant contribution to the region's economy. According to Inter-American Dialogue, remittances to Latin American and the Caribbean reached $65.5 billion in 2007, although Mexico and Brazil showed growth reductions, probably due to shifting labour demands and the current economic crisis in the USA.

These US Hispanic/Latino remittances are primarily spent on food. Cobo[5] finds that, among Colombians, shopping for groceries leads the list of expenditures derived from remittances. Several bricks-and-mortar supermarkets in Latin America are developing online capabilities in order to capitalize on this profitable market. The fees for sending money abroad are expensive, and those who receive the money often face the inconvenience of getting to a local telegraph office to complete the transaction. They also fear becoming targets of those who look for easy cash. Several bricks-and-mortar Latin American supermarkets have thus proposed an alternative solution: consumers can buy groceries and other goods directly through websites, eliminating fees for wiring money, with merchandise delivered to any local address.

E-commerce thus constitutes an important means of building social networks among Hispanics/Latinos throughout the Americas that extends far beyond the role played by traditional Hispanic media networks. As an interactive medium, the Web revolutionizes the way in which transnational communities connect, build and maintain social networks. Portes[6] has suggested that the migration process depends on and creates social networks across space. In South America Grupo Supermercados Wong bases its development on its understanding of the advantages and challenges of sustaining social networks among Peruvians abroad and their relatives in Peru.

EWong's 69 per cent market share in Lima places it among the top five enterprises in Peru.[7] Established in 1942 by Erasmo Wong, a Chinese–Peruvian entrepreneur, Grupo Supermercados Wong represents one of the most successful supermarket chains in the country with approximately 35 stores, of which 12 EWong supermarkets target upper-level consumer segments, eight Supermercados Metro offer lower prices, ten Hipermercados Metro present larger supermarket formats, and two Almacenes Eco and two American Outlets serve other consumers.

Grupo Supermercados Wong also embraces strong corporate values, including:[8] "1) the customer is our reason for being; 2) our employees are number one; 3) we seek continuous innovation; and 4) we always look for better ways to serve the customer." In pursuit of continuous innovation, EWong launched its first website in 1998, offering approximately 15,000 products and a virtual tour through the store. By February 2001 the group signed an agreement with Visa International and VISANET, Peru, that enabled Peruvians living abroad to buy groceries for their families in Peru. When ordering groceries online, customers could avoid commission fees for sending money – a common practice among banks and money wiring services such as Western Union.[9] EWong's service thus saves customers $15–20 per transaction. According to Umber Grosse,[10] EWong's global strategy is as follows:

> By 2004, more than 96 per cent of the online orders came from Peruvians living outside Peru in places with a high penetration of computers. Peruvians living in the United States used the Web site to send groceries to their families in Peru. To attract these customers, the company ran an advertising campaign in California, Florida, New Jersey, New York and Washington, DC, areas with high concentrations of Peruvians. Many customers found out about the service by word of mouth.

Until recently, mainstream marketing in the USA had largely underestimated Hispanic/Latino online transactions. In 2000 the Tomás Rivera Policy Institute[11] revealed that approximately 11 million US Hispanics/Latinos were online. In October 2003 AOL launched AOL Latino, designed to appeal to the growing number of US Hispanic/Latino online users who preferred Spanish-based Internet content for their online activities.[12] The following year the Internet Advertising Bureau estimated that 14 million US Hispanics/Latinos were engaging in online activities and designated a Hispanic Committee to track trends and changes in their online behaviour.[13] This study revealed that use of the Internet among US Hispanics equalled total Internet use in Germany (33 per cent) and surpassed its use in countries such as France (24 per cent) and Spain (23 per cent). By May 2006 Telemundo and Yahoo en Español announced their merger,[14] meaning that, for the first time, a national Hispanic television network had established business relationships with a Hispanic online service, with the stated purpose of providing online and broadcast media content for users and advertisers. Finally, in 2008 Terra.com, a digital content producer targeted towards Hispanics/Latinos, and Terra.comScore released research stating that among US Hispanics, "Internet usage now outpaces television with 56% reporting to spend at least one hour per day online vs. 50 per cent that reported spending one hour per day watching television".[15] Thus, the Web represents a broad new world for addressing Hispanics/Latinos as transnational communities and serves as a virtual space for establishing and sustaining social networks through consumption.

Laura, a Peruvian teacher who lives in Los Angeles, California, explains how important is for her to use EWong's services:

Aunt Anita never married and doesn't have kids. She is my only aunt and she was always special to me and my sister Elena, who also lives in the US. I always send money to her, but now she is in her late seventies, I'm worried that she can be robbed or that she could have an accident when she shops for groceries. You can't imagine how happy I was when I first knew about EWong's online service and home delivery. It's like having someone of my own family taking care of Aunt Anita.[16]

Consumers who receive groceries from their relatives abroad obtain more than commodities or goods. The symbolic dimension of sharing and helping transforms these groceries into love. Memory, branding and store loyalty play fundamental roles in this new trend. Peruvians abroad rely on EWong as a trustworthy partner, and, in turn, EWong leads the market with a top-of-mind awareness score of 69 per cent.[17] Yet the relationship goes beyond awareness to reach store loyalty, which suggests more than frequent visits. Consumers establish intimate personal relationships with brands to which they are loyal,[18] and EWong capitalizes on this sense of trustworthiness by allowing material and psychological connectivity between those who left the country in search of better opportunities and those who expect and need financial and emotional assistance from their relatives abroad. Among transnational communities, shopping for groceries online enhances what Calhoun and Coleman[19] call social integration, which consists of four dimensions: face-to-face relations, imagined connections, one-directional (surveillance) and systemic integration.

In traditional bricks-and-mortar environments, face-to face relations are the basis of retailing practices and often constitute a key factor for maintaining store loyalty, especially among US Hispanics/Latinos. Studies[20] reveal that US Hispanics/Latinos prefer to establish face-to-face relations with service people while shopping for groceries, because trust in these service people not only minimizes perceived risk, but also decreases the chances of cognitive dissonance. Face-to-face relations in traditional retailing spaces may also help construct a sense of belonging or, in Calhoun's terms, imagined connections. In contrast, e-commerce environments are based on virtual relations, yet Laura describes EWong's services as "having someone of my own family taking care of Aunt Anita". Social integration thus takes place when she is able to connect to her relatives abroad through a reliable electronic transaction that promises to deliver not only groceries, but also love, to her aunt.

In this sense, social integration not only benefits consumers, but also represents a gold mine for marketers. By tracking consumers' behaviours through data mining, online marketers can exert different forms of control – or unidirectional surveillance – that helps them recognize demand for products, how much money consumers spend on groceries, how often they shop online, their responsiveness to promotions and other pricing strategies, and so forth. Unidirectional surveillance thus positively affects the marketing process and helps companies achieve improved returns on their investment, increased sales and store loyalty. Systemic integration results from the convergence of different interactions, mediated by interpersonal–virtual communications, as well as economic, social, emotional and cultural needs.

This alternative way of sending remittances by ordering groceries, educational materials or school supplies online is not only convenient, but also empowering, to consumers: they can control how their money is spent and make sure that their efforts address their relatives' real needs. For example, Isabel, who studies and works in Southern California, sends money to support her relatives in Peru:

> Before using EWong, I always sent money to my son who lives with my parents. God! It was a constant struggle because the money was for groceries and oftentimes they spent it in other things that were not as important and they always argued that they needed more money for food. Now I buy the groceries online. They receive them and the problem disappeared. They can't manipulate me anymore saying that they don't have money for food.[21]

Isabel's quote illustrates how she rationalizes and maximizes the use of remittances by taking more control over distributive relations. Thus, the production of social capital through remittances may go beyond an economic dimension (the redistribution of money as value) to encompass a set of relationships, the nature of those relationships (e.g. power, gender), and the ability to mobilize social capital (either material or symbolic) to create social change, empowerment or agency. Even though Peruvians in the USA account for the greatest percentage of EWong's international consumers, transnational communities of Peruvians worldwide also collaborate to enhance their families' well-being. Online transactions can be critical to sustaining social networks for immigrants and their families, but they also provide alternative ways to manage remittances. Having control translates into empowerment not only because it eliminates uncertainty and anxiety, but also because it creates social capital. The production of social capital generates and sustains relationships that allow networks to mobilize material or symbolic resources; it is not limited to the mobilization of material resources.

Portes[22] notes that, unlike individual resources owned by disconnected persons, social capital reflects an individual's ability to mobilize these resources on demand. Nathan and Sudweeks[23] further state that "social capital is the key to control in a community, as the members of that community (with highly mobile social capital) have the greatest control over social structures." Isabel establishes priorities in terms of how much money should be spent on food and also negotiates with her mother about what kind of groceries they should buy:

> I can't just choose things and send them right away. I try to make a balance between groceries that are absolutely necessary like fish or chicken and others like some snacks and sweets that my son loves and takes to school. So, I also talk to my mother before I go online, I have a dial-up connection … We talk about what they need; she reminds me what I bought in my last online order. I never place an order without talking to her.[24]

Remittances sent as groceries thus may modify local family patterns. Usually, fathers represent the main providers, who determine the budget for groceries. Even if women shop for groceries, traditionally, the budget has been set by their husbands. In the preceding example, though, female power in the family shifts as power and control reconfigure the family as a socio-economic strategic unit.

Social support and systemic integration through online consumption among Peruvians reached a painful moment in August 2007 when a devastating earthquake (7.9 on the

Richter scale) hit Peru's Pacific coast and caused 519 deaths, destroyed more than 35 000 houses and injured thousands of people. Grupo Supermercados Wong helped the victims by sending several trucks filled with groceries and other commodities and providing stores as centres for collecting donations in Peru. EWong also enabled electronic donations for Peruvians living abroad, who wanted to help their relatives and fellow citizens. This public-relations effort, called *Donación para nuestros hermanos del sur* (Donation for our Brothers in the South), enabled Peruvians to donate groceries, medicine, and other emergency items through Grupo Wong, which delivered the goods within 48 hours. Again, social support and systemic integration resulted from the articulation of e-commerce, store loyalty and the social and cultural needs of Peruvians as transnational communities.

EWong's marketing innovations represent a growing trend in Latin America, such that several bricks-and-mortar supermarkets are implementing similar retailing strategies. The following examples illustrate how this trend appears to be unfolding in Latin America.

Argentina-based Disco,[25] established in 1961 and now owning 190 stores throughout the country, offers Disco Virtual, an online platform that allows consumers to shop for groceries or electronic devices and delivers them to their homes. In 2005 Disco Virtual achieved 25 million pesos in online transactions and listed more than 260 000 registered users.[26] Two of every 100 pesos spent buying groceries from Argentina's supermarkets on the Internet comes from Argentines abroad, particularly in the USA and Spain.[27] Incentives, such as free shipping for orders that cost more than a certain amount, can translate into more frequent purchases and greater store loyalty.[28]

Rosendo Santos sits at the computer in his Miami home three times a month to shop for his sister's groceries. This 28-year-old accountant buys a little more than $27 worth of goods per order so that he can get free shipping to his sister's home in La Plata, Argentina.

Central America also provides evidence of this trend. In El Salvador, Honduras and Guatemala, MiSuper.com offers vouchers for purchases online. Central Americans abroad can then order groceries and other products for their relatives in their countries of origin. MiSuper.com also delivers the merchandise to any local address.

For Mexicans in the USA, the Gigante supermarket chain offers Gigante Mexicard, a rechargeable debit card that can be used in Mexico and the USA. This enables Mexicans in the USA to buy groceries and other commodities for their relatives in Mexico:

> *The ISI Gift Cards are a great gift for family or friends anytime. Choose amounts from $20 to $500. The Gift Card can be picked up and used at participating stores located throughout Mexico and the United States. Select a card or create a custom card. This ensures the money is used to fit the receiver's needs. They're perfect for family or friends out of the country. It's a secure, economical, convenient and fun way to shop.*[29]

Food memories and kinship converge when consumers build social support networks through online shopping. For consumers who have left their homeland, engagement in virtual networks helps them partially overcome the distance and nostalgia. Because food practices are fundamental to building social capital and kinship, ethnic food marketing through the Web further helps consumers defy distance. In global landscapes, transnational consumers can find new ways of relocating the distribution and consumption of food online. For example, Brazilian consumers acknowledge the psychological effect that results from social integration:

My daughter lives in Florida and she shops at Pão de Web site every month. When the boxes arrive full of food and gifts it's like having her closer to us. [30]

Jonas Antônio Ferreira, the e-commerce general manager at Pão de Açúcar Supermarkets,[31] claims that, in the last decade, more than 2 million Brazilians have migrated to other countries,[32] which helps explain why Pão de Açúcar's online sales account for an average of 110 000 products daily. Most online orders come from four major Brazilian cities, although, in contrast with EWong's electronic sales, online transactions abroad represent less than 5 per cent of total sales

To a certain extent, buying groceries online for relatives abroad expands the psychological or perceived social presence of transnational consumers. Electronic transactions become a symbolic presence, such that the goods delivered represent more than their material or economic value. They convey affection, caring and, ultimately, love. In other words, consumption practices create presence, overcome distance and produce kinship through the distribution of food.

In brief, buying groceries online for relatives abroad is not only convenient for transnational consumers, but also encompasses emotional and cultural meanings that attempt to establish and maintain social networks. Food distribution online challenges traditional marketing assumptions about locality, because, despite the diaspora created by global processes, locality becomes reterritorialized in virtual spaces that create imagined communities and social networks. Traditional retailing practices assumed locality as a given, but global processes create economic, social,and cultural disjunctures, derived from migration and e-commerce dynamics, that initiate alternative spaces for establishing networks and mobilizing objects as well as social capital. Food distribution practices bring people together and help them feel closer. Online shopping thus delivers feelings of love, support and sharing, and the production of locality in this context goes far beyond a physically bounded space.

In addition to touting the convenience of sending remittances as grocery orders, several food portals targeted at US Hispanics/Latinos attempt to capitalize on nostalgic consumption. Nostalgic transnational consumers find an unrivalled market online for ethnic food delicacies and a means to re-enact their food memories. The next section thus pertains to the importance of nostalgic consumption among those who visit ethnic food portals that specialize in Latin American food.

Identity, Food Artefacts and Nostalgic Consumption Online

Consuming ethnic food and other material representations of a particular cultural identity constitutes a legitimate means of reproducing cultural capital and, ultimately, strengthening and reinventing cultural identities. Ethnic food portals specializing in marketing groceries and other food artefacts can be fundamental for transnational communities that search for special ingredients and meals that are difficult to find in mainstream stores. Food portals such as Cubanfoodmarket.com, Mexgrocer.com, Ticoshopping.com and LaCarretica.com[33] specialize in delivering Cuban, Mexican and Costa Rican food and illustrate the role of nostalgic consumption among both immigrants and tourists.

Ethnic food portals emerged as a consequence of migration, globalization and the opportunities derived from e-commerce. At first glance, ethnic food portals seem to be targeted towards transnational communities of migrants, exiles or refugees, who find a space for reasserting their cultural identity in their food practices. Sutton[34] argues that the traditional food–identity–memory equation based on the assumption that "you are what you eat" is insufficient in the face of marketing and advertising efforts to resignify and repackage food memories. He therefore calls for studies that analyse what he calls the "commodification of nostalgia", which raises interesting issues regarding behavioural patterns, online purchases, memory and the production and reproduction of cultural identity. A netnography conducted with Ticoshopping.com and LaCarretica.com, two Costa Rican food portals that deliver Costa Rican food and other ethnic paraphernalia to Costa Ricans abroad, attempts to address this issue.

Memorable Foods: Remapping Tastes and Memories in Globalscapes

Anthropological studies of food analyse food rituals and practices as key spaces for identity formation and the reproduction of cultural processes. Food memories constitute people not only as individuals but also as consumers. For example, Costa Rican ethnic food portals have been evolving since 2002, when LaCarretica.com started offering to fulfil the nostalgic consumption needs of Costa Ricans abroad. It represented a pioneer site, combining radio and television online, weather reports, legal certificates and a series of catalogues offering local salsas, cookies, beers, alcoholic beverages and other ethnic products, such as religious items and music. To accomplish its mission to meet the needs of Costa Ricans who live abroad by distributing products and services that help them feel close to their cultural roots and traditions, LaCarretica relies on high-quality customer services and communication technology, prompting consumers to describe the site as:

> ... simply fabulous. It transports you to your little country in a blink. Thanks a lot for giving us the opportunity to be close by, even if we are FAR AWAY. Best Regards to all ticos.[35]

Food thoughts and popular beliefs often travel with migrants who leave their countries to work or study. One pregnant customer placed an unusual request that illustrates the connection between food consumption and cultural beliefs: "I would like to know if you can find *arracache*. I'm pregnant. I have cravings for it. If I give birth to a baby with an open mouth, it's all your fault!"[36] *Arracache* is a root used to prepare a traditional meal called *picadillo de arracache* (chopped *arracache* seasoned with traditional ingredients). The online marketers replied to her request by admitting, "For now, we don't have access to canned *arracache* suppliers, but if we find one, we will deliver it to you. Regarding your baby, when he arrives, we have Nestlé cereals and Leche Pinito (Pinito Milk) to feed him appropriately.

The retailer thus demonstrated sympathy for the pregnant woman, but also offered her other products that could qualify as "connectors" to her home country and culture. Leche Pinito, a traditional dehydrated milk, comes from Dos Pinos RL, the largest dairy food company in the country. For more than six decades Dos Pinos has manufactured a variety of dairy products that have become food icons. Leche Pinito has been especially popular among children, who mix it with sugar and eat it as a treat. Some local sweets also include it as a main ingredient. The retailer thus activates a cultural script by recommending this product to the future mother. For several decades fresh, pasteurized milk came only from Dos Pinos, and those mothers who could not afford fresh or pasteurized milk would use Leche Pinito as an alternative way of feeding children with a reliable product that provided calcium and other nutrients. The retailer's reply relies on cultural memoirs that associate gender roles (a caring mother) with the use of traditional, local, reliable products. Thus, the message tries to persuade the young mother abroad to keep reproducing food practices from her homeland.

Food memories also highlight certain products as enablers of particular food events. Traditional food practices may be hindered in other locations in which some products are impossible to find. The websites resolve that issue; as one consumer describes, "Thanks to La Carretica we enjoyed Marfil's music, drink a *rompope* (eggnog) and pour more Lizano tabasco on rice and beans".[37] Another customer from Chicago, Illinois, exulted: "I just saw your website and let me tell you that I'm very impressed for all the things and information that you have. This is the website that we ticos[†] needed. I will order soon my 6-pack of Imperial with a heart palm can."

The arrival of unique products impossible to find at regular markets constitutes a food event, to be shared with other family members. According to one mother, LaCarretica.com brought her family in the USA together:

> Greetings! I would like to thank you for the shipment that we received yesterday. We enjoyed it in the company of my daughters, who had the idea to delight us with this mouth-watering products. We cannot find them, not even at markets that sell Central American products, because they don't carry Costa Rican food.[38]

At the end of June 2008 the most popular products on La Carretica.com included Sardimar smoked tuna cans, Volio coffee bags and tortilla presses, which reflects one of Costa Ricans' great loves: coffee. The other key to Costa Rican rituals and traditions is soccer (football), also confirmed by the site as an important means of asserting national pride and identity. Videos, t-shirts of local teams and memorabilia such as keyrings and mugs indicate that football constitutes a social practice, in which gender and national identity converge in the construction of male and female subjectivities.[39]

The consumption of coffee in Costa Rica, popularized during the nineteenth century[40] as a consequence of governmental protectionism and support for coffee producers, led to a reputation for the high standards and quality of Costa Rican coffee. Increasing interest among US and European consumers in exotic, gourmet brands inspired LaCarretica.com to promote this product category through CostaRicanCoffeeShop.com, a site launched in 2005 on which coffee connoisseurs can browse local brands and learn about coffee varieties in Costa Rica,.

This new focus reflects a response to the trends and preferences, especially among US consumers, for rare, gourmet coffee brands, locally manufactured by small coffee producers. In August 2007 Sergio Enamorado, general manager at LaCarretica.com, noted that the site would remain as a portal offering Costa Ricans abroad access to music, videos,

---

†   Ticos is a nickname referring to Costa Ricans; tradition states that Costa Ricans like to add the suffix "ito" or "ita" to nouns and adjectives to convey sympathy or closeness.

local media, news and other products and services, but it would not distribute food other than coffee bags and tuna. He explained that courier charges for food items can triple the product prices, and new US regulations for homeland security make it difficult to send some products. However, an emerging competitor, www.ticoshopping.com, may have been another significant factor prompting this change of direction.

Nevertheless, Costa Ricans abroad love LaCarretica.com because it gives them access to special products and enables them to re-enact food memories that reassert their cultural identity. In contrast, CostaRicaCoffeeShop.com provides a gateway for coffee lovers who have visited Costa Rica and discovered or experienced its coffee during their journey. As a customer from Pasadena, California, states:

Mmm.. So good! We took a coffee excursion while in Costa Rica and had a chance to try out several different brands and let me tell you – there's nothing like Dota Dark Roast. Every drop of it is gourmet quality, really.[41]

Another customer from Florida[42] explains how she learned about the product:

My in-laws brought Dota coffee from their Costa Rican trip last Christmas. I've never had a better cup of coffee! My husband is now a coffee drinker too!

A Canadian couple also describe how they enjoy Bandola coffee and have spread the news among their friends:

My husband and I were given a package of this coffee as a gift and, quite honestly, it is the nicest coffee we have ever tasted. It has a lovely smooth flavour and it's very mild. There is no bitter coffee aftertaste that is present in most coffees we've had. We can't wait to get some more. These aren't only our opinions as we served this coffee to guests and their comments were exactly the same as ours. It is, simply, a superior product that we love.[43]

Word of mouth seems to be a key means for spreading the news about new exotic products that deliver nice food experiences in the company of friends, who also enjoy drinking coffee. A US customer[44] refers to the Triángulo de Oro brand specifically:

I have shared this coffee with a number of friends and they agree that this coffee is the best. Very low acid, not too strong or heavy, best when sitting with friends who also enjoy a great coffee.

LaCarretica.com and CostaRicaCoffeeshop.com together thus offer an interesting space in which study the commodification of nostalgia for two different groups. For Costa Ricans who have left their country and live in the USA, food memories help them re-enact and reassert their cultural identity through the consumption of traditional food artefacts. Food events seem to eliminate the distance and nostalgia, even for those who travel abroad, by prompting food memories that they are willing to share with relatives and friends. US and Canadian tourists who have visited Costa Rica also maintain memories – but not only those associated with places and people. They recall commercial products and food consumption experiences and use word of mouth to direct other coffee lovers, who may not have visited the country, to rare, gourmet coffee. Consumer narratives about how they found the product build strong brand perceptions.

The next section considers a successful Costa Rican food portal that combines these two groups by serving both Costa Ricans abroad and tourists by attempting to revive their food memories through nostalgic consumption.

Ticoshopping.com: Food Memories and Nostalgic Consumption

Ticoshopping.com is a Costa Rican site that has been growing at a tremendous pace. Established in 2004, Ticoshopping.com has doubled its every year, and, according to Antonio Burgos, president and general manager, the site ranks among the top 100 000 on the Web, ranked at 1000 among Costa Rica's most visited websites. In contrast to LaCarretica.com, this site does not openly appeal to nostalgic Costa Ricans abroad, but instead promises efficiency, convenience and a secure, fast delivery:

> Our service has a worldwide covering [sic], so anyone living out of our country limits is able to get from TicoShopping.com any of the typical food, fine coffees, famous sauces, souvenirs, music, t-shirts, news, and other products we have available.

> The company's staff has a wide experience handling international sales and customer service; it also counts [sic] with a strong philosophy of respect, ethics, and efficiency to guaranty [sic] the complete satisfaction of all our visitors, and please remember: our web page is a SECURE SITE. [45]

Burgos believes that the site's competitive advantages result because it does not deal with inventories or accounts receivables. According to Burgos, these financial activities represent major expenses for businesses and make cash flow and return on investment difficult to achieve. Like LaCarretica.com and CostaRicaCoffeeshop.com, the site relies on word-of-mouth advertising to spread the word about its services and products. In turn, Ticoshopping. com considers customer service fundamental to its success. This means that every order is meticulously tracked from its departure from Costa Rica to its arrival to the shipment address. When a client complains about broken products or delays, the company replaces the products or offers discounts off future orders. This strategy enhances customers' confidence and trust in the company as it increases word of mouth as a promotional outcome.

Ticoshopping.com estimates that approximately 75 per cent of its clients are US or Canadian consumers who have visited Costa Rica, and their purchasing patterns differ from those of Costa Rican customers abroad. The US and Canadian clients usually place high-volume orders, such as 12 bottles of Guaro Cacique (pure sugarcane liquor). In contrast, Costa Ricans prefer a single product or several products in small quantities, but order long lists of different product categories, ranging from cookies and salty snacks to tuna cans or Lizano sauce. Burgos[45] describes Costa Rican customers as follows:

> I imagine them willing to take a little bit of everything we offer. I can picture tico clients sitting at the table in front of all the products they requested, examining them carefully and eating a little bit here and there, little by little.

This reverence for "lost products" relates to what Fernández[46] calls the "recapture of totality." When people migrate, they usually experience a feeling of leaving something behind in their homeland. Memories and food rituals often re-establish a sense of belonging to a totality that may have been lost in the migration process. Consuming food items that are hard to find also helps recapture the feeling of belonging to a community and re-enacting its traditions and rituals. For Costa Ricans abroad, this recapture of totality exorcises distance. Thus, online shopping for ethnic food provides consumers with the opportunity to overcome feelings of being distant and activates memories through nostalgic consumption:

> When I receive my merchandise I look like a little kid, happy and anxious. I open the box and take every item and place it on the table. I feel fulfilled, my chest is full of happiness. Then, when I pick a guayabita,‡ I transport myself to my grandmother's kitchen. I remember when my cousins and I stole guayabitas from her kitchen cabinets.[47]

However, nostalgic consumption is manifested in different ways among consumers who have travelled to Costa Rica and come back home with food memories that they wish to share with relatives and friends. Burgos suggests that this trend results from the combination of tourism and nostalgic consumption, recalling a US consumer who regularly orders food items for his *Fiesta Tica*, a Costa Rican party that he organizes for his US friends. Memories of his special vacation become a food event, at which he serves a rare sugarcane liqueur (Cacique Guaro) and Costa Rican beer to convey exotic flavours and pleasant memories of travel and leisure, re-created and shared as a ritual.

Recently, Ticoshopping.com bought a new domain (www.guaroliquor.com), where consumers can find information about local sugarcane liqueur and share their creativity by submitting original recipes. Guaro sour, Blue Morph and Pura Vida, some of the featured recipes, reinvent the way in which this liqueur traditionally is served and consumed in Costa Rica. For example, the Guaro sour clearly gets its inspiration from a traditional *pisco* sour drink, and Blue Morph recalls the blue butterfly commonly found in Costa Rica's rainforests, although it contains ingredients that local guaro drinkers would never use. Pura Vida takes its name from a local greeting, but the cocktail offers new ways of serving the liqueur. By allowing consumers to post and share their own recipes for guaro-based cocktails, www.guaroliquor.com promotes frequent visits to the site and benefits from word-of-mouth communications among Ticoshopping.com customers.

Travellers also pose strange and challenging requests to staff members. Burgos recalls a customer who requested a special order for a rare coffee brand. The customer narrated the story of his last trip to Monteverde (a popular cloud forest in Costa Rica), during which he bought a bag of Mi Negro coffee at a particular store. The brand did not appear in the Ticoshopping.com catalogue, but the client asked Ticoshopping.com to find the product so that he could place an order. Burgos, who considers himself an expert in Costa Rican coffee brands, was not familiar with it, but he and his team immediately launched a quest. They finally found a modest coffee producer located in Pavas, in downtown San José, hundreds of miles away from where the client first purchased it. Now a regular customer, the special requester orders a full supply of Mi Negro coffee every two months. As Burgos notes and this incident demonstrates, customer service provides the means to drive consumers to the site and motivates those who already use it.

On both LaCarretica.com and Ticoshopping.com, nostalgic consumption takes place in different ways. Transnational communities of Costa Ricans in the USA reawaken their

---

‡   Guava jelly covered with chocolate.

food memories with products that recall their cultural traditions and memories from their homeland. In contrast, US and Canadian tourists and travellers revisit their food memories and experiences by ordering products that they first tried abroad. However, these products and their uses change as new consumption contexts and meanings get reinvented in new recipes and cocktails.

Final Remarks

Globalization reconfigures the way in which traditional marketing practices can organize and plan the distribution of food and the delivery of culturally relevant artefacts. The findings in this research reveal how important it is for online marketing to create valuable and reliable relationships with consumers based on their articulation of corporate values, branding and retailing strategies. EWong's success illustrates how store loyalty and customer service help build social networks that constitute alternative marketing platforms. Transnational communities benefit from this infrastructure and use the Internet to forge, sustain and link societies of their origin and settlement. By establishing these networks, online consumption relocates food practices and promotes alternative social formations that demand new marketing and retailing strategies.

The first step may be to revisit stereotypes about Internet usage among Hispanics and Latinos in the USA and abroad; this market surpasses national and international boundaries. Technological convergence across the Americas is remapping the ways in which marketers can address their consumers by moving beyond locality. The penetration of broadband and mobile-phone technology in Latin America also offers a new world for marketing opportunities. Every day, more and more regions that have lacked standard telephone infrastructure gain the ability to communicate using cellphones and broadband access to the Web. Larger Hispanic/Latino portals such as Terra.com even have begun to offer services such as Terra compras (Terra shopping), that enables Latin American consumers to buy products online at US-based stores and receive the products locally in their own countries.

The online retailers use several strategies to promote frequent purchases and store loyalty, including free shipping for some orders or themed packages. Dedicated customer service that constantly tracks and solves customers complaints can increase store loyalty and improve store positioning through greater word-of-mouth effects. These effects translate into free advertising and store branding. Mergers with other online marketing firms, such as Amazon.com, eBay, or Secondlife.com, could create as yet unknown niches for ethnic food portals.

Hispanic/Latino food portals such as La Carretica.com and Ticoshopping.com not only target nostalgic transnational communities, but also invite mainstream consumers to experience new culinary styles and products. These trends are opening new distribution practices among marketers, hand-in-hand with the new global digital economy and the increasing Latinization of the US market.[48] Remittances to Latin America continue to grow, especially as Wal-Mart continues to expand its Latin American stores by buying large traditional supermarket chains in Brazil, Central America and Mexico. Wal-Mart also plans to provide financial and banking services in its stores to cash checks and send remittances. Co-branding or mergers through strategic alliances could help marketers in both Latin America and the USA face the challenges of targeting Hispanics/Latinos by moving beyond locality in the new global digital economy, where new consumption spaces continue to grow.

References

1   Portes, Alejandro (1995), *The Economic Sociology of Immigration*, Russell Sage Foundation, New York.
2   Anderson, B. (1991), *Imagined Communities*, Verso, London.
3   Kozinets, R.V. (2002), "The field behind the screen: using netnography for marketing research in online communities", *Journal of Marketing Research*, Vol. 39, pp. 61–72.
4   "Worldwide trends in international remittances" (2008), *Migrant Remittances*, Vol. 5, No. 2, p. 2. Available at http://www.thedialogue.org/PublicationFiles/Migrant%20Remittances--May%202008-FINAL.pdf (accessed June 2008).
5   Cobo Soto, Alvaro (2006), "Las cajas de compensación familiar. Un instrumento social para los colombianos", http://www.asocajas.org.co/2006/DESCARGAS/ESPAÑA/españa%20remesas.ppt (accessed June 2008).
6   Portes, *Economic Sociology of Immigration, op. cit.*; Portes, Alejandro (1997), "Immigration theory for a new century: some problems and opportunities", *International Migration Review,* Vol. 31, No. 4, pp. 799–825; Portes, Alejandro (1996), "Global villagers: the rise of transnational communities", *The American Prospect*, Vol. 25, pp. 74–77.
7   Alvarez, Novales, José Mario (nd), "Supermercado virtual", http://profesores.ie.edu/alvareznovales/Casos/Ewong.doc. (accessed June 2008).
8   Umber Grosse, Christine (2004), "Innovation and customer service at Grupo Supermercados Wong: a Peruvian success story", Thunderbird Case A07-04-0029, http://www.thunderbird.edu/about_thunderbird/case_series/2004/_04-0029.htm (accessed June 2008).
9   Alvarez, "Supermercado virtual", *op. cit.*
10   Umber Grosse, "Innovation and customer service", *op. cit.*
11   Tornazsky, Louise and Elsa Macías Sara Jones (2002), "Latinos and information technology: the promise and the challenge", Tomás Rivera Institute, http://www.trpi.org/update/informationtechnology.html (accessed June 2008).
12   AOL Latino (2003), "Timeline", http://www.aolepk.com/latino/english/timeline.htm (accessed June 2008).
13   Mack, Ann M. (2004), "IAB forms Hispanic committee", *Adweek*, http://www.adweek.com/aw/iq_interactive/article_display.jsp?vnu_content_id=2068674 (accessed June 2008).
14   LeClaire, Jennifer (2006), "Yahoo Telemundo portal caters to Hispanic market", *Tech News World*, http://www.technewsworld.com/rsstory/50445.html (accessed June 2008).
15   Terra.comScore (2008), "Hispanic digital study provides new insights into the diverse Hispanic online community", http://hispanicbusiness.com/news/2008/5/6/2008_terra_comscore_hispanic_digital_study.htm (accessed June 2008).
16   Personal communication.
17   Umber Grosse, "Innovation and customer service", *op. cit.*
18   Fournier, Susan (1998), "Consumers and their brands: developing relationship theory in consumer research", Journal of Consumer Research, Vol. 24, No. 4, pp. 343–373.

19   Calhoun, Craig and Coleman, James S. (1991), "Indirect relationships and imagined communities: large-scale social integration and transformation of everyday life" in Pierre Bourdieu (ed.), *Social Theory for a Changing Society*, Westview Press, Boulder, CO.

20   Cuellar, Sandra (2006), "The Hispanic market in the U.S. Opportunities and challenges for the food industry", http://hortmgt.aem.cornell.edu/pdf/smart_marketing/cuellar7-06.pdf; Food Marketing Institute (2002), *U.S. Hispanics: Insights into Grocery Shopping, Preferences and Attitudes*, Food Marketing Institute, Washington DC; Unilever (2006), "The U.S. market for Hispanic foods and beverages", www.unileverusa.com/Images/Hispanic%20Trip%20Study_tcm23-40305.pdf (accessed March 2008).

21   Personal communication.

22   Portes, *Economic Sociology of Immigration, op. cit.*

23   Nathan, Vivian and Sudweeks, F. (2003), "Social networks in transnational and virtual communities", *Informing Science InSITE, "Where Parallels Intersect"*, http://proceedings.informingscience.org/IS2003Proceedings/docs/192Vivia.pdf (accessed June 2008).

24   Personal communication.

25   http://www.disco.com.ar/Home/HomeDisco.asp (accessed June 2008).

26   Cáffaro, Cora (2005), "Click Caja. El Clarín de Buenos Aires", http://www.clarin.com/diario/2005/06/29/conexiones/t-1004830.htm (accessed June 2008).

27   Di Pinheiro, Raymond and Bianchi, Alejandro (2002), "Émigrés send food online to the old country", *Wall Street Journal*, 6 November, p. B3.

28   Ibid.

29   http://infinitysystemsinternational.com/main.html (accessed June 2008).

30   Di Pinheiro and Bianchi, "Emigrés send food online", *op.cit.*

31   http://www.paodeacucar.com.br (accessed June 2008).

32   Di Pinheiro & Bianchi, "Emigrés send food online", *op. cit.*

33   http://www.cubanfoodmarket.com; http://www.mexgrocer.com; http://www.lacarretica.com; http://www.ticoshopping.com (accessed June 2008).

34   Sutton, David (2001), *Remembrance of Repasts. An Anthropology of Food and Memory*, Berg, New York.

35   http://www.aboutus.org/CarRetica.com (accessed June 2008).

36   http://www.lacarretica.com (accessed June 2008).

37   Ibid.

38   Ibid.

39   Sandoval, Carlos (2006), *Fuera de juego: fútbol, identidades nacionales y masculinidades en Costa Rica*, EUCR, San José, Costa Rica,

40   Vega Jiménez, Patricia (2004), *Con sabor a Tertulia. Historia del consumo del café en Costa Rica 1840–1940*, Icafe, Instituto del Café de Costa Rica, Editorial de la Universidad de Costa Rica, San José, Costa Rica.

41   http://www.costaricancoffeeshop.com (accessed June 2008).

42   Ibid.

43   Ibid.

44   Ibid.

45   Personal communication.

46   Sutton, *Remembrance of Repasts, op. cit.*

47   Personal communication.

48   Fonseca, Vanessa (2003), "Fractal capitalism and the Latinization of the US market", doctoral dissertation, Department of Advertising, University of Texas at Austin. Available at http://www.lib.utexas.edu/etd/d/2003/fonsecav039/fonsecav039.pdf#page=3 (accessed June 2008); Fonseca, V. (2005), "Nuevo Latino. rebranding Latin American cuisine", *Consumption, Markets, and Culture*, Vol. 8, No. 2. pp. 95–130.

11 *How Consumers' Diverse Personal Values Influence the Country-of-Origin Effect*

JANAINA DE MOURA ENGRACIA GIRALDI* AND
ANA AKEMI IKEDA†

Keywords

consumer behaviour, personal values, country image, country-of-origin effect.

Abstract

This chapter addresses the question: how might consumers' diverse personal values influence country-of-origin effects? An analysis of Chinese home appliances from the perspective of Brazilian executives shows that personal values represent a multidimensional construct, such that each dimension has a different influence on the evaluation of foreign products.

In this chapter we aim to understand the country-of-origin effect; understand what personal values are and why they are important in defining people's behaviour; and learn about the relationship between values and the country-of-origin effect on the basis of the results of empirical research.

Introduction

Studies on the so-called country-of-origin effect attempt to identify processes that may help explain how the country of origin influences evaluations of a product. The

* Professor Janaina de Moura Engracia Giraldi, Professor Doctor, Faculdade de Economia Administração e Contabilidade de Ribeirão Preto (FEA-RP), Universidade de São Paulo (USP). Av. dos Bandeirantes, 3900. Ribeirão Preto (SP), Brazil. CEP: 14.040-900. E-mail: jgiraldi@usp.br. Telephone: + 55 (16) 3602 3903.

† Dr Ana Akemi Ikeda, Professor Doctor, Faculdade de Economia Administração e Contabilidade (FEA), Universidade de São Paulo (USP). Av. Prof. Luciano Gualberto, 908. Butantã, São Paulo (SP), Brazil. CEP: 05.508-900. E-mail: anaikeda@usp.br. Telephone: + 55 (11) 3818 4038.

country-of-origin construct develops from the idea that people usually make stereotyped judgements with regard to other people and countries and, consequently, towards products manufactured in those countries.[1]

The first empirical test of the influence of the country of origin on the acceptance and success of a product was conducted by Schooler,[2] who found significant differences in assessments of products that were identical in all their attributes, with the exception of the country specified by the "made in" label. Since Schooler's work, the country-of-origin effect has been the theme of more than 700 studies,[3] many of which focus on assessing the occurrence, magnitude and significance of country-of-origin effects for different products.[4]

Decades of study on the topic have led to an apparently unequivocal conclusion, however: the product's country of origin may influence consumers' assessment of the product.[5] Works within this theme indicate that the country-of-origin effect may be lessened by a range of intrinsic (that is, related to the physical composition of the product) and extrinsic (that is, related to the product but other than its physical composition) information, as well as environmental and cultural factors. Consumers' perceptions ultimately influence their choice of a product or brand – an idea common to most studies on multiple product cues.[6]

In this chapter we take Balabanis's, Mueller's and Melewar's[7] argument into account and add to the minimal academic research that investigates how cultural differences among consumers might influence their perception of different countries. In this context, we define values as the very essence of a particular culture, frequently used to define and describe different cultures.[8]

Values play an important role in the selective process of human actions and help identify how people present themselves to both themselves and others.[9] Cultural norms usually establish behavioural standards regarding how to achieve proper social relations, the means to ensure safety, good eating habits and so on.[10] Therefore, if behaviour deviates from a cultural norm, society may place sanctions or restrictions on that behaviour.

Within this context, this chapter presents the key research issue: how might consumers' diverse personal values influence the country-of-origin effect? The answer to this research question may help fill a gap in the existing body of research that relates cultural values to the country-of-origin effect.

The Country-of-Origin Effect

The country-of-origin effect, defined in various ways in the literature, refers in general to the influence of a product's country of origin on people's attitudes and behaviour towards the product (including agricultural and industrialized goods, as well as services). This effect may represent an intangible barrier to the product's entry into new markets due to the consumers' negative biases towards imported products.[11]

Over the course of more than 40 years, research on this issue has shifted from exploratory and descriptive work to the application of theory. In 1965, for example, the key issue was observing and confirming the existence of the country-of-origin effect; subsequently, research investigated which countries might be considered favourable countries of origin. More recently, researchers have argued that the important goal is to understand why the effect occurs, observe the situations in which it is most prominent, and then investigate the role that information about the country of origin plays in attitude formation and purchasing decisions.[12]

Although studies indicate that a product's country of origin may influence consumer assessments, recent discussions also note the importance of product origin in the current age of global brands.[13] Increasingly globalized production, with diversified production sources combined in the same end-product, prevent consumers from knowing anything about the product's actual country of origin, in which case the information may play only a minor role in the assessment of purchase alternatives.[14]

Therefore, for the country-of-origin effect to occur, the following conditions must hold:

- The consumer must consider information about the product's country of origin relevant to his or her choice process.
- The consumer must be sufficiently motivated to research and compare the different origins of products, which generally occurs when the perceived risk relative to the purchase is high.
- A preference for national products must exist, often linked to the consumer's patriotism or ethnocentrism, preference for foreign products or preference for specific origins associated with certain attributes.
- The consumer should consider this information as more important than other information about price, the store's reputation, perceived risk and so forth.
- The consumer can find this information easily by examining the product itself or talking with a salesperson.[15]

Although a consensus confirms that the country of origin has an impact on product evaluation, the magnitude of this effect remains a topic of debate. This debate particularly focuses on the strength of other intrinsic and extrinsic information about the product, as well as environmental and cultural factors that may facilitate or inhibit trust in the country of origin.

Personal characteristics with a potential influence on the country-of-origin effect include consumers' level of education and conservatism, age and gender, language fluency, number of cues about the product, need for cognition, motivation, degree of involvement, familiarity with the brand, and culture.[16] Furthermore, the country-of-origin effect may vary according to the country, the sample used and the products evaluated.[17]

Variables related to the type/category of the product also play a role whenever the country of origin serves as a criterion for choosing amongst alternatives.[18] For example, information about the country of origin is generally more efficient for agricultural products than for manufactured products and generates a stronger country-of-origin effect because of the historical association between agricultural production and the country or region of origin.[19] For agricultural produce, the country of origin reflects a core feature that differentiates the product from those offered by competitors.

The degree of consumer involvement with agricultural products also tends to be lower than that with manufactured products, which probably generates a greater country-of-origin effect in evaluations of agricultural products compared with manufactured ones. Consumers' perceptions of the quality of foreign products also tend to be product-specific, and food is the most culturally sensitive type of product.[20]

Because most previous research relies on manufactured products for its investigations, it might ignore a very strong country-of-origin effect. However, for this research, such a reliance does not necessarily jeopardize the results, because our objective is not to measure the country-of-origin effect itself or the strength of the relationship between personal values and the country-of-origin effect, but rather to detect which personal consumer values might have the strongest influence on evaluations of foreign products.

Other variables that may affect consumers' use of the country of origin as a purchase criterion include the level of the country development, historical associations between the country of origin and certain products (e.g. France's historical associations with clothing and food), and the strength of the relationship between the country-of-origin images and the product category, such that the images might have more "legitimacy" in certain circumstances than in others.[21] Both researchers and marketing managers require greater awareness of the influences exerted by variables that moderate the country-of-origin effect, particularly those that operate at the individual consumer level, before trying to forecast a general country-of-origin effect. Specifying such variables may improve our ability to understand and foresee country-of-origin effects on different groups of consumers in the market.

Personal Values

As a potential moderating factor of the country-of-origin effect, consumers' personal values depend strongly on the social or cultural system in which they reside.[22] Elements such as cultural similarities, social systems, social and economic class, gender, occupation, background, religious education and political preferences also may mould the value systems of a great number of people in similar ways. Whereas personality factors increase the variations among different individuals' value systems, cultural, institutional and social factors restrict these variations to a reasonably smaller number of dimensions.[23]

The various definitions of individual values converge, in the sense that they are considered the beliefs associated with desirable goals and the modes of conduct that enable the achievement of these goals.[24] Therefore, human values are personal characteristics endowed with cultural, emotional and behavioural components.

For Rokeach,[25] human values consist of desirable goals that vary in importance and serve to guide people's lives. A value therefore is a deep-rooted belief that makes a given mode of conduct or final state of existence preferable to an opposite mode of conduct or final state of existence. In turn, a system of values reflects learned organizing principles and rules that help members choose among alternatives to solve conflicts and make decisions. Rokeach believes that a person has a relatively small number of values as a whole; everybody, everywhere, has the same values to differing degrees; and the antecedents of human values may be found in culture, society, and its institutions.

For Rokeach, there are two value levels: terminal and instrumental. His Rokeach Value Survey (RVS) attempts to measure these two value levels. Terminal values relate to final desired states of existence, whereas instrumental values refer to desirable modes of conduct. Instrumental values thus reflect objectives and terminal values are needs, which represent the broadest and most personal outcomes that human beings try to achieve in their lives.[26]

Terminal values include true friendship, mature love, self-respect, happiness, inner harmony, equality, freedom, pleasure, social recognition, wisdom, salvation, family security, national security, sense of accomplishment, a world of beauty, a world at peace, a comfortable life and an exciting life. In contrast, instrumental values are being cheerful, ambitious, loving, clean, self-controlled, capable, courageous, polite, honest, imaginative, independent, intellectual, broad-minded, logical, obedient, helpful, responsible and forgiving.

Kamakura and Mazzon[27] find significant differences between the USA and Brazil with regard to terminal values. Whereas family security, a world at peace and freedom are considered the most important values in the USA, in Brazil the most important values are true friendship, mature love and happiness. Values related to family are important in both cultures, but Brazilians seem more emotional than Americans.

Instrumental values may also be divided into two groups: moral and competence values.[28] Forms of behaviour, such as honesty, lead a person to believe that he or she is behaving in a moral way. When that shows logical and intelligent reasoning, though, it indicates competence behaviour. A person may experience conflict between two moral values (e.g. behaving honestly and in a friendly way), between two competence values (e.g. imagination versus logic) or between a moral and a competence value (e.g. acting politely and offering intellectual criticism).

Terminal values are also divided into two groups: personal terminal values, which refer to the individual (e.g. inner peace, salvation) and social terminal values, which relate to interpersonal relationships (e.g. world peace).[29]

Other academic studies have tried to reduce the RVS scale into a smaller value grouping; Crosby, Bitner and Gill[30] offer perhaps the strictest.[31] On the basis of previous factor results, they argue that instrumental values should be grouped into three categories: conformity, virtuosity and self-control. They also group terminal values into four categories: idealism, security, self-actualization and hedonism.

Relationship between Values and the Country-of-origin Effect

The few studies that attempt to relate values to the country-of-origin effect use the concepts of individualism and collectivism.[32] Collectivist countries show greater bias against foreigners than individualist countries do,[33] and studies involving consumer choice indicate that collectivist countries are more averse to foreign products than are individualist ones.[34]

Collectivist consumers probably perceive foreign products as a threat to the local economy and jobs.[35] Compared with collectivists, individualists generally are less likely to make sacrifices for the benefit of their countries or any other group. Moreover, people who have a more individualistic background tend to minimize the importance of information about the country of origin and prioritize product quality.[36] Collectivists, in contrast, have a propensity to emphasize the group rather than the individual and evaluate national products more favourably, regardless of whether it is better than foreign products.

Most Latin countries, as well as the Asian ones, are considered collectivist in contrast to more individualistic Western cultures.[37] Moreover, the cultural dimension with the highest scores for Brazil (the setting of the empirical study reported herein) is "uncertainty avoidance" which indicates that Brazilian society possesses a low level of tolerance for uncertainty, does not readily accept change and tends to be very risk-averse.[38]

Another important cultural aspect for evaluating the country-of-origin influence pertains to the culture's degree of ethnocentrism. Ethnocentrism may be defined as the way in which a group perceives itself as the reference framework and classifies other groups according to its own characteristics. The more ethnocentric consumers are, the more they tend to see the purchase of foreign goods as harmful, because their consumption might harm the domestic economy, lead to job losses and be unpatriotic.[39]

In addition to demographic and psychographic characteristics, the following elements may be factors that underlie a consumer's ethnocentric tendencies: degree of openness to foreign cultures, level of patriotism, national collectivism–individualism profile and level of conservatism.[40] The opportunity to interact with other cultures by means of artefacts or interactions with people from the other cultures may also reduce consumers' prejudices and, consequently, the level of ethnocentrism.

An important study by Balabanis, Mueller and Melewar investigated the relationship between personal values and the country-of-origin effect[41] and showed that values are stronger predictors of country-of-origin effects than are demographic data, the influence of language or direct consumer contact with the foreign country. The authors point out that, although values may provide useful information for adjusting marketing programmes, using them may be successful only if the values are used on an ad hoc basis (country by country) and also take into account other contextual factors.

To determine how consumers' personal values may influence the country-of-origin effect, we undertook a field study which is discussed below, followed by a presentation of the results.

Methodology

This descriptive research (with quantitative data collection and analysis) considers two main variables: the country-of-origin effect and consumers' personal values.

Field research evaluates indirectly the country-of-origin effect, because direct evaluations are subject to bias and imprecision. This research uses the scale proposed by Nebenzahl, Jaffe and Usunier[42] to evaluate the country-of-origin effect of Chinese products, which captures the evaluative, social and emotional dimensions that respondents attribute to products. The study respondents' evaluations of people who buy products manufactured in China serve to characterize Chinese products. The sum of the scores attributed by the respondents to the 27 scale items thereby represents the influence that China's image exerts on evaluations of Chinese products.

Previous research shows that the country-of-origin effect varies according to the product category; the product analysed in this study[43] belongs to the specific category of home appliances, because China manufactures and sells such products in Brazil.

Consumers' assessments of Chinese home appliances and people who usually buy such products are collected on a 1–9 scale that indicates the degree to which respondents agree with each statement in a questionnaire. In the statistical analyses, items with negative meanings use reverse scales, such that scores closer to nine indicate more negative images associated with the product.

Furthermore, this quantitative evaluation of the country-of-origin effect asks respondents to evaluate Chinese home appliances and people who buy such products with the assumption that respondents' judgements occur on an interval scale.

The measures of consumers' personal values rely on Rokeach's RVS scale. Ample use of the RVS scale to measure values has established its psychometric properties.[44] Furthermore, Rokeach's scale is appropriate for application in Western societies, such as Brazil, and is therefore suitable for this study.[45]

As our literature review reveals, Rokeach[46] assumes two value levels, terminal and instrumental. Because instrumental values pertain to issues related to people's conduct, they should be more relevant for this study of purchasing behaviour than terminal values. Furthermore, the data collection instrument appears on an Internet page, which gives rise to concerns about the length of the questionnaire and provides another reason to include only instrumental values. The measured values are as follows: cheerful, ambitious, loving, self-controlled, capable, courageous, polite, imaginative, independent, intellectual, honest, clean, logical, obedient, helpful, responsible and forgiving.

Conceptually, measuring values through individual evaluations, rather than ranking, is a superior approach,[47] so the scale to assess values ranges from one to nine, according to their importance to the respondents. This scale is similar to that used to evaluate the country-of-origin effect. The personal values and country-of-origin evaluation scales appear in Appendices 1 and 2.

A survey method is necessary to collect the information needed to comply with the proposed objectives. The population for this research includes executives from the business and marketing areas who had taken executive MBA courses in institutions located in São Paulo state, Brazil. This state is responsible for approximately one-third of the Brazilian gross domestic product, making it the largest economy of South America and one of the biggest economies in Latin America, second only to Mexico. The total number of people included in the study reached nearly 3000.

The population of executives is a segment of interest to several companies as potential purchasers of foreign products. They can easily afford to pay for the product under investigation. In addition, because São Paulo is the wealthiest state in Brazil and one of the largest economies in Latin America, the target population should be well connected internationally.

Because this population is fairly homogenous in demographic terms, this research uses a non-probabilistic sample,[48] chosen using a convenience criterion. The ease of inviting the entire population via e-mail and uncertainty about the response rate prompted the decision to send invitations to the population as a whole, so that everyone would have the opportunity to take part in the research. The data collection took place from June to August 2006.

Results and Discussion

The total of 193 replies received corresponds to a response rate of 6.4 per cent. With regard to the sample profile, all respondents were Brazilian, with an average age of 36 years and a standard deviation of 8.5 years. Most were men (67.4 per cent), and the majority had earned degrees in engineering (27.5 per cent), business (25.1 per cent) or communication (6.0 per cent). Most respondents fell within the middle management category (19.8 per cent), followed by directors (14.6 per cent). Other employment positions cited include consultant, account manager, marketing manager, analyst, product manager, sales manager, entrepreneur and supervisor.

The measure of the degree of knowledge that respondents held about China indicates that most had some knowledge of the country: only 1.6 per cent said they knew nothing about China; 82.4 per cent had read about it; 60.6 per cent had heard about it; and 29 per cent said they knew some Chinese people. Furthermore, on a five-point scale of knowledge (1 representing "I know it very well" and 5 representing "I know nothing about it"), the average was 3.08, close to the intermediary value of the scale.

To reduce the volume of data relating to questions about the respondents' instrumental personal values, factor analysis simplifies the subsequent regression analyses.

FACTOR ANALYSIS

To determine the appropriateness of the critical assumptions necessary to carry out the factor analysis, we applied Bartlett's sphericity test. Furthermore, to measure the adjustment of the data to factor analysis, we used Kaiser-Meyer-Olkin's (KMO) test. The test results showed that the data were suitable for treatment using factor analysis, because the correlations among the variables were significant. In addition, the KMO test value for the personal value questions equalled 0.92 – an excellent result.[49]

The extraction method for the factor analysis relied on main components analysis, and the criterion for the factor extraction required eigenvalues greater than 1. Three factors emerged from the application of this criterion, which jointly explained 58.94 per cent of the elements' total variance. We rotated the factors using the Varimax rotation method to minimize the number of variables of a factor with high loadings, which made it easier to interpret the factors.[50]

We evaluated the internal consistency of the results according to Cronbach's alpha coefficient and submitted each factor to a reliability analysis. Factor 1, which comprises loving, cheerful, clean, responsible, polite, helpful, and honest personal values (in decreasing order of factor loadings), accounted for 25.58 per cent of the elements' total variance with an alpha coefficient of 0.887. Therefore, it may be considered reliable.

Factor 1 represents personal values related to the respondents' concerns about conducting themselves well and in accordance with the social rules of interaction. A similar dimension also appears in Lenartowicz and Johnson's[51] study, which they call "civility". However, we note a difference between the civility dimension and the one we observe, in that the personal values are not the same in both research efforts.

Lenartowicz's and Johnson's civility dimension consists, in decreasing order of factor loadings, of forgiving, loving, polite, obedient, helpful, cheerful and clean. Therefore, responsible and honest (part of Factor 1) join another dimension in their study, which they call "integrity" and which refers to how positively a person is evaluated by others. Thus, two of the value dimensions identified by Lenartowicz and Johnson appear joined together here. Because the personal values of loving, cheerful and clean offer the heaviest factor loadings herein, we refer to Factor 1 as civility.

Factor 2 accounts for 22.51 per cent of the total data variance; it comprises, in decreasing order of factor loadings, logical, intellectual, capable, imaginative, independent, courageous, broad-minded, and ambitious. Internal consistency, as measured by the alpha coefficient, equals 0.844, so Factor 2 may also be considered reliable.

The elements that constitute Factor 2 represent personal values related to the intellectual aspects of the respondents, who wish to follow a practical orientation in their conduct. Similar factors, called "self-direction", appear in Lenartowicz's and Johnson's[52] and Crosby's, Bitner's and Gill's[53] studies. Schwartz also uses this term for one of the ten values based on motivational objectives to represent independence in choices of actions, creation and exploration.[54]

The difference between Factor 2 and Lenartowicz's and Johnson's self-direction factor is that they do not include the capable, courageous and ambitious personal values, but instead group them into another dimension called "drive". Therefore, this research again merges two dimensions observed by Lenartowicz and Johnson.

Crosby, Bitner and Gill define self-direction as comprising ambitious, broad-minded, capable, courageous, imaginative, independent, intellectual, logical and self-controlled values (alphabetical order), similar to the results from this study; only the self-controlled value differs. We again adopt previous nomenclature and call Factor 2 "self-direction".

Finally, Factor 3 explains 10.85 per cent of the total variability of the elements analysed and consists of obedient, self-controlled and forgiving personal values, in decreasing order of factor loadings. The value of the Cronbach's alpha is 0.559, above the acceptable cut-off level of 0.50.[55] We retain Factor 3 for the subsequent analyses.

As explained previously, Lenartowicz and Johnson attribute the personal values in Factor 3 here to their civility dimension, with the exception of the self-controlled value, which they do not consider because it showed high factor loadings on more than one factor. We argue that Factor 3 relates better to Schwartz's "conformity" personal value, which represents restrictions on people's actions, inclinations and impulses that might offend or harm others and violate expectations.[56]

Furthermore, Crosby, Bitner and Gill provide evidence of a "conformity" dimension, but only obedient appears in both their dimension and our Factor 3. The other personal values in Crosby's, Bitner's and Gill's conformity dimension are cheerful, clean, polite and responsible (alphabetical order).[57] However, because obedience, tolerance and self-control may relate to submission to society norms, depending on the culture analysed, we refer to Factor 3 as "conformity".

In general, these results suggest similarity among the three personal values dimensions, whether derived from our sample or developed in theoretical studies of values. This demonstrates theoretical support for this study's empirical results and suggests face validity. The dimensions we find relate closely to those observed by previous researchers,[58] with only small differences in the values that constitute them. Table 11.1 summarizes the factor analysis results.

Crosby's, Bitner's and Gill's study was carried out in the USA, and Lenartowicz and Johnson considered 12 Latin American countries (Argentina, Bolivia, Brazil, Chile, Colombia, Ecuador, Mexico, Paraguay, Peru, Puerto Rico, Uruguay and Venezuela). This research uses only Brazilian respondents. Therefore, the differences observed among the value dimensions may indicate that the consumers' personal values can be grouped together in different dimensions, according to the thoughts and mental associations characteristic of each respondent's country. Depending on the country in which a study is conducted, some differences may mark the composition of the personal value dimensions.

We use the observed personal value dimensions in the multiple regression analysis to determine the relationship between personal values and the country-of-origin effect.

Table 11.1 Factor analysis results

Values dimensions	Instrumental values	Studies with similar results	Differences among value dimension studies
Civility	Loving, cheerful, clean, responsible, polite, helpful, honest	Lenartowicz and Johnson (2002)	Merges two dimensions from Lenartowicz and Johnson (civility and integrity).
Self-direction	Logical, intellectual, capable, imaginative, independent, courageous, broad-minded, ambitious	Lenartowicz and Johnson (2002) Crosby, Bitner and Gill (1990)	Merges two dimensions observed by Lenartowicz and Johnson (self-direction and drive). Similar to Crosby, Bitner and Gill, except self-controlled is not part of the dimension.
Conformity	Obedient, self-controlled, forgiving	Schwartz (1992) Crosby, Bitner and Gill (1990)	Similar to Schwartz's value, which represents restrictions on people's actions, inclinations and impulses. Only obedient appears in both this work and Crosby, Bitner, and Gill.

MULTIPLE REGRESSION ANALYSIS

The dimensions resulting from the factor analysis applied to consumers' personal values are the independent variables, and the country-of-origin effect is the dependent variable, represented by the sum of respondents' attributions to the image of Chinese products. With 27 variables and a 1–9 scale, the minimum expected value for the country-of-origin effect variable is 27 (27 × 1), the maximum value is 243 (27 × 9) and the intermediary value is 135 (27 × 5).

The greater the value of this variable, the more negative is the image that the respondents have of Chinese products. Because the minimum value in the database is 86, and the mean rank is greater than 149, the results show that, in general, respondents tend to evaluate Chinese products negatively.

The independent variables obtained from the factor analysis apply to personal values and correspond to the three identified dimensions (civility, self-direction and conformity). We create a composite measure from the scores to the questions that constitute the three factors. Because a different number of elements represent each personal value dimension (one dimension has seven variables, another has eight and the last has three), the independent regression analysis variables are the mean ranks of the variables that constitute the factors.

We adopt a confirmatory approach to specify the regression model, because the independent variables already are fully specified (that is, the three factors resulting from the factor analysis of the instrumental values). The regression model therefore is as follows:

$$\text{Country-of-origin effect} = \beta_0 + \beta_1 \text{ self-direction} + \beta_2 \text{ civility} + \beta_3 \text{ conformity} + \varepsilon.$$

To answer the research question, we analyse the regression coefficients of the model. Table 11.2 summarizes the estimated regression model for determining the influence of the personal values in the country-of-origin effect.

Table 11.2   Summary of the regression model

Model	R	R^2	R^2 adjusted	Standard error estimate
1	0.115	0.013	-0.003	26.86790

With regard to the statistical significance of the estimated model, this research uses a convenience sample, and we have not conducted an F-test for the determination coefficient or a t-test for the regression coefficients. Therefore, the results refer only to the sample used and should not be generalized to the research population.

Because R^2 measures the percentage of total variation in the dependent variable explained by the variation in the independent variable (with values varying from 0 to 1), we identify a weak relationship among the variables; R^2 is close to 0.[59] Therefore, the results obtained for the regression model suggest a weak dependence relationship between consumers' personal values and the country-of-origin effect. This result may reflect that the respondent population is generally sophisticated and demanding when it comes to choosing products.

We anticipated that most respondents would evaluate Chinese products negatively. However, despite this predicted negative evaluation, Chinese electronic devices usually cost approximately 30 per cent less than other brands in Brazil, which has led to market share increases for these products, from 3 per cent in 2002 to 15 per cent in 2004.[60]

Furthermore, the majority of replies about the importance of personal values concentrate at the highest points of the scale; the respondents identify 18 instrumental values as important, with some values a little more important than others. The combination of these factors may have resulted in a low R^2 for the relationship between personal values and the country-of-origin effect.

However, even when research respondents are subject to these tendencies in their evaluation of Chinese products, the moderating role of personal values still appears. This study measures not how the image of China may influence evaluations of Chinese products or the strength of the relationship between personal values and the country-of-origin effect, but rather which personal consumer values have the greatest influence on the evaluation of foreign products.

In this sense, it is more relevant to check and compare the magnitude and valence of the regression coefficients than the value of the determination coefficient (R^2) of the estimated model. Table 11.3 shows the regression coefficients as well as the tolerance values, in such a way as to enable an evaluation of the presence of multicolinearity.

Tolerance values below 0.10 denote high multicolinearity; the values in Table 11.3 are all greater than 0.10, indicating that multicolinearity might not have affected the stability of the regression coefficients. In the analyses of non-standardized regression coefficients (because we use the same measurement unit in the three independent variables), we find that the personal values dimension with the greatest β value is civility (1.982), followed by self-direction (1.003), and finally conformity (-0.380).

Table 11.3 Coefficients of the regression model

	Non-standardized coefficients		Standardized coefficients	Colinearity statistic
	β	Standard error	β	Tolerance
(Constant)	129.099	13.938		
Self-direction	1.003	2.326	0 .043	0.531
Civility	1.982	2.309	0.090	0.480
Conformity	-0.380	1.722	-0.019	0.739

Before interpreting the size and valence of the regression coefficients, it is important to note that the dependent variable represents respondents' evaluations of Chinese home appliances. The higher the values of this variable, the more negative is the image of Chinese products.

Regression coefficients express the expected change in the dependent variable for each unit of change in the independent variables. Because the coefficients of the first two personal value dimensions are positive, an increase in the importance of the civility and self-direction values leads to an increase in the country-of-origin effect variable. That is, the image associated with Chinese home appliances becomes more negative as the values of civility and self-direction grow in importance.

The civility dimension represents loving, cheerful, clean, responsible, polite, helpful and honest personal values. According to the empirical results of this research, the more important it is for respondents to behave according to the social rules of interaction, the more negatively they evaluate Chinese home appliances.

The self-direction dimension comprises logical, intellectual, capable, imaginative, independent, courageous, broad-minded and ambitious values, which may indicate that respondents are, or want to be, different than others. Because they consider themselves ambitious and successful, they do not appreciate Chinese products. In other words, the more they consider these intellectual aspects important and adopt a practical orientation in their lives, the more negatively they evaluate Chinese home appliances.

In contrast, the negative regression coefficient of the conformity dimension means that when the conformity values become more important, the country-of-origin effect variable declines. The values related to this dimension – obedient, self-controlled and forgiving – imply that the more important it is for the respondents to submit to societal norms, the more positively they evaluate Chinese home appliances, to the extent of being forgiving (tolerant) towards the products in question.

These results indicate further that personal values are a multidimensional construct, such that each dimension exerts a different influence on evaluations of foreign products. Despite having used a different value system and a different country image scale, we derive results similar to those noted by Balabanis, Mueller and Melewar.[61] In both works, the results largely indicate that the more important personal values become to respondents, the more negatively they evaluate the foreign country image.

Closing Remarks

This chapter investigates the relationship between personal values and the country-of-origin effect, using a study with Brazilian executives with executive MBA degrees in the marketing or business areas. Personal values are beliefs held by consumers, associated with desirable goals and modes of conduct that make it possible to achieve those goals. The country-of-origin effect refers to the influence of the country image on consumers' behaviours and attitudes regarding products or brands of that country.

China provides the source country for this research not only because it is one of Brazil's most important commercial partners, but also because, during the past 25 years, it has undergone impressive economic growth and a rising integration into the world economy.

By using both factor and multiple regression analyses, we find that personal values represent a multidimensional construct, such that each dimension has a different influence on evaluations of foreign products. The personal values that most affect the evaluation of foreign products are those related to the civility dimension (loving, cheerful, clean, responsible, polite, helpful and honest), followed by the values that constitute the self-direction dimension (logical, intellectual, capable, imaginative, independent, courageous, broad-minded and ambitious). The conformity dimension values (obedient, self-controlled and forgiving) have a separate and distinct influence.

Although this chapter focuses on Chinese manufactured goods rather than food products, the methodology and findings may be applicable to the food sector in many cases. For example, although food is often a hedonistic good, it also may represent a health-oriented good. Many food choices are mediated by individual beliefs and attitudes, including the factors that determine self-identity.[62]

Attributes such as the self-direction value dimension or the clean (related to food contamination issues) and imaginative (related to food neophilia – that is, the love of novelty and new things, versus neophobia, or the fear of new things or experiences) personal values should be relevant in food contexts. Because food also has powerful cultural and social connotations, attributes such as conformity and even civility value dimensions may be useful for understanding consumption behaviour.

This research provides several relevant results that can help clarify how personal values influence consumers' evaluations of a country and its products. In turn, it strengthens prior results and uncovers additional information about influences on consumers' purchasing decision processes.

Modern consumers live in an era in which citizens in many countries are beginning to question the balance of the benefits versus the demerits of a globalized economy. In many areas, particularly when it comes to food issues, a sort of consumer patriotism has been emerging, whereby consumers prefer local and national products over more remotely sourced ones. The quality of imported goods also has been cause for concern, to both consumers and governments, especially in the case of Chinese goods.

In this regard, marketing professionals and theoreticians should recognize the important role of personal values in evaluations of a country image and products manufactured in that country. The results presented here can also help them manage the use of a product's country of origin as a marketing tool. Similarly, these study findings may help government agencies responsible for the development of their country's image to adjust their brand strategies and thereby appeal to different segments of consumers according to their predominant personal values.

Regarding the methodological drawbacks of this research, we note that the target population defined for this study does not address other important purchasing segments for foreign products, such as professionals and affluent consumers who reside in regions in Brazil other than São Paulo state.

A further data limitation prevents any comparisons according to differences in the respondents' company seniority, size of the company, corporate structure or respondent's earnings. These comparisons might reveal some bias – for example, senior members of organizations might face more time constraints and refuse to reply, which may help account for the relatively low average age of 36 years among the respondents. However, we eliminated such items from the final questionnaire due to space and time constraints. The low R^2 value also indicates that some unexplained factors may require further investigation.

These research results and limitations suggest other research possibilities as well. First, the results might be more deeply investigated through other descriptive studies that use probabilistic samples to generalize the results to the populations studied. Second, this research methodology might be applied to other populations in which companies are interested to verify the consistency of the results. Moreover, comparisons with other countries could provide enriched knowledge about culture and ethnic diversities. Third, additional studies should use other scales of personal values, such as Schwartz's,[63] or other country image scales, such as that proposed by Pisharodi and Parameswaran,[64] to provide comparisons of the results pertaining to the relationship between personal values and the country-of-origin effect.

References

1. Balabanis, G., Mueller, R. and Melewar, T.C. (1999), "Country of origin images around the world: can value priorities predict them?", *Proceedings of the 28th EMAC Conference*, 1999, Berlin.
2. Schooler, R.D. (1965), "Product bias in the Central American common market", *Journal of Marketing Research*, Vol. 2, No. 4, pp. 394–397.
3. Papadopoulos, N. and Heslop, L. (2002), "Country equity and country branding: problems and prospects", *Journal of Brand Management*, Vol. 9, No. 4/5, pp. 294–314.
4. Verlegh, P.W J. and Steenkamp, J.B.E.M. (1999), "A review and meta-analysis of country-of-origin research", *Journal of Economic Psychology*, Vol. 20, No. 5, pp. 521–546.
5. Pharr, J.M. (2005), "Synthesizing country-of-origin research from the last decade: is the concept still salient in an era of global brands?", *Journal of Marketing Theory and Practice*, Vol. 13, No. 4, pp. 34–45.
6. Chao, P. and Gupta, P.B. (1995), "Information search and efficiency of consumer choices of new cars: country-of-origin effects", *International Marketing Review*, Vol. 12, No. 6, pp. 47–59.
7. Balabanis, G., Mueller, R. and Melewar, T.C. (2002), "The human values lenses of country of origin images", *International Marketing Review*, Vol. 19, No. 6, pp. 582–610.
8. Hofstede, G. (1991), *Cultures and Organizations: Software of the Mind*, McGraw-Hill, New York.
9. Rokeach, M. (1973), *The Nature of Human Values*, The Free Press, New York.

10. Assael, H. (1995), *Consumer Behavior and Marketing Action*, South-Western College Publishing, Cincinnati, OH.

11. Wang, C. and Lamb, C. (1983), "The impact of selected environmental forces upon consumers' willingness to buy foreign products", *Journal of the Academy of Marketing Science*, Vol. 11, No. 2, pp. 71–84; Agbonifoh, B.A. and Elimimian, J.U. (1999), "Attitudes of developing countries toward country-of-origin products in an era of multiple brands", *Journal of International Consumer Marketing*, Vol. 11, No. 4, pp. 97–116.

12. Ayrosa, E.A.T. (2000), "Some notes on the development of research on country-of-origin effects", *Arché Internacional*, Vol. IX, p. 26.

13. Pharr, "Synthesizing country-of-origin research", *op. cit.*

14. Usunier, J.C. (2002), "Le pays d'origine du bien influence-t-il encore les évaluations des consommateurs?", *Revue Française du Marketing*, Vol. 189–190, pp. 49–67.

15. Ibid.

16. Anderson, W.T. and Cunningham, W.H. (1972), "Gauging foreign product promotion", *Journal of Advertising Research*, Vol. 12, No. 1, pp. 29–34; Balabanis, Mueller, and Melewar, "Country of origin images around the world", *op. cit.*; Chao, P. and Rajendran, K.N. (1993), "Consumer profiles and perceptions: country-of-origin effects", *International Marketing Review*, Vol. 10, No. 2, pp. 22–39; Johansson, J.K., Douglas, S.P. and Nonaka, I. (1985), "Assessing the impact of country of origin on product evaluations: a new methodological perspective", *Journal of Marketing Research*, Vol. 22, No. 4, pp. 388–396; Maheswaran, D. (1994), "Country-of-origin as a stereotype: effects of consumer expertise and attribute strength on product evaluations", *Journal of Consumer Research*, Vol. 21, No. 2, pp. 354–365; Schaefer, A. (1997), "Consumer knowledge and country of origin effects", *European Journal of Marketing*, Vol. 31, No. 1, pp. 56–72; Shimp, T.A. and Sharma, S. (1987), "Consumer ethnocentrism: construction and validation of the CETSCALE", *Journal of Marketing Research*, Vol. 24, No. 3, pp. 280–90; Zhang, Y. (1997), "Country-of-origin effect: the moderating function of individual difference in information processing", *International Marketing Review*, Vol. 14, No. 4, pp. 266–287.

17. Martin, I.M. and Eroglu, S. (1993), "Measuring a multi-dimensional construct: country image", *Journal of Business Research*, Vol. 28, No. 3, pp. 191–210.

18. Heslop, L.A. and Papadopoulos, N. (1993), "But who knows where or when? Reflections on the images of countries and their products", in N. Papadopoulos and L.A. Heslop, *Product-Country Images: Impact and Role in International Marketing*, Haworth Press, London, pp. 39–76; Papadopoulos, N. (1993), "What product and country images are and are not", in N. Papadopoulos and L.A. Heslop, *Product-Country Images: Impact and Role in International Marketing*, Haworth Press, London, pp. 3–38.

19. Agrawal, J. and Kamakara, W.A. (1999), "Country of origin: a competitive advantage", *International Journal of Research in Marketing*, Vol. 16, No. 4, pp. 255–267.

20. Kaynak, E. and Cavusgil, S.T. (1983), "Consumer attitudes towards products of foreign origin: do they vary across product classes?", *International Journal of Advertising*, Vol. 2, No. 2, pp. 147–57.

21. Heslop and Papadopoulos, "But who knows where or when?", *op. cit.*

22. Erez, M. and Earley, P.C. (1993), *Culture, Self-Identity and Work*, Oxford University Press, New York.

23. Rokeach, *The Nature of Human Values*, *op. cit.*

24. Schwartz, S.H. (1994), "Are there universal aspects in the structure and contents of human values?", *Journal of Social Issues*, Vol. 50, No. 4, pp. 19–45.

25. Rokeach, *The Nature of Human Values*, *op. cit.*

26. Peter, J.P. and Olson, J.C. (1999), *Consumer Behaviour and Marketing Strategy* (5th edn), Irwin McGraw-Hill, Boston, MA.

27. Kamakura, W.A. and Mazzon, J.A. (1991), "Value segmentation: a model for the measurement of values and value systems", *Journal of Consumer Research*, Vol. 18, No. 2, pp. 208–218.

28. Weber, J. (1990), "Managerial value orientations: a typology and assessment", *International Journal of Value Based Management*, Vol. 3, No. 2, pp. 37–54.

29. Ibid.

30. Crosby, L.A., Bitner, M.J. and Gill, J.D. (1990), "Organizational structure of values", *Journal of Business Research*, Vol. 20, No. 2, pp. 123–34.

31. Schwartz, "Are there universal aspects …?", *op. cit.*

32. Balabanis, Mueller and Melewar, "Country of origin images", *op. cit.*; Sharma, S., Shimp, T.A. and Shin, J. (1995), "Consumer ethnocentrism: a test of antecedents and moderators", *Journal of the Academy of Marketing Science*, Vol. 23, No. 1, pp. 26–37; Watson, J.J. and Wright, K. (2000), "Consumer ethnocentrism and attitudes toward domestic and foreign products", *European Journal of Marketing*, Vol. 34, No. 9, pp. 1149–1166; Gurhan-Canli, Z. and Maheswaran, D. (2000), "Cultural variations in country of origin effects", *Journal of Marketing Research*, Vol. 37, No. 3, pp. 309–317; Hofstede, G. (2001), *Culture's Consequences: Comparing Values, Behaviours, Institutions, and Organizations across Nations* (2nd edn), Sage, Thousand Oaks, CA.

33. Hofstede, *Culture's Consequences*, *op. cit.*

34. Sharma, Shimp and Shin, "Consumer ethnocentrism", *op. cit.*; Watson and Wright, "Consumer ethnocentrism and attitudes", *op. cit.*; Gurhan-Canli and Maheswaran, "Cultural variations", *op. cit.*

35. Sharma, Shimp and Shin, "Consumer ethnocentrism", *op. cit.*

36. Gurhan-Canli and Maheswaran, "Cultural variations", *op. cit.*

37. De Mooij, M. (1998), *Global Marketing and Advertising: Understanding Cultural Paradoxes*, Sage, Thousand Oaks, CA.

38. ITIM International–Business Culture and International Management, *Geert Hofstede: Cultural Dimensions*,http://www.geert-hofstede.com (accessed February 2006).

39. Shimp and Sharma, "Consumer ethnocentrism", *op. cit.*

40. Ibid.

41. Balabanis, Mueller and Melewar, "The human value lenses", *op. cit.*

42. Nebenzahl, I.D., Jaffe, E.D. and Usunier, J.C. (2003), "Personifying country of origin research", *Management International Review*, Vol. 43, No. 4, pp. 383–406.

43. D'Astous, A. and Ahmed, S.A. (1999), "The importance of country images in the formation of consumer product perceptions", *International Marketing Review*, Vol. 16, No. 2, pp. 108–120; Nebenzahl, Jaffe and Usunier, "Personifying country of origin research", *op. cit.*

44. Kamakura and Mazzon, "Value segmentation", *op. cit.*

45. Bigoness, W.J. and Blakely, G.L. (1996), "A cross-national study of managerial values", *Journal of International Business Studies*, Vol. 27, No. 4, pp. 739–748.

46. Rokeach, *The Nature of Human Values*, *op. cit.*

47. Schwartz, "Are there universal aspects …?", *op. cit.*; Becker, B.W. (1998), "Values in advertising research: a methodological caveat", *Journal of Advertising Research*, Vol. 38, No. 4, pp. 57–60.

48. Aaker, D.A. and Day, G.S. (1983), *Marketing Research* (2nd edn), John Wiley & Sons, New York.

49. Hair, J.F., Anderson, R.E., Tatham, R.L. and Black, W.C. (1995), *Multivariate Data Analysis*, Prentice Hall, Upper Saddle River, NJ; Malhotra, N.K. (1996), *Marketing Research: An Applied Orientation*, Prentice Hall, Upper Saddle River, NJ.

50. Malhotra, *Marketing Research, op. cit.*
51. Lenartowicz, T. and Johnson, J. P. (2002), "Comparing managerial values in twelve Latin American countries: an exploratory study", *Management International Review*, Vol. 42, No. 3, pp. 279–307.
52. Ibid.
53. Crosby, Bitner and Gill, "Organizational structure of values", *op. cit.*
54. Schwartz, S.H. (1992), "Universals in the content of values: theoretical advances and empirical tests in 20 countries", *Advances in Experimental Social Psychology*, Vol. 25, pp. 1–65.
55. George, D. and Mallery, P. (2003), *SPSS for Windows Step by Step: A Simple Guide and Reference* (4th edn), Allyn and Bacon, Boston, MA.
56. Schwartz, "Universals in the content of values", *op. cit.*
57. Crosby, Bitner and Gill, "Organizational structure of values", *op. cit.*
58. Lenartowicz, T. and Johnson, J.P. (2002), "Comparing managerial values in twelve Latin American countries: an exploratory study", *Management International Review*, Vol. 42, Issue 3, pp. 279–307; Crosby, Bitner and Gill, "Organizational structure of values", *op. cit.*; Schwartz, "Universals in the content of values, *op. cit.*
59. McDaniel, C. and Gates, R. (1996), *Contemporary Marketing Research*, West Publishing Company, St Paul, MN.
60. Lahóz, André and Caetano, José R. (2005), "A China vai conquistar o mundo e sua empresa está na mira", *Portal Exame*, http://portalexame.abril.com.br.
61. Balabanis, Mueller and Melewar, "The human value lenses", *op. cit.*
62. Shepherd, R. and Raats, M.M. (1996) "Attitudes and beliefs in food habits", in H.L. Meiselman and H.J.H. MacFie (eds), *Food Choice Acceptance and Consumption*, Blackie Academic, London, pp. 346–364.
63. Schwartz, "Universals in the content of values", *op. cit.*
64. Pisharodi, R.M. and Parameswaran, R. (1992), "Confirmatory factor analysis of a country-of-origin scale: initial results", *Advances in Consumer Research*, Vol. 19, No. 1, pp. 706–714.

Appendix 1: Country-of-origin measurement scale

Household appliances made in China are:

	Totally agree						Totally disagree		
expensive products	1	2	3	4	5	6	7	8	9
products I'll be proud to show my friends	1	2	3	4	5	6	7	8	9
products I like	1	2	3	4	5	6	7	8	9
inexpensive products	1	2	3	4	5	6	7	8	9
high quality products	1	2	3	4	5	6	7	8	9
products my friends would not buy	1	2	3	4	5	6	7	8	9

A person who buys household appliances made in China:

	Totally agree						Totally disagree		
is making the best choice	1	2	3	4	5	6	7	8	9
is a gambler	1	2	3	4	5	6	7	8	9
looks for established brand names	1	2	3	4	5	6	7	8	9
is stingy	1	2	3	4	5	6	7	8	9
is paying top price for top quality	1	2	3	4	5	6	7	8	9
is a poor person	1	2	3	4	5	6	7	8	9
is getting a good deal	1	2	3	4	5	6	7	8	9
is stupid, foolish	1	2	3	4	5	6	7	8	9
is a lower-class person	1	2	3	4	5	6	7	8	9
will be satisfied	1	2	3	4	5	6	7	8	9
is unthinking, rash, naive	1	2	3	4	5	6	7	8	9
is correct in choosing the product	1	2	3	4	5	6	7	8	9
doesn't care about quality	1	2	3	4	5	6	7	8	9
is knowledgeable about the product	1	2	3	4	5	6	7	8	9
is buying a good but expensive product	1	2	3	4	5	6	7	8	9
is getting ripped off	1	2	3	4	5	6	7	8	9
cares about quality	1	2	3	4	5	6	7	8	9
is mistaken in choosing the product	1	2	3	4	5	6	7	8	9
demands high quality	1	2	3	4	5	6	7	8	9
will be dissatisfied	1	2	3	4	5	6	7	8	9
is not knowledgeable about the product	1	2	3	4	5	6	7	8	9

Appendix 2: Personal values measurement scale

Listed below are 18 values about modes of social conduct, presented in alphabetical order. To each one of these values, people attribute more or less importance, according to the way they prefer to live. Indicate how much each value below is important to you, by means of the following scale: the number "1" indicates that the value is not important at all for you, as a guiding principle for your life. On the other hand, the number "9" indicates that the value is very important to guide your life.

Value	Not important at all							Very important	
AMBITIOUS (hard working, aspiring)	1	2	3	4	5	6	7	8	9
BROADMINDED (open-minded)	1	2	3	4	5	6	7	8	9
CAPABLE (competent, effective)	1	2	3	4	5	6	7	8	9
CHEERFUL (lighthearted, joyful)	1	2	3	4	5	6	7	8	9
CLEAN (neat, tidy)	1	2	3	4	5	6	7	8	9
COURAGEOUS (standing up for your beliefs)	1	2	3	4	5	6	7	8	9
FORGIVING (willing to pardon others)	1	2	3	4	5	6	7	8	9
HELPFUL (working for the welfare of others)	1	2	3	4	5	6	7	8	9
HONEST (sincere, truthful)	1	2	3	4	5	6	7	8	9
IMAGINATIVE (daring, creative)	1	2	3	4	5	6	7	8	9
INDEPENDENT (self-reliant, self- sufficient)	1	2	3	4	5	6	7	8	9
INTELLECTUAL (intelligent, reflective)	1	2	3	4	5	6	7	8	9
LOGICAL (consistent, rational)	1	2	3	4	5	6	7	8	9
LOVING (affectionate, tender)	1	2	3	4	5	6	7	8	9
OBEDIENT (dutiful, respectful)	1	2	3	4	5	6	7	8	9
POLITE (courteous, well-mannered)	1	2	3	4	5	6	7	8	9
RESPONSIBLE (dependable, reliable)	1	2	3	4	5	6	7	8	9
SELF-CONTROLLED (restrained, self-disciplined)	1	2	3	4	5	6	7	8	9

The Near and Far East Asian Perspective

12 *Dynamics of Adi Women's Traditional Foods and Livelihoods in Varying Socio-ecological Systems of Arunachal Pradesh: A Source of Learning and Inspiration*

SUNITA MISHRA,* RANJAY K. SINGH† AND
ANAMIKA SINGH

Keywords

indigenous biodiversity, traditional foods, Adi women, knowledge networks, market, livelihoods.

Abstract

This study elaborates on the interrelationships of traditional foods with nutrition, knowledge, ecosystems and livelihoods among Adi women of Arunachal Pradesh, in north-east India. A wide range of traditional foods found in diverse ecosystems and sustained through native socio-cultural institutions and ecosystems support the livelihood systems of the Adi community in this region. Adi women identify diverse edible plants and understand methods for processing and preserving them for food security and subsistence income. Their traditional knowledge about integrating and

* Professor Sunita Mishra, Professor and Dean, School for Home Science, Babasaheb Bhimrao Ambedkar University, Vidya Vihar, Raibarelli Road, Lucknow (UP), India. E-mail: sunitasabat@yahoo.com.

† Dr Ranjay K. Singh, Department of Agricultural Extension, Central Soil Central Soil Salinity Research Institute (CSSRI), Indian Council of Agricultural Research (ICAR), Kachhwa Road, Karnal-132001, Haryana, India. E-mail: ranjay_jbp@yahoo.com. Telephone: + 91 999 664 3037.

domesticating wild ethno-botanicals into existing farming systems contributes further to food, nutritional and income security. Informal networks, formed by women, play significant roles in marketing food resources and ensuring income. Social processes such as modernization, urbanization and globalization are altering food habits in this resource-dependent region, particularly near towns and more densely settled areas.

Introduction

Learning about indigenous, biodiversity-based traditional food systems requires a process of interacting and acquiring knowledge that is unique and developed by groups of people native to a specific geographical area.[1] Throughout the world, concerns centre on the loss of traditional knowledge related to biodiversity-based foods, livelihood regimes and learning systems; many researchers have searched for ways to preserve both.[2] Ways in which traditional knowledge pertaining to local foods and livelihood systems may be lost include the erosion of vernacular languages, cultural erosion, disintegration of the extended family system and disruption of intergenerational learning chains.[3] In most communities in India, women play an important role in sustaining and promoting intergenerational traditional knowledge systems. Women in indigenous and tribal communities possesses immense knowledge of varieties of plants, their processing, their cultural importance and their mixed usage in food, medicine and materials, as well as for securing a livelihood.[4] These women do not necessarily need to understand the molecular components of food to understand the importance of the relationship between food and health or of developing a healthy diet from available resources. Rather, they perform their own informal validation through trial and error and careful observation and thereby develop the formulations and applications of a particular food. In Western science, much practical nutritional information has been derived from observation, experience and clinical trial rather than from the molecular and biochemical research with which modern food development typically is associated.[5]

The foods consumed by peoples around the world continually change over the course of history, reflecting changing technologies and skills – such as selective animal and plant breeding and domestication – as well as developments in cultivation, preservation and preparation techniques.[6] In recent decades, however, worldwide food systems have been transforming at an unprecedented rate; this dramatic change has been called "the nutrition transition".[7] In India and elsewhere, many people living in urban and industrial centres have neither the time, skills, nor inclination to acquire and prepare food in traditional ways. Massive grocery stores stocked with packaged, ready-to-eat foods and a plethora of readily available fast–food, drive-in restaurants offer a seemingly efficient, more appropriate alternative for working families.[8] The detrimental effects of these new globalized diets and food systems become evident not only in poor individual health, but also in the harms to farming systems and the management of the whole environment and livelihood system of traditional communities.[9] Many locally produced food species and crop varieties become eclipsed by industrial-scale food production. The changing scenario of food consumption patterns and acculturation processes has thus adversely affected the learning chain and the intergenerational transfer of traditional food-based knowledge and management systems in rural areas.[10]

An understanding of the role of women and the way in which they uphold the intrinsic value of local knowledge in food preparation and the conservation of related biodiversity is critical to understanding, interpreting and disseminating food-based knowledge systems. This study enables marketing executives and academicians to understand the subsistence economic value of traditional foods, as well as how women manage their resources. Systematic learning from knowledge-holders in society is an urgent need of the day, and the way in which local bio-resources used in food items reduces the dependency of rural Adi women on external markets is a key facet of this study. In recognition of the important role women play in using and conserving traditional foods and related resources, this study attempts to explore, characterize and document the dynamics of food, nutrition and livelihood among the women of the Adi tribes of north-eastern India.

Ethnography and Socio-cultural Background of Study Area

The Adi (also known as the Abor) is a major tribe living in the Himalayan hills of Arunachal Pradesh, particularly in the subtropical regions of the districts of West Siang, East Siang, Upper Siang, Upper Subansiri and Dibang Valley.[11] The East Siang district, on which this study focuses, extends over 4005 sq. km and is situated at 27.30–29.42° N latitude and 94.420–95.35° E longitude. It borders the Upper Siang district in the north, the Dhemaji district (Assam) in the south, the Dibang Valley district in the east and the West Siang district in the west. The Adi-Pasi tribe dominates the East Siang district. A network of rivers, vast open green lands and rolling hills give this region the impression of being a mystical paradise. History notwithstanding, Arunachal has large areas under forest cover (82.0 per cent) at various altitudes, including waterfalls and pools, glades, and groves, which provide a basis for the subsistence of the tribal people.[12]

The Adi are believed to have come from southern China in the sixteenth century. They reside in the far north of India and include various subtribes, which differ from one another in many of their customs and lifestyles.[13] Living in such a remote area, the people must be totally self-sufficient. The Adi practise *jhum* and wet rice cultivation and run a considerable agricultural economy. Their staple foods are rice, maize, millets, orange, pineapple, banana and forest-based traditional food products, supplemented by meat from trapping and hunting, increasingly with firearms.[14] Any issue or dispute arising over social and natural resources is dealt with through the traditional tribal institution, called *kebang*.[15] A traditional measure of a family's wealth is its possession of a *mithun*, a native ox (*Bos frontalis*), which is neither milked nor put to work, but instead given supplementary care while it grazes in the woods until its slaughter, usually at the time of a ceremonial feast. Villagers depend on traditional foods derived from diverse, boiled, wild, cultivated and weedy plants, often cooked with fish, meat and rats. Rats and squirrels are a local food delicacy.[16] Dances are a vital element of the zest and joy of living for the tribe; they are performed as important rituals, during festivals, and occasionally for recreation, and are linked with the serving of traditional foods.[17] The majority of the Adi traditionally follow the animist *Donyi-Polo* religion, which involves worship of the sun, moon and the ancestral god Abo-Teni.[18] Each deity is associated with certain tasks and acts as a protector and guardian for various concerns – food crops, home, rain – that relate to nature and have an impact on people's daily lives.[19]

Learning and Methods Applied to Traditional Foods

This study is based on three years of continuous participant observations. To achieve the study's objective, we deliberately selected the Pasighat, Roing, Mebo, Mariyang Mebo and Koyu administrative units of East Siang district, Pasighat, Arunachal Pradesh, India, on the basis of the ethnicity of the people, their high dependency on forest resources, the remoteness of the region, the diversity and endemism of plant resources (both on land and in the surrounding waters) and the communal nature of the local resources (that is, as common property, not under any exclusion legislation). Even in these areas, near towns, local resources are under increasing threat from expanding market forces, and locals sustain differing levels of resource dependence; different cultural groups (Pasi, Padam, Minyong and Pangi) coexist. From each block (Pasighat, Mebo, Roing, Mebo and Mariyang), we randomly selected a representative sample of five villages (a total of 25 villages).

In each village, we organized participatory recipe contests (traditional food competitions, organized only to gather information) with the help of a team consisting of community leaders and researchers, which enabled us to rapidly explore the relative diversity of culturally important, plant-based traditional foods.[20] Recipe contest winners were awarded first, second or third prizes, as well as two consolation prizes. Later, we interviewed these winners (totalling 75, or five from each village) separately in order to gain an understanding of the collection, processing, various aspects of use, and other dynamics of traditional food-related resources. A separate sample of 75 male, traditional knowledge-holders, compiled randomly from a voters' list provided by the *Gaon Burha*, provided data for a comparative study about gendered knowledge systems and food. To facilitate understanding and ensure the most reliable information, a local guide assisted us throughout the study. During interviews, the women described the collection and processing of foods; supplementary information pertaining to the types of vegetation and animals and their relationship with the ecology, agriculture, animals and food systems came from both men and women. In addition, we used qualitative ethno-botanical and ethno-zoological interviews to identify the uses of local species, primarily in terms of food and economics.

A focus group discussion (FGD) addressed complex issues such as processing variability, method of traditional food preparation, and sources of collection of indigenous materials and unique traditional foods. The aim here was to develop consensus data for further analysis and interpretation. In line with the UN Convention on Biodiversity recommendations, we sought prior informed consent (PIC) of the women and men in the study to confirm their property ownership of their preserved knowledge and provide them with an assured equitable benefit share in any future application.[21] If knowledge were held by the community at large, we obtained the consent of the community leader.

Traditional Foods and the Adi Community of Arunachal Pradesh, North-east India

This comprehensive study indicates that Adi women possess a wide range of knowledge about traditional foods prepared from indigenous and local wild plants, as well as indigenous agro-biodiversity. In the Appendix, we provide translations of all Adi words used in this chapter.

FOREST AND TRADITIONAL FOODS

In general, Adi community members depend on their own crops for their food, supplemented by forest plant foods and wild game and fish caught in the river. A range of traditional foods exists within the community forests, which is cooked and consumed in boiled form (see Figure 12.1).

However, consensus indicates that if a monetary value were assigned to their food, the income that they would earn from it would not be sufficient. A large percentage (70 per cent) of the respondents practise a combined strategy of growing their own food and collecting edible forest products. In addition, approximately 5 per cent of those consulted depend exclusively on forest food collection to augment their dietary needs, and 15–20 per cent exclusively depend on their own crops for their sustenance and livelihood. Because of their dependency on forest resources, most of the Adi communities living far from towns conserve their community forests to ensure food, nutritional and medicinal security. They also practise subsistence hunting for food security, for which community forests play pivotal roles. Despite considerable use of edible forest plants, this practice does not always represent a "free" good for Adi households living near more developed areas, because they do not have sufficient time to venture far into the forest to

Figure 12.1 Diversity of traditional foods prepared from forest-based ethno-botanicals

collect their food. The women run an informal market system that provides edible forest food products to town dwellers.

Those who have resided in the area for longer remember other forest products formerly used as survival food in times of shortage, particularly the pith of certain tubers and fruits like wild jackfruit and chestnut. These were necessary up until the 1970s when wet rice fields and home gardens became well-established and productive. Now these foods have become rare items in the villagers' diets. Some forest foods have made the transition from being food only eaten when times are hard fare to delicacies fit for social and cultural celebrations: these include *ongin* (*Clerodendrum colebrokianum*), *onger* (*Zanthoxylum rhetsa*), *kopi* (*Solanum torvum*), *koppir* (*Solanum khasianum*) and bamboo shoots, which, when cooked with meat, are served at various cultural occasions and festivals. Forest plants still serve as emergency food during flood and lean periods or transitions between seasons. Some such plants also have an alternative use as popular medicines. Thus, the selection and use of particular plants is based on both nutrition and medicine, linked closely with the ethnicity of the Adi tribe.

CULTURAL CAPITAL AND TRADITIONAL FOODS

Rich, diverse cultural capital is embodied within the lifestyle of the Adi community and is tied to nutritionally rich, traditional foods. On various occasions, such as festivals, particular kinds of wild game are hunted from the forest and cooked with diverse plant foods from the forest, swidden lands,‡ and kitchen gardens. Cultural events, such as marriages, dances and festivals, intertwine with the traditional ways of life and food systems. For example, a group of the Minyong tribe (an Adi subtribe) performs the *topu* dance in the *mosup* (a community hall made of bamboo and wood). During the performance, people collect the dried *mithun*, pork, dried fish, *apong* (a local, protein-rich beverage made from indigenous rice, finger millet, maize and tapioca), firewood, and local rice. These foods are communally cooked in the *mosup* and eaten during the *topu* dance.

Similarly, during festivals like *aran* (7 March), *etar* (15 May) and *solung* (1 September), dancers perform the *miri* dance while the people collect wild-animal meat and other local food items from each household; later, this food is communally cooked in the *mosup* and shared with the whole community. During the performance, the dancers sing local songs, signifying the values of plants, the forest, water, mountains and so forth, and celebrating the Adi lifestyle. Among the Minyong community, during the *aran* festival, men sing in male-only performing groups called *yongjong*; they call on each household and perform the dance. In return, each host of the *yongjong* offers dried rat and *mithun*, accompanied by local rice.

The collected food items are cooked in the community hall by the *yongjong* and then consumed by the villagers. In the transitional villages, the *yongjong* have started to sell the collected food items, whereas, in the past, any surplus food was exchanged for other food products from neighbouring tribes. Thus, a collective activity undertaken by a community group and imbued with a rich cultural heritage represents priceless capital, ensuring the exchange of local foods and providing an opportunity to learn about and share diverse, nutritionally rich foods throughout the Adi community.

---

‡   Areas cleared for temporary cultivation by cutting and burning the vegetation.

FOODS WITH MEDICINAL VALUE

Some wild plants and animal resources are consumed by Adi women specifically to cure disease and improve health. For example, bear's gallbladder is eaten during bouts of malaria, high fever and tuberculosis. Women valued boiled local chicken, wild game, fish and eggs, mixed together with such plant foods such as greens of *onger* (*Zanthoxylum rhetsa*), *ongin* (*Clerodendrum colebrookianum*), *koppir* (*Solanum khasianum*), *kopi* (*Solanum torvum*), *kekir* (*Zingiber officinalis*), *banko* (*Solanum spirale*), *marshang* (*Spilanthus acmella*), *paput* (*Gnepalium affine*), *mamang* (*Physalis minima*), *fayong* (*Polygonum* species added to enhance the flavour), *nayang* (*Erigeron canadensis*), *tangum* (*Bidens pilosa*), and *gende* (*Gynura cripidioides*), as energy-giving traditional foods. Foods that are believed to improve the digestive system include wild *owyin* and *talab* (types of onions) and *kekir* (a spice plant, hot in taste with a burning sensation). Some foods, like those made from green *koppi*, *teeta baingan* (*Solanum* species), papaya and *apong*, are eaten for their laxative qualities. Jackfruit, pumpkin and egg, among others, are regarded as hot foods for the body. Some mushroom species growing on dead wood, including *lengot*, *peki tatar*, *lolum tayin tatar* and *inyik*, are used as local vegetables and considered the most valuable source of both nutrition and income. Some food plants are used as ethno-medicine to protect against various diseases, and examples include: the leaves and fruits of *amta* (*Hibiscus sabdariffa*) used for diarrhoea and to treat dysentery; fruits of the *champa* (*Dillenia indica*), combined with fish, used to control stomach pain; *sirang* (*Castanopsis kurzii*) fruits in chutney, used to help alleviate scurvy, flatulence and toothache; *kordoi* (*Cuscuta reflexa*), used to treat jaundice; leaves of *sajna* (*Moringa oleifera*), used to help control muscle pain and treat diarrhoea; and fresh fruits of *carembola* (*Averrhoea carembola*), believed to cure jaundice. These examples indicate that the selection and use of particular plants is based on both nutrition and medicine, closely linked to the ethnicity of the Adi tribe.

A preliminary laboratory analysis (Table 12.1) indicates that the principal wild plant foods used frequently by the Adi tribe in their food systems, such as *kopi, koppir, onger, poi* (*Basella rubra*), *dhenkia saag* (*Diplazium esculentum*), *marsang, ongin, kalmu* and *rori*, have high percentages of moisture, crude protein and mineral ash. The most popular ethno-botanical, *onger* (used as a vegetable and medicine to treat diarrhoea and dysentery or mixed with pork and other meat to prevent tapeworm infection), is very rich in fat (2.51 per cent) and crude protein (5.80 per cent). *Rori* provides a fat content of 2.42 per cent and crude protein of 3.26 per cent. *Dhenkia saag*, used as an emergency food during flood conditions, is rich in crude protein (8.89 per cent) and ash (2.45 per cent). Fibre intake is comparatively minimal in the developing communities of the Adi tribe compared with more traditional, remote communities. The frequency analysis of food intake also indicates that women living near dense forests at high altitudes collect an average of 20–25 fibre- and nutrient-rich indigenous plants (trees, shrubs, creepers, climbers) from the forest and swidden lands and use them, boiled together, three times a day, whereas women living in town have a low intake of such foods.

We can infer from these examples that the culturally rich, traditional foods prepared from the forest-based ethno-botanicals not only are an integral part of the Adi diet but are also nutritionally rich. The Adi tribe's dependence on forest-based ethno-botanicals and the role of these plants in food security cannot be ignored. Self-sufficient native people living in close connection with nature and maintaining their cultural foods represent an inextricable part of nature.[22]

Table 12.1 Nutritional status of selected wild plants used in traditional foods by the Adi community

Local name	Scientific name	Edible (%)	Moisture (%)	Ash FW (%)	Crude fibre (%)	Crude protein (%)	Crude fat (%)
Koppi	Solanum torvum	83.97	76.34	0.56	9.75	4.82	0.95
Koppir	Solanum khasianum	72.90	72.98	0.44	12.44	6.33	1.73
Onger	Zanthoxylum rhetsa	48.27	75.00	0.72	8.27	5.80	2.51
Pumpkin	Cucurbita moschata	53.39	84.01	1.75	4.34	3.99	0.98
Lal ada	Zingiber sp.	81.16	89.67	1.21	11.18	2.80	2.26
Kekir	Zingiber officinalis	82.67	61.12	0.40	6.88	2.10	1.20
Poi	Basella rubra	73.18	88.26	2.60	3.68	5.15	0.86
Dhekia saag	Diplazium esculentum	49.34	90.19	2.45	8.89	8.36	0.76
Marsang	Spilanthus acmella	61.21	85.13	1.64	5.45	4.76	2.19
Ongin	Clerodendrum colebrookianum	74.35	82.35	1.85	4.36	4.76	1.65
Kalmu	A creeper	45.04	87.23	1.85	5.26	3.12	1.49
Rori	A herb	77.39	81.06	1.23	6.22	3.26	2.42
Adi dhania	Local coriander	93.47	72.54	0.82	6.92	6.42	1.14

TRADITIONAL FOODS, LIVELIHOOD AND BIOCULTURAL RESOURCE CONSERVATION

Adi women face a set of interrelated food security problems and often attempt to solve them by applying their knowledge in a holistic way. For instance, an Adi woman might view her kitchen garden not just as a source of common herbs and vegetables, but also as a complete source of food, medicine and marketable products. Her decisions about the use of one food might be affected by past acquired knowledge and perceptions of other foods found in another ecosystem. The relationship between food parts (plants, insects and animals) and the reasoning behind her decision on use depends on the types of ecosystems and social system. Traditional foods are closely tied to ethnicity, culture and ecosystem variability. Ethics, beliefs and superstitions might be important influences on what Adi women do and how ready they are to accept new practices of food preparation and processing. Trying to change traditional food practices might be difficult, because they are rooted in deeply held beliefs that underlie many other aspects of the culture. The local women's applied knowledge systems minimize risk by assuring food security and a subsistence income, rather than maximizing short-term economic profit. Beliefs can play a fundamental role in a food and livelihood system, as well as in maintaining human and environmental health. For example, holy forest groves are protected for religious reasons.

For people who otherwise have little to eat, cultural festivals celebrated once a year can be an important source of food, such as the protein-rich meat from wild game in the *etar* festival and *mithun* meat in the *solung* festival. At every Adi wedding, local rice, meat, *apong*, fish, *kebung* (Himalayan giant black squirrel), pork and *mithun* meat are served in large quantities. Adi women note that some foods, including local rice, orange, jackfruit, pineapple, banana and pork, are also important for generating income. *Mithun*, *kebung*, *apong* and local rice are considered to have the highest income potential and, as prestigious foods, represent important offerings to special guests.

Women's traditional knowledge about integrating and domesticating wild plants into existing farming systems – into both *jhum* land (slash-and-burn agriculture) and kitchen gardens – contributes further to food, nutritional and income security, and ecosystem management. For example, the domestication of *onger, marshang, oyik, banko, tangum* and *gende* in home gardens, along with *jhum* land, has helped conserve culturally and nutritionally rich foods and secured subsistence income for the Adi women living in low biodiversity ecosystems near towns or in transformed villages. On an average, an Adi woman living near the town areas earns a net profit from the recipes used in traditional foods of Rs. 50 000–70 000 per annum, a considerable sum for people living in the mountainous regions. The traditional domestication process also helps increase incremental learning and informal, location-specific experimentation about culturally and nutritionally important traditional foods required for the subsistence living in these knowledge-rich but economically poor communities. Women have developed a kind of traditional knowledge package (both hidden and visible) that includes selective harvesting, creation of micro-environments, special planting and propagation techniques, seed dispersal, and controlled burning, all of which collectively ensure that indigenous plants used in traditional food systems remain sustained in their respective ecosystems and provide a constant supply of food and income. Local availability and easy access to forest plants has also made it possible for them to use these foods not only for consumption, but also for purposes associated with cultural, social, economic, medicinal and spiritual values (see Figure 12.2).

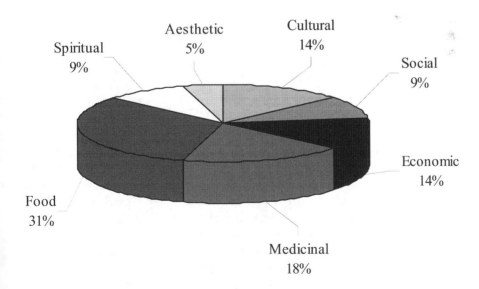

Figure 12.2 Role of forest-based, plant-based food in women's survival and livelihood

CHANGED PATTERNS AND CONSUMPTION OF FOREST-BASED FOOD SYSTEMS IN VARIOUS SOCIAL CONTEXTS

The Adi people living in and near towns are attracted to more modern foods; their use of forest-based traditional foods has decreased over time. They note that, with the passage of time, better communication, expansion of food-based markets and factors such as cultural erosion, loss of vernacular languages and the disintegration of joint family units into nuclear families have affected their use of traditional foods. The differences in traditional food use among these women are more notable than those across the generations of Adi women living in remote areas (10–20 km away from the main market). The latter group of women continue to depend more closely on forest-based traditional foods, and the change in their food use is less significant than that for Adi women living in more settled areas. Thus, the significance of forest ecosystems for Adi women in remote areas cannot be underestimated; they ensure food as well as livelihood security.

In most harsh, socio-ecological systems and remote areas where modern communication, commercialisation and market networks are weak and the light of modernity has not penetrated, the social system and the social controls for the use and conservation of indigenous resources that offer food and related livelihoods are quite strong. The degree of equitable use, conservation of traditional foods and livelihood regimes vary even among women living in different social systems. In comparison with women living in semi-rural, relatively settled areas, those living in remote, forested areas show comparatively strong ethical approaches towards accessing, harvesting, domesticating, conserving, processing, preparing and preserving food, as well as towards its use in medicine, cultural, social and spiritual contexts. The livelihood and income sources in such systems are moderate but more sustainable than any developing social system. The higher value placed on these traditional foods by women in remote rural settings, compared with women living in more settled areas, results from their greater need for self-sufficiency and their greater dependence on local resources and social networks.

Common Rationale and Hypothesis Inferred from the Traditional Foods Prepared and Consumed by the Adi Women of Arunachal Pradesh

The selection of a particular plant for food is not merely a matter of harvesting and processing. Other factors are critical, including detailed knowledge of its ecological and genetic variation, its development and propagation, its edibility, its importance for livelihood and its medicinal and therapeutic properties, all of which are determined through close observation, experience and informal experimentation by women. Table 12.2 lists some of the hypotheses and perceptions women have developed regarding traditional foods.

These informal hypotheses govern the variability of traditional foods and determine the number and types of plants to be used, alone or in combination. Traditional food consumption varies from place to place and from society to society. Even two sisters of the same parents do not always cook and process traditional foods in the same ways because of variations in their personalities, learning environments and socio-

Table 12.2   Adi women's hypotheses and perceptions about traditional foods

Traditional foods made from indigenous ingredients increase overall health and longevity.

Traditional food varieties have a special kind of aroma due to their particular genetic make-up.

Traditional beverages and fermented foods are nutritionally superior over modern foods.

Mixtures of leaves used in food preparation ensure good nutrition and provide healthful medicinal properties.

Using green leaves with meat and fish is positively correlated with avoiding side effects from frequent consumption of meat. For example, *onger* leaves can avoid tapeworm infection in the case of improperly cooked meat.

In a majority of cases in traditional cultures, livelihood and use of local foods are positively correlated, so separating traditional foods from the overall diet and livelihood is not easy; together, these factors directly and indirectly secure good nutrition.

Using a variety of foods is positively correlated with the ecosystem, cultural style, taste diversity and a subsistence lifestyle and economy.

---

environmental interactions. It is not surprising that Adi women living at varying ecological edges differ in their approaches to food use and processing techniques. These women have developed a huge informal knowledge database about what wild plants and animals to use, whether during normal times, during scarcity or in a natural disaster. For example, when food is scarce, the elders collect unique forest foods, which they consume after careful processing. The results of group discussions held with Adi elders – namely Mr Jakut Modi, Mrs Ade Modi and Mrs Tajong Tamuk – suggest that *tase*, a kind of tuber-producing tree found in hilly regions and growing up to 30–40 feet (about 10 m) in height and 1.5–2.5 feet (40–75 cm in radius) is extremely useful for food security during the droughts and the epidemic suffered by agricultural crops caused by rats. It sheds its leaves in March and April, at which time the stem can be cut down, the bark removed, and the inner pith crushed into small pieces. The pith is stored in a bamboo basket, where it ferments until juice starts to run from it. It then can be dried and consumed in two forms: *apong* and meal. The pith of this tree is considered suitable for consumption for anyone over the age of five. The taste of this tree is assessed by examining its shedded leaves. If the tree has not shed its leaves, however, the elders believe that it is not suitable to eat. *Tase* can be used as emergency food and is most often harvested during floods and droughts. *Taba* (another wild tree) is similar but used in a mixture with *tase* to enhance the taste. *Angyat* and *ayak* are local millets, consumed as nutritious foods, and especially important as emergency fare.

Overall, these discussions suggest that the Adi elders – particularly those living in remote regions – see value in the cultural landscape and their cultural traditions related to survival, both with regard to food and ecosystems. No amount of gold or currency could compensate for the loss of their traditional lifestyles or their ability to care for, and benefit from, their own homelands. Similar cases exist in other parts of the world where people of traditional communities continue to preserve their traditional lifestyles and food habits because of their high cultural norms and classic, symbiotic relations with nature.[23]

Discussion and Policy Implications for Traditional Food Systems

Traditional food systems are generally beneficial for the overall health and well-being of indigenous peoples; culturally rich, traditional foods prepared by women from local plants and wild game are perceived as nutritionally healthful in comparison with marketed commercial food.[24] As Gregory reports, wild plant foods typically are higher in calcium, iron, magnesium and vitamin C, for example, than are cultivated plants.[25] Furthermore, wild fish has less fat and, in particular, less saturated fat than farmed fish. Adi women have a similar perception of the various species of local fish and wild game found in forest areas. Availability, multi-functionality, including medicinal and cultural attributes ascribed by the Adi to the plant species are accorded and play important roles. The diversity in the informal hypothesis surrounding the selection, processing and consumption of these foods offer excellent potential for formal research and educational programmes. Such programmes may be more effective than government "top-down" policies (where actions are decided by policy-makers only) in addressing value additions, commercialization, patent rights (for the unique and functional foods), and the preservation of the ecoculture and food ethnicity of a particular locality.[26]

Traditional systems of land and resource management in the Adi area have remained largely unaltered for generations, and livelihoods continue to be subsistence-based, despite increasing economic development. However, social processes such as modernization, urbanization and globalization are beginning to alter the food habits in this resource-dependent region, particularly near towns and in more densely settled areas.[27] Women are particularly knowledgeable about culturally and nutritionally rich foods, as well as about creating varied recipes in order to maintain the diversity of supply and meet consumer demand in the local market. State governments could use such knowledge to assist and support a "bottom-to-top" approach to development programmes that promote better health, nutrition and women's empowerment through location-specific micro-entrepreneurships and educational endeavours. Furthermore, market forces might recognize the possibilities associated with developing products, micro-enterprises and channels that can bring these products to wider populations in other areas. This effort could facilitate the recognition of the nutritional and economic value of locally available plant food resources.

The recipe contests we used to collect information provided an invaluable source of learning and a means to help preserve knowledge about the use of traditional foods and their invaluable biodiversity, including raising awareness about the value of traditional foods in health and nutrition, the empowerment of women, and development. In rapidly growing nuclear family systems, the younger generation often lacks the opportunity, or sometimes the interest, to interact with elders to learn about local foods. Cultural erosion and economic and technical factors represent leading threats to the traditional system of social relations and the chain of traditional food-based learning.[28] In light of such transformations, recipe contests can provide a good source of informal education and significantly enhance and rebuild the intergenerational learning chain with regard to the value of indigenous food systems.[29] The recipe contest eco-literary tool also raise several issues related to tribal women and enables a greater understanding of their perceptions about the conservation of local knowledge about foods through various modes of materialistic and non-materialistic incentives and benefits.

Arunachal Pradesh thus has a unique opportunity to map out a people-centred development path that is both sustainable and ecologically sound. Community-based development planning and the role of women in decision-making and policy formulations about the economic aspects of traditional food resources in Arunachal Pradesh has lagged behind that other jurisdictions, resulting in slow progress on human development indicators in the state.[30] The experience of the Apatani valley in Arunachal Pradesh, where women have been involved as major stakeholders in managing bio-resources and livelihoods, should be used as a source of learning and hypotheses to initiate programmes in other areas that promote local people, particularly women, as partners in the development process, including the promotion of healthy food systems and ecosystem management. In Arunachal Pradesh there is a need to boost income opportunities and local livelihoods by promoting ecotourism and establishing small-scale industries, such as the cultivation of bamboo and other minor forest-based traditional foods that are location-specific.[31] This unique state with its 'hot spots' of enormous biodiversity hot spots and diverse indigenous peoples with unique cultures, dialects and ecosystems[32] offers an ample opportunity to gain access to, and process, different varieties of food, which can in turn sustain incomes and livelihoods within these ecosystems. These precious resources should be utilized through a participatory approach involving local women and self-help groups that work to maintain people's health, nutrition and economic wealth as well as the integrity of the ecosystem.

The involvement of researchers, markets, state governments, non-governmental organizations and local communities in collaborative investigations of local food and related health, nutrition and environmental issues could also create a new critical awareness of the values of traditional food systems. This collaboration would facilitate the transfer of traditional food-based knowledge from one place to another,[33] as well as enhance economic opportunities.[34] Systematic documentation, classification, refinement, validation of, and value addition to, traditional foods should be linked to government policies, education and research to provide the scientific and technical base required to establish organized market and micro-entrepreneurship development for these foods.

In rapidly changing socio-political and biodiversity access patterns, there is an urgent need for a comprehensive state biodiversity action plans that represent the basic foundation for culture, foods and livelihood sustenance among tribal communities.[35] The links between health and diet, as emphasized by Adi women, require even greater emphasis. These women have been identifying, accessing, grading and processing traditional foods not only for food and nutritional security, but also to ensure a subsistence income. However, as yet, their roles have not been recognised by markets or governmental agencies. Nevertheless, women's communities should have the right to control any commercialization of their knowledge and earn an equitable share of any benefits arising from its use. They should also have the right to identify opportunities for community-based food processing, quality development and marketing. Fortunately, the community is undertaking some initiatives in this respect. The recent development of community-based ecotourism and networking of food resources has improved Adi women's income and helped sustain their lifestyles[36] as has the development of informal networks between women living in remote areas, who channel resources to the local market (see Figure 12.3).

Governments must recognize traditional foods as women's choices and that they are culturally acceptable, as well as accessible. Some of the best refined and value-added foods

Figure 12.3 An organized market of traditional food-based recipes run by women in informal channels

might be promoted through cooperative societies and public food distribution systems. In addition, novel recipes and food products could be promoted and marketed in urban and town areas as functional foods that help remedy various nutrition problems and other ailments, especially in locations where people are in need but unable to access and purchase such foods. Scientific institutions can play a pivotal role in testing and validating the active ingredients and functional elements of indigenous foods, cultivated and developed organically. Such an approach can raise awareness of the importance of local foods.

These foods represent a unique culture and an important source of health knowledge that is crucial in sustaining smallholder productivity. Formal recognition of traditional foods in the mountain ecosystems of Asia, where many people rely on them for food security, demands explicit support from governmental and developmental agencies to promote their continuance and augmentation, as well as to support the empowerment of women.[37] Fortunately, this issue is receiving greater attention and thereby has the potential to fundamentally shape approaches to traditional food, nutrition, culture, livelihoods and the environment.

Acknowledgements

We are grateful to the National Innovation Foundation, Ahmedabad, Gujarat, India, for funding this study. We are also immensely grateful to the different key informants, local women, and community leaders of the villages of Pasighat, East Siang District, Arunachal Pradesh, India, who helped us build rapport and were integral parts of the study. We extend our heartiest gratitude to Professor Nancy J. Turner, School of Environmental

Sciences, University of Victoria, BC, Canada, for her painstaking job of reviewing this chapter and providing technical input for the manuscript.

References

1. Turner, N.J. and Turner, S.E. (2004), "Food, forage and medicinal resources of forests", *Encyclopedia of Life Support Systems*, EOLSS Publishers, Oxford, pp. 1–41; Singh, R.K. (2004), "Conserving diversity and culture: Pem Dolma", *Honey Bee*, Vol. 15, No. 3, pp. 12–13; Singh, R.K. (2004), "Using diversified ethnic fruits for food security and sustainable livelihoods, IK practice detail-2", http://www4.worldbank.org/afr/ikdb/search.cfm (accessed 22 October 2006); Turner, N.J. (2005), *Earth's Blanket: Traditional Teaching for Sustainable Living*, Douglas and McIntyre Ltd, Vancouver; Singh, A., Singh, R.K. and Sureja, A.K. (2007), "Cultural significance and diversities of ethnic foods of Northeast India", *Indian Journal of Traditional Knowledge*, Vol. 6, No. 1, pp. 79–94; Singh, R.K., Singh, A. and Sureja, A.K. (2007), "Traditional foods of *Monpa* tribe of West Kameng, Arunachal Pradesh: status and prospects", *Indian Journal Traditional Knowledge*, Vol. 6, No. 1, pp. 25–36.
2. Turner, *Earth's Blanket*, *op. cit.*; Singh et al., Cultural significance and diversities of ethnic foods", *op. cit.*; Singh et al., "Traditional foods of *Monpa* tribe", *op. cit.*
3. Godoy, R., Reyes-Garcia, V., Byron E., Leonard, W.R. and Vadez, V. (2005), "The effects of market economies on the well-being of indigenous peoples and on their use of renewable natural resources", *Annual Review of Anthropology*, Vol. 34, pp. 121–138.
4. Singh, A. (2007), "Traditional foods and associated knowledge systems relating to health and nutrition among Adi women of East Siang District, Arunachal Pradesh", unpublished MSc. thesis, Department of Food and Nutrition, Banaras Hindu, University (BHU), Varanasi, UP, India.
5. Milburn, M.P. (2004), "Indigenous nutrition using traditional food knowledge to solve contemporary health problems", *The American Indian Quarterly*, Vol. 28, Nos 3 and 4, pp. 411–434.
6. Ibid.; Turner, *Earth's Blanket*, *op. cit.*
7. Turner, *Earth's Blanket*, *op. cit.*; Singh et al., "Traditional foods of *Monpa* tribe", *op. cit.*
8. Turner and Turner, "Food, forage and medicinal resources", *op. cit.*; Singh et al., "Cultural significance and diversities of ethnic foods", *op. cit.*; Singh et al., "Traditional foods of *Monpa* tribe", *op. cit.*
9. Singh et al., "Cultural significance and diversities of ethnic foods", *op. cit.*; Singh et al., "Traditional foods of *Monpa* tribe", *op. cit.*
10. Brodt, S. (2002), "Learning about tree management in rural central India: A local-global continuum", *Human Organisation*, Vol. 61, pp. 58–67; Singh, "Conserving diversity and culture", *op. cit*; Singh, "Using diversified ethnic fruits", *op. cit.*
11. Hamilton, A. (1983 [1912]), *In Abor Jungles of North-East India*, Mittal Publications, Delhi.
12. Danggen, B. (2003), *A Book of Conversation: A Help Book for English to Adi Conversation*, Himalayan Publishers, Itanagar.
13. Ibid.; Lego, N.N. (1992), *British Relations with the Adis, 1825–1947*, Omsons Publications, New Delhi.
14. Danggen, *A Book of Conversation*, *op. cit.*
15. Danggen, B. (2003), *The Kebang: A Unique Indigenous Political Institution of the Adis*, Himalayan Publishers, Delhi.

16. Singh, *Traditional Foods, op. cit.*; Hamilton, *In Abor Jungles, op. cit.*

17. Mibang, T. and Abraham, P.T. (2001), *An Introduction to Adi Language*, Himalayan Publishers, Itanagar; Mibang, T. and Chaudhuri, S.K. (2004), *Understanding Tribal Religion*, Mittal Publications, New Delhi.

18. Hamilton, *In Abor Jungles, op. cit.*; Mibang and Abraham, *Introduction to Adi Language, op. cit.*

19. Hamilton, *In Abor Jungles, op. cit.*

20. Davis, A. and Wagner, J.R. (2003), "Who knows? On the importance of identifying 'experts' when researching local ecological knowledge", *Human Ecology*, Vol. 31, pp. 463–489.

21. Singh, *Traditional Foods, op. cit.*

22. Gregory, C. (2000), *Native Science: Natural Laws of Interdependence*, Clear Light Publishers, Santa Fe, NM.

23. Turner, *Earth's Blanket, op. cit.*

24. Turner and Turner, "Food, forage and medicinal resources", *op. cit.*

25. Gregory, *Native Science, op. cit.*

26. Singh, R.K. and Sureja, A.K. (2005), "Biodiversity contests: an innovative method to make knowledge dam and conserve biodiversity", paper presented at the National Symposium on Changing Concepts of Forestry in the 21st Century, Dr Y.S. Parmar University of Horticulture and Forestry, Nauni, Solan, Himanchal Pradesh, India, 21–22 October.

27. Singh et al., "Cultural significance and diversities of ethnic foods", *op. cit.*; Singh et al., "Traditional foods of *Monpa* tribes", *op. cit.*

28. Singh, *Traditional Foods, op. cit.*

29. Singh and Sureja, "Biodiversity contests", *op. cit.*

30. Singh, *Traditional Foods, op. cit.*

31. Ibid.

32. Mibang and Chaudhuri, *Understanding Tribal Religion, op. cit.*; Mibang, T. and Chaudhuri, S. K. (2004), *Folk Culture and Oral Literature from North-East India*, Mittal Publications, New Delhi.

33. Susana, G. and García, C. (2006), "The mother–child nexus. Knowledge and valuation of wild food plants in Wayanad, Western Ghats, India", *Journal of Ethnobiology and Ethnomedicine*, Vol. 2, No. 39, pp. 1–6.

34. Gupta, A.K. (1991), "Sustainability through biodiversity: designing crucible of culture, creativity and conscience", paper presented at the International Conference on Biodiversity and Conservation, Copenhagen, 8 November, pp. 8–10.

35. Pieroni, A. (2001), "Evaluation of the cultural significance of wild food and botanicals traditionally consumed in northwestern Tuscany, Italy", *Journal of Ethnobiology*, Vol. 21, pp. 89–104.

36. Singh, *Traditional Foods, op. cit.*

37. Becker, C.D. and Ghimire, K. (2003), "Synergy between traditional ecological knowledge and conservation science supports forest preservation in Ecuador", *Conservation Ecology*, Vol. 8, No. 1, pp. 1–12.

Appendix: Alphabetic Index of Adi Words and their English Translation

Adi word	English meaning
Abo-Teni	A character in spiritual stories which signify the origin of the Adi tribe.
Adi	A tribe living in the mountainous region of Arunachal Pradesh.
Angyat	Foxtail millet – a crop cultivated in the mountain region of Arunachal Pradesh and used in the preparation of beverages, as well as food, during periods of drought.
Apatani	A tribe inhabiting the Apatani plateau of Arunachal Pradesh, who are famous for their sustainable indigenous models of livelihood and farming systems.
Apong	A beverage made from rice/millets/maize/cassava.
Aran	An Adi festival during which hunting takes place and traditional foods using wild animals are prepared and consumed.
Ayak	A millet crop found in the mountain region of Arunachal Pradesh and used in the preparation of local beverages, as well as food, during drought periods.
Banko	A shrub whose leaves are used as a vegetable and for curing diabetes, malaria and high blood pressure.
Carembola/Kordoi	A fruit, commonly known in English as the star fruit, used for curing jaundice.
Champa	A tree that produces very sour-tasting fruits that are mixed with small fish while cooking to prevent them fragmenting.
Dhenkia saag	A species of indigenous fern used as vegetable and considered to be rich in protein and micro-minerals.
Donyi-Polo	The religion followed by various tribes (Adi, Nyshi, etc.) of Arunachal Pradesh in which the sun, moon and earth are major gods.
Fayong	An indigenous plant found in the forest areas, added to traditional foods to enhance flavour. Also a good source of income for Adi women.
Gaon Burha	The democratic head of village whose decision is considered supreme in all village problems and socio-political affairs.
Gende	A herb used as a vegetable during the summer season, which provides a good source of income for Adi women.
Inyik, Lengot, Lolum tayin, Peki tatar	Indigenous species of mushrooms found in the forest areas and a good source of income during the summer season.
Jhum	Swidden agriculture – a type of agriculture in which parts of the forest are cleared and burned in order to cultivate crops.
Kebung	A local term for the Himalayan giant black squirrel.
Kekir	A local variety of ginger.

Adi word	English meaning
Kopi	A vegetable belonging to the *Solanaceae* family, which provides a stable source of income for Adi women.
Koppir	A vegetable belonging to the *Solanaceae* family, which provides a stable source of income for Adi women.
Mamang	A herb used as vegetable during the summer season, which provides a good source of income for Adi women.
Marshang	A herb used as vegetable during the summer season, which provides a good source of income for Adi women.
Minyong	A subtribe of the Adi.
Mithun	Cattle (*Bos frontalis*) reared by the Adi in semi-wild conditions and representing a symbol of prosperity.
Mosup	A community hall constructed from local bamboo and indigenous palm leaves in which social, political and cultural gatherings are held.
Onger	A shrub found in forest areas and used as vegetable as well as a medicine for high blood pressure.
Ongin	A herb used as vegetable, which provides a good source of income for Adi women.
Owyin	An indigenous species of onion used as food mixed with meat from hunted animals and other meat-based foods.
Oyik	A shrub used as vegetable and as a medicine for curing diabetes, which provides a good source of income for Adi women.
Paput	A herb used as vegetable during the summer season, which provides a good source of income for Adi women.
Rori	A herb used as vegetable during the summer season, which provides a good source of income for Adi women.
Sajna	*Molinga oleifera* or the drum stick tree of which the leaves and fruits are both used as vegetable during the summer season. The leaves are a good source of iron and are used for curing various gynaecological disorders among Adi women. Also provides a good source of income for Adi women.
Solung	The Adi tribe's biggest local festival during which a *mithun* is sacrificed and various traditional foods, based on plants and crops accessed from the forest and traditional agricultural fields, are prepared.
Taba	A kind of wild tree, the inner bark of which is mixed with *tase* as a taste enhancer. Also used during periods of drought period as a survival food.
Talab	An indigenous species of onion which is mixed with meat from hunted animals' meat in food dishes and also used as ethno-medicine.
Tangum	An indigenous vegetable accessed from forest areas and used as vegetable. Also provides a good source of income for Adi women.

Adi word	English meaning
Tase	An indigenous species of tuber found in the forest regions of Arunachal Pradesh and mostly used as a survival food during periods of drought.
Topu	A dance performed by group of Adi women on various socio-cultural occasions during which various traditional foods prepared from local plants and wild animals are cooked and eaten.
Yongjong	A dance performed by a group of Adi men and associated with the cooking and eating of various traditional foods prepared from local plants and wild animals.

13 *Market Opportunities from Cultural Value Convergence and Functional Food: The Experiences of the Malaysian Marketplace*

SITI HASNAH HASSAN,* STEPHEN DANN,[†]
KHARIL ANNUAR MOHD KAMAL[‡] AND DES NICHOLLS[§]

Keywords

functional food, Malaysia, cultural value convergence.

Abstract

In this chapter we examine the role of culture and value systems in influencing functional food consumption, which remains poorly understood in developing countries. In the rapidly expanding functional food marketplace, promotions of food products focus on perceived health benefits for specific consumer groups.

We examine the role of ethnicity and the dynamics of cultural and value changes in traditional and emerging economies, explore the various influences on functional food consumption in multicultural societies, and outline lessons for businesses that compete in traditional functional food markets.

*   Dr Siti Hasnah Hassan, School of Management, Marketing and International Business, Australian National University, ACT 0200 Australia. E-mail: siti.hassan@anu.edu.au. Telephone: + 61 2612 56738.

†   Dr Stephen Dann, Senior Lecturer in Marketing, School of Management, Marketing and International Business, Australian National University, ACT 0200 Australia. E-mail: stephen.dann@anu.edu.au. Telephone: + 61 2 612 54516.

‡   Mr Kharil Annuar Mohd Kamal, School of Management, Marketing and International Business, Australian National University, ACT 0200 Australia. E-mail: khairl.mohdkamal@anu.edu.u. Telephone: + 61 2612 56738.

§   Professor Des Nicholls, School of Management, Marketing and International Business, Australian National University, ACT 0200 Australia. E-mail: des.nicholls@anu.edu.au. Telephone: + 61 2612 53367.

Introduction

In recent years food with curative properties has attracted interest among many consumers around the world, probably due to the increasing attention paid to food-related health issues, such as food's potential ability to prevent diseases and improve consumers' mental state or quality of life.[1] Initial studies established personal values as central to the motivations and underlying determinants of consumer attitudes and consumption behaviour,[2] yet most studies of functional food examine its role in developed, Western nations. The dominant national cultures in such studies tend towards individualism and the rejection of tradition in favour of modern, or postmodern, consumption values.[3] In contrast, in many developing countries, significant minority groups limit the applicability of a dominant cultural grouping,[4] such that the countries are multicultural in nature, either by quirks of geography or because they were formed as a result of interventions by an external imperial power.[5] Societies drawn together from multiple cultural groups tend towards group-identity collectivism and cultural group identity rather than dominant nationalistic traits or the more Western concepts of individualized personal values. Unlike developed Western countries, the value systems of developing multicultural societies, especially in Asia, remain significantly contested due to the high levels of social interaction and transformations in social structure.

A key element of culturally-based values in multicultural societies is the evolution of values through cultural convergence or cultural divergence. As economic, social–structural and communication systems that promote cross-cultural communication improve, the potential for convergence among culturally-based values within and between different ethnic groups increases. According to modernization theory, with time and economic development, different societies become more similar.[5] This idea receives support from neo-classical ideologues such as Francis Fukuyama,[6] who posits that all societies attain a similar economic and political system in the long term. Fukuyama also believes that capitalism and liberal democracy represent the end-states of social systems that have passed through similar phases of economic and social development. Similarly, Friedman and Zivko imagine increasing levels of similarity between nation-states at the aggregate "meta level", even as advances in market segmentation, mass customization, and individualization create increasingly fragmented markets.[7]

Due to space restrictions, this chapter does not examine the mechanisms of cultural convergence, but instead focuses specifically on how convergence might influence marketplace attitudes. For example, the three different ethnicities that co-inhabit Malaysia should become more similar after a period of rapid economic development. However, theory has not addressed the nature and level of such convergence, nor has it fully considered the contestable meaning of such convergence. Furthermore, theory does not predict the extent to which different cultures converge.[8] To avoid this controversy, this chapter focuses on a specific feature: the consumption of functional food. We thus provide an overview of how culturally-based values and individual personal values influence functional food consumption and investigate how consumers from different ethic groups negotiate and manage such values.

Functional Food

Functional food refers to a category of health-enhancing foods that are not drugs, chemicals or vitamins and are not prescribed by doctors or other formally qualified medical practitioners. Similarly, the American Dietetic Association describes functional foods as:

> ... *foods that include whole foods and fortified, enriched, or enhanced foods that have a potentially beneficial effect on health when consumed as part of a varied diet on a regular basis, at effective levels.*[9]

The International Food Information Council (IFIC) regards functional food as any form of modified food, or food ingredient, that may provide a health benefit beyond the traditional nutrients it contains.[10] In summary, functional foods include any type of food that consumers perceive as having health-enhancing properties, beyond their basic nutritional values.[11]

FOOD CONSUMPTION BEHAVIOUR

Existing studies of functional food explore trends in attitudes towards, and risk perceptions about, functional foods, as well as study market segmentations of functional food consumers.[12] Yet food consumption patterns are complex phenomena to study, because:

> ... *food-related behaviour is highly inconsistent as physical needs, temporary moods, attitudes, traditions, food supply situations, acquired knowledge of nutrients and food ingredients, etc. interact at different levels and to a varying extent.*[13]

Functional food consumption also depends on various personal and cultural values, which may change over time and vary according to segmentation factors such as gender, social class, age, education and culture.[14]

CULTURAL CONVERGENCE AND FUNCTIONAL FOOD

Cultural convergence is increasingly visible as a primary driver of functional food consumption. Culturally-derived health beliefs affect food choices and prohibitions, which differ from culture to culture. In line with economic theory, culture probably shapes tastes and preferences. That is, if culture consists of a system of shared beliefs, and people in that culture share tastes and preferences, tastes and preferences have been shaped by the boundaries of culture.[15] Consequently, cultural divergence should create increased barriers to cross-cultural functional food consumption, whereas cultural convergence should create opportunities for consumers to experiment with functional food alternatives from other cultural groups. Cultural convergence in this sense may serve as a facilitator that removes the perception of foreignness from functional food from different cultures, such that previously culturally specific functional food may become palatable to members of other cultures. In the case of Malaysia, this convergence has tended to follow the dominant values of the Malay Muslim majority, which enjoys entrenched systems that safeguard and promote Malay rights, resulting from the social contract established when Malaysia achieved independence in 1957. This system remains operational despite concerns that it may jeopardize ethnic harmony. Nevertheless, consistent with our argument about cultural convergence, more and more Malays, especially those with higher education, are moving away from this system of Malay dominance.

The Malaysian Case Study: Functional Food in a Multicultural Context

This chapter outlines various influences on functional food consumption in a contemporary, multicultural society. The development of the model focused on functional food cultural convergence in the multicultural framework of Malaysia, where each of the three dominant Malaysian ethnic groups (Malay, Indian and Chinese) have their own beliefs about foods, well-being, and traditional functional foods. For example, the Malay cultural group uses herbs and plant roots as traditional dietary supplements, Malaysian Indian communities relate health foods with their traditional Ayurvedic practices, and Chinese groups believe that the foundation of human health is the therapeutic use of food. However, their distinction is blurring as health-conscious consumers from all three ethnic groups become willing to try alternative ethnic or culturally-based functional food – as long the option does not conflict with their own core cultural principles and values.

METHODOLOGY

For this Malaysian functional food case study, we use Venkatesh's ethno-consumerist methodology, which provides an in-depth understanding of cross-cultural consumer experiences in a given culture.[16] For support, we also implement the means–end chain methodology recommended by Gutman to identify consumption motives and values.[17] In addition, we adapt Glaser's and Strauss's approach to grounded theory methodology to enable the use of constant comparative analysis.[18] Data compared within a single interview, between the same cultural ethnic groups and between different ethnic groups, provide cross-checks for social and cultural factors and minimize issues surrounding the misappropriation of cultural artefacts during the coding and analysis. Coding is central to the transformation of the data to theory, in that our objective for this study is to identify relevant cultural objects, practices and experiences that influence functional food consumption. The analyses used in the process reveal key conceptual structures, social histories and individual consumer memories that in turn identify the factors that influence functional food consumption.

CORE CATEGORIES OF FUNCTIONAL FOODS

The main core categories reflect the central themes of the data, revealed as an outcome of the selective coding process.[19] The core categories governing function food consumption are cultural values, cultural convergence, value negotiation, health motives, knowledge and personal values, all of which appear in the proposed functional food consumption model.

Model of Preference Formation for Functional Food

Through our case study research, we derive a series of propositions that explain the selection of function food in a multicultural society. The model has six separate propositions:

- Proposition 1: Culturally-based values underpin consumer preferences for functional food.
- Proposition 2: Knowledge plays an important role in influencing preferences towards functional food.
- Proposition 3: The perceived healthiness of functional foods affects the consumption of such food.
- Proposition 4: Over time, cultural values in relation to functional food preferences converge due to social interaction.
- Proposition 5: Consumers negotiate and manage their conflicting cultural values by categorizing, prioritizing and balancing.
- Proposition 6: Consumers' personal values are more influential than their cultural values in functional food consumption.

Figure 13.1 illustrates these propositions.

PROPOSITION 1: CULTURALLY-BASED VALUES UNDERLIE CONSUMER PREFERENCES FOR FUNCTIONAL FOOD

Each ethnic group has specific traditional cultural practices and beliefs that are reported to benefit their members. Culturally-based values underpin consumer preferences by affecting all aspects of food behaviour, food choices and food consumption. As both

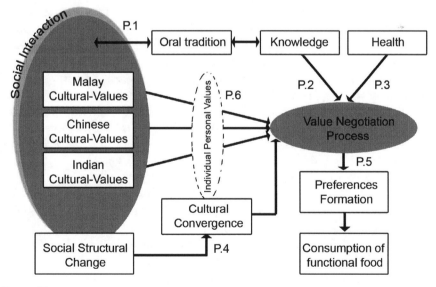

*P= Proposition

Figure 13.1 Substantive theory of functional food consumption in multicultural societies

Fieldhouse and Sobal argue, food, eating and nutrition depend heavily on custom and culture.[20] Cultural value differences among consumers influence such issues as healthy eating, adequate levels of sleeping, exercise and vitamin intake.[21] Consumption of functional foods to prevent or cure illnesses therefore reflects cultural variation among the three ethnic groups – Malays, Chinese and Indians – in Malaysia

Culturally-based values do not directly influence functional food consumption, but instead are subject to various filters and interact with other factors, such as oral traditions and food beliefs. Oral tradition provides a valuable source of learning, understanding of own culture and development of cultural values.[22] Oral traditions inherited from previous generations also are an integral part of the transference process associated with learning culture values and thereby influence the consumption of functional food.

Knowledge of functional foods through oral tradition has a strong influence on food selection. According to Bakker, even though written records of cultures may exist, some aspects of culture, customs and traditions are most effectively passed on through the oral traditions.[23] In the case of functional food, oral tradition represents a preferred and trusted source, because the tradition itself gets passed on during the performance of functional food preparation and selection.[24] Children learn the importance of certain foods and their effects when they are growing up as part of the transference of family traditions from generation to generation.[25]

Another mediating influence pertains to the beliefs attached to certain foods. Malays use herbs and plant roots from the rainforest as traditional supplements, as do the Chinese, who relate functional foods to traditional Chinese medicine using knowledge derived from Chinese philosophical and religious teachings affiliated with Confucianism, Buddhism and Taoism. Malaysian Indians, in contrast, relate functional food to their cultural interpretation of traditional Ayurvedic practices. All three ethnic groups have their own beliefs and practices in choosing food that may provide health benefits. The similarities in these belief and knowledge probably result from the influence and exchange of information in Malaysia during earlier centuries which promoted a shared cultural framework;[26] in the seventeenth century the Malay peninsula served as a trading centre for travellers from China and India and, during this period the cultures exchanged medical ideas and goods, with the consequence that Malay food beliefs have been influenced by travellers from South-east Asia, China and India, as well as Arabs who were responsible for bringing Islam to the peninsula. Moreover, within the context of their multicultural society, the three ethnic groups continue to interact and exchange information between each other. As a result, knowledge about food classification is becoming very widespread among Malay, Chinese, and Indian ethnic groups, who obtain further knowledge from reading, word of mouth, advertisements and their own experiences.

Malays, Chinese and Indians similarly classify foods, illnesses and traditional remedies according to the intrinsic qualities of human bodily effect as "hot" or "cold". This classification is important in choosing which functional food to consume. Each food has a different effect on different people, so consumers must find the food that is compatible with their individual body systems. This knowledge is passed on verbally and shared among community members. Cold food sometimes has an "airy effect" and can cause discomfort, so,participants from all three ethnic groups universally said that they add certain ingredients, such as spices (e.g. pepper, cumin, garam masala, extra garlic, ginger) to balance it.

Cultural values encompass historical, traditional and spiritual antecedents of functional food consumption, in that they represent the influences taught to a consumer as part of his or her upbringing in a society. For example, the cultural values associated with religious beliefs influence the perception of different food products as acceptable or unacceptable; Islam classifies various foods as either *halal* or *haram*, Judaism uses the kosher/non-kosher categorization, and Hindu beliefs proscribe the consumption of any living animals, such as cows. Table 13.1 outlines the subcategories that encompass the influence of cultural values on functional food.

PROPOSITION 2: KNOWLEDGE PLAYS AN IMPORTANT ROLE IN INFLUENCING PREFERENCE TOWARDS FUNCTIONAL FOOD

Consumers use nutritional knowledge to link diet and health and change their eating habits accordingly, although knowledge alone is unlikely to be effective in maximizing a healthy lifestyle. According to Nestle et al., the level of health knowledge is moderate among consumers,[27] but many do not know how to apply this knowledge effectively or refuse to practise it, even when they know the health benefits of consuming healthy food(s). Consumers get information about functional food from various sources, such as formal or informal learning, mass media, advertising and oral tradition. Nevertheless, word of mouth or oral traditions are easier to access and practise in developing, traditional societies.

Table 13.1 Cultural value and functional food

Conceptual category	Property
Traditional functional food	Ethnic tradition/cultural ritual Common food in the culture Symbolic food
Food belief	*Bisa* (allergic) – Malay culture Cold and hot foods in Malay and Indian culture Yin and yang – Chinese culture Airy food in Malay culture
Religion	*Halal* (Malay)* Beef (Indian, Hindu) Pork (Malay) Alcohol (Malay) Vegan (Hindu and Buddhist) Vegetarian (Hindu and Buddhist)
Oral tradition	Inherited knowledge/heritage Trusted information Testimony and evidence
Family upbringing	Family tradition Regular meal since childhood Familiarity

* *The* Malay sample population self-identified as Islamic, or adherents to the dominant Islamic cultural values of *halal/haram*

Some modernized versions of traditional functional food brands are very common in health-food markets. Advertisements for Malay traditional herbal products stress beauty and appearance (e.g. radiant skin, slim figure, slower ageing process). These products are usually advertised on television, radio and in magazines, targeting young women who are concerned about their image. Thus, in addition to representing cultures and customs, food provides other benefits, such as nutritional value, pleasure, satisfaction, sharing and giving, and social interaction.

Knowledge is a component of the value negotiation process by which the consumer draws on prior learning, experience and other accessible information to determine the value of a functional food product as a means of assisting or enhancing their current state of health.[28] As a set of learned information, knowledge is also influenced by cultural values, traditional knowledge and oral histories within a cultural group, as well as external influences such as research, media or other communications exposure. Table 13.2 outlines the subcategories that encompass knowledge and functional food.

Participants indicate that, apart from oral tradition, they get most of their knowledge about functional food, including other ethnic groups' functional food, from media such as newspapers, magazines, books and television shows. Some knowledge comes from making friends from different ethnic groups. In relation to functional food consumption, consumers in multicultural communities, regardless of their ethnicity rely on knowledge they receive from oral tradition, word of mouth and mass media, and seem to share it with others. Therefore, greater understanding that health-related foods provide health benefits beyond basic nutrition drives demand for, and consumption of, that food.

PROPOSITION 3: THE PERCEIVED HEALTHINESS OF FUNCTIONAL FOODS AFFECTS THE CONSUMPTION OF SUCH FOOD

The perceived health-enhancing properties of some functional foods motivates some people to consume them on the basis of their belief that functional foods provide health benefits beyond basic nutritional needs, including the prevention of modern lifestyle diseases. Thus, there is a perception that these foods help consumers care for themselves and live healthily. For instance, the Chinese believe that foods and medicine have equal importance in preventing and treating disease; they come from the same source, are based on the same basic theories, and have the same uses.[29] Chinese functional foods include mushrooms, ginseng, green tea, the hawthorn fruit and its extracts, and the Chinese wolfberry, believed to prevent cancer and offer other health benefits. Indian

Table 13.2 Knowledge and functional food

Conceptual category	Property
Formal	Education
Informal	Experience
Personal	Oral tradition
Impersonal information	Word of mouth
	Reading (newspapers, magazines, books)
	Mass media (TV, radio, catalogue, direct mail)

functional foods include turmeric, curcumin, asafoetida, cinnamon, plus various Indian spices, herbs and plants. In addition to making the food tastier, these foods are believed to promote optimum health. Malay functional food includes pegaga (*Centella asiatica*), tongkat ali (*Eurycoma longifolia*), kachip fatima (*Labisia pothoina*) and red yam. Increasing scientific evidence supports the functional role of these foods in human health; for example, turmeric, green tea, mushrooms,and red yams may help prevent cancer and other illnesses.[30] Other studies show inextricable links between traditional food resources and benefits to nutrition and health in traditional and developing societies.[31]

Food consumption represents part of a consumer's identity, because the process of consumption involves tradition, social commitment and health concepts.[32] Health provides an important motivation for food choice,[33] and as consumers grow more aware and conscious of the importance of health, they search for food that can help keep them healthy, prevent diseases and improve their mental state and quality of life.[34]

Health motives may be important factors in consumers' choice to consume functional food. Participants who are older (including those who have a history of health problems in the family or currently suffer from a health problem) are likely to be more concerned with consuming specific functional foods that might cure or prevent heart disease, diabetes, cancer, hypertension and many other debilitating diseases. These participants recall oral tradition and culturally-based functional food from their own culture and other cultures. Generally, they are more flexible in accepting traditional or modern functional foods, as long the food gives them curative benefits. In contrast, young and healthy participants are less concerned about oral tradition or health-related foods,[35] probably because they do not think that it is necessary to take specific functional food or other health foods while they are still young and healthy. Many say that they will be more concerned about the issue when they grow older or face health problems.

The health motive for functional food consumption is thus the most straightforward motive: Functional foods are perceived as a form of health product, consumed as both a proactive measure and a reactive agent to assist recoveries. Table 13.3 outlines the subcategories that encompass this motive.

Health motives also are a specific form of value negotiation, representing the pragmatic use of the health benefits of functional food as a self-medication technique. A similar

Table 13.3 Health motives

Conceptual category	Property
Ageing	Getting older
Health history	Family health background
Necessity	Healthy life style
	Preventing illness
	Treating illness
	Curing illness
	Enhancing health
	Keeping youthful

form of product value statement likely is associated with vitamin and herbal supplements commonly sold to assist recovery from colds or influenza.

PROPOSITION 4: OVER TIME, CULTURAL VALUES IN RELATION TO FUNCTIONAL FOOD PREFERENCES CONVERGE DUE TO SOCIAL INTERACTION

To a certain degree, cultural practices change or converge over time.[36] The data show that cultural convergence occurs due to changes in socio-economic development, mainly because of urbanization, modernization, industrialization and globalization. Social changes can also cause changes in lifestyle and value systems. For example, economic development may be a form of social change, because economic development tends to lead to shifts away from absolute norms and values towards rational, tolerant, trusting and participatory values.[37] Evidence from previous research indicates that value systems vary because of differences in income, occupation, living conditions, and length and intensity of exposure to another culture within any ethnic group.[38] In this study, participants (especially young and educated ones) have no problem accepting either functional foods that are common within their given culture or other culturally-based functional foods that are culturally acceptable. They are willing to try a given functional food if scientific evidence supports its use and trusted persons recommend it.

Social interaction among the ethnic groups also promotes cultural convergence over time. Living in close proximity fosters interactions and solidarity between members of different ethnic groups, which prompts the acceptance of others' culturally-based functional food. Constant interaction ensures more mutual understanding and respect, whereas lack of interpersonal interaction tends to reinforce stereotypes and hostility at the group level.[39] Indian or Chinese participants who grew up in Malay neighbourhoods or worked or socialized with Malay peers have no problem adopting Malays' culturally-based functional food. Similarly, Malays who grew up in Chinese or Indian neighbourhoods or worked with other ethnic groups have no problem adopting other culturally-based functional food as long the food is *halal* (that is, processed according to Islamic rules). In other words, Malays have no problem accepting Chinese or Indian functional foods that are based on herbal plants, fruits, leaves or roots, as long there are no animal-based ingredients or alcohol in them. Participants who work in public sectors, such as members of the police force or schoolteachers, tend to accept culturally-based functional foods because they socialize and work with other ethnic groups. Additional evidence indicates that Malays, Chinese and Indians adopt and share each ethnic group's cooking styles; most of the culturally-based food ingredients from the three ethnic groups can be obtained easily from grocery stores.

To a certain degree, then, cultural practices change and converge over time. Lee and Tse argue that some consumption behaviours may be ingrained in ethnic identity and others not.[40] Culturally-based food behaviour in functional food consumption converges over time. Cultural value convergence in turn means that the cultures of the three ethnic groups tend to become more alike as a result of increasing social interactions.

Based on evidence and available literature, Figure 13.2 illustrates how socio-economic development can cause a structural change that encourages social interaction and leads to changes in lifestyle and the value system. Over time, these changes promote cultural convergence with regard to functional food consumption

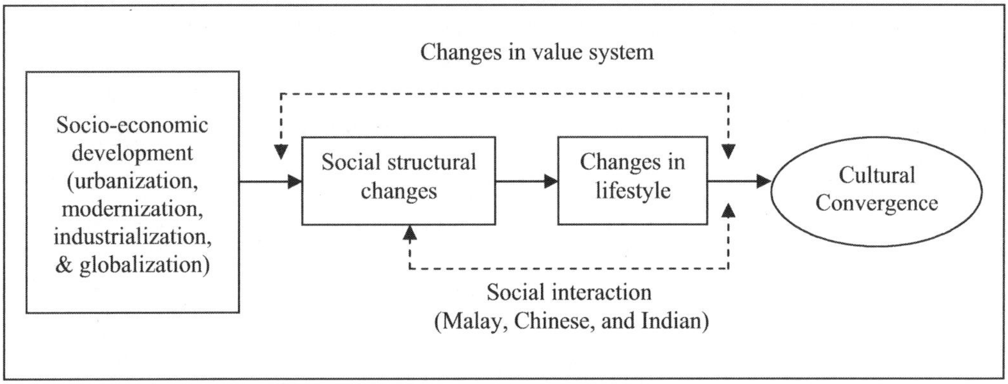

Figure 13.2 Cultural convergence in multicultural societies with regard to functional food consumption

Cultural convergence represents the recognition of the changing nature of the world, including rapid developments in society brought about by economic development, urbanization and access to the influences of other cultures through modernization. Table 13.4 outlines the subcategories of the cultural convergence factors.

The role of cultural convergence factors on the consumption of functional food also becomes evident when we consider four categories, including Western functional foods, as a part of the decision-making framework for functional food consumption. This analysis also suggests a potential market opportunity for Western food that can be demonstrated to have key health-assisting factors associated with consumers' traditional functional food choices.

PROPOSITION 5: CONSUMERS NEGOTIATE AND MANAGE THEIR CONFLICTING CULTURAL VALUES BY CATEGORIZING, PRIORITIZING AND BALANCING

Participants do not spend considerable time thinking when they make consumption choices, nor are they aware of their values until they face conflicting values, especially

Table 13.4 Cultural convergence factors

Conceptual category	Property
Economic development	Social change
	Social interaction (workplace, school, neighbour, friends)
	Education
	Knowledge
	Socio-economic change
	Urbanization
	Industrialization
	Modernization
	Globalization: Western functional food, Jamu (Malay, Indonesian), Ayurvedic (India, mainland), and traditional Chinese medicine (China, mainland)

when their personal values conflict with religious values. A variety of culturally-based and modern functional foods are available in the market, some of which conflict with religion, custom, food beliefs or personal values. The participants appear to negotiate these values unconsciously every time they make a decision to consume or not consume the selected functional food, as supported by the literature[41] and observational data. Table 13.5 outlines a saliency concepts value negotiation.

Participants' past choices and experiences with functional food are important sources of evidence about traits or abilities; these choices can become binding precedents. Although choices made over time may exhibit serial dependencies, the preferences that underlie these choices are stable. Therefore, at some point during consumption, consumers manage to align their value system with their own strategies until they find what they want. Eventually, the interaction of experience and preference influences their consumption habits.

Participants negotiate values in functional food consumption in several ways. During food choice or consumption, they must address conflicting value systems. According to Kamakura and Novak,[42] a consumer's value system provides an important tool for dealing with conflicting values during decision-making. A value system is unique to each consumer, which makes consumption choices in personal food systems rather complex. Consumers may have a set of common values in their value system, but the way in which they order and prioritize those values differs, even if they share similar cultural backgrounds. Social and lifestyle changes make food-related choice decisions more

Table 13.5 Illustration of the saliency concepts value negotiation

Participant	Incident
P1 Malay	I do not totally reject traditional or totally accept modern functional food. *Knowledge from reading and talking to others* is important. *Testimonial and experience* from others are also very important in influencing which *health or functional food I choose*. I need some kind of *evidence* to make [the] right choice. Other important things are the *taste, smell, price, availability of the food and how easy [it is] to prepare or to consume it*.
P2 Malay	As long it gives me *all the benefits for good health, suitable with [sic] my body system* and *halal*, then I has [sic] no problem with it. I can *tolerate* it even though I prefer the traditional health food. But nowadays there are *various choices of functional food products* in the market.
P1 Chinese	I look at the *benefits* first. I'm not a conservative person. I'm very open in accepting modern health foods. I think *knowledge* and *time* are very important factors in the decision to choose whatever food you eat. When you are busy … you will just eat whatever is *convenient* to you. You really don't have time to read and to look for the most suitable food for yourself.
P3 Indian	I don't have problem to [sic] consume modern functional food because it is very *convenient to consume* this product although most of the time I prefer the traditional one. But I have to make sure there are *no animal-based ingredients* in the food. *As a Hindu I don't take beef.*

complex, and people must negotiate values even within themselves, especially if they take a long-term view.

Food-related values in personal food systems may also conflict because of changing lifestyle patterns and life-course experiences related to food.[43] Consumers adopt three strategies during the value negotiation process for their personal food systems. First, they categorize foods and eating situations; second, they prioritize conflicting values for specific eating situations; and, third, they balance this prioritization across personally defined timeframes. As consumers negotiate and manage conflicting values throughout the food consumption process, their value systems change too. Changes in consumption practices may force cultural convergence, or even cultural divergence, within and between ethnic groups in a multi-ethnic nation.

Value negotiation represents the factors that the consumer uses to create his or her own mental models of what constitutes functional foods. These factors include external influences of advertising, word of mouth and product endorsements, as well as internal factors such as personal experience and subjective judgements on the success of the product in delivering health benefits compared with the total time, effort and monetary costs, as Table 13.6 illustrates.

Classic marketing influences also play a role in the establishment and maintenance of the perceived efficacy of the functional foods through factors such as pricing, branding, paid endorsements, advertising and the packaging of functional foods into convenient units.

PROPOSITION 6: CONSUMERS' PERSONAL VALUES ARE MORE INFLUENTIAL THAN CULTURAL VALUES IN FUNCTIONAL FOOD CONSUMPTION

Values are intangible outcomes or ends that can be categorized as attributes, consequence and values. As a whole, values represent hierarchically structured attributes, leading to benefits, which in turn produce value satisfaction. Functional food attributes are therefore

Table 13.6 Value negotiation factors

Conceptual category	Property
Health motive	Health benefits, effectiveness, end results, side–effect, necessities
Knowledge	Oral tradition, word of mouth, testimony, advertisement
Religion and food belief	*Halal* (Malay), beef (Indian Hindus), pork (Malay), alcohol (Malay), vegan (Hindu and Buddhist), vegetarian (Hindu and Buddhist), compatibility with body system
Price and brand	Affordability, buy trial product, certified by health authority
Time constraints	Convenience, ease of preparation and use, taste
Resources	Affordability, accessibility, availability

a means for consumers to obtain desired ends through the benefits yielded by those attributes; these reflect their personal values.

Rokeach introduced instrumental values and terminal values, whereby consumers may apply either or both sets to achieve their goals.[44] Instrumental values reflect a chosen way of reaching end values, such as certain behavioural characteristics that appear socially desirable, including ambitiousness, honesty, responsibility, obedience and courageousness. Terminal values reflect the end-states themselves, the ultimate, idealized modes of living, such as inner harmony, happiness, family security, a comfortable life and wisdom.

Individual personal values vary from consumer to consumer and sometimes may not represent cultural values. Some consumers' personal values provide the underlying determinants of their attitudes and consumption behaviour. In this sense, according to Rokeach, an individual value is "an enduring belief that a specific mode of conduct or end-state of existence is personally or socially preferable to an opposite or converse mode of conduct or end-state of existence".[45] Furthermore, Schwartz and Bilsky define values as "the designation of whose interests the attainment of each value serves. Values may serve individualistic interests (e.g. pleasure, independence), collective interests (e.g. equality, responsible), or both types of interests (e.g. wisdom)".[46]

Consumers learn and develop their values throughout their lives. Self-conception, self-esteem, personal experience and changes in society can alter or shape individual personal values.[47] In Malaysia, rapid structural changes and social transformations are leading to a new modern generation that differs from previous generations.[48] Malaysia offers an example of a fast-moving, developing country with rapid technological advancements and social transformations.

Social transformations affect consumers' core values. Consumers may possess few culturally based values but acquire hundreds of personal values throughout their lives,[49] particularly in the context of functional food consumption. Evidence from the data analysis and existing literature shows that participants acquire knowledge of functional foods from various sources; in addition to cultural values they acquired from their ancestors, they develop and acquire personal values throughout their lives.

Personal values thus represent the consumer's internal "black box" of influences that affect functional food decisions. These influences range from the internally mediated rewards of inner harmony to the externally mediated influence of traditional laws. In relation to functional food consumption, consumers may use terminal values to obtain the desired modes of life, such as inner harmony or happiness; instrumental values provide the means of achieving these terminal values, as Table 13.7 summarizes.

The role of personal values for functional foods is akin to the influence of psychographic variables in standard decision-making processes. These internal factors are difficult to control in a marketing exchange, although they can be accessed by aligning the functional food's branding and perception with the key influences – for example, "pleasure, happiness, and an exciting life" could easily be adapted as a positioning statement for a brand.

MANAGERIAL IMPLICATIONS

Studying functional food in Malaysia provides useful tools for understanding how consumers from multicultural societies undergoing rapid transition manage conflicting

Table 13.7 Values from the Hierarchical Value Map (HVM) analysis

Terminal values	Instrumental values
Happiness	Responsibility
Inner harmony	Obedient
Pleasure	Loving
Family security	Independent
Freedom	Self-controlled
Self-respect	
Social recognition	
Comfortable life	
Exciting life	

values in their functional food consumption. Such societies undergo rapid structural changes and social transformation due to economic development, and, as such, they represent an emerging trend in the study of consumer value systems.[50] Although functional food provides a medium for understanding the influence of culturally-based values on consumption, this study may also be generalized to any type of product for which consumption is strongly based on cultural values.

For traditional functional food, marketers might begin with an ethnically-based promotion, which they should change as the product becomes more acceptable to other ethnic groups. The ethnic dimension of the product can create a "mystical aura" that marketers can capitalize on in their future marketing efforts. For modernized functional food, we suggest a strategy of promoting both ethnic and mass appeal simultaneously, because the popularity of certain products, such as traditional functional foods, may depend on the ethnic dimension. These strategies rely on the crucial assumption that a degree of cultural convergence exists in the society.

Lessons from the Malaysian Study

Due to their close proximity, each major ethnic group in Malaysia probably acquires practices and beliefs from the other cultures. With time, views about functional foods held by the Malays, Chinese and Indians may converge. The lack of sufficient evidence about the culturally-based values or attitudes towards functional foods in multicultural societies demands a theoretical model that can link multicultural values, oral tradition, social interaction and cultural convergence and thereby clarify consumer consumption. This study provides such knowledge with a model that may applied to other types of products in which cultural values strongly influence consumption.

In Malaysia, consumers can usually be slotted into segments delineated by their ethnic group. We suggest that a better communication strategy might increase favourable perceptions of functional food as a whole. The rigid ethnic-based strategy should give way to a more flexible strategy, with marketing programmes acceptable to all people across ethnic groups. Functional food producers should also design and manufacture food products that are acceptable to all ethnic groups. This effort must be undertaken delicately, because even as manufacturers attempt to make such products acceptable to consumers from various ethnicities, they must retain a unique ethnic or cultural component. If producers pursue

238 The New Cultures of Food

the lowest common denominator, the product loses its ethnic and cultural flavour; on the other hand, an overreliance on ethnicity and cultural components may make that product unattractive to people from other cultures. This balance is very delicate, and in this regard, perhaps, cooperation with the government is required.

Furthermore, the Malaysian government may need to address gaps in food education and information regarding the universality of culture-specific functional food items. However, we recommend that any such campaign should take great care to allow the retention of the underlying cultural identity of such products, rather than attempting to extract them from their traditional meanings by presenting their broader health benefits solely to the wider community. Nevertheless, this strategy should still communicate the ability of functional foods to deliver health benefits to a wider market rather than focus specifically on an ethnic cohort.

Since the model we present derives from research into the consumption of functional foods, it may not apply directly to other food products. However, food consumption literature and observed trends suggest that its key factors should generalize to other food consumption contexts. We do not examine the rate of convergence, which probably involves a long-term process when we consider socially mediated values. Although cross-cultural product adoption may occur in the short and medium terms, the incorporation of a culturally-based functional food into another culture is often a function of generational change. Finally, the lack of a control group might be justifiably perceived as a weakness of this study; however, need not invalidate the study conclusions, because the study is exploratory in nature and instead formulates six propositions. Further studies should refine, modify or uncover additional propositions; additional research might also attempt to design a more robust method of testing these propositions.

Conclusions

This study reveals that values and health motives are significant factors that help explain the consumption of functional food products. Given the nature of functional food as a traditional cultural artefact, it can be confined within cultural boundaries. Thus, functional food is a type of culturally-based food that is unique to those within that culture or ethnic group. Over time, though, pervasive cultural changes brought about by intergroup communications, economic development and greater social interaction promotes a certain level of cultural convergence in functional food consumption. Such a convergence should guide efforts to promote functional foods in Malaysia by both the private sector and the government. Finally, we stress that, even though convergence presents an opportunity for cross-cultural marketing, both the private sector and the government must simultaneously maintain the ethnic and cultural character of the functional food while taking the opportunity to market these culturally unique products across different cultures.

References

1.   Ahmad, S. (1996), "Research and development on functional foods in Malaysia", *Nutrition Reviews*, Vol. 54, No. 11, p. 169; Poulsen, J.B. (1999), "Danish consumers' attitudes towards functional foods", working paper, Aarhus School of Business, MAPP; Hasler, C.M. (1998),

"Functional foods: their role in disease prevention and health promotion", *Food Technology*, Vol. 52, No. 11, pp. 63–70; Milner, J.A. (1999), "Functional foods and health promotion", *Journal of Nutrition*, Vol. 129, No. 7, p. 1395S; Bech-Larsen, T. and Grunert K.G. (2003), "The perceived healthiness of functional foods: a conjoint study of Danish, Finnish and American consumers' perception of functional foods", *Appetite*, Vol. 40, No. 1, pp. 9–14.

2. Scott, J.E. and Lamont, L.M. (1977), "Relating consumer values to consumer behavior: a model and method for investigation" in T.W. Greer (ed.), *Increasing Marketing Productivity*, American Marketing Association, Chicago, pp. 283–288; Homer, P.M. and Kahle, L.R. (1988), "A structural equation test of the value-attitude-behavior hierarchy", *Journal of Personality and Social Psychology*, Vol. 54, pp. 638–645.

3. Douglas, S.P. and Craig, C.S. (1997), "The changing dynamic of consumer behavior: implications for cross-cultural research", *International Journal of Research in Marketing*, Vol. 14, No. 4, pp. 379–395; Finucane, M.L. and Holup, J.L. (2005), "Psychosocial and cultural factors affecting the perceived risk of genetically modified food: an overview of the literature", *Social Science & Medicine*, Vol. 60, No. 7, pp. 1603–1612; Steenkamp, J-B.E.M. and Burgess, S.M. (2002), "Optimum stimulation level and exploratory consumer behavior in an emerging consumer market", *International Journal of Research in Marketing*, Vol. 19, No. 2, pp. 131–150.

4. Durvasula, S. et al. (1993), "Assessing the cross-national applicability of consumer behavior models: a model of attitude toward advertising in general", *Journal of Consumer Research*, Vol. 19, No. 4, pp. 626–636.

5. Douglas and Craig, "The changing dynamic of consumer behaviour", *op. cit.*; Finucane and Holup, "Psychosocial and cultural factors", *op. cit.*; Eisenstadt, S.N. (1965), "Transformation of social political, and cultural orders in modernization", *American Sociological Review*, Vol. 30, No. 5, pp. 659–673.

6. Fukuyama, F. (1992), *The End of History and the Last Man*, Simon & Schuster, New York.

7. Friedman, T.L. (2006), *The World is Flat: A Brief History of the Twenty First Century*, Penguin, London; Zivko, T. (2006), "The economic-cultural context of the EU economies", *Kybernetes*, Vol. 35, Nos 7–8, pp. 1024–1036.

8. Inglehart, R. and Baker, W.E. (2000), "Modernization, cultural change, and the persistence of traditional values", *American Sociological Review*, Vol. 65, No. 1, pp. 19–51.

9. American Dietetic Association Report (2004), "Position of the American Dietetic Association: functional foods", *Journal of The American Dietetic Association*, Vol. 104, No. 5, pp. 814–826, at p. 817.

10. IFIC (1998), "Backgrounder: functional foods", *Food Insight Media Guide*, International Food Information Council Foundation, Washington, DC.

11. Ibid.; Kuhnlein, H. (1984), "Traditional and contemporary Nuxalk foods", *Nutrition Research*, Vol. 4, No. 5, pp. 789–809.

12. Frewer, L.J., Scholderer, J. and Lambert, N. (2003), "Consumer acceptance of functional foods: issues for the future", *British Food Journal*, Vol. 105, Nos 10–11, p. 714; Weststrate, J.A., van Poppel, G. and Verschuren, P.M. (2002), "Functional foods, trends and future", *British Journal of Nutrition*, Vol. 88, No. S2, pp. 233–235; de Heer, A.J. (2002), "Communication barriers in the market for functional foods: the dilemma of using health claims in business-to-consumer communication" in *Communicating Health and New Genetics*. Finnish Information Studies, Åbo, Tampere, and Oulu.

13. de Heer, "Communication barriers in the market", *op. cit.*, p. 58.

14. Mennell, S., Murcott, A. and Van Otterloo, A.H. (1992), *The Sociology of Food, Eating, Diet and Culture*, Sage, London.

15.   Verbeke, W. and López, G.P. (2005), "Ethnic food attitudes and behaviour among Belgians and Hispanics living in Belgium", *British Food Journal*, Vol. 107, Nos 10–11, p. 823.

16.   Venkatesh, A. (1995), "Ethnoconsumerism: a new paradigm to study cultural and cross-cultural consumer behavior" in J.A. Costa and G. Bamossy (eds.), *Marketing in the Multicultural World*, Sage, London, pp. 26–67.

17.   Gutman, J. (1982), "A means–end chain model based on consumer categorization process", *Journal of Marketing*, Vol. 46, No. 2, pp. 60–72.

18.   Glaser, B.G. and Strauss, A.L. (1967), *The Discovery of Grounded Theory*, Alinde, Chicago.

19.   Charmaz, K. (1983), "The grounded theory method: an explication and interpretation" in R.M. Emerson (ed.), *Contemporary Field Research: A Collection of Readings*, Waveland Press, Prospect Heights, IL, pp. 109–126; Strauss, A.L. and Corbin, J. (1998), *Basics of Qualitative Research: Techniques and Procedures for Developing Grounded Theory* (2nd edn), Sage, Thousand Oaks, CA; Schreiber, R.S. (2001), "The 'how to' of grounded theory: avoiding the pitfalls", in R.S. Schreiber and P.N. Stern (eds.), *Using Grounded Theory in Nursing*, Springer, New York.

20.   Fieldhouse, P. (1986), *Food and Nutrition: Customs and Culture*, Croom Helm, London; Sobal, J. (1998), "Cultural comparison research designs in food, eating, and nutrition", *Food Quality and Preference*, Vol. 9, No. 6, pp. 385–392.

21.   Pachter, L.M., Sheehan, J. and Cloutier, M.M. (2000), "Factor and subscale structure of a parental health locus of control instrument (parental health beliefs scales) for use in a mainland United States Puerto Rican community", *Social Science & Medicine*, Vol. 50, No. 5, pp. 715–721.

22.   Chamarik, S. (1999), "Oral tradition in Thailand: a development perspective" paper presented at "Collection and Safeguarding the Oral Tradition":,A Satellite Meeting of the 65th IFLA Council and General Conference, 16–19 August, Khon Kaen, Thailand, http://www.ifla.org/IV/ifla65/65sc-e.htm (accessed 2 February 2009).

23.   Bakker, E.J. (2003), "Homer as an oral tradition", *Oral Tradition*, Vol. 18, No. 1, pp. 52–54.

24.   Ibid.

25.   Ahmad, "Research and development on functional foods", *op. cit.*

26.   Laderman, C. (1983), *Wives and Midwives: Childbirth and Nutrition in Rural Malaysia*, University of California Press, Los Angeles.

27.   Nestle, M. et al. (1998), "Behavioral and social influences on food choice/discussion", *Nutrition Reviews*, Vol. 56, No. 5, p. S50.

28.   Verbeke, W. (2005), "Consumer acceptance of functional foods: socio-demographic, cognitive and attitudinal determinants", *Food Quality and Preference*, Vol. 16, No. 1, pp. 45–57; Wansink, B. (2001), "When does nutritional knowledge relate to the acceptance of a functional food?", http://www.consumerpsychology.com/insights/pdf/funcfoodsknow.pdf (accessed 5 January 2005); Bhaskaran, S. and Hardley, F. (2002), "Buyer beliefs, attitudes and behaviour: foods with therapeutic claims", *Journal of Consumer Marketing*, Vol. 19, No. 7, pp. 591–606; IFIC (1999), "Functional foods: attitudinal research (1996–1999)", International Food Information Council Foundation, Washington, DC; Hilliam, M. (1996), "Functional foods: the Western consumer viewpoint", *Nutrition Reviews*, Vol. 54, No. 11, p. S189.

29.   Weng, W. and Chen, J. (1996), "The Eastern perspective on functional foods based on traditional Chinese medicine", *Nutrition Reviews*, Vol. 54, No. 11, pp. S11–S16.

30.   Ahmad, "Research and development on functional foods", *op. cit.*; Krishnaswamy, K. (1996), "Indian functional foods: role in prevention of cancer", *Nutrition Reviews*, Vol. 54, No. 11, p. S127; Fujiki, H. et al. (1996), "Japanese green tea as a cancer preventive in humans", *Nutrition Reviews*, Vol. 54, No. 11, p. S67; Chang, R. (1996), "Functional properties of edible mushrooms", *Nutrition Reviews*, Vol. 54, No. 11, p. S91.

31. Singh, A. (2007), "Traditional foods and associated knowledge systems relating to health and nutrition among Adi women of East Siang district, Arunachal Pradesh", unpublished, Department of Home Science and Nutrition, Banaras Hindu University, Varanasi, Uttar Pradesh; Singh, A., S. R.K., and Sureja, A.K. (2007), "Cultural significance and diversities of ethnic foods of northeast India", *Indian Journal of Traditional Knowledge*, Vol. 6, No. 6, pp. 79–104; Singh, R.K. (2004), "Conserving diversity and culture – Pem Dolma", *Honey Bee*, Vol. 15, No. 3, pp. 12–13; Singh, R.K., Singh, A. and Sureja, A.K. (2007), "Sustainable use of ethnobotanical resources", *Indian Journal of Traditional Knowledge*, Vol. 6, No. 3, pp. 521–530; Singh, R.K., Singh, A. and Sureja, A.K. (2007), "Traditional foods of Monpa tribe of West Kameng, Arunachal Pradesh", *Indian Journal of Traditional Knowledge*, Vol. 6, No. 1, pp. 25–36.

32. Singh, A. (2007), "Traditional foods and associated knowledge systems", *op. cit.*; Kuhnlein, H. (2007), "Indigenous people's food systems: a wealth of knowledge in food and food composition", paper presented at the Seventh International Food Data Conference: Food Composition and Biodiversity, 21–24 October, Brazilian Network of Food Data Systems (BRASILFOODS) and FAO, University of Sao Paulo (USP), Brazil.

33. Lappalainen, R., Kearney, J. and Gibney, M. (1998), "A Pan EU survey of consumer attitudes to food, nutrition and health: an overview", *Quality and Preference*, Vol. 9, No. 6, pp. 467–478; Steptoe, A., Pollard, T.M. and Wardle, J. (1995), "Development of a measure of the motives underlying the selection of food: the food choice questionnaire", *Appetite*, Vol. 25, pp. 267–284.

34. Ahmad, "Research and development on functional foods", *op. cit.*

35. Turner, N.J. and Turner, S.E. (2004), "Food, forage and medicinal resources of forests", *Encyclopedia of Life Support Systems*, EOLSS, Oxford, pp. 1–41; Turner, N.J. (2005), *Earth's Blanket: Traditional Teaching for Sustainable Living*, Douglas and McIntyre Ltd, Vancouver; Pretty, J.N. (2007), *The Earth Only Endures: On Reconnecting with Nature and Our Place in It*, Earthscan, London.

36. Samson, C. and Pretty, J. (2006), "Environmental and health benefits of hunting lifestyles and diets for the Innu of Labrador", *Food Policy*, Vol. 31, pp. 528–553; Turner, N.J. and Turner, K.L. (2007), "Traditional food systems, erosion and renewal in Northwestern North America", *Indian Journal of Traditional Knowledge*, Vol. 6, No. 1, pp. 57–68; Singh, "Traditional foods and associated knowledge systems", *op. cit.*; Pretty, *The Earth Only Endures*, *op. cit.*

37. Inglehart and Baker, "Modernization, cultural change", *op. cit.*

38. Bronfenbrenner, U. (1986), "Ecology of the family as a context for human development: research perspectives", *Developmental Psychology*, Vol. 22, pp. 723–742; Hoff-Ginsberg, E. and Tardiff, T. (1995), "Socioeconomic status and parenting" in M.H. Bornstein (ed.), *Handbook of Parenting*, Erlbaum, Hillsdale, NJ, pp. 161–188; Super, C.M. and Harkness, S. (1986), "The developmental niche: a conceptualization of the interface of child and culture", *International Journal of Behavioral Development*, Vol. 9, pp. 545–569.

39. Tan, C.B. (1982), "Ethnic relations in Malaysia" in D.Y.H. Wu (ed.), *Ethnicity and Interpersonal Interaction: A Cross Cultural Study*, Maruzen Asia, Republic of Singapore, pp. 37–61.

40. Lee, W. and Tse, D.K. (1994), "Becoming Canadian: understanding how Hong Kong immigrants change their consumption", *Pacific Affairs*, Vol. 67, No. 1, pp. 70–95.

41. Connors, M. et al. (2001), "Managing values in personal food systems", *Appetite*, Vol. 36, No. 3, pp. 189–200.

42. Kamakura, W.A. and Novak, T.P. (1992), "Value-system segmentation: exploring the Meaning of LOV", *Journal of Consumer Research*, Vol. 19, No. 1, pp. 119–132.

43. Connors et al., "Managing values", *op. cit.*

44. Rokeach, M. (1973), *The Nature of Human Values*, The Free Press, New York.

45. Ibid., p. 5.

46. Schwartz, S.H. and Bilsky, W. (1990), "Toward a theory of the universal content and structure of values: extensions and cross-cultural replications", *Journal of Personality & Social Psychology*, Vol. 58, No. 5, pp. 878–891 at p. 882.

47. Rokeach, M. (1979), *Understanding Human Values: Individual and Societal*, The Free Press, New York; Singh, "Conserving diversity and culture", *op. cit.*

48. Embong, A.R. (1998), "Social transformation the state and the middle classes in post-independence Malaysia" in Z. Ibrahim (ed.), *Cultural Contestations: Mediating Identities in a Changing Malaysian Society*, ASEAN Academic Press, London, pp. 83–116.

49. Yau, O.H.M. (1994), *Consumer Behaviour in China: Customer Satisfaction and Cultural Values*, Routledge, London.

50. Douglas and Craig, "The changing dynamic of consumer behaviour", *op. cit.*; Embong, "Social transformation", *op. cit.*

14 *Influence of the* Halal *Certification Mark in Food Product Advertisements in Malaysia*

SITI HASNAH HASSAN,* STEPHEN DANN,† KHARIL ANNUAR MOHD KAMAL‡ AND ERNEST CYRIL DE RUN§

Keywords

halal, brand, advertising, Malaysia.

Abstract

In this chapter we propose a review of the influence of *halal* certification on consumer perceptions of food quality. As one of the few systematic studies that examines the influence of the *halal* sign in advertising as a quality assurance marker, this research investigates the use and effectiveness of consumers' perceptions of *halal* certification as a quality assurance mark in the context of the Malaysian multicultural society. Malaysia is moving to become a global hub for *halal* certification and production.

We will also assess the influence of the *halal* mark as a quality assurance symbol; examine the results of experimental studies regarding the use of *halal* in advertisements;

* Dr Siti Hasnah Hassan, School of Management, Marketing and International Business, Australian National University, ACT 0200, Australia. E-mail: siti.hassan@anu.edu.au. Telephone: + 612 612 56738.

† Dr Stephen Dann, Senior Lecturer in Marketing, School of Management, Marketing and International Business, Australian National University, ACT 0200, Australia. E-mail: stephen.dann@anu.edu.au. Telephone: + 61 2 612 54516.

‡ Mr Kharil Annuar Mohd Kamal, School of Management, Marketing and International Business, Australian National University, ACT 0200, Australia. E-mail: kharil.mohdkamal@anu.edu.au. Telephone: + 612 612 56738.

§ Associate Professor Dr Ernest Cyril de Run, Deputy Dean (Research and Postgraduate), Faculty of Economics and Business, University Malaysia Sarawak, 94300 Kota Samarahan, Sarawak, Malaysia. E-mail: drernest@feb.unimas.my. Telephone: + 60 82 581388, 581688 extension 2283.

and expand on the limited research on the use of *halal* as a form of semiotic indicator of food standards.

Introduction

Rapid global growth in the recognition of the *halal* mark as a benchmark for safety and quality assurance is presenting marketers with a new market opportunity that simultaneously meets the needs of the broader Muslim consumer market and can be leveraged as a quality mark for non-Muslim consumers. *Halal* is a broad term that encompasses the whole aspect of a Muslim's life, and, in the context of food consumption, the term denotes that the particular food is permissible to be consumed. In Malaysia a third-party organization appointed by the government or authorized through the top Islamic bodies in a country assign *halal* certification marks.

Understanding the Market for *Halal* Food Products

The *halal* food market has been driven primarily by the needs of Muslim consumers whose product preferences are governed by *halal* rules. The Muslim market worldwide is estimated to comprise approximately 2 billion consumers, with the estimated global *halal* food trade averaging from US\$150–500 billion. The traditionally non-Islamic market of the USA spends approximately US\$12 billion annually on *halal*-accredited food.[1] Currently the *halal* food market worldwide is estimated to be worth approximately US\$2.1 trillion a year.[2]

The Qu'ran offers specific guidelines about how Muslims should choose and consume their food, which are included in the terms *halal* and *haram*. *Halal* means "permitted or allowed" to Muslims.[3] Most meat and vegetables are considered *halal* except for pork, its byproducts and certain other products.[4] To further complicate matters, food can fit into nine levels between *halal* and *haram*, including *makrooh* and *mashbooh* products.[5] If a product has received *halal* certification, it is deemed fit for consumption by Muslim consumers.

Haram refers to prohibited foods. Foods considered *haram* include pork meat and pork byproducts; animals improperly slaughtered or dead before slaughtering; animals killed in the name of anyone other than Allah; alcohol and intoxicants; carnivorous animals; birds of prey; land animals without external ears; blood and blood byproducts; and foods containing any of the above. Those foods that are not clearly *halal* or *haram* are referred to as *mashbooh*, meaning doubtful or questionable. Foods containing ingredients like gelatine, enzymes and emulsifiers are *mashbooh* because the classification of these ingredients is difficult. Although the Qu'ran provides guidelines, ultimately, it is the level of individual piety that guides Muslim consumer behaviour in choosing to consume or not to consume a particular food product.

In general, the concepts of *halal* and *haram* cover everything about Muslims' life and day-to-day behaviour. *Halal* refers to activities that are explicitly permitted or not explicitly prohibited by the religion. *Haram* refers to the activities that are not permitted or are prohibited by the religion. This prohibition is based on interpretations of the Qu'ran and the Hadith by learned scholars of Islam, known as the *ulamak* or *ulema*. This chapter restricts the concepts of *halal* and *haram* to food and other edible products. *Halal* foods are visually similar in appearance to other foods, set apart instead by their nature, processing, ingredients, handling and subjection to specific butchering techniques.[6] Readers who wish to understand the principles of *halal* and *haram* in Islam more closely might refer to books written by Al-Qaradawi and Azimabadi.[7]

Economic Benefits, Regional Growth and Government Strategies

The existence of a large, segmented and reachable Muslim market offers great opportunities for businesses.[8] The Malaysian government, sensing this potential demand, has categorically stated that it intends to be the *halal* food hub in South-east Asia. In line with this objective, the Malaysian government oversees *halal* certification through the Department of Islamic Development Malaysia (JAKIM), which provides a contrast with other countries: In Indonesia, *halal* certification can be obtained from the Indonesian Muslim Scholar Assembly, which operates as an extra-government authority.[9] In the USA, a non-Muslim country, the Islamic Food and Nutrition Council of America provides *halal* certification,[10] and Australia, another non-Muslim country, has four *halal* certification organizations involved in accrediting domestic and export meat and non-meat products: Australian *Halal* Food Services, the *Halal* Certification Authority Australia, the Islamic Coordinating Council of Victoria and the Australian Federation of Islamic Councils.

Is *Halal* Accreditation Key to Islamic Food Marketing Success?

Prior research in food marketing pertaining to *halal* food or *halal* food ingredients has generally been limited to the discussion of possible opportunities[11] or certification issues.[12] Current thinking on *halal* food is therefore based on the preconceived notion that certification will have an immediate and positive impact on the purchase behaviour of Muslims. This thinking is partly based on uncritical acceptance by media and government agencies in Malaysia,[13] as well as the limited research and thinking about the impact of *halal* certification on the preferences of non-Muslim consumers.[14]

The importance of the *halal* sign can be illustrated best when the foods in question are roughly similar in all aspects except for their *halal* certification. When presented with a choice of two similar food products, Muslim consumers are more likely to consume the *halal* accredited food, and devout Muslims regard the *halal* sign as a primary determinant of their food preferences in any situation. Consequently, *halal* accreditation ranges between a valuable competitive edge to an absolute necessity for food products targeted at markets with large proportions of Islamic consumers.

Prior Research

Because research on *halal* food and *halal* accredited food is relatively novel, problems arise in attempting to define the literature. One way to overcome this issue is to include all literature about *halal* and *haram* in Islam. However, this method is not feasible for this particular chapter due to space limitations. Another means follows an eclectic approach, taking bits and pieces of related literature that best explain the usage of the *halal* sign and accreditation within the marketing discipline. In the context of this chapter, this approach is more appropriate; this research therefore examines the *halal* sign as a brand mark that provides both an endorsement of the product and a statement of product quality.

Halal Marks and Advertising Literature

Advertising represents a multifaceted mechanism that informs, persuades, reminds and adds value to the consumer while also assisting a company's other efforts in terms of pricing, design and distribution of a product.[15] According to the American Marketing Association's definition of marketing, advertising constitutes part of marketing's role to create, communicate and deliver value to consumers. To this end, *halal* certification is a marketing tool, because it can create value by offering a message (safe food), communicating this offering (accreditation demonstrating the safety of the product) and delivering value (providing trustworthy information to assist informed decision-making).[16] Certification can be used particularly as a means to inform, persuade and remind Muslim consumers that the food product is safe for consumption. Towards this end, by communicating a safety message, the certification can add value for consumers and marketers alike, because the *halal* mark indicates the food is both physically and spiritually safe for consumption.

The persuasive ability of advertising can also become manifest through indirect means, such as creating favourable predispositions towards certain products. Attitudes are learned behaviours that can be taught or changed through marketing communications,[17] and attitude is a key link between the consumer's perceptions of important purchase attributes, such as price or quality, and actual behaviour in purchasing a product.[18] Attitudes towards brands result from the importance and relevance of the brand's attributes and benefits, which, in the context of the *halal* certification symbol, confer the key attributes of spiritual and physical safety, as well as the brand's respect for the Islamic faith.[19] The *halal* certification thus may predispose consumers to have favourable attitudes towards a certified product.

Advertising and Intentions to Purchase

Marketing communications literature establishes the value and role of advertising as a mechanism for influencing purchase intentions.[20] Specifically, a range of practical and theoretical studies indicate that the following theoretical constructs have positive influences on purchase intentions and behaviour:

- *Attitude toward brands*: in the case of *halal*, a brand mark leads Muslim consumers to feel positively toward the *halal* symbol as a trusted icon of spiritual and physical safety.

- *Product claims*: features of the product communicated through the advertising and, with the endorsement of a *halal* mark, communicate product quality standards and adherence to specific religious practice in the preparation of the food products.
- *Source credibility and corporate credibility*: this is positively influenced by the third-party nature of the *halal* accreditation, improving the reputation of the firm that has taken the time, effort and costs to adhere to the elements of the Islamic faith required for *halal* accreditation.

SIMILARITY–ATTRACTION THEORY

Similarity–attraction theory states that the more similar one's attitudes and beliefs are to a specific other; the more likely the consumer will be attracted.[21] This is particularly true with regard to salespeople's similarity to prospects from the perspective of the observable and internal aspects of salespeople's performance.[22] The more similarities salespeople can identify with their prospects, the better their performance. This can also be the case in negotiations with different cultures[23] – if a company knows that the more similar it appears to its target group, the better the reaction will be, it can use this information to target specific groups.

This reasoning might apply to the issue of *halal* signs in advertisements, such that Muslim respondents may be more attracted to such products because they reflect their attitudes and beliefs. In contrast, non-Muslim respondents should have a neutral, less positive, or even negative, reaction to the use of *halal* signs. The difference in their reactions may be due to how non-Muslims perceive Islam, such that the reaction of non-Muslims is likely to correlate with their favourability or negativity towards the faith.

SPEECH ACCOMMODATION THEORY

To reach a specific group, communication must accommodate that group. Speech accommodation theory (SAT) notes that different language speakers tend to accommodate other language speakers when delivering a message and can obtain a positive response when they do so.[24] *Halal* signs in advertisements clearly attempt to accommodate Muslim respondents and therefore should provoke a positive response from them. Non-Muslim respondents are unlikely to see themselves as being accommodated and should react accordingly (that is, with a negative perception [attenuated] and no reciprocation of accommodation).[25] Similar studies carried out in Malaysia, using the language in an advertisement or packaging as a cue, support SAT.[26]

The Role of Third-party Certification

Prior research into third-party accreditation and standards shows that consumers perceive the quality and attributes related to the certification positively and regard the neutrality of the third party as a positive indicator of the credibility of the accreditation endorsement.[27] Consumers might use certification marks for one or more of the following functions at the time of the purchase decision: as a general aid at the time of purchase;[28] as a protection evaluation;[29] as unbiased information about the product;[30] or as a guide for the selection of products with certain attributes above some stated, perceived or expected general standard.[31] By gaining a seal or certification of endorsement from a third party that is well respected by consumers, a company can achieve brand differentiation and attract perceptions of improved quality, without any substantive modification to the original product.[32] Obviously, in the case of the *halal* certification, the product must reach a minimum set of standards to qualify for the accreditation, so non-*halal* complementary products would need to engage in product modification to acquire accreditation. However, consumers do not always use a third-party endorsement to assess the believability of a claim in an advertisement.[33]

Halal Certification Context

The *halal* certificate represents a third-party certification of the physical creation process of food products and, as such, represents a form of warranty or guarantee of the quality of the merchandise. *Halal* marks can be viewed as a form of third-party endorsement by the government and other key Islamic accreditation agencies that enforce the *halal* standard accreditation criteria. Organizations providing *halal* accreditation vouch that producers follow the appropriate standards; as such, it is an evaluative opinion of approval that the food is safe for consumption, and the *halal* sign further offers an implicit warranty of the quality of the product.

As prior research and business experience indicates, information provided by third-party certification marks may be classified into three major categories.[34] First, the accreditation may confer a form of warranty such that the certifier typically takes on limited responsibility regarding the consumer's purchase of the product. Second, the accreditation may indicate that the certifier presents an evaluative opinion of the product in the form of either certification of approval. (Similarly, non-certification indicates implicit disapproval.) Third, the third-party accreditation may represent a factual assessment of the product's quality and adherence to appropriate production processes.

Field-testing the *Halal* Accreditation Mark

EXAMINING THE IMPACT OF HALAL

Although *halal* accreditation is widespread, no major empirical studies address the influence of the *halal* signage on purchase decisions by Muslim and non-Muslim consumers. The current rationale for government and corporate support for this signage is based on the untested belief that Muslim consumers will respond positively to foods certified as *halal* and that non-Muslims will not be offended by the presence of such signage. This situation prompts three research questions to begin to examine quantitatively the influence of accreditation on purchase decisions.

- Do *halal* signs used on food products actually elicit positive responses from consumers?
- Are Muslim consumers reacting favourably to the *halal* sign?
- Do non-Muslims consumers have a favourable response to the use of *halal* signs? If not, are non-Muslim consumers at least neutral towards the presence of *halal* accreditation?

The research investigates the impact of a *halal* sign as both an advertisement and a signifier of third-party accreditation in order to determine how these factors influence Muslim and non-Muslim responses to *halal* accreditation. The *halal* sign may be seen as a means of accommodating a specific target market. By including a *halal* sign in an advertisement, a company appears to overtly pursue the Muslim market, so the company must know whether this effort will result in Muslim consumers developing positive attitudes and behaviours towards the company. At the same time, companies should be concerned about the reaction of non-Muslims and whether there will be any backlash against their efforts to accommodate Muslims.

In the case of the *halal* accreditation, a confounding issue relates to the speech accommodation principle; because *halal* accreditation is a certification of adherence to both religious beliefs and a series of specific procedural protocols, the accreditation may be perceived as an accommodation to the practice of Islam and non-accommodation to the faith values of non-Islamic customers. This research therefore also tests whether significant observable positive and negative responses to *halal* accreditation depend on respondents' religious orientations. By displaying advertisements with and without the *halal* sign, this research determines if the *halal* signs used on food products actually elicit positive or negative responses from consumers through testing and contrasting the means of the various measurements provided by Muslim and non-Muslim respondents. The data can thus indicate whether non-Muslim consumers have a favourable, or at least neutral, response to the use of *halal* signs.

TESTING HALAL ACCREDITATION

Accreditation testing involves an experimental, two-by-two factorial design to determine the reactions of Muslim and non-Muslims to *halal*-endorsed or non-endorsed advertising. Quasi-random convenience sampling elicited 250 Muslim and 250 non-Muslim respondents, chosen at random by the survey administration teams from among attendees at a series of government-sponsored seminars. No selection criteria consider gender, ethnicity or age. The survey instrument used existing measures from advertising and marketing communication literature, including company credibility,[35] company image,[36] perceived sensitivity,[37] attitude of consumers towards the company,[38] attitude toward the advertisement,[39] attitude toward the brand,[40] purchase intentions[41] and target of the advertisement.[42]

Stimulus Material

The design of the advertisement is an important issue, because it must be realistic and portray the correct elements and language. Because chicken must be prepared under *halal* rules to be acceptable for Muslim consumption, this study uses an advertisement for a fictional brand of roasted chicken, and thereby minimizes any potential bias from prior history with the brand, to ascertain the importance of *halal* as an influence in the absence of prior knowledge of the brand. Because the existing *halal* or *haram* status of an established brand might be known by respondents, the use of the new brand reduces the risk of contamination of the decision process.

Results

DESCRIPTIVE ANALYSIS

The descriptive analysis for both advertisements, with or without the *halal* sign, by religion appears in Tables 14.1 and 14.2. For all attitudinal and behavioural variables tested, Muslims reacted more positively towards advertisements with *halal* signs compared with the advertisements that lacked *halal* signs. The highest score occurs for sensitivity displayed by the advertiser toward Muslims, which indicates that the accommodation attempt was successful. These differences are significant, indicating support for the use of *halal* signs in advertisements.

Similar findings emerge for the non-Muslim respondents, who also reacted more positively towards advertisements with *halal* signs, although they tended not to agree that the advertiser was sensitive to their needs.

Tables 14.3 and 14.4 report the Bonferroni t-tests of the differences in the reactions of Muslims and non-Muslims towards advertisements with and without *halal* signage.

The findings in Table 14.3 are surprising, in that, on nearly every variable, non-Muslims outscore Muslims. The only variable on which Muslims score higher is sensitivity, demonstrating that the advertisement appears to accommodate Muslims. This finding is surprising, because the *halal* sign reportedly provides a Muslim-based sign, yet non-Muslims score higher on the attitudinal and behavioural variables. Nevertheless, the Muslim respondents' scores are also high.

Table 14.1 Statistics for Muslim respondents

	Sample	Size	Mean	Standard deviation	Variance	Mean standard error
Buy product/ brand*	*halal*	125	4.36	1.762	3.103	0.1576
	non-*halal*	125	2.664	1.486	2.209	0.1329
Attitude towards ad*	*halal*	125	4.237	0.9083	0.8251	0.08124
	non-*halal*	125	3.887	0.7926	0.6282	0.07089
Attitude towards brand*	*halal*	125	4.444	1.345	1.809	0.1203
	non-*halal*	125	3.258	1.299	1.686	0.1162
Attitude towards company*	*halal*	125	4.256	1.122	1.258	0.10031
	non-*halal*	125	3.456	1.11	1.231	0.09925
Sensitivity toward ad*	*halal*	125	5.296	1.645	2.706	0.1471
	non-*halal*	125	2.712	1.473	2.17	0.1318
Recommend to other*	*halal*	125	4.504	1.776	3.155	0.1589
	non-*halal*	125	2.68	1.473	2.171	0.1318

* Significant at p < 0.001 (two-tailed).

Table 14.2   Statistics for non-Muslim respondents

	Sample	Size	Mean	Standard deviation	Variance	Mean standard error
Buy product/ brand*	*halal*	125	5.32	1.383	1.913	0.1237
	non-*halal*	125	4.112	1.602	2.568	0.1433
Attitude towards ad*	*halal*	125	4.87	0.7913	0.6262	0.07078
	non-*halal*	125	4.282	0.7881	0.6211	0.07049
Attitude towards brand*	*halal*	125	5.328	1.094	1.197	0.09786
	non-*halal*	125	4.332	1.068	1.14	0.09549
Attitude towards company*	*halal*	125	4.93	0.8145	0.6634	0.07285
	non-*halal*	125	4.15	0.9153	0.8378	0.08187
Sensitivity towards ad	*halal*	125	3.62	1.491	2.223	0.1334
	non-*halal*	125	3.672	1.412	1.992	0.1262
Recommend to other*	*halal*	125	5.504	1.248	1.558	0.1117
	non-*halal*	125	4.624	1.372	1.882	0.1227

* Significant at $p < 0.001$ (two-tailed).

Table 14.3   Bonferroni test for advertisements with *halal* signage

Variable	Religion	Mean	SD	N	t	df	p	Bonferroni adjusted p significant? (test at 5%/5 = 1%)
Buy product/ brand	Muslim	4.36	1.76	125	−4.79	248	0.00	Sig
	Non-Muslim	5.32	1.38	125				
Attitude towards ad	Muslim	4.24	0.91	125	−5.85	248	0.00	Sig
	Non-Muslim	4.87	0.79	125				
Attitude towards brand	Muslim	4.44	1.35	125	−5.74	248	0.00	Sig
	Non-Muslim	5.33	1.09	125				
Attitude towards company	Muslim	4.26	1.12	125	−5.40	248	0.00	Sig
	Non-Muslim	4.93	0.81	125				
Sensitivity towards ad	Muslim	5.30	1.65	125	8.46	248	0.00	Sig
	Non-Muslim	3.62	1.49	125				
Recommend to others	Muslim	4.50	1.77	125	−5.15	248	0.00	Sig
	Non-Muslim	5.50	1.25	125				

The findings in Table 14.4 support the effectiveness of accommodating Muslims by using *halal* signs. Muslims score significantly lower in all aspects studied, whereas non-Muslims continue to score highly. When there is no *halal* sign, Muslims do not express favourable attitudinal and behavioural responses. In the same situation, non-Muslims still react positively, but less positively than when a *halal* sign appears.

Finally, a basic model consisting of the buying decision as the dependent variable, with brand attitude, advertisement sensitivity, and recommending to others as independent variables, includes the dummies for *halal*/non-*halal* foods and for Muslim/non-Muslim consumers. Table 14.5 shows the ANOVA results for Muslim consumers, which indicate that the coefficients for the models are significant.

Table 14.6 provides the ANOVA results for non-Muslim consumers. With the exception of the *halal* variable, the coefficients for the models are significant. These results are in line with the descriptive statistics discussed at the beginning of this section.

Discussion of the Field Test Result

The findings of this study must be considered within the context of the study country. Muslims are the dominant group in Malaysia,[43] so their reactions are probably based on a dominant group schema, whereas non-Muslims react according to non-dominant groups schema.[44] The findings support this line of thought, yet with a twist. Non-Muslims' reactions are more positive compared with Muslims' reactions when they see an advertisement with *halal* signage. The strength of this reaction indicates a strong understanding of Muslim (dominant group) requirements by non-Muslims.

Table 14.4 Bonferroni test for advertisements without *halal* signage

Variable	Religion	Mean	SD	N	T	df	p	Bonferroni adjusted p significant? (test at 5%/5 = 1%)
Buy product/ brand	Muslim	2.66	1.49	125	−7.42	248	0.00	Sig
	Non-Muslim	4.11	1.60	125				
Attitude towards ad	Muslim	3.89	0.79	125	−3.90	248	0.00	Sig
	Non-Muslim	4.28	0.79	125				
Attitude towards brand	Muslim	3.26	1.30	125	−7.12	248	0.00	Sig
	Non-Muslim	4.33	1.07	125				
Attitude towards company	Muslim	3.46	1.11	125	−5.36	248	0.00	Sig
	Non-Muslim	4.15	0.92	125				
Sensitivity towards ad	Muslim	2.71	1.47	125	−5.26	248	0.00	Sig
	Non-Muslim	3.67	1.41	125				
Recommend to others	Muslim	2.68	1.47	125	−10.78	248	0.00	Sig
	Non-Muslim	4.62	1.37	125				

Table 14.5 ANOVA results for Muslim consumers

Source of variation	df	s.s.	m.s.	v.r.	cov.ef.	F pr.
HALAL1	1	8.271	8.271	6.05	0.74	0.015
Covariates	2	322.244	161.122	117.81		<.001
Brand Att.	1	272.765	272.765	199.44		<.001
Recommend	1	49.479	49.479	36.18		<.001
Residual	246	336.444	1.368		1.94	
Total	249	838.464				

Table 14.6 ANOVA results for non-Muslim consumers

Source of variation	df	s.s.	m.s.	v.r.	cov.ef.	F pr.
HALAL1	1	2.505	2.505	2.32	0.82	0.129
Covariates	2	290.056	145.028	134.34		<.001
Brand Att.	1	281.254	281.254	260.52		<.001
Recommend	1	8.802	8.802	8.15		0.005
Residual	246	265.576	1.08		2.08	
Total	249	646.836				

Nevertheless, the findings support normative claims; Muslims will buy products that have *halal* signage. When an advertisement depicts *halal* signage, Muslims react positively: they buy, recommend, have positive attitudes towards the brand and company, and believe that the advertiser is sensitive to their needs. Products produced with *halal* certification are readily accepted by Muslim consumers, as well as consumers from other religions.

In the context of Malaysia, non-Muslims also respond positively, except for the sensitivity variable. In other words, they accept that this type of product labelling provides them with enough information about the product's quality and the company's status and therefore would purchase and recommend the product. The functions of the label work well with the non-dominant group. Nevertheless, they also demonstrate knowledge that they are being sidelined and believe that the advertiser is not sensitive to their own needs.

Halal certification is a third-party certification mark, which classifies it as a factual certification. The common view is that such a mark is a source of information with the potential to assist consumers in their buying decisions.[45] The findings here confirm this idea, because both Muslim and non-Muslims use the certification as a source of information to determine their attitudinal and behavioural reactions.

The more problematic part of these findings involve the results for non-Muslims' purchase decisions, for which the *halal* coefficient is not significant. Some ambivalence appears in their response, indicating that, even though they understand and react positively to the use of *halal* certification, it is not a major factor when they decide to purchase. Perhaps there is no other choice for non-Muslims in matters of certification in Malaysia; for example, although kosher products are available to non-Muslims in the USA, they are not available in the Malaysian food market. Furthermore, non-Muslims lack other religious-based certifications that they may use as a point of reference.

Study Contributions

This study contributes to the field of advertising, especially with regard to the impact of using religious or ethnically-based advertising. These findings suggest that, by using certified *halal* signage, a company may be able to segment and target the Muslim market while still enjoying positive reactions from the non-Muslim market. Companies can create products differentiated by labelling that targets specific groups.

Managerial Recommendations

Several managerial recommendations emerge from this study. These recommendations cover the implications of *halal* certification and its value for both Muslim and non-Muslim consumers.

Understandably, many companies in Malaysia are eager to tap into the global *halal* market. They may even believe that *halal* certification acts a passport to profitable markets. However, they may also obtain a false or premature sense of their competitiveness, because the process of achieving *halal* certification provides a modern or sophisticated flavour to their offerings. An aspect of the *halal* certification requires ISO compliance, so companies and marketers may believe that an ISO-compliant *halal* standard provides Malaysia and its companies with a competitive edge. But this belief must be backed up with further evidence that is difficult to obtain and not yet fully demonstrated.

Halal certification remains an integral part of the regulatory framework in the Malaysian food industry; companies probably do not think twice about implementing the steps to obtain it. However, in response to the Malaysian government's initiative to "go global" with *halal* certification, a major question should be obvious: what are the reactions of Muslim and non-Muslim consumers to *halal* certification in pluralistic societies? This implication has been somewhat ignored in the rhetoric that appears in newspapers and Internet-based reports.

This issue relates to marketers' sensitivity to non-Muslims, potential unintended effects of targeting, and the reaction of dominant versus non-dominant groups to such efforts.[46] In many countries, Muslim societies coexist with non-Muslims, and in countries where Muslims form the majority, regulations are likely to demand that food producers be sensitive to Muslims' religious requirements. In such situations, sensitivity to non-Muslims may be forgotten. According to theory, the dominant group culture (Muslims) often do not recognize the non-dominant group culture (non-Muslims).[47] Studies have yet to investigate the reactions of Muslim and non-Muslim consumers to the use of *halal* signs in products sold to both Muslim and non-Muslim markets. Intuition suggests that food producers and marketers may assume no adverse reactions by non-Muslims, but this intuition may be incorrect. Non-Muslims might still buy the foods with *halal* certification, because they may have no choice, but what happens when those choices become available?

This issue is perhaps more important in countries with sizeable Muslim niche markets but in which the majority of the population is non-Muslim. Marketers have to attract Muslim consumers, the targeted market, but remain aware of the sensitivities of the dominant non-Muslim market. The non-dominant group culture, Muslim, recognizes its own culture, and the dominant group culture, non-Muslim, probably does not regard the targeting of a specific subpopulation as a threat to itself or the broader market.[48] In this regard, Malaysia offers an excellent test case because of its sizeable non-Muslim market, which is actually larger than the Muslim market solely in terms of income per capita. Thus, determining how these two market segments react to *halal* certification in Malaysia offers a first step in helping companies that aspire to follow the government's lead in promoting *halal* food certification globally.

The Value of *Halal* Accreditation for Muslim Consumers

These findings strongly support the notion that *halal* signs used on food products actually elicit positive responses from consumers. Muslim consumers react favourably to *halal* signs and less favourably when there is no *halal* sign. Thus, there is value to Muslims in the use of *halal* signs in advertisements. First, including the *halal* sign shows Muslim consumers that the advertiser is sensitive to their needs and is trying to reach out to them. This effort already represents a benefit for any company that wishes to target Muslims. Second, by depicting the *halal* sign, a company reaffirms that it has followed all the religious requirements of Muslims and made the product safe to consume, which eliminates doubt and worry for the consumer. A company can use the *halal* sign as a method of targeting Muslim consumers and should ensure that all its marketing communications include a *halal* sign. Leaflets and other modes of communication could educate consumers about the steps to achieve and maintain *halal* certification. Such communications can continue to reassure the Muslim masses and further strengthen the company's claim of being *halal*.

Value of *Halal* Accreditation for Non-Muslim Consumers

Halal accreditation also elicits significant positive reactions from non-Muslim consumers, although it is not a significant factor in their buying decisions. Therefore, companies cannot be lackadaisical when producing a product and aim just for the Muslim market, which could cause them to lose the non-Muslim market. That is, companies cannot rely solely on *halal* certification signage, but must also offer products or services that non-Muslims appreciate and want, based on their quality, branding, differentiation and marketing. *Halal* certification signage helps, but it is not a cure-all. Furthermore, the findings from Malaysia do not necessarily generalize to other countries, especially those in which Muslim consumers are the minority. In such contexts, *halal* certification signage might appear in small print, at the back of the product packaging, to appeal to the Muslim market. Non-Muslim consumers may find blatant *halal* certification signage insensitive to their needs or, at worst, offensive, and they may prefer other forms of certification. Muslim consumers in majority non-Muslim consumers' markets tend to read the ingredients and contents of the food carefully. Without *halal* certification signage, they normally look out for *haram* ingredients, such as an animal-based substance (gelatine, enhanced, natural animal-based flavour) or alcohol to assist their decision-making.

Potential Costs of *Halal* Accreditation

Although the findings indicate support for the *halal* sign for both Muslim and non-Muslim markets, negative reactions are possible from certain consumers, largely due to its close association with a specific religion. Companies should note this potential cost before committing to the use of *halal* signage. They also should understand that, for non-Muslims, a *halal* sign is not a significant reason for purchasing a product. The certification is for Muslims, not for non-Muslims. As such, companies must decide who their target market consists of and why they buy. They also must clearly understand that a *halal* sign does not guarantee sales.

Implementing Third-party *Halal* Certification: The Malaysian Government Case Study

The Malaysian government has long recognized the importance of *halal*-certified food and states its aim to become the *halal* food hub in South-east Asia, through sites in Pahang and Penang, identified as *halal* food hubs. Northport at Port Klang is also rapidly redeveloping to become a major player as a *halal* distribution centre. The government has introduced many incentives to develop and exploit Malaysia's potential as an international *halal* food hub, and establishing the Halal Industry Development Corporation represents another step towards this end.[49]

Several government measures attempt to promote Malaysia as a producer of quality, convenient, *halal* foods.[50] These measures include incentives targeted at Malaysian companies, such as small and medium-sized enterprises (SMEs) that are eligible for a wide range of incentives to support their efforts to gain access to the *halal* market. Grants for business planning and development, product and process improvements, productivity and quality improvements, certification, market development, and brand promotion are now available. Investment tax allowances of 100 per cent on qualifying (approved) capital expenditures span five years for companies that produce *halal* foods. Finally, companies receive a double tax deduction on expenditures for obtaining *halal* certification and accreditation, from the year of assessment.[51]

Another incentive is the streamlining of the bureaucracy that regulates the *halal* certification process. Initial plans to use a private company, Ilham Daya Sdn Bhd (IDSB), to issue *halal* certification failed.[52] The government then decided to cancel privatization plans for the issue of *halal* certificates and has reappointed JAKIM (Department of Islamic Development, Malaysia) to issue the certificates.[53] JAKIM has been entrusted with the responsibility of ascertaining the *halal* status of abattoirs or processing plants that intend to export *halal* products to Malaysia. This exercise involves not only an official site inspection of plants, but also an examination of how *halal* status is maintained and monitored at all times. JAKIM also has established a set of guidelines for the appointment of reputable and reliable foreign Islamic bodies or organizations for the sole purpose of monitoring the *halal* status of all these plants.[54]

Halal certification can therefore be seen as a quality certification accreditation that is becoming increasingly important for enhancing the competitiveness of companies in the global market, especially the Muslim market. The Malaysian government's twofold response encourages companies to obtain *halal* certification and streamlines the regulatory process for *halal* certification.

Acting on the *Halal* Accreditation Advantage

The following recommendations may enable companies to benefit from *halal* accreditation:

- Use *halal* signs in all advertisements and marketing communications.
- Explain that *halal* accreditation is a form of certification that the company wishes to have, not a comment on culture and religion.
- Explain the process of obtaining *halal* certification and efforts to keep *halal* certification.
- Engage in continuous reviews of the effect of *halal* signs on various consumers.
- Undertake continuous reviews of the *halal* accreditation process in the company.

Future Research

The results and managerial recommendations indicate that further research should consider the effects of the *halal* certification signage on consumer behaviour. Further examinations might address the different reactions to *halal* certification signage, such as perceptions of the image of the company. In Malaysia, non-Muslims probably do not find the *halal* certification signage offensive because they are familiar with the sign and constitute the non-dominant group. Reactions of non-Muslims in other situations, such as when they are the majority, require exploration. Additional studies could consider the possibilities of other forms of certification marks, whether religious or non-religious, especially in secular nations, to determine whether there is demand for non-religious forms of certification for *halal*. Further examination is also needed into the cognitive processes that may influence consumer behaviour in other countries: the result in this chapter may not be applicable to multicultural societies with a minority Muslim population. Finally, this study does not differentiate between different market segments within the sample; this remains an area for further research into the reactions of differing market segments to the *halal* mark.

Conclusions

This study serves as an initial investigation of the implementation of *halal* signs in Malaysian advertisements. Its main objective is to determine the reactions of Muslim and non-Muslim consumers to the use of *halal* signs in advertisements. The findings indicate that

Muslims react more positively to advertisements with *halal* signage than they do to those without. Non-Muslims also react positively, although they believe that the advertisers are not sensitive to their needs, as do Muslims when the advertisements do not portray *halal* signage. Also, in contrast to Muslims, among non-Muslims, *halal* certification signage is not a significant variable in their purchase decisions. Ideally, for Muslim consumers, *halal* certification indicates that the food products have met the requirements laid down by Sharia law, whereas for non-Muslim consumers, *halal* represents a symbol of the quality and safety of a product produced strictly under the *halal* certification system. The findings suggest that by using *halal* certification signage, companies can target Muslims but not reduce the favourable responses from non-Muslims.

References

1. Yusof, Hakimah Mohd (2004), "Halal certification scheme", *Standards and Quality News*, Vol. 11, No. 4, pp. 4–5; Berry, D. (2000), "What is halal?", *Dairy Foods,* Vol. 101, No. 4, p. 36.
2. Anonymous (2007), "Northport helps halal products players reach out to the world", *New Straits Times*, 15 January.
3. Berry, "What is halal?", *op. cit.*; Eliasi, J.R. and Dwyer, J.T. (2002), "Kosher and halal: religious observances affecting dietary intakes", *Journal of the American Dietetic Association*, Vol. 102, No. 7, pp. 911–913.
4. Berry, "What is halal?", *op. cit.*
5. Eliasi and Bwyer, "Kosher and halal", *op. cit.*
6. Canadian Council of Muslim Theologians (2007), "Halal guidelines", http://www.jucanada.org/halalguidelines.htm (accessed 23 July 2007).
7. Al-Qaradawi, Yusuf (1982), *The Lawful and the Prohibited in Islam [Al-halal Wal Haram Fil Islam]*, Islamic Book Service; Azimabadi, Badr (2000), *The Permitted and the Prohibited in Islam: Al-halal vs. Al-Haram*, Talha Publications, Lahore.
8. Turcsik, R. (2001), "Kosher and halal: more than just product", *Supermarket Business*, Vol. 56, No. 11, p. 81.
9. Ahmad Ludjito, H. (2007), "The role of ulama (Islamic scholars) in dealing with bioethical issues in Indonesia", http://www.eubios.info/EJ76/ej76d.htm (accessed 23 July 2007); Maxhalal (2007), "Malaysian halal certification", http://www.malaysiahalalfoods.com/halalcert.html (accessed 23 July 2007).
10. Islamic Food and Nutrition Council (2007), "Islamic Food and Nutrition Council", http://www.ifanca.org/index.php (accessed 23 July 2007).
11. Bernama (1999), "Melaka to set up first halal food industry in the region", 24 November, p. 1; Karijn, Bonne et al. (2007), "Determinants of halal meat consumption in France", *British Food Journal*, Vol. 109, No. 5, p. 367.
12. Berry, "What is halal?", *op. cit.*; Anonymous (2003), "Issuance of halal certification to be standardized", *New Straits Times*, 21 March, p. 6; Mermelstein, N.H. (1997), "Halal certification standards", *Food Technology*, Vol. 51, p. 134.
13. Anonymous (2000), "Form body to protect halal hub aspirations", *New Straits Times*, 14 April; Zurinna, Raja Adam (2007), "HDC strategies to make Malaysia global halal hub", *New Straits Times*, 18 April, Business Times.
14. Karijn et al., "Determinants of halal meat production", *op. cit.*
15. Belch, G.E. and Belch, M.A (1998), *Advertising and Promotion*, Irwin/McGraw-Hill, New York.

16. Rice, G. and Al-Mossawi, M. (2002), "The implications of Islam for advertising messages: the Middle Eastern context", *Journal of Euromarketing*, Vol. 11, No. 3, pp. 71–96.

17. Rossiter, J.R and Percy, L. (1998), *Advertising Communications and Promotion Management* (2nd edn), McGraw-Hill, New York.

18. Lutz, R (1992), "The role of attitude theory in marketing" in H. Kassarijian and T. Robertson (eds), *Perspectives in Consumer Behavior*, Prentice Hall, Englewood Cliffs, NJ, pp. 317–339.

19. Keller, K.L. (1993), "Conceptualizing, measuring and managing customer-based brand equity", *Journal of Marketing*, Vol. 57, No. 1, pp. 1–22.

20. Lafferty, B.A. and Goldsmith, R.E. (1999), "Corporate credibility's role in consumers' attitudes and purchase intentions when a high versus low credibility endorser is used in the ad", *Journal of Business Research*, Vol. 44, pp. 109–116; Lafferty, B.A, Goldsmith, R.E. and Newell, S.J. (2002), "The dual credibility model: the influence of corporate and endorser credibility on attitudes and purchase intentions", *Journal of Marketing Theory and Practice*, Summer, pp. 1–12.

21. Byrne, D. (1969), "Attitudes and attraction", *Advances in Experimental Social Psychology*, Vol. 4, pp. 35–89; Byrne, Barbara M. and Campbell, T. Leanne (1999), "Cross-cultural comparisons and the presumption of equivalent measurement and theoretical structure: a look beneath the surface", *Journal of Cross-Cultural Psychology*, Vol. 30, No. 5, pp. 555–574.

22. Lichtenthal, J. David and Tellefsen, T. (1999), *Towards Buyer–Seller Similarity*, Pennsylvania State University, University Park; Smith, J. Brock. (1998), "Buyer–seller relationships: similarity, relationship management, and quality", *Psychology and Marketing*, Vol. 15, No. 1, pp. 3–21.

23. Francis, June. N.P. (1991), "When in Rome? The effects of cultural adaptation on intercultural business negotiations", *Journal of International Business Studies*, Vol. 22, pp. 403–428; Pornpitakpan, Chanthika (2004), "The persuasiveness of source credibility: a critical review of five decades' evidence", *Journal of Applied Social Psychology*, Vol. 34, No. 2, pp. 243–281.

24. Giles, H., Taylor, D.M. and Bourhis, R.Y. (1973), "Toward a theory of interpersonal accommodation through speech accommodation: some Canadian data", *Language in Society*, Vol. 2, pp. 177–192.

25. Simard, L., Taylor, D.M. and Giles, H. (1976), "Attribution processes and interpersonal accommodation in a bilingual setting", *Language and Speech*, Vol. 19, pp. 374–387.

26. de Run, E.C. (2005), "Does targeting really work? The perspective of a dominant group", *International Journal of Business and Society*, Vol. 6, No. 1, pp. 27–51; de Run, E.C. (2007), "Ethnically targeted advertising: views of those not targeted", *Journal of Asia Pacific Marketing and Logistics*, Vol. 19, No. 3; de Run, E.C. and Chin, S.F. (2006), "Language use in packaging: Malay and Chinese consumer reactions", *Sunway Academic Journal*, Vol. 3, pp. 133–145.

27. Parkinson, T.L. (1975), "The role of seals and certifications of approval in consumer decision making", *Journal of Consumer Affairs*, Vol. 9, Summer, pp. 1–14; Laric, M.V. and Sarel, D. (1981), "Consumer (mis)perceptions and usage of third party certification marks, 1972 and 1980: did public policy have an impact?", *Journal of Marketing*, Vol. 45, pp. 135–142.

28. Phelps, D.M. (1949), "Certification marks under the Lanham Act", *Journal of Marketing*, Vol. 13 (April), pp. 478–505; Taylor, D.A. (1958), "Certification marks – success or failure", *Journal of Marketing*, Vol. 22 (July), pp. 9–46.

29. Laric and Sarel, "Consumer (mis)perceptions", *op. cit.*

30. Bennett, J.T. and McCrohan, K.F. (1993), "Public policy issues in the marketing of seals of approval for food", *Journal of Consumer Affairs*, Vol. 27, No. 2, pp. 397–415.

31. Kamins, M.A. and Marks, L.J. (1991), "The perception of kosher as a third party certification claim in advertising for familiar and unfamiliar brands", *Journal of the Academy of Marketing Science*, Vol. 19, No. 3, pp. 177–185; Parkinson, "The role of seals and certifications", *op. cit.*

32. Ibid.
33. Beltramini, R.F. and Stafford, E.R. (1993), "Comprehension and perceived believability of seals of approval information in advertising", *Journal of Advertising*, Vol. 22, No. 3, pp. 3–13.
34. Laric and Sarel, "Consumer (mis)perceptions", *op. cit.*
35. Coulson, R. (1980), "Corporate credibility: what it's all about", *Business Quarterly*, Vol. 45, No. 1, p. 71; Newell, S.J. and Goldsmith, R.E. (2001), "The development of a scale to measure perceived corporate credibility", *Journal of Business Research*, Vol. 52, pp. 235–247.
36. Fombrun, C.J. (1996), *Realizing Value from the Corporate Image*, Harvard Business School Press, Boston, MA; Gray, Jennifer, Armstrong, Gillian and Farley, Heather (2003), "Opportunities and constraints in the functional food market", *Nutrition and Food Science*, Vol. 33, No. 5, p. 213.
37. Koslow, S., Shamdasani, P.N. and Touchstone, E.E. (1994), "Exploring language effects in ethnic advertising: a sociolinguistic perspective", *Journal of Consumer Research*, Vol. 20, pp. 575–585.
38. Gregory, Gary D., Munch, James M. and Peterson, Mark (2002), "Attitude functions in consumer research: comparing value-attitude relations in individualist and collectivist cultures", *Journal of Business Research*, Vol. 55, No. 11, pp. 933–942; Simard et al., "Attribution processes", *op. cit.*
39. Ford, J.B., LaTour, M.S. and Henthorne, T.L. (1995), "Perception of marital roles in purchase decision processes: a cross-cultural study", *Journal of Academic Marketing Science*, Vol. 23, No. 2, pp. 120–131.
40. Biehal, G., Stephens, D. and Curlo, E. (1992), "Attitude towards the ad and brand choice", *Journal of Advertising*, Vol. 22, No. 3, pp. 19–36; Gardner, M.P. (1985), "Does attitude to the ad affect brand attitude under a brand evaluation set?", *Journal of Marketing Research*, Vol. 22 (May), pp. 192–198; Mitchell, Andrew A. and Olson, Jerry C. (1981), "Are product attribute beliefs the only mediator of advertising effects on brand attitude?", *Journal of Marketing Research*, Vol. 18, No. 3, p. 318.
41. Beltramini and Stafford, "Comprehension and perceived believability", *op. cit.*; Maheswaran, Durairaj and Sternthal, Brian (1990), "The effects of knowledge, motivation, and type of message on ad processing and product judgments", *Journal of Consumer Research*, Vol. 17, No. 1, p. 66; Schlinger, M.J. (1979), "A profile of responses to commercials", *Journal of Advertising Research*, Vol. 19, No. 2, pp. 37–48.
42. Koslow et al., "Exploring language effects", *op. cit.*
43. Invest East (2007), "An analysis of the world Muslim population by country/region", http://www.factbook.net/muslim_pop.php (accessed 24 July 2007).
44. Brumbaugh, A.M. (1995), "Managing diversity: a cultural knowledge approach to communicating to multiple market segments", doctoral dissertation, Duke University; Brumbaugh, A.M. (2002), "Source and nonsource cues in advertising and their effects on the activation of cultural and subcultural knowledge on the route to persuasion", *Journal of Consumer Research*, Vol. 29, No. 2, pp. 258–269.
45. Bennett and McCrohan, "Public policy issues", *op. cit.*
46. de Run, "Does targeting really work?", *op. cit.*; de Run, "Ethnically targeted advertising", *op. cit.*
47. Brumbaugh, "Managing diversity", *op. cit.*; Brumbaugh, "Source and nonsource cues", *op. cit.*
48. Ibid.
49. Anonymous (2006), "Corporation a boost for halal industry", *New Straits Times*, 9 May.
50. Anonymous (2007), "Malaysia Hab Antarabangsa", *Berita Harian*, 26 June.

51. Anonymous (2007), "Chapter 21 development of the halal industry", http://www.btimes.com.my/Current_News/BT/imp3_pdf/chapter02.pdf/ (accessed 26 July 2007).

52. Anonymous (1998), "Call to review rates for halal certification", *Business Times*, 21 December; Anonymous (1999), "Halal license rates will scare producers", *Business Times*, 15 February.

53. Anonymous (2007), "Sijil halal JAKIM", http://www.halaljakim.gov.my/ (accessed 23 July 2007).

54. Ibid.

15 Asian Food and Drink: Change, Renewal and Stability in Handsworth

SURESH H. PATEL[*†] AND KULDIP GUJRAL[‡]

Keywords

Asian food, change, ecological, fusion, Handsworth, renewal, retail, stability.

Abstract

In this chapter we investigate change and renewal in the Asian food and drink industry in Handsworth, Birmingham. Specifically, we explore why the Asian food industry has been so successful on Soho Road; use Goad maps[§] to illuminate the nature and dynamics of the Asian food industry; conceptualize and reconstruct the journey of independent food outlets across a timescale; and, finally, evaluate the change, renewal and stability of the food sector and individual food businesses during the past 50 years.

Introduction

The UK food industry, whether in the form of production, processing, manufacture, distribution or retail, represents an important component of the economy at both national and local levels. Nationally, the food chain employs 12.5 per cent of workers and accounts for 8 per cent of the U.K. economy.[1] The UK market consists of more than 60 million consumers, approximately 83 per cent of whom live in England.[2] These consumers benefit from living in a developed and industrialized country with a strong, stable economy and high disposable income levels. Although it is a highly urbanized

*   Professor Suresh H. Patel, Birmingham City University, Business School, Perry Barr, Birmingham, B42 2SU, UK. Telephone: + 44 121 331 5202. E-mail: Suresh.H.Patel@bcu.ac.uk.

†   The author acknowledges the help and contribution of Mr. Nilan Patel in preparing the charts, illustrations and tables for this chapter.

‡   Mr Kuldip Gujral, Birmingham Chamber of Commerce, 75 Harborne Road, Edgbaston, Birmingham, UK. Telephone: + 44 121 607 1767. E-mail: kgujral@birminghamchamber.org.uk.

§   Goad maps have been produced by Goad since 1966 for shopping and district centres and are still published on a scale of 1:1056 (1 inch to 88 feet). Revisions are produced every two years. The Map Library maintains a collection of Goad archival material, including letter books.

nation, the UK places a high value on country living. In addition, consumers sustain a thriving organic sector and are very concerned with food safety, despite being the greatest consumers of snacks, confectionary and convenience foods in Europe.

Several factors contribute to the vitality of the local retail market and the viability of individual businesses. The most fundamental is the relative size and capacity of the market in terms of potential customers and their characteristics, including the number, type and class of customers; their employment and income or asset situation; and their tastes and cultural preferences. In this chapter we investigate which types of establishments can best support a particular type of retail market and review the key drivers, in the pre- and post-late 1970s, of the growth of the Asian food industry in a small area, as well as strategies to cultivate growth, underlying retail theory and future assessments.

Most industry experts believe that ethnic minority consumers are a key group to target; ethnic food sales are rising at 14 per cent a year in Europe and 5 per cent in the USA.[3] Minority consumers account for only a small proportion of ethnic food spending, yet group trends often drive mainstream ethnic food consumption. Marketers thus must understand minority trends to increase their sales of ethnic food products. Spending on ethnic food in the USA, which now consists of 11.8 per cent of all retail food sales, has grown at an average annual rate of 4.9 per cent during the past five years.[4] In Europe the market is growing almost three times as fast, although total sales still account for less than 1 per cent of retail food spending.

The past generation has seen dynamic growth in the consumption of ethnic foods among both ethnic minority and majority communities, in and outside the UK.[¶] Consumers increasingly seek more authentic ethnic tastes – for example, whereas Indian foods previously had been anglicized to accommodate UK consumers' palates, these consumers now demand spicier dishes.

Handsworth is a vital urban centre for Asian customers and a source of employment opportunities for the local population. The initial entry of the Asian community into the food sector has stemmed from the cultural predilection for entrepreneurship, its social status and linkages with wholesale and import distribution. Subsequent entries are outcomes associated with the state of the economy, contracting labour market opportunities and relative earning capacity.

Once they are established, these businesses grow in scale and scope by utilizing a combination of strategies to penetrate both existing and new markets. Evidence points to a wider Asian customer base from various towns and cities, particularly through the improved transport network of coach companies, rail connections and flights from Birmingham International Airport to the subcontinent and other Asian countries. Asian food and drink products are also penetrating the local white population due to acculturation and a greater awareness of Asian cuisines, groceries and drinks.

Background

The overriding objectives of this chapter are threefold. The first is to identify key drivers that support the Asian food and drink sector. The second is to explore the growth of the Asian food and drink business by plotting the evolution of the Asian food and drink

---

¶   Total expenditures on ethnic eating, including restaurants and takeaways, are estimated to be more than £1 billion annually. There are an estimated 6,000 Chinese restaurants, 5,500 Indian restaurants and 300 Thai restaurants in the UK.

sector in Handsworth during the past 50 years. This involves: identifying the magnitude of the aggregate growth of the Asian food and drink sector in Handsworth; examining the different entry and exit strategies of Asian entrepreneurs in the food and food and drink industries in the context of the economy; exploring the different business strategies adopted by the Asian business community to gain a competitive advantage in the food and drink sector; and identifying changes in the food and drink business sector, store channels and non-store channels. The third and final objective is to assess and evaluate the implications of structural change, renewal and stability in the Asian food and drink sector.

Research Strategy

The information in this chapter is based on primary and secondary research. Primary research involved on-site examinations of the retail milieu through mystery shopping to develop a contemporary portrait of road-level development. Daily trips from home to work and from work to home provided an effective tool for monitoring the evolution of road-level retail development. This information was supplemented by the formal use of Goad maps, which provide historical information about the business units, trade functions and type, customer merchandise and physical parameters of the premises, including the site, location and logistics.

A review of existing academic literature, including surveys, methodologies and findings, also supports the research effort. Secondary research also entailed gathering data from relevant trade, business and government sources, including company literature and Internet sources. The analysis of consumer demographics comes from Mintel Market Research Survey data.

We further talked to experts in the food and drink industry, academic institutions and trade bodies and analysed information from grocery industry magazines, trade journals and bulletins. Some experts provided insight into the progress of individual food businesses over the course of many years. They thus confirmed the ownership dynamics, patterns of family ownership and diversification of business opportunities beyond the study area into other regions and international activity.

We used a series of indicators based on information contained in Goad maps to observe activity by retail and service-oriented businesses and determine underlying change and growth. The Goad maps of Handsworth (Soho Road) include:

- major and minor side roads and streets flowing out;
- scaled premises, drawn to size;
- property numbers;
- business names;
- nature of activities;
- occupied premises;
- vacant premises and sites.

Using this methodology, we were able to identify trade opportunities and problems and observe patterns of growth, succession and decline. Reasonably reliable information is available about several parameters, which gave us a sound understanding of the viability of individual businesses and the vitality of particular sectors over a long period of time.

Finally, the mystery shopping effort consisted of telephone calls and visits to supermarkets, restaurants and butchers to monitor customer service. We entered the places of business and acted like normal customers to evaluate the quality, mix and match of merchandise, shop layout and displays, and fixtures and fittings. As mystery shopping elicits better responses and results in more valuable and realistic feedback, it provides an important contribution to the overall approach. We also undertake a catchment area analysis of the location.

Definitions

The Asian category includes Mixed-White and Asian, East Asian and West Asian groups, as Table 15.1 shows. Not all data from the 2001 census allow for the amalgamation of these categories. For statistical and practical reasons, we cannot always analyse the data in terms of each individual subcategory, but the sample for the broad category of Asian-owned businesses is large enough to allow a fairly robust analysis. When practical or useful, we analysed some subcategories to determine whether any significant differences existed.

According to the *Population Census*,[5] the total UK population numbers more than 1 million, and approximately 14 per cent is Asian (including, for the purposes of this report, the Census categories Asian or Asian British, Mixed – White and Asian, and Chinese).

The food and drink industry is extremely diverse, and any classification that uses only one system can prove difficult. Bases of classification might include legal form, operational structure, range of merchandise, degree of service, pricing policy, location, size of outlet or method of customer contact. Some overlap occurs between categories, which continue to blur as firms diversify and respond to changing environments. We used a combination of classifications based on operational structure (e.g. independent trader), range of merchandise (e.g. groceries), and location (e.g. Soho Road).

Finally, we adopted central place theory, which defines a central place as a settlement that provides one or more services for the population living around it. Simple, basic

Table 15.1 Classification of the Asian category

Asian		Other
South Asian	East Asian	West Asian
Asian – British	Chinese	Turkish
Asian – Indian	Japanese	Kurdish
Asian – Pakistani Other Asian	Middle Eastern	
Asian – Bangladeshi		
Asian – Other		
Mixed – White and Asian		

services (e.g. grocery stores) are of low order, whereas specialized services (e.g. universities) are of high order. A high-order service implies low-order services around it, but not vice versa. Settlements that provide low-order services are thus low-order settlements, and those that provide high-order services are high-order settlements. The sphere of influence includes the area under the influence of the central place.

Study Area

Soho Road (A41) is part of the Handsworth area of Birmingham, which lies in the north-west of the city. The A41 road is a ribbon-developed shopping district, with food and drink stores alongside other rows of shops on both sides of the road. A high volume of vehicular and pedestrian traffic moves along this stretch and gives access to the M5 motorway at West Bromwich, junction 1, and the A34 Walsall Road feeder to the M6 motorway at Great Barr Scott Arms, junction 7. The area is known for Asian shopping, cultural centres and a thriving clientele.

According to the Population Census, 25 634 people resided in Soho in 2001.[6] The 4.8 km^2 area has a high population density of 5369 people per km^2, compared with 3649 people per km^2 for Birmingham. The age of the population can be broken down as follows: 27.9 per cent aged younger than 16 years; 59 per cent aged between 16 and 59 years; and 13.1 per cent aged older than 60 years. The average age was 31.2 years, compared with 26 years for Birmingham as a whole. The minority ethnic population consists of 76.2 per cent (19 522) of the ward's population, compared with 29.6 per cent for Birmingham overall. Some 9 313 (53.3 per cent) of the population aged 16–74 years worked or were seeking work, compared with 60.4 per cent for Birmingham overall (see Table 15.2).

Soho Road in Handsworth is a district shopping centre, similar to those often found in suburbs or inner-city recovered areas, often known as secondary shopping centres. The population served can range from as few as 10 000 to as many as 80 000 people. The main attributes of a district shopping centre include a complete range of convenience goods and services and a choice of traders for all these goods, as well as a proportion of more popular comparison good shops and service outlets, a sufficient population and easier accessibility.

The catchment area analysis shows what entices the shoppers living within a shopping centre's sphere of influence into the centre and away from other shopping influences. Specifically, the business attractions of the centre include: niche stores; the kinds and selection of merchandise offered; delivery, credit and other retail services; the reputation of key retailers; banking and car-parking facilities; social and amusement attractions; area population; the density and class of customers; transportation and car ownership; and the topographical nature of market. Additional factors include the relationship of the site to the main shopping centre, the accessibility of the site and the strength of business interception.

During the 1950s and 1960s the Asian food and drink industry was in its infancy, largely occupied by early migrants who acted as pedlars and hawkers and who took products from one household to another on a irregular basis. They recognized the potential captive audience and the increasing numbers of immigrants from the Indian subcontinent. New arrivals settled in densely populated inner-city wards of metropolitan

Table 15.2 Ethnic groups, total population, Soho ward

	All People	White			Mixed				Asian or Asian British				Black or Black British			Chinese or other	
		British	Irish	Other White	White and Black Caribbean	White and Black African	White and Asian	Other Mixed	Indian	Pakistani	Bangladeshi	Other Asian	Black Caribbean	Black African	Other Black	Chinese	Other ethnic group
TOTAL PERSONS	25 634	5250	563	299	718	56	207	243	6851	3587	994	592	4647	368	620	176	453
Males	12 611	2668	272	167	334	24	58	110	3380	1893	479	359	2044	172	268	93	250
Females	13 023	2582	291	132	384	32	109	133	3481	1694	515	233	2603	196	352	83	203
Age																	
0–4	2253	291	7	28	116	3	48	53	502	454	160	50	349	38	78	17	49
5–15	4511	646	25	21	282	20	74	91	1318	780	248	102	896	85	179	30	134
16–29	6221	1087	56	137	172	14	39	52	1711	1251	303	181	787	96	147	62	126
30–49	7069	1525	130	67	125	15	38	45	2038	703	178	176	1557	113	191	35	133
50 to pensionable age	2262	780	136	24	6	3	7	-	619	199	47	48	330	19	6	12	26
pensionable age to 74	1929	518	134	11	12	3	-	-	440	137	50	22	547	14	17	15	9
75 and over	989	403	75	11	5	-	-	-	233	43	8	13	181	3	3	5	6
Country of Birth																	
UK	16 783	5150	167	63	682	37	189	191	3697	2068	489	274	2887	116	574	68	131
Outside UK	8851	100	396	236	36	19	18	82	3154	1519	505	318	1760	252	46	108	322
Economic Activity																	
In employment [11+][13]	7434	1773	159	80	128	12	27	33	2249	789	170	169	1434	100	162	28	51
Unemployed	1879	375	45	26	49	10	15	15	447	229	61	43	389	39	72	14	50
Economically inactive	8168	1762	252	133	138	11	42	51	2112	1272	347	215	1338	103	127	82	183
Not aged 16 to 74	8153	1340	107	60	403	23	123	144	2053	1297	416	155	1426	126	259	52	159
General Health																	
Good health	16 128	2957	232	200	529	48	170	186	4373	2428	681	387	2804	287	406	125	335
Fairly good health	6222	1472	187	68	144	4	28	37	1511	798	236	134	1237	74	170	40	82
Not good health	3284	821	144	31	45	4	5	20	977	361	77	71	636	27	44	11	35
Limited long-term illness																	
Has a limiting long-term illness	5183	1390	229	45	97	-	26	38	1441	533	144	103	988	32	74	33	43
Does not have a limiting long-term illness	20 449	3860	334	254	621	54	181	225	5420	3087	850	489	3559	336	546	143	410
Resident Type																	
Living in a household	25 067	4905	527	285	697	54	205	240	6812	3551	993	535	4598	265	613	175	451
Living in a communal establishment	578	345	36	14	21	-	3	3	49	36	-	5	49	3	7	3	3

Note: Cells in this table may have been adjusted to avoid the disclosure of confidential information.

cities, such as Birmingham. The itinerant experiment was proving successful, which attracted interest in wholesaling.

The Digbeth Wholesale Market was populated by important members of the Asian communities, including K. Butt, M. Sharif, A. Bidwalla and I. Desai, who acted as intermediaries between exporters from the Indian subcontinent and the retailers of Handsworth. The wholesalers imported goods and sold them to retailers in Birmingham.[7]

Drivers of the Asian Food and Drink Sector

The drivers of the development of the Asian food and drink sector include both macro- and micro-environmental forces, which differ in prominence between the pre- and post-1970s phases. The circumstances and conditions in which Asian food and drink businesses have emerged requires the consideration of two principal factors: changes in the size, composition and spatial distribution of the Asian and white communities; and changes in the industrial and occupational structure and associated level of earning opportunities for the Asian community.

PRE-LATE 1970S

Changes in the size, composition and spatial distribution of Asian and white communities

One of the most important drivers determining demand for Asian food and drink is population size. The major infusion of New Commonwealth immigrants in Birmingham during the 1950s and 1960s resulted from the Immigration Act of 1962, heralded as the "beat the ban rush". Push factors included the building of the Mangla Dam in Mirpur, which displaced large sections of the local Pakistani population who received compensation for their troubles.[8] Pull factors such as labour shortages and earning opportunities were also very important for the chain migration of this group. Active recruitment by British firms in the Indian subcontinent played a part in attracting individual families within extended networks, villagers and those involved in specific occupations defined by the voucher schemes at the time. The result was that whole families, villages and occupational communities were attracted to emigrate to the UK, which created dense clusters of Asian communities living side-by-side – a ready-made market ripe for exploitation.

The number of people born in the New Commonwealth residing in Birmingham rose from 5000 in 1951 to 30 000 in 1961, and five years later the population had increased to 50 000.[9] Government controls subsequently steadily curtailed the number of new immigrants; by the late 1970s most of the entrants were family dependents. The incoming population produced wide disparities in settlement patterns, generating differentials in the size and composition of different wards.[10] For example, a large concentration of Hindus and Sikhs appeared in Soho ward, and the remainder of these groups settled in adjoining Sandwell. In Soho ward, the Asian electorate rose from five persons in 1956 to 3124 by 1971. In the subsequent five years the electorate increased further to 4593. This population thus came to represent approximately one-third of the total electorate in the ward.[11]

Several academics offer explanations for this process of residential movement and settlement; This tradition goes back at least to Homer Hoyt who in 1939 articulated his influential notions of filtering and vacancy chains, based on his observations of how households move between neighbourhoods over time".[12] The outbound movement of prior, existing populations out of an area then opened opportunities for the inbound movement of new populations, seeking opportunities in housing, employment, self-employment and education, and joining existing members of their families and communities.

Changes in the industrial and occupational structure and associated level of earning opportunities for the Asian community

The ecological succession process also affected the occupations, employment and self-employment of the local population.[13] Immigrants poured into unfilled vacancies, and white communities moved into housing in better areas in the suburbs.[14] The promotion of white employees and high job turnover in certain industries created further vacancies for immigrant labour. With regard to self-employment, most white-owned businesses were withdrawing from an area that was changing residentially and becoming cosmopolitan.[15] Because the existing business community was not aware of distinctive Asian tastes in food and drink and lacked contacts and networks to source these products, it could not compete with emerging Asian food businesses. Hence, occupational succession, whereby the local white community abandoned food businesses, opened opportunities for new communities.

Another important factor was the relative earning capacity of food businesses compared with other towns and cities and other employment opportunities, such as the manufacturing sector. Fewer food businesses existed in Birmingham than, for example, Bradford or Manchester because wages were higher in the Birmingham manufacturing industry than in the woollen or cotton industries in Bradford and Manchester.[16] This distinction made it attractive for people to work and remain in employment rather than become self-employed. Another reason related to the economic cycle and national variations. During times of expansion, the proportion of job vacancies rose higher than the national average, whereas during times of contraction, unemployment fell lower than the national average. In addition, earning capacity provided an important reason for the consumption of Asian food and drink. The Inland Revenue's Income Census for 1959–60 showed that the average person's income from employment in the West Midlands region increased to 4 per cent above the UK average. The Family Expenditure Survey for 1961–63 also revealed incomes per household in the West Midlands even higher than those in London and the South East, reaching 13 per cent above the average for Great Britain as a whole.

Thus, both ecological and occupational succession processes combined to create an Asian food and drink sector. Cultural proclivity, as well as economic opportunity factors, played an important part at this stage of development.

POST-LATE 1970S

The prominence of cultural drivers declined after the late 1970s as immigration was curtailed and the Asian food and drink market came close to being adequately served. The comparative advantage of Birmingham for the Asian community in terms of lower employment (not business), higher earnings and stability was also to disappear and reverse.

The late 1970s marked the start of a major recession. Immigration controls tightened, and unemployment increased. Uniquely, unemployment grew faster in the West Midlands after 1979 than in any other region and was more pronounced in the inner city.[17] Low levels of investment in the West Midlands and a concentration in a narrow range of engineering industries was singled out as a major threat to the future of the region.[18] One-third of manufacturing jobs that existed in 1978 disappeared. The Asian community was heavily concentrated in these industries and therefore very vulnerable. Many lost their jobs, and others experienced a reduction in real income even if they continued employment. The effect in the Handsworth ward was very significant. Between 1976 and 1981, 4272 jobs disappeared in the manufacturing industry in the Handsworth, Lozells and Soho subregion. Some 84 per cent of these job losses resulted from the contraction and closure of large companies.[19]

The annihilation of the industrial base during these years turned the region from an industrial heartland to an industrial wasteland. Between 1971 and 1984, in the Partnership area (the inner city), manufacturing jobs fell by 58 per cent compared with 31 per cent for Great Britain overall. Unemployment in Handsworth, Lozells and Soho reached 38 per cent in 1985 – three times the national average.

Disadvantaged positions in the wage economy were identified as the principal motivation for a majority of Asians to move away from wage employment and take greater control of their own livelihoods. Self-employment represented the best, even though a risky, option at the time. The food and drink sector offered less risk and uncertainty and low barriers to entry. The food sector also offered a stepping stone to entry into more diversified trades later. Unlike previous migrants who entered the food trade with little qualification, this group was much more educated, at degree and postgraduate levels.

The determinants and implications for Asian food businesses after the late 1970s were influenced more by economic factors and structural cycles, including higher unemployment, increasing redundancies, lower wages and less disposable income.

Food and drink outlets provided a springboard for many people to expand, diversify and develop other retail opportunities as part of a long-term strategy. A close look at the growth of the Asian food and drink sector, businesses, stores, and merchandise will help clarify the trends and strategies that underlie this field of enterprise.

Growth of the Asian Food and Drink Business

Growth in the Asian food and drink business occurs at five levels: sector, business, food/non-food, non-store channel, and merchandise.

SECTOR

The seeds for the emergence of Asian food entrepreneurs were sown by an increasing Asian population, expanding cultural tastes, demand for Asian goods and the ability to speak Asian languages; in this context, fixed shops provided a place where owners' and consumers' status and cultural ties could be reinforced. Asians came from countries with different languages, cultural values, traditions, beliefs, religions, personality characteristics, occupational skills and so forth. In addition, many Asian groups had different motivations for moving to the UK, which often affected their desire and need to assimilate. Food and drink businesses primarily provided sole-purpose outlets, such as grocers, butchers, restaurant/cafes and off-licence operators.

The grocery trade made an attractive proposition for many Asians who wished to turn to self-employment. It offered prior product knowledge, low barriers to entry, self-consumption, a foothold in business and a stepping stone towards a long-term strategy of engaging in a more diversified business sector.[20]

In 1959 only one Asian grocer existed, and its primary role was to meet the needs of visiting people from the Indian subcontinent who had semi-permanent status. However, between 1961 and 1971 the number of grocer outlets increased marginally from two to seven, a threefold increase (see Table 15.3). The real expansion in the numbers of grocers came four years later. In 1975 the number shot up to 16, a more than sevenfold increase from 1961. The number of grocers fluctuated little up to 1981 and marginally increased thereafter to 21 by 1986. Wholesale grocers opened their first outlet in 1973. Since 1986 the independent grocery market has matured and attracted the attention of larger supermarkets in the vicinity. Approximately 33 per cent of grocery outlets have ceased to operate from the same premises, falling from 21 in 1986 to 13 by 2006.

The number of butchers experienced a less dramatic pattern. The first outlet opened in 1962, and one to two outlets remained the constant number until 1981. In 1981, three outlets were recorded, rising to five in 1985 and eight by 1987. The increase was largely due to demand for *halal* meat among the increasing Muslim population from the Indian subcontinent, as well as Eastern European and other Asian countries.

Table 15.3 Expansion and contraction of Asian food outlets, 1961–1983

Food business	1961	1962	1963	1964	1965	1966	1967	1968	1969
Grocers	2	3	3	3	2	2	3	4	5
Butchers		1		1		1	2	1	1
Restaurants				1	1			1	1
Cafes									
Bakers									
Pubs									

Food business	1970	1971	1972	1973	1975	1977	1979	1981	1983
Grocers	2	7	7	8	16	15	14	17	19
Butchers	1	1	1	2	1	2	2	3	3
Restaurants		3	2	2					
Cafes	1	2	1	1	2	4	8	8	9
Bakers							1	2	2
Pubs							2	2	2

Both restaurants and cafes started late; the first outlet only appeared in 1964. After 1971 we begin to see marginal growth to five outlets, fluctuating around this level until 1977. The real growth in numbers started in 1979 (eight outlets), increasing to 13 by 1986. Growth continued to 19 stores by 2006. On Holyhead road, a Kwik-Fit auto garage was converted into a high-class restaurant offering vegetarian food.

Growth in sandwich shops resulted from health and lifestyle trends replacing traditional bakers. The number of bakers increased from one outlet in 1979 to three in 1987 and stayed steady thereafter. Off-licences started with one operator in 1967, increasing to two by 1981, and remaining constant thereafter. Pubs established in 1979 increased to three by 1985 and doubled by 1987 (see Table 15.4).

BUSINESS

The growth pattern of individual food and drink businesses reveals resilience, change and renewal. Individual food and drink business strategies reflected the following variations:

- change from non-food to food functions;
- change from one food to another food in the same premises;
- change from existing food to metamorphosed food premises;
- change from one type of food ownership to another;
- change from food to vacant premises.

For example, Paz Food became vacant while the Greggs bakery (non-Asian) and Sangam Confectioner filled vacant premises. Some outlets changed from food to non-food activity – for example, D & B Grocer became Streetwise clothing. Other activities changed

Table 15.4   Expansion and contraction of Asian food outlets, 1985–2007

Food business	1985	1986	1987	1989	1991	1993	1996
Grocers	20	21	20	19	20	17	18
Butchers	5	5	8	7	9	9	7
Restaurants and Cafés	13	13	15	16	14	16	17
Bakers	2	2	3	2	2	2	3
Pubs	3	3	6	7	7	6	6

Food business	1998	2000	2002	2004	2006	2007
Grocers	15	14	14	13	13	13
Butchers	7	7	7	7	7	7
Restaurants and Cafés	17	18	18	19	19	19
Bakers	3	3	3	3	3	3
Pubs	6	6	7	7	7	7

in the same food sector, such as Wing Li takeaway becoming Sang Ley takeaway and Lal & Sons Butchers transforming into Halal Meat Butchers. The Havmor Supermarket premises restructured into two outlets: a vacant unit and Gill Supermarket.

Other trends reflect the conversion of basement floors for cooking, outside catering and kitchenette, and the use of upper floors for other purposes. Strategic development of the Handsworth Market has replaced the former food stalls, and the purpose-built Kwik Save (now owned by Somerfield) has intensified competition.

FOOD/NON-FOOD

During the study period, compound businesses that stock some degree of food and drink products have grown. These include chemists, newsagents, cinemas and Indian clubs. The Asian Cinemas and Indian Clubs stock certain food and drink items, but in limited supply. The chemists and newsagents stock mainstream food and drink items.

NON-STORE CHANNEL

An increasing number of food outlets are exploring alternative and complementary non-store channels, such as selling on the Internet or online shopping, mobile delivery and warehousing.

MERCHANDISE

The mixture of merchandise is changing and following different market niches and emerging tastes for fusion, tropical, exotic, healthy, lifestyle and organic products. Evidence suggests a growing trend whereby grocery stores moving into Handsworth stock larger product lines and designate more shelf space to both ethnic and mainstream food. This approach has proved successful, insofar as shoppers from both majority and minority communities find it convenient to stock up on non-ethnic and national brands at the same time.

Several major transitions in product development, diversification and franchising have taken place during the reporting period. For example, the sandwich franchise Subway opened on Soho Road, which represents a diversification from conventional ownership. The franchise is also experimenting with new products, such as aloo tikka and paneer tikka, aimed at vegetarian consumers.

Growth Strategies and the Central Place Theory

Having considered the various levels at which Asian food and drink businesses have grown, this section examines the growth strategies behind these growth patterns. The growth strategies recognize that no business can stand still, but instead must adapt to change. As Figure 15.1 depicts, growth may be pursued through a four major routes, related to the type of merchandise offered and the customers chosen as the target market.

The penetration strategy requires the food operator to seek aggressively to increase its market share. This strategy has been pursued by those who have increased their market

	Customers	
Merchandise	Penetration	Market Development
	Merchandise Development	Diversification

Figure 15.1 Growth strategies

share at the expense of smaller stores. There is a limit to the growth possible with a penetration strategy, which relies on existing merchandise.

The merchandise development strategy can achieve additional growth by adding new merchandise to appeal to existing customers and generate extra sales. For example, newsagents have added new food merchandise to expand their businesses.

The market development strategy can be pursued in two ways. First, new customers might be sought in geographic areas not currently served. Second, the strategy might involve attracting customers from the same geographical area through, for example, high-order food retailing. The Khazana restaurant has attracted customers from a wider catchment area who do not use the Soho Road shopping facility.

The diversification strategy involves offering new merchandise for new target customer groups; it is therefore the most expansive, riskiest and the most rewarding of the growth strategies.

For retailers, an integration strategy seeks to minimize conflict in the distribution channel by taking ownership of channel members through acquisitions or mergers. East End Food Ltd manufactures its own products and sells them through various retail outlets that are members of the Shopeasy symbol group, supported by East End Foods Ltd.

Store image and customer service strategies communicate the store personality through the exterior of store, window displays, and the interior design and layout.

The range of strategies used cannot solely explain why the food industry has remained stable on Soho Road compared with independent outlets elsewhere. We find strong theoretical evidence in support of the central place theory, which seeks to explain the size and spacing of human settlements. The theory rests on the notion that centralization is a natural principle of order and that human settlements follow it. Created by the German geographer Walter Christaller, central place theory further suggests that laws determine the number, size and distribution of towns and their functions as markets.[21]

To develop the theory, Christaller used two concepts: threshold and range. Threshold is the minimum market (population or income) needed to bring about the sale of a particular good or service. Range is the maximum distance that consumers will travel to acquire goods, because, at some point, the cost or inconvenience outweighs the need for the good.

As a result of these consumer preferences, a system of centres of various sizes emerges. Each centre supplies particular types of goods, forming levels of hierarchy that suggest several generalizations about the spacing, size and function of settlements:

- The larger the settlements, the fewer in number they will be, such that there are many small villages but relatively few large cities.

- The larger the settlements grow in size, the greater the distance between them, such that villages usually appear close together, whereas cities are spaced much further apart.
- As a settlement increases in size, the range and number of its functions increase.
- As a settlement increases in size, the number of higher-order services increases, such that a greater degree of specialization occurs in the services.

The higher the order of the goods and services (more durable, valuable, and variable), the larger the range of the goods and services, and the longer the distance people are willing to travel to acquire them.

Examples of low-order goods and services include newspaper stalls, groceries, bakeries and post offices. These offerings are supported by a relatively smaller threshold population and demand. Examples of high-order goods and services include jewellery, large shopping arcades and malls, which are supported by a much larger threshold populations and demand.

Christaller further deduced that settlements would tend to form in a triangular/hexagonal lattice, which represents the most efficient pattern for travel between settlements (according to stacking theory).

The validity of central place theory may vary with local factors, such as climate, topography, history of development, technological improvement and the personal preferences of consumers and suppliers. However, it does a reasonably good job of describing the spatial pattern of urbanization. No other economic theory explains the hierarchy of urban centres. As Heilbrun notes, "A hierarchy is by definition a systematic arrangement of the classes of an object."[22]

In this case, the "object" consists of economic centres, both large and small. The central place hierarchy describes the relationship between a central place (higher-order) and its tributary areas (lower-order). Furthermore, central place theory enables us to understand why independent convenience outlets manage to perform better; they are closely linked to the geography of comparison goods and service outlets. High-order retailing instead draws on customers from a wider radius, which benefits the convenience food sector. Independent food outlets elsewhere are fragmented and do not benefit from the range or threshold discussed for this area.

Future Assessments and Implications

TRENDS

A future assessment of the supply of Asian food and drink can be undertaken by reviewing the demand trends for Asian food and drink goods and services. Demand by the Asian community and the majority community relates to various factors, including culture, religion, immigration, employment, home cooking, income, health, dietary, transport, family size, ageing and so forth.[23]

IMMIGRATION

Immigration rates will not reach previous levels; immigration is currently limited to the specific needs of industries and Eastern European countries. Polish immigration has been increasing, but these immigrants are likely to generate their own food business opportunities to service their own communities.

FAMILY SIZE

Traditionally, Asian family sizes have been larger than that of the average white family. Despite some evidence of convergence in a few subgroups, wide disparities still exist between white and other Asian subgroups, to the extent that in Bradford the total white population has been declining, while the Muslim population has been increasing to the extent that the overall population of Bradford has increased.[24]

AGEING

Life expectancy in Britain has been rising; in a day, it may rise by almost "5 hours".[25] The impact of this development is mind-boggling; people who reach the age of 60 years by 2031, will live for another 20–25 years. By 2051 an average man is expected to live 19 more years, and women are expected to live 21 years longer.[26]

LIFESTYLE

Long work hours that leave little time for food preparation and poor diet choices have contributed to increasingly frequent health and weight issues in the UK, the most overweight nation in Western Europe. If the current trend continues, it could match US obesity levels. The country has generally adopted a service economy, with many adults working in desk jobs. In addition, UK lifestyles are increasingly sedentary, and UK workers work the longest hours in Europe; approximately 20 per cent work more than 48 hours a week. The number of working women has also risen considerably, to the point that approximately two-thirds of working-age women are economically active.

CULTURE

Asians have strong ties to their native food cultures and continue to retain their identities within the UK host culture. The extent to which native British consumers are adapting and have adopted the food consumption patterns of various minority ethnic groups is also notable. Consumer acculturation is a process by which people acquire skills, knowledge and attitudes relevant to their functioning as consumers in the marketplace.[27] Acculturated consumers try new ways of shopping and encounter new products. Consumers thus might learn and adopt all new consumer behaviours, or maintain their consumer practices from their homeland or heritage, or form completely new behaviour patterns that combine the homeland and new culture patterns.[28] For example, British Indians have significantly influenced British popular culture through Indian restaurants, most of which are actually run by owners of Bangladeshi origin. Chicken tikka masala has surpassed fish and chips in terms of popularity and become Britain's most popular national dish, even though it is a British Asian invention, not known in India until it was introduced in response to requests by many British.

DIVERSITY

Demand for Asian goods can vary from one subgroup to another and depends on taste, style, religious beliefs and culture. For example, Hindus do not eat beef, and Muslims do not eat pork or drink alcohol. Observant Muslims only eat *halal* food and drink. The current UK Muslim population is estimated to be 1.9 million (3.2 per cent) and increasing.[29] Their spending power is estimated to be £20.5 billion, and the *halal* market itself is worth £700 million. A niche sector, this fragmented market consists of many independent small retailers. However, examining all the similarities and differences among Asian subgroup segments and their consumer behaviours is beyond the scope of this investigation. Of particular note, though, are the differences among first-, second- and third-generation Asians, in that older communities rely more on traditional Asian food than do younger Asians, who tend to eat more mainstream food.

HEALTH

In parts of the health sector some opportunities may exist that are subject to strong current consumer trends (e.g. health consciousness, upmarket consumer bases, ageing population). However, the tightening regulatory environment and the distribution structure, controlled by a few major players, may limit these opportunities. Total deaths from coronary heart disease among minority ethnic communities is 40 per cent higher than the national average, and Asians under the age of 40 years are three times more prone to heart disease than the national average.[30] Diabetes-related deaths among Asians are also three times greater than the national average.

Indian cuisine needs to move from being a popular occasional meal option to an everyday meal option, with the flexibility of other staples of the British diet, such as pasta. Rice is a popular and versatile accompaniment to different cuisines, and, as far as consumers are concerned, it is a healthy food item. Convincing consumers to adopt Indian food into their diets will require a major perceptual readjustment, however.

FUSION

A new emerging trend, "fusion food", is becoming increasingly popular and has proven to be an excellent avenue for introducing new flavours and products to the general population. Fusion food blends flavours and ideas from different cultures and ethnicities to develop a brand-new dish. The blending of different ethnic spices is becoming so popular that manufacturers are beginning to incorporate different flavours into their prepackaged foods. These fusion foods continue to grow in popularity because they offer an opportunity for consumers to taste different cuisines in one central place.

MERCHANDISE

Larger stores are stocking a range of Asian food and drink items, but their out-of-town location means that only consumers with cars can access such goods. Because this type and mix of merchandise suffers high barriers to sourcing, product knowledge and supply chain availability, it is difficult for non-Asians to supply and distribute Asian food. Future opportunities will largely depend on the ability of suppliers to reflect demand trends.

Home-grown

An Asian-owned company has developed the market for growing Asian speciality vegetables in Shifnal, Shropshire, on a 600-acre site. Its sales are increasing and reaching Scotland and Ireland.[31] This development should have a direct impact on the distribution pattern of Asian vegetables in the foreseeable future; these vegetables currently are imported from the Indian subcontinent and other countries.

Premium

Ready-made and ready-to-cook meals offer huge growth areas and provide a massive opportunity for Indian food, if companies can develop the right proposition.

Conclusions

The food industry makes an important contribution to the UK economy in terms of wealth creation, employment generation and area regeneration. The role of the Asian food sector within this industry, particularly in highly Asian-populated areas such as Soho Road, Handsworth, is therefore critical to the regeneration and health of that locality.

During the past 20 years, the market share of larger grocery retailers has increased significantly, which means greater buying power for large retailers and therefore lower prices than those set by smaller retailers. The largest retailers can invest the cost advantages they enjoy on account of their greater buying power in improved customer facilities or reduced prices, which can drive greater sales and thus even greater buying power. The recent move by large grocery retailers into small-format stores in high street locations, together with extended opening hours, has cost small retailers their previous comparative advantage associated with convenience. These changes are the result of market forces, which suggests that no public policy intervention is required on the grounds of economic efficiency.

Using a multifaceted methodology, we provide an informed study of the Asian food industry in Handsworth. Desk research and discussions with experts, together with mystery shopping and Goad maps, enable us to trace the evolution of Asian food outlets over a 50-year period and assess catchments and customer profiles.

The Asian food and drink industry has evolved as a result of different combinations of ecological factors, such as immigration, ethnicity and settlement, as well as economic factors such as employment and income. The prominence of ecological factors in the pre-late 1970s and the prominence of economic factors since the post-late 1970s have largely shaped the development of the food industry in two stages. Demographic changes and labour market disadvantages have driven much of the retail change over the decades, as retailers have responded to shifts in demand associated with the lifestyles of different groups. Employment status and rising income also have played their part in fuelling retail change and consumer behaviour.

On Soho Road, the changing landscape has been captured by Goad data that show business, occupant and premises characteristics over a long period. The data show change, renewal and stability in certain food businesses, as well as their survival and succession strategies. As the experts note, several succession strategies exist, including product development, market penetration, business development and business diversification. The food industry had provided a stepping stone for many independent retailers to expand, diversify and develop new opportunities in the long term.

The structure of retailing in Handsworth has changed in ways similar to the retailing industry in the rest of the UK,[32] although there are also some significant differences resulting from its unique geography and ethnicity. Central place theory helps us understand the development of the comparison goods sector and how it creates additional benefits by increasing the range (maximum distance) and threshold (minimum market). For example, when high-order stores such as jewellers and shoe shops cluster together, they encourage people to travel greater distances and increase the market size for food operators.

Various key trends and merchandise development needs must be taken into account in assessing the foreseeable future, including the nature and extent of immigration, shifts from urban to rural areas, family size, ageing populations as a result of higher life expectancies, altering lifestyles, consumer acculturation and diversity, health and food fusion, premium products, niche and specialist food retailing, and organic food.

The Asian food sector will continue to grow in line with the overall growth of the economy, providing employment and greater contributions to economic activity. The long-term structure of Asian food retailing also depends on the pace of economic development, the emergence and speed of adoption of new technology (e.g. e-commerce, teleshopping), planning regulations and regeneration, and the rate at which consumers adopt new buying patterns.

The important contribution of the Asian food sector provides the potential for further development. A fuller recognition of its key role in the regional economy and future policy formulation, together with an integration of its interests with other aspects of economic policy and regeneration (including enterprise strategy) should be promoted. In encouraging sustainable food retail development and growth, responsibility also lies with the industry itself. Trade representative and associations, together with the state, should provide a facilitating, enabling environment.

This study reveals significant structural changes, which will continue. A strategic response and initiatives are required to improve the competitiveness of the sector. The House of Commons has an opportunity to extend the role of district shopping centres,[35] which have been forced to compress between high streets and out-of-town shopping centres.

References

1. PACEC (1998), *The Food Supply Chain in the West Midlands Region*, Final Report, prepared by Public and Corporate Economic Consultants (PACEC) for the Rural Development Commission West Midlands Region.
2. Euromonitor International (2004), "Global market information database for agriculture and agri-food Canada: Retailing in the United Kingdom", October.
3. The World Factbook (2006), "United Kingdom", 29 June, https://www.cia.gov/cia/publications/factbook/geos/uk.html#Intro (accessed 5 July 2006).
4. Ibid.
5. *Population Census* (2001), Office for National Statistics, London.

6. Ibid.
7. Patel, S. (1987), "Patterns of growth: Asian retailing in inner and outer areas of Birmingham" in S. Vertovec. (ed.), *Aspects of the South Asian Diaspora: Oxford University Papers on India*, Volume 2, Part 2,Oxford University Press, Oxford.
8. Patel, S. (1988), "Nature and dynamics of Asian retailing in UK", unpublished doctoral thesis, Open University, Milton Keynes; Saifullah-Khan, V. (1982), "The role of culture of dominance in structuring the experience of ethnic minorities" in C. Husband (ed.), *Race in Britain*, London: Hutchinson.
9. Ward, R. and Sims, R. (1981), "Social status, the market, and ethnic segregation" in C. Peach, V. Robinson and P. Smith (eds), *Ethnic Segregation in Cities*, Croom Helm, London.
10. Patel, "Nature and dynamics of Asian retailing", *op. cit.*
11. Ward and Sims, "Social status, the market and ethnic segregation", *op. cit.*
12. Cited in Holloway, S.R., Ellis, M. Wright, R. and Hudson, M. (2005), "Partnering 'out' and fitting in: residential segregation and the neighbourhood: contents of mixed-race households", *Population, Space and Place*, Vo. 11, pp. 299–324; See also Hoyt, H. (1939), *Structure and Growth of Residential Neighborhoods in American Cities*, Federal Housing Administration, Washington DC.
13. Ibid.
14. Allen, S. (1971), *New Minorities, Old Conflicts*, Random House, New York; Allen, S. et al. (1973), "Self-employed and business activity" in S. Allen, S. Bentley and J. Bornat (eds), *Work, Race and Immigration*, University of Bradford, Bradford; Anwar, M. (1979), *The Myth of Return: Pakistanis in Britain*, Heinemann, London; Aurora, G.S. (1967), *The New Frontiersmen: A Sociological Study of Indian Immigrants in the United Kingdom,*, Popular Prakashan, Bombay.
15. H. Aldrich (1980), "Asian shopkeeper as a middleman minority" in A. Evans and D. Eversley (eds), *The Inner City: Employment and Industry*, Heinemann, London, pp. 389–407; H. Aldrich et al. (1981), "Business development and self-segregation: Asian enterprise in three cities" in C. Peach, V. Robinson and S, Smith (eds), *Ethnic Segregation in Cities*, Croom Helm, London, pp. 176–192; H. Aldrich et al. (1982), "From periphery to peripheral: The South Asian petite bourgeoisie in England", in I.H. Simpson and R. Simpson (eds), *Research in the Sociology of Work*, Vol. 2, JAI Press, Greenwich, CT, pp. 1–32; H. Aldrich et al. (1984), "Inter-ethnic competition for business sites", paper presented at the annual meeting of the American Sociological Association; H. Aldrich et al. (1984), "Ethnic advantage and minority business development" in R. Ward and R. Jenkins (eds), *Ethnic Communities in Business*, Cambridge University Press, Cambridge, pp. 189–210.
16. Ward, R. (1983), "Ethnic enterprise in Britain", *SSRC Newsletter*, Vol. 49; Ward, R. (1983), "Middleman minority, ethnic niche, replacement labour or general migration? Patterns of South Asian settlement in Britain", paper presented at the Mid West Sociological Society Conference, Kansas City; Ward, R. (1983), "Ethnic communities and ethnic business", *New Community*, Vol. 2, pp. 1–9.
17. Public Sector Management Research Unit (1985), *The Effect of Recession on West Midland's Economy*, Working Paper Series, Aston Business School.
18. West Midlands County Council (1984), Report, West Midlands Low Pay Unit, Birmingham.
19. G.J. Dear (1985), *Handsworth/Lozells September 1985: Report of the Chief Constable, West Midlands Police*, West Midlands Police, Birmingham.
20. Patel, "Nature and dynamics of Asian retailing", *op. cit.*
21. Beguin, H. (1992), "Christaller's central place postulates: Commentary", *Annals of Regional Science*, Vol. 26, Issue 3, pp. 209–229.

22. Heilbrun, J. (1992), "Art and culture as central place functions", *Urban Studies*, Vol. 29, Issue 2, pp. 205–215. Quote referenced at: http://swevashtick.blogspot.com/2008/10/uofa-asu-challenge-can-panarchy-and.html.

23. USDA Foreign Agricultural Service (2006), "United Kingdom HRI Food Service Sector: Eating out passes home food consumption in UK 2006", *Gain Report*, No. UK6027, 23August, http://www.fas.usda.gov/gainfiles/200608/146208793.pdf (accessed September 13, 2006).

24. Patel, "Patterns of growth", *op. cit.*

25. Visco I. (2001). *Ageing Populations: Economic Issues and Policy Challenges*, Organization for Economic Cooperation and Development, Paris.

26. Ibid.

27. Penaloza, L. (1989), "Immigrant consumer acculturation", *Advances in Consumer Research*, Vol. 16, pp. 110–118.

28. Wallendorf, M. and Reilly, M. (1983), "Ethnic migration, assimilation, and consumption", *Journal of Consumer Research*, Vol. 10 (December), pp. 292–302.

29. Mintel (2002), "Market intelligence food and drink, UK", January.

30. Mintel (2007), "Market intelligence Indian foods – UK", January.

31. Harper Adams Report (2006), *New Opportunities in the Fresh Produce Market: Feasibility Study*, Ref: BG/FD5008/F, Harper Adams University College, Newport.

32. Dawson, J. (2004), "Retail change in Britain during 30 years: strategic use of economies of scale and scope", Centre for the Study of Retailing in Scotland, Research Papers in Retailing, No. 0402.

33. House of Commons All-Parliamentary Small Shops Group (2007), *High Street Britain: 2015*, APPSSG, London.

16 Retail-led Regeneration: Government Initiatives to Support Asian Food

SURESH H. PATEL*† AND KULDIP GUJRAL‡

Keywords

retailing, regeneration, government initiatives, food businesses, Shopwell, Shopeasy, Asian trade link.

Abstract

In this chapter we propose to examine why and how independent Asian food retail businesses contribute to the regeneration of distressed areas. Thus, we attempt to answer the following questions. First, is the reluctance of larger stores to enter disadvantaged areas linked to local trends and the characteristics of marginal markets? Second, do smaller independent food retailers regard these areas as an economic opportunity and compete against the entry of larger stores? Third, and finally, what government initiatives might help strengthen the contribution of independent food retailing to deprived areas?

Introduction

This chapter explores the political dimensions of the survival of independent retailing, as well as the drivers of a range of policies, including regeneration,[1] entrepreneurship,[2] health[3] and dietary changes.[4] The impetus for planning and regeneration comes from the Department of Communities and Local Government (DCLG), which in May 2007 announced the government's Planning White Paper, highlighting major reforms to the UK's planning system. One of the four key pillars is of particular significance for

---

* Professor Suresh H Patel, Birmingham City University, Business School, Perry Barr, Birmingham, B42 2SU, UK. Telephone: + 44 121 331 5202. E-mail: Suresh.H.Patel@bcu.ac.uk.

† The author acknowledges the help and contribution of Mr. Dhanay Patel in preparing the charts, illustrations and tables for this chapter.

‡ Mr Kuldip Gujral, Birmingham Chamber of Commerce, 75 Harborne Road, Edgbaston, Birmingham, UK. Telephone: + 44 121 607 1767. E-mail: kgujral@birminghamchamber.org.uk.

supermarkets because it pertains to the development of a "planning system to support town centres in a positive way".[5]

In a conference entitled "Disadvantaged or Under-served?" championed by a former Birmingham MP, the Rt Hon. Lord Rooker, UK Minister for Regeneration and Regional Development, highlighted the importance of regeneration schemes as making sound economic sense to business:

Just like anywhere else, to be genuinely sustainable, disadvantaged areas need homes, jobs, services and infrastructure to be in balance in an attractive and welcoming environment ... what we must do is harness the power of retail, commercial property – in fact business as a whole – as a beneficial engine of change.[§]

A review of the literature pertaining to small-scale retailing reveals a range of issues at the national and local levels, including food deserts,[6] buying power, access to healthy food,[7] social inclusion[8], crime, skills, sustainable communities and so forth[9] that independent food retailers face in deprived areas, as well as views about investment potential for the area. For instance, Furey and colleagues believe that food deserts have been compounded by the effect of large grocery retailers locating on the periphery of towns and the subsequent displacement of independent retailers.[10] The Competition Commission, however, finds no link between the locational strategies of supermarket operators and restricted access to groceries.[11]

This chapter considers the trends and issues in deprived areas, the resulting consumer issues and business challenges, the social benefits of retail-led regeneration and the characteristics of marginal markets (including the key issues of, and benefits for, Asian food retailing). This research reviews real-life, retail-led regeneration initiatives aimed at supporting Asian food businesses and maximizing retail's contribution to urban regeneration. It concludes with the main conclusions of this analysis.

Framework of Reference

TRENDS AND PATTERNS

The UK retailing sector has changed significantly in recent years, with larger retail businesses growing at the expense of small retailers. Traditional, local, independent convenience stores have been rapidly declining by up to 2000 per year.[12] Of the 278 630 shops that operate in the UK, approximately half are owned and managed by a sole trader, and a further 103 000 have fewer than five employees.[13] According to a recent research report, there are more than 68 000 black and minority ethnic (BME) retailers in the UK and almost 4000 BME wholesalers.[14] The total number of staff working for BME retailers and wholesalers is more than 373 000, and in 2005–06, the BME and wholesale sector had a combined turnover of £32.96 billion, almost 12 per cent of UK retail sales.[15]

Have the changes in retail size and structure and the characteristics of distressed areas consolidated the survival and, in some cases, renewal of the Asian food retail sector? Can

§   It seems ironic that one of the food retail development schemes covered in this chapter originated in his constituency and benefited the West Midlands as a whole.

the demographic portrait of the West Midlands provide an idea of the potential that may exist for independent Asian food retail activity?

To gain an understanding of the characteristics of local people within the West Midlands region, the Population Census[16] shows that the population of the West Midlands in 2001 was 5 267 000 (10.7 per cent of the population of England). In relation to most southern counties, the West Midlands region is one of the slowest growing in terms of population, with a lower percentage of people in the 30–44-year age group, in good health and economically active, in professional and technical occupations, including owner occupiers and occupation owners.

In addition, the West Midlands has the highest percentage of people in the 10–14-year age group, married, and with dependent children, as well as the highest average household size, after London. The number of ethnic minority people and those employed in manufacturing demonstrate the potential purchasing power, diversity and concentration of the population. However, this potential is constrained in that the West Midlands contains the highest incidence of people with long-term illnesses, and without qualifications, the most social renting, and the highest unemployment in the 16–74-year age group, as well suffering acute deprivation (see Table 16.1).

Despite the slow growth, the changing structure of the food retail industry, the characteristics of the deprived areas and the potential opportunities arising from demographic evidence, to date there has been little analysis of the development of independent Asian food retail businesses across the West Midlands.

Retail decentralization, to the extent that it has occurred in the West Midlands, also follows the rest of the UK, in that the region has seen many out-of-town developments, including an increase in the number of retail warehouse parks, during the past 30 years. The shift to out-of-town locations is commonly cited as the reason for the decline of town centres and independent food stores. To address the decline in town shopping centres, the government introduced PPG6 (Planning Policy Guideline) in 1996 to encourage new retail and leisure development in town centres. However, little is being done to protect independent food retail outlets. It is important to understand the characteristics of underserved markets or markets that larger stores cannot reach. Also, it is pertinent that key issues and benefits arising out of Asian food retailing are considered in this analysis.

The capacity and conditions in the West Midlands are ripe for slower growth and constrained market performance in the Asian food sector. The Asian retail community needs to work hard to mainstream its products and services in order to move from an ethnic niche to a mainstream market economy.

Characteristics of Marginal Markets

These socio-economic characteristics underlie this analysis which attempts to understand why larger retailers will not enter an area (or a marginal market) unless there were an economic case for doing so, and thus why some areas might not be served.[¶] The marginal markets can therefore be regarded as unprofitable by larger food stores because they

---

[¶]   Marginal markets in a retailing context appear where large food stores have inadequate access to localized communities for reasons associated with geography, ethnicity, culture, religion, disposable income, buying power, population density and other invidious factors –.and where small, independent food retail units can fulfil a viable role.

Table 16.1   Socio-economic characteristics of the West Midlands

Age profile

- Fewer people in the 30–44 age group (21.9 per cent compared with 22.6 per cent in England), but more in the 10–14 age group (6.9 per cent compared with 6.6 per cent in England).

Marital status

- Above average proportion of adults who are married.
- Highest proportion of households with dependent children (30.7 per cent compared with 29.5 per cent for England).

Ethnic origin

- With the exception of London, lowest proportion of people identifying themselves as White (88.8 per cent compared with 90.9 per cent for England as a whole).
  Above average proportions of White Irish, Mixed White and Black Caribbean, Indian, Pakistani, Bangladeshi and Black Caribbean people.
  - Indian people form 3.4 per cent of the population of the West Midlands, including 8 per cent or more in Wolverhampton, Sandwell and Coventry.
  - Pakistani people form 2.9 per cent of the region's population, with the majority living in Birmingham.
  - Since 1991, the proportion of the population identified as White has fallen from 91.8 per cent to 88.8 per cent.
  - The Asian or Asian British group has increased from 5.6 per cent to 7.3 per cent.
  - The new "Mixed" group formed 1.4 per cent of the 2001 population.
  - The proportions of the West Midlands population born in England was 89.1 per cent, higher than for England as a whole (87.4 per cent), but lower than for any region except for London and the South East.

Religion

- The proportion of people who state that their religion is Christian is higher in the West Midlands (72.6 per cent) than for England (71.7 per cent).
- After Christian, the most common religion in the West Midlands is Muslim (4.1 per cent of the population).
- The West Midlands has a higher proportion of Sikhs than any other region (2 per cent compared with 0.7 per cent for England).
- Lowest proportion of Jewish people of any other region (0.1 per cent compared with 0.5 per cent for England).

Health

- The West Midlands has a slightly lower proportion of people in good health than the average for England as a whole (67.2 per cent compared with 68.8 per cent for England).
- Slightly higher proportion with a long-term illness than England as a whole (18.9 per cent compared with 17.9 per cent).

Economically active

- The West Midlands has a lower proportion of economically active people than England as a whole (65.9 per cent compared with 66.9 per cent nationally).
- The proportion of people aged 16–74 who are unemployed is higher than for England as a whole (3.8 per cent compared with 3.3 per cent for England).
- The West Midlands has the highest proportion of people working in the manufacturing industry (20.8 per cent of people aged 16-74 in employment compared with the average for England of 14.8 per cent).
- The West Midlands has the lowest proportion of people working in associate professional and technical occupations (e.g. engineering technicians, nurses, artists), the second highest proportion working in skilled trades (gardeners, electricians, cooks) and as process, plant and machine operatives (e.g. quarry workers, bus drivers). It also has the second lowest proportion of people working in personal service occupations (e.g. nursery nurses, barbers).

Table 16.1 *Concluded*

Qualifications

- The West Midlands has an above average proportion of people aged 16-74 with no qualifications (33.9 per cent).
- Is the second lowest region for both level 3 (2 A-levels or equivalent) at 7.4 per cent, and level 4/5 (degree, professional qualification or equivalent), at 16.2 per cent.
- Sandwell district has the highest proportion in England of people aged 16-74 with no qualifications (45.6 per cent). Stoke-on-Trent unitary authority (42.9 per cent) and Walsall (42.7 per cent) are also in the top ten for no qualifications.

Owner-occupation

- In the West Midlands, 69 per cent of households are owner-occupiers, ranging from 60 per cent in Birmingham, Sandwell and Wolverhampton to 83 per cent in Staffordshire, Moorlands and Bromsgrove.
- The West Midlands has an above average proportion of social renting (council, housing associations). Thirty per cent of households rent from a social landlord in Sandwell and 29 per cent in Wolverhampton. Ten per cent of households in the West Midlands rent from a private landlord – the second lowest proportion among English regions.
- The highest rates of private renting in the region are in South Shropshire (16 per cent) and Bridgnorth (15 per cent).
- The West Midlands has the highest average household size of the English regions (2.41 compared with 2.36 for England as a whole).

Deprivation

- Areas of high deprivation tend to be urban-based, and the most deprived ward in the West Midlands is Aston which ranks 27 in England.
- 40–46 per cent of the population of Sandwell, Walsall and Wolverhampton and 36 per cent in Birmingham live in the most deprived 10 per cent of wards in the country.

generally are characterized by low-income households, high unemployment rates, low levels of skills among the local labour supply, low levels of car ownership, high levels of crime (actual and perceived) and poor health among the resident population.

Most reports into retail-led regeneration have attempted to draw out the challenges businesses face in looking to invest in underserved areas. Retailers face higher operating costs or lower revenues in urban deprived areas compared to elsewhere. The GLA Economics Study[17] identifies a number of factors:

- Retailers often need to stock a different product mix to suit the needs of urban consumers, especially where there are large, ethnically diverse populations.
- Local labour supplies are less skilled than in other areas.
- Underserved markets consist of low-income households, and this threatens store profitability.
- There is a lack of suitable premises and costs of store development are higher in urban areas.
- Crime and the fear of crime in deprived areas are higher than elsewhere.
- Insurance is less available and more expensive due to "redlining"** practices used by companies to identify risky areas.

** Redlining refers to the practice whereby insurance companies identify high-risk areas and avoid underwriting in them.

- Some areas have low levels of car ownership or suffer from other factors that make consumer access to the store problematic.

In contrast, in addition to the private benefits, increasing retail provision in an underserved area may serve to regenerate such areas by promoting social inclusion and physical and economic regeneration.

SOCIAL INCLUSION

Social inclusion issues can be addressed by retail-led regeneration schemes in a number of ways. The local resident population can gain better access to retail facilities by increasing the retail portfolio and merchandise mix in underserved areas. Independent food outlets can reduce the time and cost required to travel to more distant shops and offer a greater range of speciality, healthy and organic goods and services. Thus, if the new retail provision brings good-quality and fairly-priced grocery to an area, it is argued that the health of the neighbourhood population may improve.[18]

Fragmented, dispersed and localized food retailing brings new job opportunities to the local population. By providing retail employment in one area, there could be a net gain in an underserved area, where, by definition, there are fewer competing stores compared with other areas.

ECONOMIC GROWTH

Literature on retail-led regeneration schemes focus on out-of-town centres, town/city centre management and large anchor stores rather than isolated, dispersed, fragmented or independent outlets. It is debatable which type of retail offering – large multiple retailers or small independent retailers – provides the most benefits to a local economy. The New Economic Foundation argues that big-box retail developments "not only exploit neighbourhood communities by offering low wage jobs but that they also cause the inevitable decline of High Streets and traditional retail business by displacement of local businesses and the extraction of large operating profits from the local economy which slows down the regeneration process".[19]

Can independent Asian food retail stores contribute to, and act as, catalysts for reviving the local economy and increase the circulation of money? Many locations are too small for large retailers to consider investing in, and, in such cases, there is a need for small independent stores. The following evidence illustrates this view:

- According to a report by the Department of Health,[20] large retailers generally consider neighbourhoods consisting of around 3000–4000 households as too small for investment.
- A study by the convenience chain Mace shows that small neighbourhoods can sustain small stores if they sell the right product mix to suit the community.[21]
- Research by the Work Foundation suggests that the answer lies in clustering large and small retailers in underserved areas. Evidence suggests that the outlets or stores of large retailers (particularly when the stores are large) draw foot traffic to a particular area. In this way, the large retailer store acts as an anchor for an area, allowing other retailers, including small retailers, to develop alongside the large retailer's store.

- Research into small retailers suggests that they need to focus on quality or specialize in a certain retail niche to compete effectively with large retailers.[22]

PHYSICAL REGENERATION

Government planning policy (as set out in Planning Policy Guideline 6) has dictated that the first preference for the location of new developments is town-centre locations, followed by edge-of-town, and only then in out-of-town sites if no suitable alternative can be found. Independent food outlets are bringing vacant, unused and derelict premises back into use in deprived areas, thereby improving the environment, reducing crime and enhancing the quality of life.

Key Issues and Benefits of Asian Food Retailing

A series of key issues associated with operating food retail businesses in distressed areas can be identified:

- higher costs and lower revenues;
- low-income households;
- high unemployment rates;
- less skilled populations;
- low availability of suitable sites to develop;
- high crime rates;
- insurance difficulties;
- large, ethnically diverse populations that require a different mix of products compared with the mainstream population.

An alternative view supports the assertion that an economic case for businesses to invest in many underserved and deprived areas is both vital and viable. The private benefits that arise from operating in distressed areas include:

- higher returns on commercial property;
- little or no competition from other retailers;
- large supplies of readily available local labour;
- potential access to profitable ethnic markets.

As a result, some commentators argue that many independent food operators may be "cash-poor" in terms of business survival but "asset-rich" as far as property ownership and appreciation is concerned.

There are wider economic, physical, and social inclusion benefits to be derived from independent Asian food retailing, such as the following:

- Retail development offers residents of disadvantaged communities and co-ethnics access to retail goods and services.

- The retail industry is a valuable form of employment for many groups in the labour market, partly due to the high proportion of part-time employment opportunities available compared with other sectors of the economy.
- Entry into retail employment requires few qualifications and is consequently a valuable form of employment in deprived areas that exhibit large populations with low entry-level skills and high unemployment rates.[23]
- The development of urban areas often requires the development of brownfield sites, which can considerably improve the quality of the local environment.
- The pressure on rural land increases when new retail centres are built on greenfield sites.

In recent years a number of studies and initiatives, mostly in the USA, have attempted to demonstrate the significant commercial opportunities in deprived areas. They argue that the business opportunity lies in the fact that deprived areas have high population densities, a large supply of unemployed labour, and often good transport links, which can draw consumers from outside the initial catchment area.

Methodology

An evaluation of three government-led initiatives in the West Midlands was carried out, following discussions with local authorities, government agencies, and university and independent consultants. The rationale for the choice of initiatives reflected what was happening on the ground, the visibility of the impact of support, the availability of appropriate material and regeneration funding. The selection involved narrowing down a small number of potential initiatives to a list that reflected regional variation in the West Midlands.

The initiatives selected have the following characteristics: concerted interventions to improve the supply of good-quality food through retail channels to the urban population, with the principal benefits of health; competitively priced products; promotion of own-label merchandise and multi-buys; offers; and preferential discounting. These development initiatives incorporate an integrated approach, which includes elements such as training, skill development, environmental protection, loyalty and other social benefits.

The initiatives offered a range of experience within the Asian food and drink industry. The following schemes are included:

- Shopeasy in inner part of the West Midlands;
- Asian Trade Link across the West Midlands;
- Shopwell in Sandwell.

For each initiative, the information and evidence obtained pertain to the characteristics of the initiative and location, the stimulus that made the business innovate and adapt, how the business addressed the needs and the lessons learned. The research study is designed to support the development of local and central policy. Therefore, the approach derives from:

- substantial consultation and scoping since 2003.

- a series of five issue papers of specific interest.
- three action learning sets to forward developmental practice in specific areas.
- a dissemination programme of interim and final reports, workshops, and conferences.
- a three-year summative evaluation of impacts and added value

The central questions that this research investigates are as follows:

- What are the key issues at the national and regional levels and the contextual influences that have shaped the independent food retail sector?
- What aims have the initiative partners brought to the sector in terms of resources, skills, attitudes and aspirations?
- What objectives, priorities, structures and processes have been developed through the initiatives?
- What policy statements support these initiatives?
- What strategies lend support to food retail development initiatives?
- What partnership arrangements exist to develop these initiatives?
- What have the initiatives achieved?
- What recommendations can be reached from the evaluation?

The initiatives illuminate what is happening, but cannot offer a sufficient basis for statistical inferences from which to make generalizations. Instead, the evaluation method offers a deeper understanding of variations among schemes and the reasons for change. The three initiatives represent a range of circumstances but, together, depict very different sets of themes and partnerships:

- The Shopeasy scheme was founded on the principle of "strength through unity" or the Asian concept of *Shakti* – a collective response of individual, isolated and fragmented food retailers.
- The Shopwell scheme was based on improving the healthy options and changing the terms and display of merchandising offering.
- The Asian Trade Link (ATL) scheme involved training provision to improve the competitiveness of the business.

The initiatives also often involved local, regional, and national partners, including the specialist sector, and geographic expertise.

Results and Analysis: Government Initiatives

This section reviews government-led initiatives. The conceptual framework includes policy and strategies, evidence of need and rationale, partnerships, descriptions, aims, objectives and delivery, outcomes and evaluation. It is useful to view the conceptual framework according to a circular flow. Most initiatives begin with a strategic and policy context, because funding is contingent on those contexts. Evidence of need and the rationale is established on the basis of the policy and strategy within the geographical area. A partnership is formed to support the policy, strategic and, sometimes, implementation statements. A project description is articulated and an aim determined. To move from the current what and where to the desired where and what, a set of objectives are identified and implemented for delivery. The implementation process involves inputs, throughput and outputs. At the expiration of the project, a set of outcomes will have been achieved. The outcomes are evaluated against set targets and the lessons learned, and then fed back into improved policies and strategies (see Table 16.2).

At this stage, two pertinent questions arise. First, how do the initiatives compare and, second, are their experience similar or different? Each of the questions is answered in the following.

The policy and strategy differ for each initiative, with Shopwell relying on a combination of national (Neighbourhood Renewal) and local (Local Agenda 21, Walking Strategy, Health Plan and Business Plan) strategies. In contrast, the policy impetus for Shopeasy came exclusively from regional and subregional strategies (Regeneration Zones). The strategies for ATL come from a mixture of national action plan and household surveys, together with international reports and academic research.

Evidence of need and rationale differ in focus. Shopwell is predominantly related to health, neighbourhood renewal, and access to retail outlets, in contrast to Shopeasy, which is explicitly focused on business dynamics and specific issues affecting business survival. The ATL is concerned primarily with the underrepresentation of disadvantaged groups.

The type and stakeholding of partnership vary with the initiative. A wide range of partners is engaged in the Shopwell initiative, led by local authorities but with stakeholders involved in vertical integration (e.g. farmers, manufacturers, wholesalers, distributors, educational minority, African-Caribbean associations). In contrast, the local authority is a small partnership, comprising Business Link, a wholesaler, retailers and a university, for the Shopeasy initiative. The partnership model is also different for the ATL initiative, with a smaller number of partners – namely, a university, retail advisers and independent retailers.

The descriptive focus of Shopwell is on consumption, in contrast to Shopeasy, which targets purchasing, and ATL, which focuses on training.

The Shopwell scheme is founded on the AIDA model (Awareness, Interest, Desire and Adoption), which encourages customers ultimately to create sustainable and healthy lifestyles. The Shopeasy scheme pertains to improving the competitiveness of the firm by changing the image and improving the quality of shops. The ATL focus is on training for management development and creating website presence.

The objectives and delivery modes, mechanisms and direction also vary. Shopwell is primarily concerned with increasing physical walking and the consumption of food and drink. Shopeasy has multiple objectives, including training in merchandising and purchasing reinvesting. ATL is preoccupied with addressing market failure within the Asian business community and tackling skills development.

Given the differing aims, objectives and delivery, it is unsurprising that Shopwell is geared towards achieving value and volume sales increases, compared with Shopeasy, which invests in increased shop layout, expansion, loyalty credits and sales. ATL focuses on training, seminars and management awareness.

Table 16.2 Conceptual evaluation framework

Food Retail Development Initiative (FRDI)	Shopwell	Shopeasy	Asian Trade Link (ATL)
Policy and strategies	The Policy Action Team 13 of the National Strategy for Neighbourhood Renewal (1999). Shopwell Business Plan – *A Report for Sandwell*, NRF 6. "Sandwell Health Plan", Department of Health (1999). *Saving Lives: Our Healthier Nation*, Cm. 4386, The Stationery Office/Department of Health (1999). The Local Agenda 21 Strategy for Sandwell. The Walking Strategy. Sandwell Metropolitan Borough Council (2001).	The South Black Country and West Birmingham Zone – known as "The Arc of Opportunity". The EBNS Regeneration Zone. Reflecting the pillars of the West Midlands Regional Economic Strategy: Thriving Enterprise. Thriving People and Communities. Environment and Infrastructure.	Labour Force Survey (A Government Action Plan for Small Business – the Evidence Base, (www.sbs.gov.uk) (2004). The SBS Household Survey (2005). The GEM Report (2003). Ethnic Minority Enterprise: Policy in Practice (2001).
Evidence of need and rationale	Neighbourhood renewal. Access to affordable fresh food. Access to retail outlets. Deprived communities. Poor nutrition leading to low birth weight. Later development of disease. Reduce risk of cancer from food and vegetables cooked by caterers. Directives on food supplements and traditional herbal medicines.	Decline of small food stores. Barriers affected trade position, survival and growth. Poor environment, e.g. adverse physical dilapidation, environmental degradation. Social issues such as rising crime. Business issues, such as lack of affordable insurance.	Black and minority ethnic people underrepresented. Concentration of black and minority ethnic people in certain sectors and industries. Lack of use of publicly-funded business support agencies. Improve retail management.
Partnership	The consultants engaged suppliers, farmers and dried food merchants and delivered a training programme in partnership with: Fresh Solutions (a company specializing in fresh produce training and consultancy). Hyperama (leading wholesaler specializing in the supply of quality produce. Sandwell Retail Association. Sure Start. Sandwell Citizens Advice Bureau. Sandwell Healthy Schools Scheme. Sandwell PALS (Patient Advice and Liaison Service). ACHIS (African Caribbean Health Improvement Service).	Birmingham City Council (Economic Development Department). Business Link Birmingham and Solihull (BLBS). East End Foods PLC. Birmingham City University (BCU). Cadbury, while not partners, have supported the project. Five local retailers have been members of the project steering group for the SRB 6 programme.	Asian Trade Limited, a not-for-profit organization, limited by guarantee. Leeds Metropolitan University. Small Business Service/DTI Phoenix Fund. Retail advisers. Independent retailers.

Table 16.2 *Continued*

Food Retail Development Initiative (FRDI)	Shopwell	Shopeasy	Asian Trade Link (ATL)
Description	Improve food and vegetable consumption in Sandwell.	Symbol group including group purchasing, training.	Help independent retailers become better businesses by providing advice, support and information.
Aim	Increase awareness. Encourage food and vegetable consumption. Improve local accessibility. Create, sustainable, healthy neighbourhood retailing.	Change image of local shops. Improve quality of shopping. Help small retailers compete with supermarkets and superstores.	Provide and promote accessible, high-quality and web-based services. Training in retail management, merchandising.
Objectives and delivery	Increase physical activity, e.g., walking. Increase food and vegetable consumption.	Training and advice in retail management and merchandising. Symbol group collaboration. Attracting more customers. Selling more profitable lines. Reinvesting in shop. Passing benefits to customers.	Connect with the diversity agenda. Help disadvantaged community groups. Increase participants in enterprising education and training. Raise skill levels. Support and evaluate the establishment of business. Improve and enhance community cohesion.
Outcomes	Volume of sales increased for 3 stores by 139%, 229% and 189% over one year (2005–06), respectively. Value of sales increased for 3 stores by 56%, 117% and 105% over one year (2005–06), respectively.	In Sparkbrook, 120 businesses were visited, 42 recruited, and 51 people trained. Six retailers had invested £60,000 between them by January 2002. 15 retailers had taken part in the programme in the SRB 6 areas, out of a target of 20. Benefits for participating retailers included: improved service to customers and average increase in turnover of 5%. Benefits for East End Foods: greater loyalty amongst participating retailers and increased sales; stronger position for negotiating discounts with their own suppliers. Benefits for Business Link Birmingham and Solihull: enhanced profile in Asian business community; participating retailers taking advantage of further BLBS services (e.g., advice on use of IT; e-Club). Benefits for residents in regeneration areas: access to improved local shopping.	The generation of leads and the provision of ongoing support through the engagement of cash-and-carry outlets have met their target in Birmingham and West Yorkshire with a modest shortfall in Leicester (three outlets). The target in relation to the mystery shopper visits has been exceeded in all three locations, whilst in Leicester the original target has been exceeded by 50%. On core outputs: Birmingham: overperforming on SME–assisted learning opportunities; achieving target outputs on jobs created; underperforming on workshops and seminars; underperforming on jobs safeguarded. Leicester: achieving target output on jobs created and underperforming on SME-assisted workshops and seminars; learning opportunities and jobs safeguarded. West Yorkshire: overperforming on SME-assisted workshops and seminars; learning opportunities and jobs created; underperforming on jobs safeguarded.

Table 16.2 *Concluded*

Food Retail Development Initiative (FRDI)	Shopwell	Shopeasy	Asian Trade Link (ATL)
Evaluation	Capital grants purchased and/or renew assets, e.g. equipment, machinery, fixtures and fittings. Increased fresh produce sales had a positive effect on sales of other items. Display, variety, price, quality and freshness were important in tempting customers to buy. All stores wanted to expand their range of fresh food.	The evaluation indicated strong support for the initiative both from the stakeholders and retailers. The retailers emphasized the benefits of discounting, multi-buys, fascia improvements and merchandising display. The project was praised by Barbara Roche MP in her ministerial address at the BURA/BRC Retail and Regeneration Conference on 6 June 2003.	From the ATL Retail Programme Mr Rasool received advice and guidance on improving shop floor layout, shop front window display and consumer/buyer behaviour. The support and guidance provided him with effective strategies to design and implement an impressive and practical floor layout and window displays. In addition, it helped inform understanding of how changes in consumer tastes, demands and behaviour may affect the business, in order to compete with the likes of direct competitors, ASDA and Morrisons.

Shopwell sees tangible value in terms of physical grants and improvement works, renewing assets and increasing sales of health food. Shopeasy, too, sees tangible benefits in terms of fascia renovation, discounting and merchandising display. The scheme receives ministerial attention. The ATL appears to generate intangible benefits, which are purely advisory and training-related.

Policy: Lessons from the Field

This study identifies a blind spot in existing national government policy for recognizing the diverse contributions of Asian retail food outlets and supporting and sustaining this sector. There has been little or no support available for small retail firms, particularly in the food and drink sector, until recently, despite their positive performance resilience during recessions and recoveries over generations. A single, coherent statutory provision on independent retail development is still missing, but, as these initiatives illustrate, national policy is beginning to embrace the sector from a range of perspectives. One such example is the support that comes from improving health inequality and nutrition amongst low-income communities; improving local neighbourhoods and increasing community capacity in deprived areas; and retail provision, sustainability and competitiveness.

This review shows that, although urban deprived areas present retailers with a host of challenges, there are many small-scale business opportunities in these areas, which can overcome and outweigh such challenges. A number of issues emerge from the case studies regarding which action should be considered. Arguably, part of the role of the public sector in encouraging retailers to enter deprived areas is to promulgate existing evidence about the benefits of investing in deprived areas more effectively.

The evidence from regeneration initiatives and reports across the USA and the UK demonstrate that the characteristics of deprived areas can create good business opportunities. Some advantages of businesses operating in deprived underserved areas include:

- Commercial property in deprived areas achieves higher returns than commercial property in other UK areas.
- Underserved markets are likely to have high levels of untapped demand.
- Many deprived areas provide access to underserved ethnic markets.
- Underserved markets offer little competition from other retailers.
- Deprived areas tend to have a large, readily available, local labour supply.

As well as these private benefits, increased retail provision can bring many social or economic benefits to disadvantaged communities, such as physically regenerating sites and their surroundings. The regeneration of brownfield sites can contribute to the economic regeneration of an area by significantly improving the appearance of the location, which can help to attract further business to the surrounding area. Reviving the local economy and generating employment opportunities can contribute to the economic regeneration of deprived areas as more businesses enter an area after initial investors demonstrate the area's profit potential, which in turn leads to more job creation. Moreover, retail employment often provides a stepping stone to employment in other sectors of the economy, thus spreading the effects of the retail-led regeneration into other areas of the economy.

Addressing issues of social inclusion by increasing retail provisions in underserved and deprived areas can address the issues of health exclusion by providing communities with improved access to goods and services and providing the resident population with employment opportunities. Increasing the number of retail jobs available can help engage groups that face particular barriers in accessing employment opportunities. The government inquiry should assess the precise role that independent food retail businesses play in deprived areas and support a proactive business case.

This chapter highlights the interplay of a complex series of factors and their effects on broad social, economic, regulatory and commercial factors, which influence the pattern we see today. Some trends seem likely to continue; others are much more uncertain.

Conclusions

An emerging body of evidence describes the negative impact of the demise of independent food retailing in local economies, such as the impact on health and the local economy when local food retailing is allowed to collapse;[24] the impact of retail concentration and the creation of food deserts;[25] and concerns about health inequalities.[26] However, some evidence points to business opportunities that could be exploited from investing in deprived, underserved markets.[27] In addition to private commercial benefits, there are wider economic and social benefits to disadvantaged communities that come from an increase in retail development. Smaller independent food retailers see these areas as an economic opportunity and compete or militate against the entry of larger stores.

Government initiatives are increasingly seen as an instrument for delivering many policy objectives. This chapter offers insights into the merits of supporting independent food retail outlets, in that they provide a vital link to regenerating local communities. Significant structural change is underway in the independent food retail sector, and a strategic response is required from the industry, as well as from its trade and representative associations. There is a need for the independent food retail sector to increase levels of information being diffused about the changes taking place, their vital role and their contributions to gross domestic product. The sector should increase collaboration with regard to technology, management practices and increase purchasing power. It also needs to work closely with other sectors of economic activity, such as banking, finance and insurance, to improve the range and quality of services it offers.

The study sheds light on the opportunities for food retailing in deprived areas; however, the independent food retail sector experiences a wide range of issues vis-à-vis larger stores. Government needs to extend its current inquiry into the role of independent stores to identify their potential effects on the neighbourhoods they serve.

References

1. GLA Economics (2005), "Retail in London Working Paper B: Retail and regeneration", http://www.london.gov.uk/mayor/economic_unit/docs/retail_wpb_retail_and_regeneration.pdf.

2. House of Commons All-Parliamentary Small Shops Group (2006), *High Street Britain: 2015*, APPSSG, London.

3. Cummins, S., Findlay, A., Petticrew, M. and Sparks, L. (2005), "Do large scale food retail interventions improve diet and health?", *British Medical Journal*, Vol. 330, pp. 683–684; Cummins, S. and Macintyre, S. (2002), "Food deserts – evidence and assumption in health policy making", *British Medical Journal*, Vol. 325, pp. 436–438; Wanless, D. (2004), *Securing Good Health for the Whole Population*, Report for HM Treasury, London; Department of Health (1999), *Reducing Health Inequalities: An Action Report*, DOH, London; Department of Health Policy Action Team 13 (1999), *Improving Shopping Access for People Living in Deprived Neighbourhoods*, http://www.dh.gov.uk/en/Publicationsandstatistics/Publications/PublicationsPolicyAndGuidance/DH_4008831.

4. Department of Health (2003), *Food and Health Action Plan. Food and Health Problems: Food and Health Analysis for Comment*, DOH, London. Available at: http://www.dh.gov.uk/prod_consum_dh/groups/dh_digitalassets/@dh/@en/documents/digitalasset/dh_4065834.pdf.

5. Communication received from Maria Cryan, of Quintus Public Affairs Ltd.

6. Furey, S., Strugnell, C. and McIlveen, H. (2001), "An investigation of the potential existence of food deserts in rural and urban areas of northern Ireland", *Agriculture and Human Values*, Vol. 18, pp. 447–457.

7. Department of Health (2004), *Choosing Health: Making Healthier Choices Easier*, White Paper on Public Health, November, Cm. 6374, Stationery Office, London; Cummins, S. and Macintyre, S. (1999), "The location of food stores in urban areas: a case study of Glasgow", *British Food Journal*, Vol. 101, No. 7, pp. 545–553; Lang, T. and Caraher, M. (1998), "Access to healthy foods: Part II. Food poverty and shopping deserts: What are the implications for health promotion policy and practice?", *Health Education Journal*, Vol. 57, pp. 202–211; Caraher, M., Kirk, K., Lang, T. and Carr-Hill, R. (1998), "Access to healthy foods: Part I. Barriers to accessing healthy

foods: Differentials by gender, social class, income and mode of transport", *Health Education Journal*, Vol. 57, pp. 191–201.

8. Office of the Deputy Prime Minister, Research Report 6, "Changing Practices: A Good Practice Guide for Businesses Locating in Deprived Areas", Case studies, British Retail Consortium and Neighbour Renewal Unit, http://www.renewal.net/Documents/RNET/Policy%20Guidance/Changingpracticescase.pdf.

9. Ibid.

10. Furey et al., "An investigation of the potentail existence of food deserts", *op. cit.*

11. Competition Commission (2000), *Supermarkets: A Report on the Supply of Groceries from Multiple Stores in the United Kingdom*, The Stationery Office, Norwich.

12. GLA Economics, "Retail in London", *op. cit.*

13. Ibid.

14. Centre for Retail Research (2006), *Diversity in Shopping: A Report on UK Based Minority Ethnic Retail Business*, Report for VISA Europe, Nottingham.

15. Ibid.

16. Population Census (2001), Office for National Statistics.

17. GLA Economics, (2005), "Retail in London Working Paper G: Small retailers", http://www.london.gov.uk/mayor/economic_unit/docs/retail_wpg_small_retailers.pdf.

18. Department of Health Policy Action Team 13, *Improving Shopping Access*, *op. cit.*

19. The New Economics Foundation (2003), *Ghost Town Britain II: Death on the High Street*, NEF, London, p. 2.

20. Department of Health Policy Action Team 13, *Improving Shopping Access*, *op. cit.*

21. Ibid.

22. GLA Economics, "Retail in London Working Paper B", *op. cit.*

23. Ibid.

24. Dowler, E., Turner, S. and Dobson, B. (2001), *Poverty Bites: Food, Health and Poor Families*, CPAG, London.

25. Marsden, T., Harrison, M. and Flynn, A. (1998), "Creating competitive space: exploring the social and political maintenance of retail power", *Environment and Planning*, Vol. 30, pp. 481–498; Guy, C. (1998), "Off-centre retailing in the UK: prospects for the future and implications for town centres", *Built Environment*, Vol. 24, No. 1, pp. 16–30.

26. Caraher et al., "Access to healthy foods: Part I", *op. cit.*; Lang and Caraher, "Access to healthy foods: Part II", *op. cit.*

27. New Economics Foundation, *Ghost Town Britain II*, *op. cit.*

17 *Shaping the "Authentic": Marketing Ethnic Food to Consumers*

EMMA DRESSLER-HAWKE* AND JULIANA MANSVELT†

Keywords

ethnic food, acculturation, authenticity.

Abstract

In New Zealand supermarkets, the volume of "ethnic" food products has increased substantially during the past two decades. This study explores the availability, location and shelf position of ethnic foods with a view towards determining how authenticity gets shaped in four New Zealand supermarket chains. The results indicate that ethnic food is primarily integrated into mainstream product lines, with some food aimed more specifically at ethnic populations, separated into specialist ethnic sections. Supermarkets identified as serving populations of higher socio-economic status tend to have a greater range of both mainstream and specialized ethnic products. Retailers and marketers must therefore negotiate the concepts of familiarity, risk, authenticity and convenience to appeal to increasingly multicultural mainstream audiences.

Introduction

CONCEPTUALIZING ETHNIC FOOD AND CONSUMER RELATIONSHIPS

Researchers have long identified a relationship between consumer identities and food. Food is a necessary part of material life, but it is also an important source of cultural

*   Dr Emma Dressler-Hawke, Department of Communication, Journalism and Marketing, Private Bag 11 222, Palmerston North, New Zealand. E-mail: E.K.Dresler-Hawke@massey.ac.nz. Telephone: + 64 6 350 5799 ext 7141.

†   Dr Juliana Mansvelt, School of People, Environment and Planning, Massey University, Palmerston North, New Zealand. E-mail: J.R.Mansvelt@massey.ac.nz.

capital that implies status, knowledge and even luxury. If "we are what we eat",[1] as well as what we do not eat, then food origins and their place and cultural associations are critical.[2] Purchasing and eating food may be associated with the construction of social imaginaries, which situate people's food consumption practices within wider sets of social meanings.[3] Consequently "eating habits both symbolize and mark the boundaries of cultures".[4] This role is particularly significant with regard to the marketing of ethnic foods, for which the association of food commodities with different cultures or places can encourage important, favourable associations of products with individual and group identities and thus enable consumers' purchases to play a role in establishing social difference or distinction from others.[5]

The marketing of "ethnic food" is a challenging subject for researchers, not least because of definitional issues regarding what constitutes "ethnic food" and for whom the term applies. We may consider ethnic consumers as individuals who belong "to a group that share one ethnicity different from that of the mainstream population",[6] but how that group is defined depends on the place and culture.[7] For Western consumers, ethnic food often refers to Mexican, Italian, Chinese, Japanese, Thai, Caribbean, Middle Eastern and North African food,[8] but, in New Zealand, Dutch and Pacifica foods might also be added to the list. Maori foods, associated (at least initially) with the indigenous people of New Zealand, remain largely undifferentiated as an ethnic category on supermarket shelves, even though they may involve different gathering, sourcing, preparation and eating practices.

Although multi-ethnic eating habits are not new, having been a feature of exploration and colonization since at least the sixteenth and seventeenth centuries,[9] the practice has intensified in recent years. For example, the growing popularity of Chinese and Indian cuisine in the UK since the 1960s has encouraged more diversity within the sector.[10] Regional and cultural eating habits persist, so even though food products and preparation are more homogeneous, ignoring the ethnicity of target audiences could mean alienating nearly one-third of potential patrons,[11] prompting even transnational food firms such as Burger King and Denny's Restaurants to focus on ethnic customers. Other companies seek to promote ethnic foods as a means to deploy imaginative geographies aimed at encouraging groups of consumers to "taste the world" as part of imaging food and its place in their own and others' everyday lives.[12] Although individual and social preferences for ethnic food may play an important part in food consumption, they form in relation to the distribution and accessibility of products and techniques of marketing, advertising, packaging, branding and in-store sales strategies. For example, the shift in status of sugar from a luxury to an everyday item between the eighteenth and nineteenth centuries had less to do with consumers' cultural preferences than with the practices of processors and distributors, designed to ensure continued profitability.[13]

From an acculturation point of view, cooking ethnic foods at home by mainstream consumers is also important. The processes of selection, purchase, preparation and consumption of ethnic food at home represent a personalized adaptation of culturally foreign or strange commodities, culinary practices, and/or tastes.[14] Fast-changing food trends also have implications for foods, such as a demand for Italian dishes influenced by preferences for low-carbohydrate foods or the increased popularity of the Mediterranean diet.[15] As ethnic foods penetrate markets and distribution networks, becoming readily available in restaurants and on food tables at home, and as they assume ordinary prices and can be knowledgeably prepared by consumers, they may take on the status of, and become fused with, everyday grocery items.[16]

Processes of globalization also have resulted in the diffusion of food products, production, preparation and consumption practices across national boundaries, resulting in greater availability, affordability and exposure to previously "foreign" food. Regional cultural and regional food practices and processes are thus no longer only localized,[17] and ethnic food has become the "spice" to liven up mainstream cultures.[18] Western consumers have been introduced to new forms of ethnic food through travel, restaurants, recipes and cooking programmes, as well as through television, the Internet and various forms of advertising. The new sophistication of shoppers appears to be expressed in their desire to find more restaurant-inspired offerings in their supermarkets, such that much of what was considered ethnic food 50 years ago now seems to be mainstream.[19] Products such as sushi, once considered unique or unusual, are now commonplace in many countries outside Japan. This trend extends beyond food dishes to exotic fresh fruit and vegetables and cuts of meat. Consumer exposure to new food practices and preferences has also been linked to altered food preparation and display practices, such as the Asian preferences for live or whole fish, identification of kosher or *halal* foods, and changed framings of healthy diets.[20]

Despite these trends towards increasing homogenization of food preferences on supermarket shelves, numerous stores still cater to specific ethnic groups, and shopping venues remain a significant part of ethnic identity.[21] Ethnic foods may differ in taste, shape, texture, availability, quality, price, cooking techniques, seasonality, meal structure and timing, and sourcing.[22] In New Zealand's increasingly multicultural society Asian supermarkets, speciality product stores (e.g. Dutch shops) and open-air markets all cater to the needs of a range of consumers from different ethnicities. Recent developments also include speciality food stores with an online presence or entirely Internet-based retailers (e.g. Tokyo Food which caters to Japanese consumers). For those recently arrived in a new country, food may remain the only link to a life left behind, yet, even then, the integration of traditional foods and new food products in the new place may be a conscious identity choice.[23] For retailers involved in serving a primarily ethnic market, sourcing speciality products, finding and targeting ethnic groups, and establishing a coherent customer base remain challenges.[24] For mainstream retailers, the challenge centres on effectively serving a multicultural customer base.

Consumers also face complex choices with regard to selecting food products, caught as they are in transnational networks[25] and having to make decisions that may involve new identifications, knowledge and even food preparation practices.[26] According to the National Restaurant Association,[27] three distinctly different segments of people relate to ethnic cuisines differently: the "culture oriented", the "restaurant oriented" and the "preparation oriented". The first group are sophisticated and adventurous consumers who enjoy new cuisines. The second group seeks good taste and a good atmosphere. The last group represents those who like to prepare food at home using ethnic ingredients and cooking styles to create healthy foods with an authentic ethnic flair. As consumers become more discerning and aware of flavours, pressure seemingly increases for foods that are sold in mainstream stores and supermarkets to become more authentic.

Consequently, marketers face an inherent dilemma in creating place or cultural associations. The packaging, marketing and branding of goods as "authentic" can provide a source of differentiation from everyday food – a means of social distinction for niche consumers. Alternatively, products may be marketed and assimilated into the prevailing food culture of the predominant market, increasing their presence and saleability in mainstream food spaces but reducing their differentiation and identity value. The resulting tension between the marketing of ethnic food as authentic versus mainstream appears increasingly blurred in so-called fusion food, which represents the amalgamation of ideas and flavours, as in naan bread pizza.[28]

RETAILING ETHNIC FOOD: THE INTEGRATION OR SEPARATION OF ETHNIC PRODUCTS ON NEW ZEALAND SUPERMARKET SHELVES

The remainder of this chapter examines the sale of ethnic food products in four leading New Zealand supermarkets in order to reflect on how this dilemma may be negotiated on store shelves. The market research reported herein explores differences in store display and audience to reflect on the ways in which ethnic food may be shaped as an "authentic" product, both separated from, and assimilated into, other food ranges. It intends to provide a snapshot that captures the availability of ethnic food to consumers.

Methodology

A single-wave data collection in May 2007 used observational strategies in four leading supermarkets (New World, Pak 'N' Save, Countdown and Woolworths). These supermarkets service consumers of varying socio-economic status in the Manawatu region of New Zealand. The supermarket data came from a convenience sample of 50 participants (overall age range 18–51 years, mean age of 35 years). Each participant rank-ordered the four supermarkets from 1 (servicing the lowest socio-economic consumers) to rank 4 (servicing the highest socio-economic consumers). The reporting of the results identified each supermarket only by a letter: A, B, C or D.

Defining ethnic food is problematic because it represents a complex and dynamic category. Many items that were previously considered ethnic – such as Japanese noodles, burritos and tacos – have become part of the mainstream diet in New Zealand. For the purposes of this research, the term "ethnic food" refers to products from a particular ethnic group, whether racial, national or cultural.[29]

The foods classified as ethnic may then be segmented by nationality (Indian, Chinese, Mexican, Japanese, Dutch) and divided into product categories, such as hardware (chopsticks, sushi rollers), bulk bins (dried nuts and fruits), biscuits/snacks/crackers (rice crackers, biscuits), confectionery (lollies, sweets), cooking sauces (ready-to-use sachets, bottled sauces, cooking pastes, tamarind sauces/pastes, condiment sauces), vegetables and fruits (fresh, dried, canned), rice (basmati, jasmine, long and short grain, sushi rice, rice paper), noodles (oriental noodles, instant noodles, cup noodles), pasta (Italian), cooking needs (prepacked spices, herbs and seasonings, coconut cream, milk powder, tofu, vinegars and oils), soups (soup mixes, instant soups), and beverages (tea, coffee). These categories further subdivide into frozen (seafood range, pastry, breads, vegetables), chilled (cheese, meat, fish), and ambient (pasta). For each supermarket, the ethnic products consist of two major categories: mainstream and ethnic. In the ethnic section, the products are also distinguished as products with labels printed in English and products with labels printed in their native languages.

Several forms of foods do not appear in the assessment because they have become so assimilated into mainstream culture that they can no longer be considered ethnic, including chocolate (Toblerone, Lindt, Guylian) and herbs and spices (cinnamon, coriander, ginger). The final analysis records 708 ethnic products from 18 countries in the four selected supermarkets.

Results

The results indicate wide variation in ethnic products among the four leading supermarkets. Assessments of Supermarket A consistently report that it services low socio-economic consumers, followed by Supermarkets B and C, and Supermarket D was perceived to service high socio-economic consumers (Friedman test, $p = 0.00$). Supermarkets A and B are discount operations, offering the lowest prices, and they carry fewer brands and package sizes than Supermarkets C and D. This distinction is especially noticeable for ethnic food products. Supermarket A carries 124 items, Supermarket B carries 177 items, Supermarket C has 197 items, and Supermarket D offers 210 items. Furthermore, multiple brands provide the same ethnic products, especially those with mainstream status, such as tea, tofu, pasta, packet sauces and soy sauce. Consequently, commonalities mark both products and brands across the four supermarkets. Many products appear in both the mainstream and ethnic sections of the supermarket – specifically, 11 products from Supermarket A, 16 products from Supermarket B, 16 from Supermarket C, and 22 from Supermarket D. The number of products found in both sections thus increases with the ranking of the socio-economic status of the supermarkets, which implies greater availability and visibility of ethnic food products in stores that serve higher socio-economic consumers.

Overall, 351 ethnic products (49.6 per cent) achieve mainstream status (e.g. fruit and vegetables, prepacked spices, breads, noodles, pasta, oils, sauces, coconut creams). Approximately 248 ethnic products (35 per cent) are positioned in the ethnic section of the supermarket, of which 109 products (15.4 per cent) appear in the ethnic section and had labels printed in their native languages. Figure 17.1 shows the differential quantities of ethnic food products that gained mainstream status among the supermarkets servicing consumers of varying socio-economic status.

Most ethnic products were convenience-style foods; ready meals and snacks form significant proportions in all supermarkets. The notable presence of ready-made cooking sauces and condiments in sachets, bottled sauces, cooking pastes, tamarind sauces/pastes and condiment sauces provide the added option of allowing the addition or omission of extra ingredients to accommodate individual preferences.

Major ethnic groups differ not only from one another, but also within each segment. For example, Asian products appeared most prevalent in all four surveyed supermarkets, but they were mostly Chinese, Indian and Japanese, with only a handful of Thai, Vietnamese or Korean products available.

Analyses of the packaging indicate that many products suggest cooking processes, such as adding vegetables and meats to the "authentic" base sauce, which enables consumers to complete the cooking process themselves. Hence, the cooking process is fluid and negotiated, allowing for the personalization of taste and ingredients. Despite the wide availability of flavours (e.g. korma, tikka masala, tandoori, madras), the actual range is very limited.

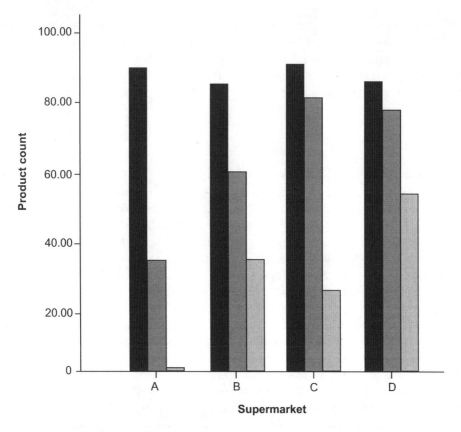

Figure 17.1 Ethnic products from four selected supermarkets

There was a distinct absence of ethnic fusion foods marks in the four surveyed supermarkets. With this approach, the food preparation styles of various ethnic groups combine to provide a unique flavour or dish and create new versions of mainstream products such as pizzas, pastas or stir fries. Examples of such products include Thai lasagne, Mexican pizza or Japanese enchiladas.

Assimilation and Separation of Ethnic Foods in Ethnic Food Marketing

ASSIMILATION OR ACCULTURATION AS A GUIDING CONCEPTUAL FRAMEWORK

The results indicate that supermarkets are responding to consumers' growing interest in foods from different countries. However, the range of ethnic products differs in supermarkets of varying socio-economic status, suggesting that ethnic foods have a larger consumer base in more affluent supermarkets – a finding consistent with the prevalence of ethnic food consumption among more affluent consumers.[30] Also, in common with existing research and market commentaries, many ethnic products have become assimilated into mainstream products,[31] reflecting current marketing strategies to focus less on meeting the needs of fragmented, diverse and/or particular cultural communities and more on marketing products to appeal to a general and generic audience. The notion of "authenticity" becomes a vehicle for encouraging mainstream consumers to make adventurous purchasing decisions. Marketers endeavour to make the authentic accessible to consumers through the availability of a range of tastes, but also differentiate products through packaging and product positioning, whether in the ethnic or mainstream sections of the supermarket. The shaping of authenticity requires a complex field of managerial practices and marketers' imagination, such that mainstreamed products present as "authentic tastes of the world" and coexist with products located in ethnic sections, often more readily identifiable as ethnic by country-of-origin label, packaging and language. The retailer's and marketers' task of framing authenticity becomes further complicated by the range of consumer orientations, from ethnic consumers seeking familiar food to Westernized consumers seeking, but not necessarily knowing what constitutes, an authentic ethnic experience or taste.

Consumer goods transmit cultural meaning and expectations, such as presenting the preparation of exotic ethnic food as fast, fun, non-threatening and easy. The process of selection, purchase, preparation and consumption of ethnic food at home has been simplified in the form of packets that demonstrate "simple three-step" cooking processes and feature serving suggestions. This information provides consumers with easy access to ethnic food and helps them use culturally unfamiliar products, because identification and recognition of unfamiliar ingredients remains a gradual and time-consuming process. Consumers are less likely to be intimidated by ethnic ingredients or foods if they have directions on how to use them.[32]

The concept of acculturation is useful for describing the processes at work. Specifically, acculturation pertains to the ways in which groups of individuals of different cultures come into continuous, first-hand contact with products, followed by subsequent changes in the original cultural patterns of either or both groups.[33] It is a more appropriate term than assimilation, which occurs when immigrants shift to the culture of destination and new cultural patterns become the same as those of the destination culture. Acculturation, in contrast, incorporates changes in both groups.

Consumer and retailer awareness and acceptance of ethnic food as an "everyday" food also results from processes of globalization, including international trade, migration and tourism. These factors encourage greater availability and diversity of products on supermarket shelves, as well as facilitating processes of acculturation. Measures to remove the "foreignness" of food commodities and associated food practices are important to the successful marketing of products to mainstream consumers.[34] Placing ethnic foods among more familiar products and marketing them in ways that evoke both familiarity (i.e., in New Zealand, using the English language and promising ease of cooking and preparation) and difference (i.e., "bring Asia home", "create the exotic with ease") is critical. Products in specialized food aisles also represent a common and international trend in supermarkets that intend to cater more specifically to ethnic shoppers.[35]

ETHNICITY AS A MARKETING TOOL

If ethnicity has become a marketing tool, it is not an easy one for marketers to wield. Removing consumer risk and familiarizing consumers with ethnic products through mainstreaming on supermarket shelves requires establishing and maintaining a degree of distance and separation from other foods to achieve an edge in the market that resonates in notions of distinctiveness and adventure. British curry consumers, for example, have expressed a desire for variety, extending beyond the traditional range of Indian curries.[36] Given the cultural and identity value that people may obtain when they seek to expose themselves to new foods and tastes, the task of marketing ethnic foods to multicultural audiences becomes a matter of balancing familiarity and distance, comfort and risk, and security and adventure. Products available on New Zealand supermarket shelves appear to cater to such dichotomies, with ready-made cooking sauces, for example, coming in different grades of spiciness (mild to hot).

The tension identified between consumers who strive for greater authenticity and social differentiation and those who seek to fuse Western ideas and flavours through mainstreamed ethnic products poses substantive challenges for manufacturers and marketers wanting to position their products in the market. For food to be seen as ethnic, they must make the products stand out as innovative and different. As ethnic foods become part of everyday diets, some manufacturers have realized greater differentiation is a key to maintaining market share. In Britain, for example, five standardized dishes constitute 80 per cent of the Indian curry market (tikka masala, korma, balti, madras and rogan josh).[37] As competition for shelf space increases, emerging premium products claim authenticity through associations with curries from Kerala and dishes from northern India.[38] Product innovations also involve calculated risks, so firms can overcome the challenge of developing high-end premium or experimental products by producing a relatively stable range of products for mainstream tastes and new flavours/ varieties that keep consumer interest high for short periods of time.[39] For smaller firms, securing points of difference and sales is more challenging because shelf space remains dominated by big brand/size producers, such as the Indian food producers, Sharwoods and Pataks.[40]

Considerations in Marketing Ethnic Food to Cosmopolitan Consumers

The results from New Zealand reveal different shelf space and marketing techniques; products appear differentiated on the basis of whether they are designated for ethnic markets or mainstream consumers, and higher economic status supermarkets tend to stock more ethnic foods with greater variety. This situation prompts questions about the characteristics of the markets being targeted and served. As ethnic food has become more cosmopolitan, the marketing choice must trade off marketing mainstream products to an increasingly ethnically diverse assortment of customers or retailing specifically to ethnic groups.[41] Jannoff[42] believes that the best ethnic food marketing spreads commodities throughout the store, enabling consumers to see a wide variety of products. Carrying ethnic goods alongside other products extends the product range and variety, providing greater choice for all consumers. Ethnic foods incorporated into traditional product categories can also make it easier for people to bring exotic and new tastes home. However, since a significant core of ethnic customers lives in the store market area, the separation of ethnic products and marketing them specifically to ethnic groups can be a profitable strategy.

Laroche et al.[43] also suggest that marketers should consider products to ascertain which of their facets relate to traditional (ethnic) consumption patterns and which are unfamiliar. Such an analysis can then serve as a basis for identifying the benefits and implications of products with a mainstream or ethnic presence and identity. Exposure to a range and variety of ethnic foods is increasingly important in shaping food preferences and behaviours, so marketers need to be attuned to the possibilities for promoting ethnic products to diverse or fragmented market segments, such as through media coverage, television cooking programmes and education. The impacts of celebrity cooking programmes (and their associated advertising and promotion), such as British chef Jamie Oliver's, have been notable not only for introducing potential consumers to new cooking techniques and foods, but also for having demonstrable effects on the sales of spices on supermarket shelves.[44] However, the mainstreaming of ethnic food in supermarkets may create a challenge for marketers in terms of quantifying and tracking trends in food preferences and consumption.[45]

Consequently, managing product categories is not simply a matter of deciding on whether to market to ethnic and/or mainstream consumers but also demands research on shoppers and neighbourhoods, focusing on establishing relationships with groups and addressing them with the right messages.[46] Only then it is possible to address consumers' need for variety and understand the factors that affect consumer behaviour and demand. Studies of mainstream consumers, for example, reveal a desire for healthier ethnic alternatives (i.e. Indian food cooked in less ghee), posing challenges for producers that want to tap into trends for vegetarian, low-carbohydrate, low-fat and antioxidant foods.[47] Such trends will also have different ramifications for fresh, frozen and ambient products. The degree to which groups of people are ethnocentric – concerned with the appropriateness and morality of consuming foreign-made goods – is also an important parameter that influences purchasing intentions.[48]

Marketing Ethnic Food for Ethnic Consumers

When they choose to appeal directly to specific ethnic groups, marketers must consider the practical and imagined needs of ethnic consumers and the appeal of available products. In culturally diverse societies, marketers of ethic products face numerous challenges, including how best to reward and foster long-term consumer relationships. Effective customization, responsiveness and personalization depend on knowing the characteristics of potential consumers.[49] Researchers must consider consumer learning and food sourcing networks, penetrate cultural and language barriers, and understand the brand preferences of ethnic and non-ethnic customers, particularly with regard to different product lines (e.g. chilled versus frozen, ambient, fresh fruit and vegetables, meats) and the sourcing strategies favoured by such groups.[50] Several specialist e-retailers have emerged in New Zealand in recent years (e.g. Tokyo Food, an online supermarket catering to Japanese consumers, and Moshims Indian Supermarket), offering a much greater range of ethnic products than is available in the four surveyed supermarkets.

Changes in demographics can also have a direct impact on the sales, marketing and positioning of ethnic foods, especially when more ethnic customers start shopping in mainstream stores and more ethnic foods move from niche to mainstream status.[51] Lewis notes the dangers of underestimating the purchasing power of niche markets, particularly when ethnic populations are geographically proximate to, or growing faster than, mainstream populations.[52] It is also necessary to discover ways in which such populations may differ with regard to education, generational attitudes and behaviours, travel and exposure to international commercial cultures, because these factors influence lifestyle choices and associated food preferences. An American study of immigrants shows they tend to discard the eating habits of their parents or grandparents and adopt standard American diets, reserving their ethnic cuisine for special occasions.[53] There may also be a need to consider which products might be demanded at certain times of the year for celebratory or religious purposes and the prices consumers might be prepared to pay.[54]

Conclusions: Mainstreaming Ethnic Food – Possibilities and Constraints

The mainstreaming of ethnic food products in supermarket shelves identified in New Zealand supermarkets implies both possibilities and constraints for manufacturers, retailers and marketers. Although mainstreaming and assimilation provide greater exposure to ethnic products and encourage acculturation, they also increase familiarity, reducing ethnic products to the status of everyday consumables and thereby minimizing their novelty and foreign value. The challenge for retailers and marketers interested in retailing to mainstream (but increasingly multicultural) markets is to find ways of retaining the authenticity and exoticness of the commodity while ensuring ease of preparation and minimal risk for consumers. This research touches on some ways in which these goals may be attained through packaging (e.g. three-step easy methods), but a detailed analysis of how authenticity, familiarity, safety and risk interact and may be maintained is required for differing food categories, prices and individual commodities.

Although the sample for this study is small, the study purpose is not to be representative of ethnic production, but rather to highlight the key dimensions that marketers and retailers should consider when presenting ethnic food. This snapshot of the products made available to New Zealand consumers illustrates the complexity of shaping authenticity. The research also aligns with a research agenda towards the role of food consumption in a global economy and emphasizes the importance of food distribution and consumption spaces for creating social identities. The next step, therefore, is to explore consumer meanings, choices and experiences of such foods and consider how identity may be formed through food practices and preferences.

The difficulties associated with categorizing food as ethnic or mainstream have also been highlighted. For informed and rigorous research to occur, it first must explore the meaning of ethnicity in the twenty-first century and the emerging significance of ethnicity for ethnic and non-ethnic consumers. Careful unpacking of the images and claims made in the name of authenticity would also be beneficial. This process should uncover the changing shape of the consumption of ethnic products and reveal the benefits, consequences, trade-offs and implications for manufacturers, marketers and consumers. Such changes no doubt will be directed by image management and economic profit. Furthermore, tracking the general movement of ethnic food production to monitor demand and shifting perceptions of ethnic food is recommended. For example, despite the limited offerings on New Zealand supermarket shelves, interest in fusion foods among consumers and industry representatives is growing.[55] These foods place less emphasis on the authenticity of the ethnic food and instead focus on their similarity to other food products, which suggests that they may be a potential avenue for increasing product ranges and markets.

Ethnic food is a dynamic and lucrative market, and much of the consumption of ethnic products has been driven by non-ethnic consumers eating more convenience-style food.[56] In developing ethnic food products, manufacturers confront the complex challenge of meeting seemingly opposing dichotomies: ethnic food remaining authentic while avoiding the liabilities associated with culturally foreign objects. Success in creating ethnic food does not depend on the capacity to produce authentic food, but rather on how well food companies and marketers can accommodate increasingly demanding consumers who seek the variety and distinctiveness associated with the image of authenticity. Ethnicity is thus being marketed, packaged and sold, all the while shaping the "authentic" to make it more compatible with mainstream values and expectations.

References

1. Gabbacia, D. (1998), *We Are What We Eat. Ethnic Food and the Making of Americans*, Harvard University Press, Cambridge, MA.
2. Bell, D. and Valentine, G. (1997), *Consuming Geographies: We Are Where We Eat*, Routledge, London.
3. Cook, I., Crang, P. and Thorpe, M. (1999), "Eating into Britishness: multicultural imaginaries and the identity politics of food" in Seymour Roseneil (ed.), *Practising Identities, Power and Resistance*, Macmillan, Basingstoke, pp. 223–248; Domosh, M. (2003), "Pickles and purity: discourses of food, empire and work in turn-of-the-century USA", *Social & Cultural Geography*, Vol. 4, No. 1, pp. 7–26.
4. Gabbacia, *We Are What We Eat, op. cit.*, p. 8.
5. Bell and Valentine, *Consuming Geographies, op. cit*; Cook, I. and Crang, P. (1996), "The world on a plate: culinary culture, displacement and geographical knowledges", *Journal of Material Culture*, Vol. 1, No. 2, pp. 131–153.
6. Pires, G. and Stanton, J. (2000), "Marketing services to ethnic consumers in culturally diverse markets: issues and implications", *Journal of Services Marketing*, Vol. 14, No. 7, pp. 607–618 at p. 607.
7. Stewart, A. L. (1994), "Europeans embrace tastes of ethnic food", *Marketing News*, 17 January, p. 10; Hamlett, J., Bailey, A.R., Alexander, A. and Shaw, G. (2008), "Ethnicity and consumption: South Asian food shopping patterns in Britain, 1947–75", *Journal of Consumer Culture*, Vol. 8, No. 1, pp. 91–116.
8. Reynolds-Zayak, L. (2003), "New product opportunities identified for ethnic foods at the winter fancy food show, San Francisco", *Agri-Food Trade Service*, http://atn-riae.agr.ca/events/e3493.htm (accessed 26 July 2007).
9. Gabbacia, *We Are What We Eat, op. cit.*
10. Mintel International Group Ltd, (2006), "Abstract, Ethnic Restaurants and Takeaways – UK – June 2006", Mintel International Group Ltd, Global Information Inc, http://www.the-infoshop.com/study/mt42272-restaurants.html (accessed 26 July 2007).
11. Perlik, A. (2005), "Minority matters", *Restaurants and Institutions*, 15 March, pp. 36–38.
12. Appadurai, A. (1990), "Disjuncture and difference in the global cultural economy", *Public Culture*, Vol. 2, No. 2, pp. 1–24.

13. Mintz, S. (1985), *Sweetness and Power. The Place of Sugar in Modern History*, Viking Penguin, New York.

14. Jamal, A. (1996), "Acculturation: the symbolism of ethnic eating among contemporary British consumers", *British Food Journal*, Vol. 98, No. 10, pp. 12–26.

15. Riell, H. (2005), "Newest ethnic explosion", *Frozen Food Age*, Vol. 54, No. 1, p. 29.

16. Gabbacia, *We Are What We Eat*, *op. cit.*

17. Cwiertka, K. (2001), "Introduction" in K. Cwiertka and B. Walraven (eds), *Asian Food: The Global and the Local*, University of Hawaii Press, Honolulu, pp. 1–15.

18. Hooks, B. (1992), *Black Looks: Race and Representation*, South End Press, Boston, MA.

19. Howell, D. (2004), "Ethnic interests see better slotting", *DSN Retailing Today*, 5 January, p. 23.

20. Barry, J. (1999), "Foreign affairs", *Progressive Grocer*, Vol. 78, No. 8, pp. 76 81.

21. Wang, L. and Lo, L. (2007), "Immigrant grocery-shopping behavior: ethnic identity versus accessibility", *Environment and Planning A*, Vol. 39, pp. 684–699.

22. Cwiertka, K. (2001), "Eating the homeland. Japanese expatriates in The Netherlands" in K. Cwiertka and B. Walraven (eds), *Asian Food: The Global and the Local*, University of Hawaii Press, Honolulu, pp 133–152.

23. Ibid.

24. Lewis, L. (1998), "Culture shock", *Progressive Grocer*, Vol. 77, No. 4, pp. 22–27.

25. Dwyer, C. and Jackson, P. (2003), "Commodifying difference: selling EASTern fashion", *Environment and Planning D: Society and Space*, Vol. 21, pp. 269–91; Jackson, P. (2002), "Commercial cultures: transcending the cultural and the economic", *Progress in Human Geography*, Vol. 26, No. 1, pp. 3–18.

26. Hamlett et al., "Ethnicity and consumption", *op. cit.*

27. Food Marketing Institute (1998), "Language of the food industry", http://www.fmi.org/facts_figs/glossary_search.cfm?keyword=ethnic%20foods (accessed 20 May 2007).

28. Chomka, S. (2002), "Food's foreign affair", *Food Manufacture*, NPD Supplement, December, pp. 8–11.

29. Food Marketing Institute, "Language of the food industry", *op. cit.*

30. Awbi, A. (2006), "UK suppliers urged to target European ethnic food demand", http://www.foodanddrinkeurope.com/news/ng.asp?id=66178-ethnic-food-heinz-amoy (accessed 12 September 2007).

31. Halpern, M. (2006), "Flavour nation", *Marketing Magazine*, Vol. 111, No. 3, pp. 10–12.

32. Halpern, M. (2006), "Global grocery shopping", *Marketing Magazine*, Vol. 111, No. 8, p. 4.

33. Jamal, "Acculturation", *op. cit.*, p. 13.

34. Ibid.

35. Barry, "Foreign affairs", *op. cit.*

36. Jamal, "Acculturation", *op. cit.*

37. Bell, I. (2005), "Analyst comment", *Marketing*, 22 June, p. 37.

38. Bainbridge, J. (2005), "Added spice", *Marketing*, 16 November, pp. 36–37; Chomka, "Food's foreign affair", *op. cit.*

39. Perlik, A. (2005), "Opportunity knocks", *Restaurants and Institutions*, 15 March, pp. 40–43.

40. Bell, "Analyst comment", *op. cit.*

41. Duff, M. (2005), "Ethnic goes mainstream where tastes are cosmopolitan", *DSN Retailing Today*, 10 January, p. 23.

42. Jannoff, B. (1999), "Foreign affairs", *Progressive Grocer*, Vol. 78, No. 8, pp. 76–80.

43. Laroche, M., Chankon, K. and Tomiuk, M.A. (1998), "Italian ethnic identity and its relative impact on the consumption of convenience and traditional foods", *Journal of Consumer Marketing*, Vol. 15, No. 2, pp. 125–151.

44. Bainbridge, "Added spice", *op. cit.*

45. Halpern, "Flavour nation", *op. cit.*

46. Dowdell, S. (2005), "Who's your ethnic?", *Progressive Grocer*, Vol. 84, No. 12, p. 3.

47. Chomka, "Food's foreign affair", *op. cit.*

48. Kavak, B. and Gumusluoglu, L. (2007), "Segmenting food markets. The role of ethnocentrism and lifestyle in understanding purchasing intentions", *International Journal of Market Research*, Vol. 49, No. 1, pp. 71-94.

49. Pires and Stanton, op. cit.

50. Omar, O. E., Hirst, A., and Blankson, C., (2004), "Food shopping behaviour among ethnic and non-ethnic communities", *Journal of Food Products Marketing*, Vol. 10, No. 4, pp. 39–57.

51. Janoff, "Foreign affairs", *op. cit.*

52. Lewis, "Culture shock", *op. cit.*; Javed, S. (2000), "Ethnic e-tailer builds expertise in untapped market", *Marketing News*, 9 October, p. 24.

53. Brown, L.K. and Mussell, K. (eds), (1984), *Ethnic and Regional Foodways in the United States*, University of Tennessee Press, Knoxville.

54. Lewis, "Culture shock", *op. cit.*

55. Halpern, "Flavour nation", *op. cit.*; International Food Industry Trends (n,d.), http://www.fryfoodtech.com (accessed 3 March 2008).

56. Hensen, S. and Jaffee, S. (2005), "Jamaica's trade in ethnic foods and other niche products. The impact of food safety and plant health standards", Agriculture and Rural Development Discussion Paper 18, The World Bank, http://siteresources.worldbank.org/INTARD/Resources/JamaicaStandardsF_final.pdf.

Index